The GOLDEN AGE of CRAP

77 B-Movies From the Glory Days of VHS
2nd Edition

NATHAN SHUMATE

Copyright © 2010, 2011 by Nathan Shumate. All rights reserved. Reproduction of material from within this book by photographic, digital, or other methods of electronic storage or retrieval is prohibited without permission in writing from the publisher.

Layout and cover design by Nathan Shumate

All images within are used within the intent of the Fair Use Doctrine and should not be construed as a challenge to their legal owners.

Published 2011 by Cold Fusion Media Empire

1468 N. 350 West
Sunset, UT 84015

www.coldfusionmedia..us
www.nathanshumate.com

TABLE of CONTENTS

Introductory Prefatory Foreword..5
Introduction to the Second Edition..7
Prologue..9

Endgame (1983)..11
Warrior of the Lost World (1983)...15
Night of the Comet (1984)..19
Radioactive Dreams (1984)..22
Blood Cult (1985)...25
Cemetery of Terror (1985)...28
Future Hunters (1985)..32
Pray For Death (1985)..38
Trancers (1985)...40
Land of Doom (1986)...44
Night of the Creeps (1986)...47
The Ripper (1986)...50
The Supernaturals (1986)...53
Warriors of the Apocalypse (1986)..56
Bad Taste (1987)...60
The Barbarians (1987)..62
Black Cobra (1987)...66
Forever Evil (1987)...69
Hell Comes to Frogtown (1987)..72
Nail Gun Massacre (1987)...75
Plutonium Baby (1987)..78
Redneck Zombies (1987)...82
    Producer Ed Bishop's Comments...85
Friday the 13th Part VII: The New Blood (1987)...88
Killer Klowns From Outer Space (1988)..91
Nightfall (1988)...94
Phantasm II (1988)...97
Pumpkinhead (1988)..100
Vice Academy (1988)..104
Zombie 4: After Death (1988)..107
Chopper Chicks in Zombietown (1989)..111
Moontrap (1989)...121
The Dead Next Door (1989)..124
    Writer/Director J.R. Bookwalter's Comments..................................127
The Dead Pit (1989)...129
The Laughing Dead (1989)..133
Dark Heritage: The Final Descendant (1990)...136
Evil Spirits (1990)...140
Mindwarp (1990)..143
Robot Ninja (1990)...146
    Writer/Director J.R. Bookwalter's Comments..................................150

Solar Crisis (1990)..152
The Invisible Maniac (1990)...156
America's Deadliest Home Video (1991)..159
Godzilla vs. King Ghidora (1991)...162
Kingdom of the Vampire (1991)...146
    Director J.R. Bookwalter's Comments...171
Night of the Day of the Dawn of the Son of the Bride of the Return of the Revenge of the Terror of the Attack of the Evil Mutant Hellbound Flesh Eating Subhumanoid Living Dead, Part 2 (1991)...173
Auntie Lee's Meat Pies (1992)..176
Excessive Force (1992)...179
Fortress (1992)...182
Knights (1992)...185
Prototype X29A (1992)..189
Split Second (1992)..193
Carnosaur (1993)...198
Return to Frogtown (1993)..202
Zombie Bloodbath (1993)..205
Abraxas, Guardian of the Universe (1994)..209
Immortal Combat (1994)...212
Necronomicon: Book of the Dead (1994)...216
Rockwell: A Legend of the Wild West (1994)...221
Addicted to Murder (1995)..224
Armageddon: The Final Challenge (1995)...227
Creep (1995)..231
Cyberzone (1995)...235
    Screenwriter William C. Martell's Comments..238
Death Machine (1995)..241
Dragon Fury (1995)...244
Gunfighter's Moon (1995)..247
Invisible Mom (1995)...250
    Screenwriter William C. Martell's Comments..253
Terminal Rush (1995)..254
The Mangler (1995)...258
Crossworlds (1996)..262
Sci-Fighters (1996)..265
Street Corner Justice (1996)..268
Victim of Desire (1996)..271
    Screenwriter William C. Martell's Comments..274
Bleak Future (1997)...276
Hostile Intent (1997)..279
Free Enterprise (1998)...282
The Lost World (1998)...284
Six-String Samurai (1998)...288

Epilogue..290
Index...293

INTRODUCTORY PREFATORY FOREWORD

Why are you listening to what I say?

As with most members of my generation, I blame everything on my parents.

I was raised by a mother and father who exhibited sober caution in the molding of young minds. They didn't want to expose me, their firstborn, to influences which many childrearing experts and religious leaders were decrying as deleterious. The list of TV programs I couldn't watch in my tender years would stagger you; it certainly sparked the humor of my classmates, who would all come to school having seen all the same shows the night before (this was back in the days of the monoculture). It didn't help that there were only two TV channels where I grew up, neither of which wanted to waste precious broadcast time on the kind of kid-friendly schlock that filled Saturday afternoons in other markets. I didn't even see by first *Godzilla* movie until I was seventeen, though not for lack of trying. (It was *Godzilla 1985*. I was underwhelmed.)

Oh, but I read. I read anything fantastic or speculative, anything which bore no resemblance to the rural boredom in which I was raised. Science fiction, fantasy, even horror, although my father frowned on Stephen King and his imitators. And I read movie books from the library, survey volumes which described all of the franchises from Universal and Hammer, all of the B-movie space aliens and giant bugs which really didn't look so bad in the publicity photos which these books reproduced in glorious black and white. By the time I got out of public school, I knew far too much about movies I had never seen, and I had one rock-solid belief: *I had missed out.*

The decades since then have been, in one sense, an attempt to reclaim a missed childhood. I am not currently twelve years old, of course; I am a college-educated adult with a mortgage and mature political views and a very few gray hairs that I can hide by careful combing. And I come to the movies I watch as a Bachelor of Arts in English Literature, *summa cum laude*; few of the movies I watch can stand up to the scrutiny I put them under. But every once in a while, I find an unambitious B-movie that, I realize, I would have thought totally rocked when I was in junior high. And every once in a greater while, I find one that makes me feel like I am regressed to that age when spectacle and chutzpah could cover a multitude of production sins, and *awesomest* is a perfectly legitimate adjective. It's finding those rare, happy accidents amidst the pits of factory-produced entertainment sausage that keeps me ladling out more of the same.

The reviews in this book all began life as first drafts on my website, Cold Fusion Video Reviews (www.coldfusionvideo.com), from which they have been studiously revised. The name of the site is taken from a flash-in-the-pan news story at the tail end of the '80s of two research physicists who thought they had discovered the Grail-like process room-temperature (i.e., "cold") fusion, and called a press conference instead of submitting their findings for peer review. After the hoopla, it turned out that no one could replicate their results; red faces all around.. If you don't remember the story, that's okay; the researchers were at the University of Utah, the state in which I now make my home, so the story's stuck in the regional memory. Locals can still be a little titchy about it. I picked that name for my site because A) it sounded cool, and B) it exemplified the discovery of excellence in a B-movie: it's unlikely, it's damned near impossible to replicate, but when and if it happens... *Zowie*. (I did not consider the fact that there's an application server software package called Cold Fusion, so including that term in my site name would confuse the hell out of search engines.)

The movies in this book are linked by having gotten most or all of their exposure through the medium of home video. Quite a few of them did have some form of theatrical release, especially the earlier ones, but the number of people who can remember having seen them on the big screen is dwarfed by those who first saw them on rented videocassettes. I've organized the reviews in this book by chronological order of the movies' releases, so that you can get a sense of the order in which they would likely have been seen by a B-movie aficionado of the time. I don't claim that these individual reviews coalesce into a comprehensive portrait of the era by the end of the book; it is, rather, a sampling of dubious statistical validity of the movies that were known to B-movie fans almost solely from their appearance on the video store shelves, a snapshot of an epoch. I can't say that *you have missed out* if you have never seen some of these movies; in many cases, the review is more entertainment than the movie being reviewed. (Readers on my website often ask me to cover more movies that I hate, because my reaction to them is the most fun to read. That's sort of like encouraging a singer who can only hit the high notes when he bashes his thumb with a hammer.)

At any rate... I think there was a conclusion around here somewhere, but I'll be jiggered if I can find it. I guess the point, if point there be, is that I hope you enjoy seeing these movies through my eyes, be they mature adult eyes or those of my inner twelve-year-old.

P.S. This book fits perfectly on the back of the toilet. I'm just saying.

-April 2010

INTRODUCTION to the SECOND EDITION

Trust me to miss the boat by being too early.

When this book originally came out in 2010, there was no such thing as "VHS nostalgia." Frankly, I'm still skeptical on most days that such a thing exists, but the evidence for it is around us. Books and Facebook pages and documentaries and whatnot showcase individuals and organizations which look back to the days of rental VHS with fondness, and which seek out to collect those films which have not yet gotten any sort of DVD or streaming release.

As such, the original edition of this book was often cited as being of interest specifically to VHS collectors. I should thank those who pursue this unlikely hobby, as their interest has managed to make *The Golden Age of Crap* the most consistently selling of everything I've written. To make the book even more interesting and useful to those aficionados—and to the rest of you, I hope—I've incorporated full-color reproductions of videocassette covers, movie posters, and other images of interest. I've also added an index, so that the misguided soul who wants to use this book as a reference work of sorts may continue in those misguided ways.

By the way, the website at which the initial drafts of all these reviews was posted, Cold Fusion Video Reviews, is no more. By the summer of 2011, I was experiencing bad movie burnout, and announced that I was moving to a reduced posting schedule—which, as it turned out, was a *non*-posting schedule. (The last movie reviewed on the site? 1993's *Leprechaun*.) Then, in the spring of 2013, the website's hosting company had a massive server outage which exposed the fact that they had not actually been backing up as they had promised. The entire coldfusionvideo.com site, as well as several others I ran, were kaput. I managed to scrape substantially all of the text of the movie reviews thanks to archive.org, but the task of reposting over six hundred movie reviews in a new WordPress installation was too daunting; I kept pretending that I would indeed do such a thing, but eventually I faced reality and let the domain lapse.

Which means that, aside from archive.org, this book, in either edition, is the only source for these reviews. That should make you feel better about paying to get content which was originally given away for free. (I hope you enjoy the arrangement; I have plans to bring out a *Golden Age of Crap II* in the semi-near future, as well as at least one *Silver Age of Crap*, culled from the DVD rental era.)

However, the loss of the website means that I can freely add a couple of features that I had kept out of the first edition: namely, the "Notable Totables" of breasts, explosions, etc. Contrary to what some detractors had said, I don't rate the movies *by* such metrics, but you can get a better feel for what the movie offers—or, rather, what it tries to offer—its viewers by those totals.

-March 2021

A NOTE on SOURCES

No, I don't have the largest collection of international VHS tapes in existence. While several in my personal possession grace the following pages, I had to use external sources for many of them, especially those from overseas releases. My main source was "the internet." Perhaps you've heard of it?

While scans without a watermark are obviously ideal, the watermarks to be seen on many of the best scans indicate to you whom to thank for them. I would like to call attention especially to the site VHSCollector.com, from which an embarrassing number of the scans to follow were "borrowed." There are people out there doing God's work, folks, and my hat's off to them for preserving what they can of a vanishing format and its cover art.

PROLOGUE
How We Got Where We Were

Hollywood went through one of its periodic paradigm shifts in the '70s. Before that, the gap between studio movies and B-movies had been significant, but not unbridgeable. B-movies got their start in a symbiotic relationship with their more expensive cousins in the first half of the 20th century; most movie houses showed double features, and a "B-movie" was the cheaper feature made expressly to fill out the second half of a program. The A-movie/B-movie partnership started dissolving in the '50s and '60s, thanks to Technicolor and Cinemascope on the studio side (innovations introduced to combat the influence of television) and drive-in double features composed solely of what had formerly been "B-movies" on the other (designed to attract the teenyboppers, who were looking for trash instead of epics). But the big blow was dealt by two movies in the '70s: *Jaws* (1975) and *Star Wars* (1977).

Before that, there had been no blockbusters, no summer movie season, no cross-promotion in toy stores and Happy Meals. Suddenly, mainstream Hollywood started making most of their money from so-called "tentpole movies," features which opened wide all across the U.S. and were heavily promoted and merchandised in order to recoup their ever-increasing costs. The *Star Wars* trilogy offers a good example of the latter: the production budget for *Star Wars* was $13 million, *The Empire Strikes Back* (1980) was $18 million, and *The Return of the Jedi* (1983) was $32 million—and any studio which didn't put comparable cash into their intended moneymakers wasn't going to fill enough seats to break even. Theatrically-released B-movies (the productions of Roger Corman and Charles Band, for example, and the horror flicks and historical epics churned out by the Italian film industry for American consumption) didn't have the appeal to compete for cinema-goer dollars, and began to be edged out of the marketplace.

But as the cheap filler feature was slowly disappearing from the big screen, a new distribution model was springing up thanks to the introduction of consumer-grade videocassette recorders. The original superstars of the video rental market were the expected blockbuster favorites (the first movie I saw on video was *Star Wars*, and I assume I'm not alone in that), but distributors also found that there was a higher demand for niche genres and B-movies on video than there had been in the theater, as well as back-catalog features that never saw the light of a theatrical re-release.

Hollywood had been afraid that VCRs would kill the movie industry. Now within a few short years, not only were studios counting on videocassette profits as part of their calculus for theatrical features, the low-end production companies had found that the rental economy could be central to their profitability. There may not have been enough of an audience for a cheap sci-fi or horror or action movie to fill a cinema all at once during a theatrical release, but a videocassette of that same feature sold to a rental store for $50 to $80 could reach a respectable audience one person at a time over a number of years and turn a profit. The B-movie had come home...

ENDGAME (1983)

For an "Endgame" champion in the year 2025, there's only one way to live. Dangerously.

aka *Endgame—Bronx Lotta Finale*

- Directed by "Steve Benson" (Joe D'Amato)
- Written by "Steve Benson" and Aldo Florio
- Starring Al Cliver, "Moira Chen" (Laura Gemser), George Eastman, Jack Davis and Al Yamanouchi

I enjoy this movie. I don't try to defend it, I just enjoy it. Back in high school, I caught it on late-night TV (for some reason one of the local channels broadcast Italian and unknown '70s sci-fi and fantasy movies almost continuously after midnight; I didn't realize at the time what a treasure it was). And unlike most things/people I fell for in high school, I haven't completely outgrown it.

In this future, there are only two environments: the city, which is just as dirty and urban as you'd expect with large junky areas uninhabitable except by scavengers and mutants; and the countryside, which is arid and looks generally like gravel yards. The only remnants of civilization are in the cities, where a brutal televised game called "Endgame" takes people's minds off their troubles. It's a fun little gladiatorial contest pitting one prey against three hunters in a broad section of the decimated city, each with three weapons. Fights to the death are permitted and encouraged.

Our hero is Ron Shannon, champion Endgame player, who probably picked up his fighting skills defending his last name in the playground. (Shannon is played by Al Cliver, born "Pierluigi Conti," a big blond fellow who was one of the go-to lead actors for cheap Italian exploitation flicks shot for the U.S. market, despite the fact that he didn't speak English.) His hunters are Aldridge, an Africanesque warrior, Mantrax, a diminutive white-guy martial artist, and Karnak, a Cossack-style meanie. Karnak (played by Italian exploitation regular George Eastman) is the one to watch; he and Shannon grew up

together, which means he was probably the one beating up Shannon on the playground (because "Karnak" just oozes toughness). All of them all wear some kind of facepaint, usually with a motif of a fireball around the eye; it's a nifty little cultural feature for Endgame players, and it showed up in my Halloween costume the year after I first saw this.

While Shannon creeps through the darkened city (oddly enough, it's never day there) and his hunters follow, we're also introduced to "Security Service" troops, Nazi-like stormtroopers doing the bidding of the fascist government. (No, I mean really Nazi-like; they wear German helmets, gas masks at all times, and long double-breasted trenchcoats, and even their insignia looks like the double lightning bolt of Hitler's SS.) Their business is massacring the mutant communities growing up in the rubble, since the mutants have telepathic abilities. (Seems to me, then, that the SS shouldn't be able to creep up on the mutants, but there you go.)

We're also introduced to the weakest series of scenes in the movie... a bunch of brown-uniformed generals sitting around a table making nefarious plans. The problem here is that everyone goes to great lengths not to mention what they're actually discussing; they just say things like, "If this continues, it will ruin all of our plans!" I know it's meant to be vaguely ominous, but it comes off as vaguely bureaucratic instead.

Back to the chase, as it were. In the course of defeating the first two hunters, Shannon also rescues a mutant girl (the beauteous Laura Gemser of the *Emanuelle* movies, here billed as "Moira Chen") from some raggedy scavengers. She returns the favor by telepathically helping when Karnak finds him; with her unseen aid, Shannon defeats Karnak in front of the TV cameras, but then spares his life. Because he's the hero, that's why.

He then saves the mutant girl Lilith again, this time from stormtroopers, and they discover together the aftermath of an SS massacre. The only two survivors are the mutant boy Tommy (Christopher Walsh) and Professor Levin (Jack Davis), a neurosurgeon studying the mutants who believes they are the glorious next step in human evolution.

Shannon shelters them at his apartment, and a proposition is tabled: if he will help Lilith and a few other mutants out of the city to a rendezvous point two hundred miles away in the next two days (by December 25th—I'm sure that's supposed to be meaningful, but nothing is ever done with it), he'll be paid in massive quantities of gold. The professor makes here a case for the perfection of an all-psychic society; no guile, no dishonesty, no telemarketers...

Meanwhile, Colonel Morgan (Gordon Mitchell), leader of the Security Service, visits Karnak. He points out Lilith's presence in some stills taken from the televised Endgame footage; if she were a mutant, he points out, then Shannon may have won unfairly. And that's enough to set Karnak off.

Shannon assembles the obligatory merc team to help him: the local dojo master (Gus Stone) and a mysterious martial artist named "Ninja" who works out there (Hal Yamanouchi), an overweight neo-barbarian named Kovack (Mario Pedone), and an old half-Indian named Kijawa (Nat Williams). Plus cannon fodder named Stark (Frank Ukmar). (Don't worry, he'll be dead real soon.)

Before he can leave the city, Shannon is hunted down by Morgan and his troopers; he's about to bite it, but suddenly Karnak steps out of nowhere and blasts the troopers. It's that honor-among-rivals thing; no one's going to take Shannon down except Karnak, and he's going to do it in his own time.

In their convoy of two motorcycles, a big van with a machine gun crow's nest, and Shannon's own souped-up apocalypsemobile, they start the journey with Lilith, Tommy, the professor, and a half-dozen other mutants (not telling the mercs, of course, of their mutant status).

And hey—it's finally day time! The wasteland, it seems, is an overcast but under-precipitated place, with the occasional trashed car littered with mutant bodies. These mutants, though, are different than the urban kind; theirs is a regressive mutation, which means that some have *Planet of the Apes* faces, some have webbed fingers and hokey patches of scales, etc. Bet we'll see more of these guys.

Their next encounter is probably the niftiest: they come upon a decrepit warehouse complex (amazing how no single-family farmhouses ever survive the apocalypse), where they meet about a hundred blind monks, dressed in black robes. To the travelers' amazement, the monks attack *en masse*. Their secret, Lilith discovers psychically, is that they have a captive psychic mutant whom they force to transmit the sight from the travelers' eyes to the monks. What we're treated to here is tons and tons of cowboy shooting—you know, the kind where the cowboy fires a single shot and five Indians fall dead. Except the mercs are going at it with machine guns; black-robed bodies fall in waves, until finally Shannon bursts into the building where the captive is held, and kills him; suddenly the monks all wander around, bumping into things. (The only member of the convoy to be lost here was Stark. Told you not to get attached to him.)

Taking leave of the monks, the party moves out and finds a place to stop and rest. Shannon watches Lilith with Tommy, and finds out that the kid's a powerful telekinetic, which is a new mutation. He's so powerful that Lilith has to keep his mind in check all the time. Gee, yet on the surface he's just a cute mop-headed kid. Hmm, bet he won't be useful later. (Oh yeah, we also get to see, peering over a sand dune... Karnak watching them. Don't those psychic senses have any early-warning function?)

Next the travelers find a cadre of massacred travelers... but almost too late, Lilith blurts out that it's a trap. Alas, it's true, and the professor takes a bullet, never to see his beloved guileless society. (Excuse me while I wipe away a tear.) Hefty barbarian Kovack then gets all huffy because Lilith's obviously a mutant, and he didn't agree to risk his life for some mutant, but Shannon rightly points out that what they're risking their lives for is the gold.

Alas, the conversation gets no further, because they then find themselves surrounded by a regressive mutant biker gang. Time for some more cowboy shooting; in the fray, Ninja and Kijawa go down (and, one assumes, Kovack; we never see him die, but he abruptly disappears from the movie—serves him right, the prejudiced bastard). And the fat scaly leader of the mutants grabs Lilith for himself. Can't say as I blame him; he's traveling with two topless women from his harem, and I really would have appreciated it if they'd put their tops back on, if you know what I mean.

Finally, with Karnak's sudden help, the others defeat the mutants and get away. Shannon feels the need to go back for Lilith, and Karnak goes along. They follow the mutants back to their stronghold, yet another abandoned industrial site. While they wait for nightfall to sneak in, Lilith stoically gets raped by the scaly guy. (More on this later.)

After disabling all the (unguarded) bikes, Shannon and Karnak sneak into the midst of the soundest-sleeping mutants you ever did see. I mean, they all sleep in one big room, flopped all over each other, and Shannon and Karnak still manage to kill the single guard, sneak in, rescue Lilith, kill the scaly guy, and make it out. Or almost; someone

wakes up after Shannon and Lilith have escaped, leaving Karnak to fend for himself.

Shannon and Lilith meet up with the convoy (now protected only by Dojo Guy) and make it to the rendezvous point. Unfortunately, they're met there by Colonel Morgan and a crapload of stormtroopers, and Dojo Guy bites it. As their final defense, Shannon has Lilith release the blocks on Tommy's powers, and the little kid cheerfully destroys troopers right and left; they're blown around by a sudden windstorm, the machine gun on the crow's nest mows them down by itself, troopers burst into flames, the troopers truck rises into the air and drops on a handful of them—and as a final touch, Morgan's own gun turns around and forces itself into his mouth. Blam.

Then Tommy's back to his smiling self. (I'm thinking years and years of therapy here.)

The rendezvous helicopter lands, and two guys in medical white deliver a big box of gold to Shannon. (Wow! It's like Christmas or something! See, because it's December 25th and… never mind.) Lilith invites him to join them in their new society, but Shannon declines, saying that he's part of the world of the past. They leave, and Shannon's about to pick up his gold, when bullets pepper the ground. Karnak's alive after all. After divesting themselves silently of weapons, they give each other that little "amiable enemies" smile, and launch themselves at each other. Freeze frame. The end.

The most surprising thing about this movie is its restraint—especially when you realize that director "Steve Benson" is none other than Joe D'Amato, the auteur behind almost 200 movies including notorious exploitationers like *Anthropophagus* (1980) and *Porno Holocaust* (1981) and *Caligula 2* (1982), along with standard B-level stuff like the *Ator the Fighting Eagle* sword-and-sorcery trilogy. In fact, the entire thing is completely under-key. Everybody's a stoic; even the rape of Lilith has very little impact. And when Laura Gemser's breasts make little impact, you know you're in an alternate universe.

This is actually indicative of the biggest flaw of the movie: it doesn't build to anything. The one big battle scene, against the blind monks, takes place halfway through; by contrast, the rescue mission is anti-climactic. Nothing ever reaches critical mass.

On the other hand, there's plenty going for this movie. The initial Endgame sequence is well-done, especially the constant sponsor's messages for Life Plus, the miracle protein drink. There's an actual plot behind everything, simple though it is, and there are enough interesting episodes to keep it from dragging horribly.

Hey, I know I'm trying desperately to defend this movie. What can I say? It doesn't rub me the wrong way, and given the median quality level of dystopian/ post-apocalyptic movies (especially Italian ones), that's saying something.

Some Notable Totables:
• body count: 161
• breasts: 8
• explosions: 6
• dream sequences: 0
• ominous thunderstorms: 0
• actors who've appeared on *Star Trek*: 0

WARRIOR of the LOST WORLD (1983)

IN ANOTHER TIME... IN A WORLD RULED BY TYRANNY AND VIOLENCE... ONLY ONE MAN CAN STOP THE NIGHTMARE!

- Written and directed by David Worth
- Starring Robert Ginty, Persis Khambatta, Donald Pleasence, Fred Williamson and Harrison Muller
- Produced by Roberto Bessi and Frank Hildebrand

"Oh, are the meek inheriting the earth?"

Yes, another post-apocalyptic movie, and one bankrolled by Italians and shot outside of Rome. But this one at least has an American director in deference to the movie's main intended audience, and that's not just an anglicized pseudonym; David Worth has helmed many solid American productions, such as *Lady Dragon* (1992) and *Lady Dragon 2* (1992), and *Shark Attack 2* (2002) and *Shark Attack 3* (2003). USA! USA!

Thanks to the conventions of the genre, we know to expect some sort of preamble or screencrawl at the beginning of most post-apocalyptic movies (because without them, we'd be entirely unfamiliar with the idea of nuclear holocaust and its aftermath, right?). But it's rare to have one so full of chunky exposition as this one. There's so much exposition here, in fact, that I'll just reproduce it verbatim for you (quirky punctuation intact) instead of trying to summarize it:

**In another time, in a distant land…
Generations after the radiation wars and the collapse of nations, government, finance, and com-munications, there came into existence a new Dark Age of Tyranny.**

As each Sector adapted its' own rules for survival, the evil despot PROSSER brought to power a Congress to enforce his "Laws and Obligations" and armed a deadly Militia, The Omega, to destroy the Outsiders who were trying to establish a more tolerant society- The New Way.

The region beyond the control of The Omega is the Wasteland, a forbidden zone populated by roving tribes of desperate Marginals who engage in a barbaric struggle for territory and survival.

> Meanwhile, high in the mountains, living among the ruins of past civilizations, dwells a small group of Mystics called the Enlightened Elders. It is here that the Outsiders, led by McWAYNE and his daughter NASTASIA gain inspiration in their struggle against PROSSOR and The Omega.
>
> Now, into this time of conflict and rebellion, astride his supersonic speedcycle, rides one man... a fearless survivor, who was destined to become the...
>
> WARRIOR of the
> LOST WORLD

Why did I share all of that with you? Merely to demonstrate how much of the backstory of this movie was only alluded to obliquely in the movie itself, and had to be spelled out in the preamble. Face it, when your movie starts with a screencrawl longer than a full page of script, you know you've got problems.

The titular Warrior, never called by name and identified on the video cover only as "the Rider" (the late Robert Ginty, looking like Russell Crowe with his light beard), is meant to be cut from that same "loner drawn to a cause" cloth as Han Solo. (What, the "In another time, in a distant land" part of the crawl didn't clue you in to impending *Star Wars* pretentions?) And like dear Captain Solo, the Rider is graced with a distinctive vehicle—which in this case also plays the role of sidekick. Because the bike can talk. Sort of. This was the year after *Knight Rider* hit the airwaves, so talking vehicles were all the rage. But instead of measured and erudite tones, the cycle speaks in almost-incomprehensible synthesized speech. Not to worry, though, because everything it says also blinks on its little screen for us to see. And it says/blinks everything three times. (Those of you who were unfortunate to have been exposed to the *Mighty Hercules* cartoon in your youth, please join me in some unwelcome "Newton!" "That's me! That's me!" flashbacks.)

The worst part here, though, isn't the bike. It's Ginty's reaction to it. With every line he utters in "conversation" with the cycle, you can see how disgusted he is at playing opposite the world's most annoying vocoder. (Fifteen years later, Liam Neeson would emulate his performance every time he was asked to "act" opposite a CGI character to be added later.)

Anyway. Mr. Badass Rider and his annoying two-wheeled sidekick go cruising along the (surprisingly well-maintained) deserted roads of the Wasteland, annoying Omega troopers for no apparent reason and getting into ever-so-exciting chases and crashes. He then moseys through an auto salvage yard, populated by New Wave punks. And evading them with more explosions and what not, he then proceeds to ride directly into a cliff face.

No, really. The cliff was actually part of the "wall of illusion" that the Enlightened Elders placed around their Shangri-La, and the bike was on autopilot while the Rider was shooting back at his pursuers, and artificial intelligences don't usually notice mental illusions ('Like, what wall?"). But the Rider himself, we are told, got through the wall because he is pure of heart, underneath it all. So the toga-draped mystics heal him by shining flashlights on him, while blaxploitation star Fred Williamson stands by and... um... collects his paycheck, I guess. (He really didn't need to be in this movie for any reason, but this was during the period in which you simply couldn't make an Italian post-apocalyptic movie without casting Fred Williamson somewhere.)

The Elders inform the Rider that he's been chosen to do heroic stuff for them—specifically, to rescue Professor McWayne, currently in Prossor's custody and scheduled for execution. The Rider will have none of it, naturally, until McWayne's daughter Nastasia (Persis Khambatta, coasting out the last of her fifteen minutes of fame from *Star Trek: The Motion Picture* (1979)) aims a handgun at his balls to convince him. "An offer he can't refuse," indeed.

Their plan is awfully simple: in stolen jumpsuits that look just like what everyone wears in the city, the Rider and Nastasia slog through the big ol' secret tunnel that none of the bad guys know about. Along the way they meet up with some tarantulas and snakes (just to remind us that *Raiders of the Lost Ark* (1981) was a much better movie), and some zombified mutants (just to remind us that the movie we're watching has an Italian pedigree). The tunnel comes out into a somnambulistic nightclub, where the entertainment could be described as "bondage vogueing." And then they trot through the 1984-ish city, where blank-faced citizenry wanders around under the omnipresent voice of Prossor spouting Newspeak like "Work is everyone's freedom." I guess not many people have the day off, because there are only a couple dozen assembled in the outdoor amphitheater where Professor McWayne (Harrison Muller) is scheduled to meet his end.

And then they rescue him. Really, it's almost that simple; the Rider grabs a gun from an Omega soldier and starts shooting. Dozens of other Omegas helpfully run into the path of his bullets. Nastasia grabs a gun, and so does McWayne, and together they decimate the lion's share of the Omega organization. I've seen first-level videogame fodder with a better sense of self-preservation. Hell, I've seen Tetris blocks with a better sense of self-preservation. I take back every disparaging word I might ever have said about Imperial Stormtroopers.

But fortune occasionally favors even the terminally wall-eyed, and a single Omega bullet manages to strike its intended target, puncturing Nastasia's leg right before she can hop aboard their conveniently-stolen helicopter. The Rider has no chance but to leave without her. "But she's my daughter!" McWayne protests. (Gosh, sir, I'd forgotten about that. That just makes everything different, don't it?)

Despite the fact that two people with no tactical support managed to run rough-shod across several dozen of Prossor's best, McWayne decides that the only way to rescue Nastasia—and while they're at it, completely destroy the whole system of fascist suppression and ickiness—is to do the whole "unite the tribes" bit. Which leads us to what pretty much qualifies as the centerpiece of the movie, as all of the various groups of "Marginals" come together in one place to kick the tar out of each other. (The TV's busted, you know.) And because it's virtually required in all post-apocalyptic milieus, the tribes each have a gimmick going. You've already met the New Wavers; but on top of them, we now have a karate gang! Beerbellied rednecks! Paramilitary types! And hairy-pitted Amazons! Given that these are the choices of social strata in the post-nuclear world, I certainly hope that the first bomb to hit lands directly on me and chars me to a cinder.

At McWayne's urging, the Rider wins the admiration of all the groups by beating up their champions. (In keeping with the imitation of all things Harrison Ford, he also gets the snot smacked out him in the process.) Then McWayne makes a speech so lame, I honestly expected the Marginals to turn their backs on him—he goes on and on about "marginalized by society" and "fascist oppression" and such. But somehow, this inspires them to sacrifice themselves against overwhelming odds. Boy, if such a poor orator can rally them to war in thirty seconds, I'd love to see how long it would take a good ol'-fashioned tent preacher to bring them all to Jesus.

In the meantime, though, Nastasia has been in the clutches of Prossor (Donald Pleasence). He's got that manner of affected distraction so common to world-conquering potentates, which also means that Pleasence doesn't need to break a sweat to collect his paycheck.

And then things roll toward their obvious conclusion. I suppose it's a sign of the political times I live in that the whole idea of instantaneous, complete regime change by a couple of VW busloads of ill-armed misfits is so ridiculous that I don't even want to try to suspend my disbelief. (On the other hand, when the regime in question has about one hundred cross-eyed troops, and their "unbeatable weapon" is a slow-moving garbage truck with a flamethrower attached)

Oh, and I don't mean to be tossing out any real spoilers, but here's a nickel's worth of free advice for all prospective Evil Overlords out there: I know you really love irony, but wait to savor it until victory is assured, okay? I mean, yes, there's something delicious about brainwashing your arch-nemesis' daughter and using her to shoot her father, but schemes like this never ever work.

So. Aside from the copious *Star Wars* and *Raiders* "homages," is there anything at all good to say about this movie? Well, I did cheer at one point. It was when the damned bike got run over by the garbage truck and "died." Then, shades of R2-D2, somebody rebuilt it for the happy finale. Grrr.

Some Notable Totables:
- body count: 119
- breasts: 0
- explosions: 13
- ominous thunderstorms: 0
- dwarfs: 1 (among the beerbellied rednecks)
- actors who've appeared on *Star Trek*: 2
  - Persis Khambatta (Nastasia) played Ilia, the Federation's least likely sex symbol, in *Star Trek: The Motion Picture*
  - Fred Williamson ("Henchman") played "Anka" in the classic episode "The Cloud Minders"

NIGHT of the COMET (1984)

IT WAS THE LAST THING ON EARTH THEY EVER EXPECTED.

- Written and directed by Thom Eberhardt
- Starring Robert Beltrane, Catherine Mary Stewart, Kelly Maroney, Sharon Farrell and Mary Woronov
- Produced by Wayne Crowford and Andrew Lane
- Executive produced by Thomas Coleman, Michael Rosenblatt and Sandra Scheik

It's kind of funny that, of the three movies that made Catherine Mary Stewart's face familiar to fanboys in the '80s (the other two being *The Last Starfighter* (1984) and *Weekend at Bernie's* (1989)), two of them spend an odd amount of time fussing around with videogames. But then, we are speaking of two movies that came out in 1984. There are worse pop-cultural trends to have one's face associated with (lambada immediately comes to mind).

Stewart plays Regina, an eighteen-year-old movie theater usher with an obsession for an unnamed videogame and a projectionist pseudo-boyfriend Larry (Michael Bowen) who makes some money sneaking movie prints out for bootlegging. His apropos pick for the December night in question is *It Came From Outer Space*—apropos because this also happens to be the night that a much-anticipated comet is grazing the earth's atmosphere for all to see. Supposedly, this comet hasn't been around for 65 million years—*when the dinosaurs suddenly went extinct*. (How, one wonders, would you calculate an ellipse that big from the scanty data they'd have?) And everyone's out ready to party while watching the lightshow, just like they later would in *Independence Day* (1996).That doesn't sound ominous, does it?

Regina and Larry spend the night in the steel-lined projection room in order to sneak the print back first thing in the morning, while everyone else is out gazing at the tremendous one-night-only lightshow. (Obviously, this was made in anticipation of the return of Halley's Comet in 1986; given the thunderous zap-filled display here, people who first saw this movie and then expected the real comet to be in any way analogous were presumably greatly disappointed.) "Everyone else" includes Regina's überbitchy stepmother Doris (Sharon Farrell), who's stepping out with the neighbor while Dad, a Green Beret, is off fighting some Central American war. Regina also has a younger cheerleader sister, Samantha (Kelly Maroney), who takes off after being decked by the step-mom, and spends the night in a gardening shed.

And that's good, because aside from those few people who've spent the night in metal-shielded locations, every other danged person (and, presumably, animal) who is exposed to the comet's radiation ends up... Well, remember that old *Star Trek* episode where a disease eventually reduces the crew of another starship to a handful of rock salt inside a collapsed uniform? Sorta like that, except it's a handful of red dust instead of rock salt. (Leftover supplies from *V: The Final Battle* (1984)? I dunno.)

This is, frankly, the best part of the movie: The sun coming up through red-tinted smog on an L.A. where no one—absolutely no one—is in evidence. Streets are completely empty, except for piles of clothing on sidewalks and the occasional car still running at a stoplight, with ironic Christmas music ("It Came Upon a Midnight Clear") playing on the radio. Sprinkler heads pop up and automated store lights come on; aside from that, nothing. Nothing except our few survivors.

And some zombies. Apparently, people who had only minimal protection didn't get turned to dust, at least not immediately; instead, they become pasty-skinned, sore-covered, white-eyed zombies craving human flesh, a fact discovers when Larry, miffed that his contact hasn't come back with the movie print, ventures obliviously out the back door and gets himself eaten.

Regina ventures out a different door, takes about ten minutes of wading through dusty clothes to finally clue in (a zombie attack also helps spur her mental processes—fortunately, Daddy taught his daughters to take care of themselves), and makes her way home, where she and the returned Samantha commiserate. And then they have a brainstorm: the radio has been belching out low-grade 1984 rock-pop incessantly since the movie started! Let's go find the DJ!

Unfortunately, what they thought was a live on-air personality turned out to be pre-recorded voice tracking (bane of all radio everywhere, if you ask me), but the trip does have a bonus, in that another survivor had the same idea: Hector (Robert Beltrane, later to star in TV's *Star Trek: Voyager*), a trucker who had survived by sleeping in the back of his cab. Boy, good thing that it was a young and hot and personable trucker instead of some groady old stinking road-goat who survived, huh?

And it's here where you might want to go and fix yourself a snack and leave the video going. Because it looks like writer/director Thom Eberhardt had a beginning and an ending, and hoped to fudge his way through the middle. It didn't work, and so the entire second act is padded like a couch cushion, with scene after scene in the neon-lit studio, accompanied by synth keyboards and drum machines. (I loved the '80s as much as anyone, but lackluster music is bad no matter what the decade.) We're so desperate for story here, we even fall back on that old shocker, the nightmare-within-a-nightmare. Then Hector heads up to check on his mother in San Diego (and encounters a zombie child—and I can't tell whether the scene was being played as comedy or not), and the girls go on the requisite shopping trip, to the accompaniment of "Girls Just Wanna Have Fun." (There is no way ever to do a shopping mall scene in a zombie movie without echoing *Dawn of the Dead* (1978), and very few movies can stand the comparison.)

It's only after the girls are attacked by half-zombified night shift stock boys who've taken over the mall that we get the other plot thread we've been waiting for: another group of survivors from a think tank installation, led by Dr. Carter (the ubiquitous character actor Geoffrey Lewis), is rounding up the surviving onesies and twosies, over the objections of sullen think-tanker Audrey (Mary Woronov). It's from them that we learn that even after-the-fact exposure can start an individual on the path from normal to zombie to a puff of dust. And that rash that Samantha's developed? We don't call that a good sign.

There is a nifty plot twist in the last ten minutes, and since it's one of the things done right, I won't spoil it for you. But I will say that, coming as it does on the tail end of almost an hour of waffling non-story, it's too late to fuel the fires of enthusiasm. And the fact that the great adventure of the climax is almost comically simple for the protagonists to accomplish doesn't help things.

What is kind of surprising, though, is the almost Pollyanna-ish conclusion, which has Regina, Samantha, Hector, Samantha's plot-contrivance boyfriend (you can't have a post-apocalyptic society rely on polygamy, after all), and two rescued children setting out to re-establish civilization mainly by putting on a happy face. Apparently, the continuation of electrical power in the city is taken for granted (how else will the '80s music continue forever?), and no one seems to wonder what they're going to survive on in an urban environment once the canned goods are gone (or how the ecosystem will be impacted by the complete dearth of animal life—which, technically, is never mentioned, but seems to be a common-sense extrapolation). That's even ignoring the miraculous (by divine screenwriter fiat) non-issue of everyone's eventual zombification.

More than anything, the entire feature seems to be a set-up for the real story, or at least the story I'd like to see—to wit, deciding whether to try to continue 20th-century civilization in a city being retaken by entropy or to head out and start over with a clean slate (with a gene pool too small to be viable anyway). But *Night of the Comet* didn't impress anyone enough to spur a sequel.

Some Notable Totables:
- body count: 12 (plus, like, everybody in the world)
- breasts: 0
- explosions: 1
- dream sequences: 1 (or 2, depending on how you count a dream-within-a-dream)
- ominous thunderstorms: 2
- actors who've appeared on *Star Trek*: 1
  - Robert Beltrane (Hector) played Commander Chakotay on *Star Trek: Voyager* (the "*Night of the Comet*" of *Trek* series)

RADIOACTIVE DREAMS (1984)

Just your typical action-adventure-science-fiction-musical-fantasy in the post-nuclear world.

- *Written and directed by Albert Pyun*
- *Starring John Stockwell, Michael Dudikoff, Lisa Blount, George Kennedy, and Don Murray*
- *Produced by Moctezuma Esparza and Tom Karnowski*
- *Executive produced by H. Frank Dominguez*

Time spent watching an Albert Pyun movie does not contribute to your life. It only leaves you that much closer to the inevitable end of your days.

Unless, of course, you watch them in order to write sarcastic and occasionally amusing reviews at great length. Then they're just more fertile grist for the mill. Go me!

Radioactive Dreams was only Pyun's second movie, after his fairly well-received (for him) debut *The Sword and the Sorcerer* (1982). At least, as schlockmeisters go, this second film was sufficiently different in concept that he didn't get pegged as a one-trick pony. (Compare his output to, say, the output of select Italian directors: "Hey, this time, instead of a South Asian cannibal tribe, let's make a movie about a *Central American* cannibal tribe!") And as concepts go, it's not bad: a pair of boys, locked in a bomb shelter for fifteen years with nothing but old pulp novels to read, emerge into a post-apocalyptic wasteland steeped to their eyeballs in hard-boiled clichés. There's certainly potential in that logline, so much so that a modified version of it was turned into the moderately entertaining comedy *Blast From the Past* in 1999.

But this is Albert Pyun we're talking about here, a singular director whose great talent has turned out to be sucking all of the color out of whatever movie he directs, a man who could render a week of hedonistic debauchery as a grey, lackluster experience.

As we begin in the far-flung future of 1996, our two lads are playing in the woods near where a couple of crooks (one of whom is George Kennedy) are hiding out or stowing loot or something at a convenient bomb shelter. Then a mushroom cloud goes off on the horizon, and the crooks kindly toss the two boys into the shelter and seal them in alone.

Fifteen years later, our heroes have grown up into Phillip (John Stockwell) and Marlowe (the *American Ninja* himself, Michael Dudikoff). And yes, character names are going to be that blatant all the way through; Pyun is after all the director who, five years later, named all the characters in *Cyborg* (1989) after guitars. You can bet the departed souls of the classic private eye novelists sure appreciate this "homage."

Anyway. They've finally found a way to break out of the locked bomb shelter, so they give each other haircuts, get themselves some stylin' (circa 1940) threads (from where? don't ask) and head out in their classic car that doesn't mind having sat unmaintained for fifteen years.

The world is the standard arid desert landscape, but it doesn't take long before the two boys run across, almost literally, a blonde being chased by mutants. The girl is Miles Archer (Lisa Blount, and yes, I did warn you about the character names), and despite Marlowe's instant infatuation, she's not exactly as she appears. Before she leaves them at a nearby working phonebooth in the middle of nowhere (!), she accidentally lets two red keys fall out of her pocket. These keys are the plot's McGuffin, as helpfully explained in the title card before the opening credits; they belong to the single nuclear warhead that wasn't launched in the civilization-frying exchange. Whoever holds the keys, therefore, has the most powerful weapon in the world.

The boys soon run into another hapless waif, and this time it's Phillip's turn to be smitten; she's Rusty Mars (Michele Little), sort of a hippy chick as filtered through '80s pop culture. In fact, everyone they meet has a different pop-cultural gimmick. They rescue Rusty from a couple of nine-year-olds in leisure suits (are juvenile actors allowed to drop that many F-bombs in their dialogue?), and she leads them on to Edge City, a collection of bombed-out buildings populated by enclaves of greasers, cannibal hippies, New Wavers, etc. And all of it is accompanied by one of the most annoying post-*Flashdance*/*Footloose* synthpop soundtracks of all time. We even get a three- minute music video segment that might entirely sap the will to live of an unprepared audience.

Again—there's potential in the concept. But Albert Pyun seems congenitally unable to craft a coherent storyline,
or use the tools of cinema to tell one effectively, so what we get here seems so disjointed it verges on the surreal. The mood shifts from ostensible comedy to ersatz pathos at the drop of a hat; impromptu speeches from character to character are interspersed with a bad copy of a hard-boiled voiceover delivered by Phillip, sounding more like a morose teenager trying to impress with his "depth" than the tarnished angels of the golden age of private eyes. And where else are you going to find a director so enamored of slow-motion that he shoots the entire five-minute climactic action scene that way? Of particular note is Michael Dudikoff as Marlow, the goofier of the two heroes (as opposed to John Stockwell's Phillip, the whiny naysayer). It's

one of those odd little twists of fate that Dudikoff shot another movie that same year that got him more recognition, *American Ninja* (1984). The odd quirk of fate is that his *American Ninja* character is defined by his stolid reserve, whereas *Radioactive Dreams* shows that there was some talent for physical comedy lurking in the boy. Not that Pyun knew how to draw it out of him; thanks to clueless direction, Dudikoff simple comes across as a bad Buddy Hackett imitation with hormones.

As often happens in Pyun movies, there is a single scene that stands out as being good—if, that is, it were a part of another movie in which it didn't seem so out of place. Here, it's the scene in which Phillip is gently seduced by Rusty, and though he really doesn't want to show it, he's scared out of his wits. It's a well-done scene, very honest and almost poignant, and it desperately wants to be in a better movie than this. (In case you're wondering, no, Phillip doesn't end up getting any; it turns out that Rusty is simply baiting a trap for the local cannibal club.)

As you can guess from his position in the credits, George Kennedy does show up again toward the end. However, I had a really hard time following exactly what his position in the plot was; I was too busy keeping up the one-man chant of "End! End! End!" I think it may have been more a matter of Pyun saying, "Dammit, I paid for him, I'm going to use him!"

You may reasonably be thinking, from the foregoing description, that this was ostensibly a comedy. Honestly, I can't tell if it was meant to be or not. There are scenes which are pretty obviously meant to be humorous, but they uniformly fall flat from heavy-handed execution. And the serious parts are so ploddingly serious that they tend to dispel any awareness of satirical intent.

When the end result of a production turns out to be a very bad movie, the writer can often say, "It's not my fault; the director screwed with the script." And the director can in turn declare, "It's not my fault; you should have seen the script they gave me to work with." But when the writer and the director are the same person—and that person just happens to be Albert Pyun—you've got no choice but to believe that this is pretty much how he intended the movie to be. So what, then, can we make of the fact that, after this, he has directed a full forty-four more movies?

Truly, the world in which that can happen, the world in which we live, is stranger and more frightening than any radioactive wasteland.

Some Notable Totables:
- body count: 26
- breasts: 2
- explosions: 20
- ominous thunderstorms: 1
- actors who've appeared on *Star Trek*: 1
  - Hilary Shepard ("Biker Leader") played "Hoya" in the *DS9* episode "The Ship," and "Lauren" in the episodes "Statistical Probabilities" and "Chrysalis"

BLOOD CULT (1985)

A NEW EXPERIENCE IN TERROR AWAITS YOU!

- *Directed by Christopher Lewis*
- *Written by Stuart Rosenthal*
- *Starring Juli Andelman, Charles Ellis, James Vance, Bennie Lee McGowan and Josef Hardt*
- *Produced by Linda Lewis*
- *Executive produced by Bill F. Blair*

Up until the mid-'80s, Hollywood studios had been content to license their theatrical product to third parties for videocassette distribution. Then they finally wised up and realized the looming revenue potential in the home video market, and instead of licensing their features, they began to put together in-house video distribution divisions. As the stream of studio-produced content dried up, one distributor wondered if, for the amount he would normally pay to license a theatrical feature, he could produce an original feature-length movie and distribute it himself. Thus *Blood Cult* was born: shot on twin Sony Betacams in nine days for a price tag of $27,000, it holds the singular honor of being the first feature ever made specifically for direct-to-video distribution.

And you know that if I spend the first paragraph focusing on a movie's history, it's because the movie itself is somewhat underwhelming. I've certainly seen much worse horror films, but if it weren't for *Blood Cult's* pioneer status in video distribution history, it would scarcely be memorable in any other regard.

The opening gives us a clear picture of where we're headed: a darkened sorority house at night, a co-ed alone in the house taking a shower, a prowler creeping through the house with a shiny meatcleaver. You might want to consider this an homage to Hitchcock and Carpenter (director Christopher Lewis certainly wants you to, according to the DVD commentary), but even by 1985 such a setup had been wiped so clean of originality that it's nothing but a pat little cliché. But what they lack in originality, the filmmakers certainly demonstrate in patience; it's a full five minutes from the establishing shot of the sorority house until the prowler makes himself known to the co-ed as he tries to break down the bathroom door. A quick chop-chop-chop later, and he exits with the co-ed's freshly showered arm, leaving behind a small gold medallion with a dog's head on it.

From there, we go to another sorority house a couple of nights later; a co-ed wakes in the night to find that the prowler's there in the bedroom, having already decapitated her roommate. He doesn't kill this one; he just beats her unconscious with her roommate's severed head. We are now almost fifteen minutes into the movie (including a screencrawl giving the setting as "Central State College" somewhere in the Midwest); you may well conclude that not exactly going to be flooded with plot here.

The two slasher setpieces taken care of, we can finally meet our protagonist, septuagenarian Sheriff Wilbois (Charles

Ellis). Wilbois is very clearly out of his depth; he's a common-sense peacekeeper in the heartland who's never had to deal with anything as gruesome as a serial killer. Fun fact: the script predates the distributor's direct-to-video brainstorm by several years, and in fact had originally been written to feature an elderly Buster Crabbe (!) as the sheriff, until his death spoiled the project. Ellis is no Buster Crabbe, but he's probably an even better fit for an aging smalltown lawman who wants to preserve his town, the university, and his upcoming chances at reelection.

Sheriff Wilbois does have an ace in the hole: his daughter Tina (Juli Andelman) works at the university library, and thus helps her father cross-reference the occult significance of the dog-headed medallions. On the minus side, Tina's boyfriend is Joel (James Vance), world's ugliest grad student, who seems to like nothing better than to demonstrate Tina's lousy taste in men by kissing her repeatedly in front of Daddy.

Right, the medallions. The dog face links them to a 17th-century witchcult which would build a frankensteined meat effigy in order to curse magistrates and other authority figures. This would be the point for Sheriff Wilbois to wonder if someone has it in for him personally, but he never does. Instead, he spends plenty of time running back and forth between the dean's office and his own sheriff's station, assigning never-seen deputies to guard the sorority houses while the bodies continue to pile up. (Though if you ask me, any co-ed who

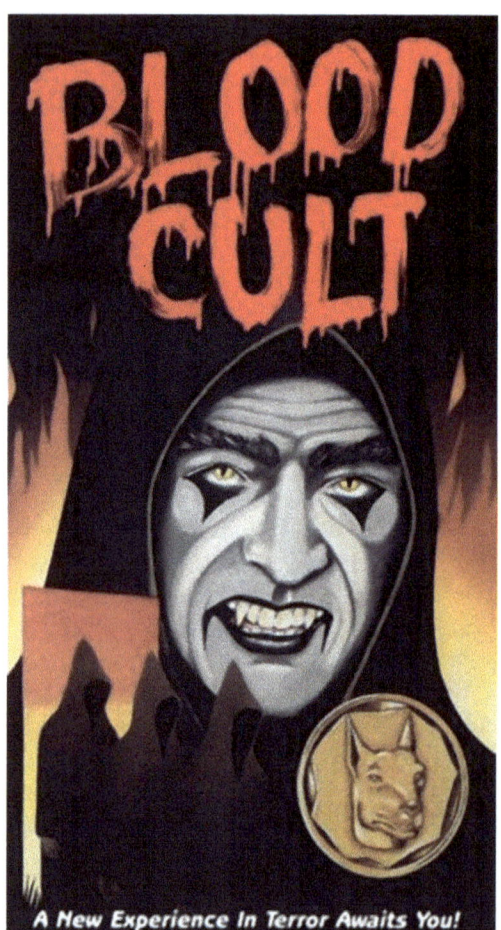

A New Experience In Terror Awaits You!

ventures out after dark alone while a serial killer preys on sorority girls is just doing her part to cull the herd.) The sheriff has few leads until he notices that the book identifying the medallion says that that witchcult's rites always took place out in the country at night, with bonfires and chanting and such. And it just so happens that his department took a complaint call from a farmer who claimed that "poachers" were lighting fires in the nearby woods in the middle of the night, and had also decapitated his dog.

If the movies you've seen recently have had too little padding for your tastes, this one should fill the ticket. The sheriff spends a lot of time going between the library and his office, with plenty of footage of the transit in between. (Thrill to the sensible ten-and-two steering action!) Even some of the gore scenes seem more like filler than in the standard slasher flick; when a pair of severed fingers are discovered nonsensically in somebody's cafeteria salad, one gets the feeling that they were there not for the gross-out factor, but simply to give an excuse to follow a diner all the way through the long cafeteria line.

When I say that acting is at the level of community theater, I'm not hurling an insult, I'm acknowledging where the director found most of his cast. As such, I suppose they're adequate, though nowhere near natural. And of course, once some characters are revealed as cultists, they begin speaking in that stilted "Ooh, I'm a cultist!" monotone though their diction in previous scenes had all been well-adjusted. (Make your own Tom Cruise joke, okay?)

The extent to which there *are* cultists is left annoyingly ambiguous, as most of what we see of them comes after Wilbois, traipsing through the woods at night to find the poachers, gets hit on the head; what he sees of a cult rite is therefore either seen blearily through a concussion, or entirely an hallucination. If what we see is true, it doesn't make much sense that a witchcult whose main distinguishing characteristic is rituals against magistrates should then handle the sheriff with kid gloves and even make overtures to him. But then, as the director admits in the commentary, a lot of this really doesn't make sense in retrospect. And what does make sense is available on film in the older movies they cribbed from.

While those of us who enjoy "microbudget" genre cinema should appreciate the movement that *Blood Cult* engendered, it doesn't follow that we must therefore treat this movie as "the *Citizen Kane* of direct-to-video." This outing proved that it could be done, and with the right distribution strategy could be done profitably. But it took later filmmakers, following and broadening the trail, to show that it could be done well.

Some Notable Totables:
- body count: 6, plus 1 dog
- breasts: 0
- explosions: 0
- ominous thunderstorms: 1
- dream sequences: 1—or was it?
- actors who've appeared on *Star Trek*: 0

CEMETERY of TERROR (1985)

aka *Cementerio del Terror*

- *Written and directed by Ruben Galindo Jr.*
- *Starring Hugo "Stieglitz" (Stiglitz), Usi Velasco, Erika Buenfil, Edna Bolkan and Maria Rebeca*
- *Produced by Raul Galindo*
- *Executive produced by Rodolfo Galindo*

Far be it from me to rely on over-broad generalizations—except when it suits my purpose—but when considering foreign cinema, one can usually divide any country's output into one of two camps:

1. Films in which both the stories told and the techniques used to tell them reflect the mores, tropes and symbols of the native culture—movies that could literally have been made nowhere else, by no one else.

2. The same old crap that gets cranked out and exported by American tripe factories. But this time, we made it! It's schlock in our own language! Woo!

Cemetery of Terror falls solidly into the second category. I speak no Spanish and had to rely on the subtitles, but I feel safe in saying that my poor opinion of this movie cannot be blamed on subtleties of Mexican culture or cinematic tradition I didn't pick up on. (Upon which I did not pick? Whatever.) No, I think we can blame the essential dumbness of the movie, a language which is spoken the world over.

Our "star power," such as it is, is provided by Hugo Stiglitz (you may not know the name, but this Mexican-born actor is currently credited with over 200 Spanish-language movie roles). Stiglitz plays Dr. Cardan, and you will grasp the essence his character immediately when I tell you that Dr. Cardan is exactly like Donald Pleasence's Dr. Loomis from the *Halloween* movies, except that Loomis didn't feel the need to keep his shirt unbuttoned practically to the navel. (And aren't we all glad.) We are introduced to Cardan in that most heroic of tableaus, "man asleep in front of staticky TV." Cardan is dreaming about… well, I could keep you in suspense until the random images get explained a few scenes later, but let's just connect the dots right now: Cardan is dreaming about his patient Devlon (Jose Gomez Parcero), a serial killer who is of course a being of "pure *ee*-vil," yada yada yada. We don't see Devlon's face for several scenes, and when we do it's something of a letdown, as Devlon looks like nothing more than a mean-spirited homeless man. His hands, though, are oddly misshapen and claw-like. A good thing for him, too; let the other cinematic mass murderers rely on wimpy tools and weapons—not Devlon. Machetes? Chainsaws? Garden Weasels™? Bah. Devlon uses nothing but his bare hands to claw and carve up his victims, and if that means that most death scenes are going to be poorly edited and unconvincing approximations of people receiving flesh wounds, well, that's just the price you have to pay for keeping it real.

The dream Cardan has involves Devlon stalking a lone woman in an office building at night, killing her, and then catching a bazillion bullets from the police who show up. And wouldn't you know it, that's exactly what he finds out happened during the night when the police call in the morning: Devlon escaped from the psychiatric hospital, went on a spree, and got taken down.

Cardan immediately goes to the station to argue with Captain Ancira (Raul Meraz) that Devlon the Satanist needs to be cremated immediately because he's pure *ee-vil*, but Ancira holds to procedure, which involves an autopsy and then just a normal burial. They're probably not even going to chain up the corpse in the casket or anything.

Meanwhile, we've had the pleasure of meeting most of the rest of our cast: three medical students, Jorge, Oscar, and Pedro (Cervando Manzetti, Rene Cardona III, and Andres García Jr.), and their girlfriends, Olivia, Marianna, and Leena (Edna Bolkan, Jacqueline Castro, and Erika Buenfil), and no, there is no pressing need to differentiate them. The boys have a terrific idea: how about we tell the girls that we'll take them to some posh jet-set party, and instead take them for a private kegger and nookie session at that spooky old abandoned house? Won't that be fun! Yeah, the girls will really think that's funny! Also, sweetie, instead of that mink stole I promised you for your birthday, here's some cat poop! Funny, huh? Hey, why are you hitting me? What's gotten into you?

And somewhere in here, when we're not watching our six twentysomethings on a pointless waterskiing excursion (*"This scene sponsored in part by the local tourism board"*), we also meet small group of children: two are Captain Ancira's, two are neighbor kids, and Tonny (Eduardo Capetillo), the oldest (probably fourteen) is an orphan being raised by his sister. Their only purpose at this stage of the movie is to demonstrate that Halloween, as celebrated in Mexico, sucks. Yes, this is Halloween night, though that fact is only mentioned in the children's scenes (it's never noted, for instance, whether the "jet set" party was meant to be themed), and I think there's exactly one cheap brittle plastic mask between all of the children. They also have a jack-o-lantern, carved out to function as a real lantern. And that's it. Enjoy yourselves, kids!

So our three groups of people approach the evening thus:

The twentysomethings arrive at the abandoned house and gain entry through the open basement door. As absolutely no one would have suspected, the girls are seriously pissed and refuse to kanoodle. The guys then get an even more brilliantly brilliant idea: it's a well-known fact that fear makes women melt into the arms of whatever men happen to be adjacent, so let's creep them out! By stealing a corpse from the morgue! And taking it to the enormous cemetery just around the corner! And attempting to raise the dead, using this big black book full of spookiness we found in the upstairs room of the house with "devlon" painted across the cover! (Seriously, could you cram more bad ideas into a single scheme? Wait, they left out "Let's eat and then immediately go swimming.")

The kids, as soon as they all link up, immediately decide to go over to the big-ass cemetery because ~~the dead have the best candy~~ it's Halloween, and it'll be spooky. Wherever it is they're starting from, the cemetery is pretty far away, which conveniently takes them out of the picture until needed.

Dr. Cardan forges the signature and seal of the local judge on an order for Devlon's immediate cremation, and he and Captain Ancira drive over to the morgue (with Ancira idly wondering aloud how Cardan got the order signed with the judge out of town that week—boy, he's a sharp one!). By the time they get there, though, the medical boys have jimmied the lock on the back door, stolen the ugliest corpse on the premises—Devlon's, naturally—and stuffed it in the back of their hatchback. Question: Aren't bodies in the morgue usually stripped down? Because Devlon's still dressed in his molester trenchcoat and hobnailed boots.

Cardan is obviously anxious about this—

either that, or his bladder is sending out distress calls—so he steals Ancira's car to drive around town, looking for a stray corpse. How did he steal the car? Well, Ancira got out to use a phone booth because his wife had called the station, anxious about her kids. Let's just look at the timeframe here: there's never a clock to be seen in this movie, but the trick-or-treaters were instructed to be back by 10 o'clock. By this time, they haven't even arrived at the cemetery which was their destination when they left their own block, so I have a hard time believing that it's suddenly so late that mothers are freaking out.

The twenty-somethings get the body back to the center of the cemetery, and Jorge starts reciting "Satan, come hither" texts from the big black book, in a scene that calls to mind the equally lame *Children Shouldn't Play With Dead Things* (1972). As ominous thunder sounds and torrents of rain fall (immediately followed by a shot of the glowing full moon in a cloudless sky), they decide to abandon the enterprise—and the body—and make for the abandoned house. Naturally, as soon as they scamper for shelter, Devlon sits up. Hey, whaddaya know! The movie's about to start!

(Note: Immediately thereafter, the trick-or-treaters arrive at the cemetery. Where it is not raining. Or even damp. Continuity is more than a suggestion, you know?)

Now. Six victims in the abandoned house, all in some stage of kanoodling (fear, rain—whatever gets the girls to shiver, makes them horny!). You would be surprised to see how quickly Devlon kills them all, usually with his bare hands. Only one of the deaths is really worth mentioning on its own, and that because of incompetence: Oscar has been out on the porch swing with Marianna and goes in to freshen up her drink. By the time he gets back, Devlon has dragged her off. Oscar finds her body in the long grass and cautiously looks right, looks left—slash! Devlon's cruel nails strike out of nowhere, even though Oscar is standing in the middle of the back lawn, well-lit enough to read a newspaper. And again—look right, look left —slash! Seriously, where is Devlon supposed to be hiding?

The only other detail of note: As has been demonstrated many times by slasher flicks, a man's ears stop working when he's aroused, meaning that it's always the girl who hears something and insists on investigation.

So, we're now 55 minutes into the movie… and we've exhausted our convenient pool of victims. Yes, there are the kids (who are just now reaching the center of the cemetery), but you and I both know that it's the rare and ambitious horror film which will allow a child to be killed, and this movie simply isn't that ambitious. So instead of any more gore, we're instead given a chase scene which lasts for the rest of the movie. The kids get spooked by a falling tree and mysterious flames from a grave, they run to the abandoned house, they see the bodies and catch Devlon's eye, they run back to the cemetery with Devlon in pursuit, they stumble around crying and telling each other to hurry up, and then graves start opening and zombies start chasing them too. (Jorge's incantation? Devlon's native Satanic power?

Does it matter?) The kids make it aaaall the way back through to the front gate (odd that there's no fence or wall around the back end of the cemetery, separating it from the abandoned house), which is magically locked, and it almost looks like they might get trapped…

…When Cardan drives up in his stolen police car. How did he know to show up there? He didn't. Ever since he stole the car, over half an hour of the movie ago, we've kept cutting back to shots of him speeding through the city, looking frantically out the windows. I guess, then, that it's only pure chance that brings him to this exact spot right when he's needed to bust down the gate. Even then, the car immediately conks out, so he and the children, yes, have to run all the way back through the cemetery, toward the house. Why to the house? Because Cardan mentions that they have to destroy Devlon's book, and Tonny replies that he saw a big black book in the house. (I'd be more accepting of this whole book-as-McGuffin gimmick if it were written on parchment or illuminated in blood or something, but it's pretty clearly a press-printed book, which means it's not unique; why is the physical book itself such a powerful talisman?)

I realized that this movie had no more to offer me when Cardan hands one of the children a crucifix to keep the zombies back, and it works. Um, this is a Mexican Catholic cemetery; it's chock-full of crosses, with which the zombies seem to have no particular problem. This is the level of thinking that informs the entire movie; it's called "going into production with a first-draft script," and it means that the story is divided almost completely into two unrelated chunks, with the "star power" of Hugo Stiglitz given nothing to do for most of the movie.

In other words… Yup. Just like its American precedents.

Some Notable Totables:
- body count: 9
- breasts: 0
- explosions: 1
- dream sequences: 1
- ominous thunderstorms: 3
- cars that won't start for no reason: 1
- actors who've appeared on *Star Trek*: 0

FUTURE HUNTERS (1985)

WHEN A CHANCE ENCOUNTER BECOMES A DEADLY ADVENTURE.

- Directed by Cirio H. Santiago
- Written by J.L. Thompson
- Starring Robert Patrick, Linda Carol, Ed Crick, Bruce Li and Richard Norton
- Produced by Anthony Maharaj

As far as I can tell, every inch of footage appearing in *Future Hunters* was shot specifically for this motion picture. Nevertheless, it feels like it was constructed entirely of repurposed stock footage, mainly because the script is a stitched-together conglomeration that would do Dr. Frankenstein proud. I think I can even discern which borrowed elements were used to make the initial pitch: "It's part *Terminator*, part *Raiders of the Lost Ark*! And we'll shoot it in the Philippines to save money!" But that doesn't even begin to do justice to this hack job, which also manages to incorporate *The Maltese Falcon* (1941), *Romancing the Stone* (1984), *The Road Warrior* (1981), any of several hundred interchangeable kung fu movies, every "lost world of Amazons" movie ever made, and maybe even the midget spy thriller *For Your Height Only* (1981). Oh, and it sucks, too.

As a voiceover narration helpfully informs us, the story begins in 2025, almost forty years after the world falls down and goes boom. One man, Matthew, is trying to find the legendary Spear of Longinus, the fabled implement which pierced Christ's side and thus gained phenomenal (though vague) powers, one of which is to travel through time. Matthew is trying to go back forty years and keep the holocaust from happening. Yes, all of this information (and more!) is contained in the narration; why bother with that namby "visual storytelling" when you can just unload efficient exposition?

And yup, there's Matthew (Richard Norton) himself, driving a MadMaxMobile across an arid landscape, pursued by two more such contraptions. As usual, gasoline doesn't seem to be in short supply; neither do the bullets which Matthew's pursuers expend in automatic weapons fire. But Matthew outranks them there—they've got machine guns, but he's got a grenade launcher!

Unfortunately, Matthew is himself outgunned by the warlord Zaar (David Light), who has a number of tanks at his disposal. Matthew is captured and dragged to a bad matte painting of a fortress, escapes, runs next door to the mission-style church (which everyone calls "the temple") and, lo and behold, this is where Zaar is keeping the spear! How convenient!

At least someone did some research for the script. I read a book a few years back that purportedly told the true story of the spear of Longinus (though it was similarly vague on what the spear could actually do apart from poking crucified messiahs), and the prop they use here does look like the picture in the book. Well, except for the animated glow that pulses through it when Matthew picks it up. I'm hoping that real mystically-charged artifacts have better special effects. Oh, and although everyone calls it the "spear," it's actually just the spearhead—it's a lot easier to run around with a desperately-sought artifact when it isn't seven feet long.

Anyway. Zaar orders his tanks to fire on the temple rather than let Matthew get it. Everything explodes…

…And we roll opening credits and cut to 1986. The back of the video gives the release date as 1989, but that's easy enough to explain—the movie was made in 1985, but couldn't find anyone desperate/stupid enough to distribute it for four more years.

So. 1986, same church out in the desert, though it doesn't look much better for wear than it does in forty years. In fact, the entire landscape is just as arid and deserted as it is in the future. Are you sure there was a nuclear apocalypse? (The matte painting is notably absent, though.) A young couple is exploring the abandoned church. Actually, only Michelle (Linda Carol) is exploring it, because she wants to be an anthropologist in addition to a café owner because her dad died and all he left her was a bunch of money. Her boyfriend Slade (Robert Patrick) is just hanging around, waiting for her to be done; in addition, he helpfully gives us the chunk of Michelle's backstory above through some exceptionally clumsy dialogue. (Well, exceptional compared to most movies, not to what follows in this one.)

As they get ready to leave, a small biker gang (a ganglet?) rides up and proceeds to molest them, because there's nothing bikers like better than checking in on small abandoned churches in the desert to see if there's anyone there to rape. They kick the tar out of Slade, and are about ready to take turns with Michelle, when post-apocalyptic warrior Matthew wakes up inside the church with the spear in his hand—he's been blown backward in time! He comes out of the church and makes short work of the bikers (one of them melts into ash when stabbed with the spearhead), but takes a bullet in a vital organ.

Michelle and Slade try to get him to a hospital, but he gives them the spear and a short, nonsensical description of it and its powers before he expires in their backseat. His last words are to find someone named "Hightower" who knows all about the spear's power and destiny. (That, and the fact that he didn't know what they meant when they said they were "outside L.A." I can understand his confusion—I mean, is Los Angeles supposed to look so much like the Philippines?)

Slade's one of those "don't get involved" people, and wants Michelle to forget all about it after they ditch the corpse with the police, but he didn't see someone melt to ash like she did. Plus, I guess he doesn't have the soul of a wanna-be great anthropologist. No, he's just a cropduster mechanic. (Gee, wonder if that will come in handy later.) And she's not the only one who thinks the spear might be important; when they're back at the café, a trio of standard-issue heavies come in, demand the spearhead, and demonstrate that they really don't know how to wreck a restaurant very well. They then leave because… um… customers are coming. (Curses! In a café, of all places! Foiled again!)

Michelle finds Professor Hightower's work in the library; he's one of the foremost experts on the spear of Longinus, and wouldn't you know it, he's a member of the faculty right here at the local university. (In L.A., I mean. Where this is taking place. Not in the Philippines, where of course this is not taking place.) Unfortunately, Hightower has disappeared somewhere around Hong Kong on one of his expeditions, according to Professor Fielding (Ed Crick), who offers to take the spear off her hands. When she refuses, he then offers to put Hightower in touch with her as soon as he resurfaces, and she gives him her address. (Let's see—you want the professor to contact you, and you know that bad guys are trying to take the spear by force; wouldn't leaving your phone number be more appropriate? On the other hand, the bad guys seemed to intuit who she was and where she ran her café, so…)

Well, more bad guys pursue them down a lonely street (in L.A., dammit, not the Philippines, despite the jungle encroaching on the shoulder of the road!), and only her defensive driving skills keep them alive. She and Slade decide that the most sensible thing to do would be to fly to Hong Kong and try to find Hightower. After all, there are only six million people in the city, all speaking a language they don't know; how hard could it be?

Plus, they do have an advantage: Slade has a friend in Hong Kong. What's more, he drives a taxi (and who better to track someone down than a taxi driver?). And what's even more, he's Bruce Li![1] That's quite the ace in the hole, especially when (after driving around pointing at the tall buildings —these three minutes brought to you by the Hong Kong Tourism Commission) Slade and Li take a trip to the Forbidden Pagoda of the Silver Fox, where Hightower was rumored to have been. Well, they don't find Hightower, but they do find an old kung fu master who cops a "Which part of 'forbidden' don't you understand?" attitude and wipes the floor with Slade.

But—did I mention? Slade's friend is Bruce Li! Which means that for the next ten minutes, we're going to forget about the plot and watch Li and the kung fu master whup on each other. We even get those exaggerated hand-to-hand sound effects that were notably absent when the master beat up Slade.

It seems like the bout will go on forever—it certainly tries to—but it's mercifully cut short when a mysterious sniper shoots the kung fu master, although he apparently meant to plug Slade. Slade and Li make a half-hearted effort to find the sniper, but get sidetracked into looking around the pagoda for signs of Hightower. Then after ten seconds of diligent searching and finding no obvious graffiti on the walls that says "Hightower was here but went thataway," they shrug their shoulders and trot on their merry way. (They also find no one else taking care of the pagoda. I guess one kung fu master per historic landmark is sufficient.)

They get back to the hotel just in time to catch Michelle once more entertaining thugs (but this time, it's Asian thugs) who're on the trail of the spear. More fighting ensues (man, they oughtta bottle that Bruce Li and sell him in corner stores), and the thug leader spills the beans about Hightower being somewhere in—the Philippines! Boy, I thought we'd never get there! And extra weirdness: Hightower is supposed to be looking for the fabled Venus Valley, an Amazon-inhabited lost world somewhere in southeast Asia where the shaft of the spear is hidden; the spear and the shaft have to be brought together to have any power (excepting, one assumes, that whole "traveling through time" thing, and that "turning the impaled to ash" thing).

So. Over to exotic Manila we go, where Slade and Michelle ooh and ah some more at the buildings (these three minutes brought to you by the Philippine Tourism Commission). But there's a mysterious someone who's waiting for them—an evil, nefarious white supremacist who wants the spear to rid the world of all the inferior races, even if it takes a nuclear cleansing! We don't see his face right off, but that's okay; he's got the most overacting hands I've ever seen, which makes up for it. And really—given that there are absolutely no other characters it could possibly be (unless you think it's Bruce Li), I'll just clue you in: it's Professor Fielding, the guy from the university who offered to relieve Michelle of the spear. And let's just think about this: A), how can someone on an academic's salary afford a foreign villa, plus all the equipment for his neo-Nazi army? and B) would a white supremacist be really happy to have his secret hideout in the Philippines, surrounded by, you know, all those brown people (quite a few of whom are among his foot soldiers)?

Fielding's goons try to nab Slade and Michelle at the hotel; many luggage carts and potted plants figure in the ensuing chase, as you can well imagine. The goons grab Michelle, and Slade follows in a convenient vehicle back to Fielding's lair. Apparently the international date line runs right through the Philippines, because mid-pursuit it changes from pitch-black night to the middle of the

---

[1] That's "Li," not "Lee"; he was one of the dozen or so semi-lookalike martial artists who tried to make a career out of being Bruce Lee's "successor" after Lee's death.

day. Slade, ex-Marine that he is, fights his way through Nazi fodder to the inner room where Fielding and his chief goon loom over Michelle and the much-sought Professor Hightower (Paul Holmes), the latter manacled to the wall. Fielding triumphantly pulls the spear from Michelle's shoulder bag, and he and his entourage leave. Kill the captives here and now? Nah—not when he can fire rockets at his own villa from a helicopter to kill them, right? But Slade and Michelle had enough time to escape the villa first (Hightower, not so much), and gee, wouldn't you know it, there's a second chopper right there, ready to go. Heck, an extra copy of Fielding's flight plans to the Venus Valley are sitting right there on the seat.

It's one thing for a movie not even to try. It's another when it proudly displays the fact, practically walking up to you, slapping you in the face, and proclaiming, "We're not even trying!"

But this chase doesn't get very far, because Fielding has a remote explosive wired to his second chopper. But he waits long enough before pushing the button that Slade and Michelle can jump to safety in the water. And it's only a minor delay; on land, Slade immediately finds a small aircraft hangar and steals a single-prop plane. And of course, he's got the flight plan memorized, so off they go after Fielding again. But now there's no place to land near the right coordinates, and they're almost out of fuel, so they have to bail out again (using a parachute this time) while the plane crashes.

(You'd like to think we're somewhere near the end now, wouldn't you? Wouldn't you? Ha ha ha ha HA HAHAHAHAHA*cough* cough… Hack…)

We'll cut short their bickering "banter" in the jungle; suffice it to say that, for the first time since I originally saw *Romancing the Stone*, I really wished I were watching it again instead. But that's all cut short when they stumble, yes, right into the Nazi camp and into Fielding's clutches. Michelle's again almost about to be given the "rough love"

treatment by one of the Nazis (boy, does *she* ever attract Mr. Wrong) when the camp is attacked…

…By Mongols.

Just reliving the scene as I write about it makes me want to poke at my cerebral cortex with a straight pin until I skewer that specific memory. Why are there Mongols on horseback, with swords and primitive firearms, inhabiting a Philippine jungle? Not only is there no answer, no one even acts like it's a question.

Cue a really boring battle between Nazis and Mongols as a lot of extras we've never seen before get killed. Ten minutes later, when the smoke clears, Slade and Michelle have once again escaped into the jungle with the spear. And there, they meet…

Okay, let me preface this. I'm thinking that the original intention was to get this movie into drive-ins, and the assumption was that by this time, just about everyone there would be making out and paying no attention to the screen. (After all, who wouldn't be turned on by all the "jungle bickering" bits? Not to mention all of the "Michelle almost gets gang-raped yet again" scenes.) And you know, if I were at the drive-in for this flick, I'd neck with just about anything to distract me from the feature. But you really have to feel bad for anyone who was getting hot 'n' heavy, happened to glance up at the screen, and saw…

…Midget Filipino cavepeople.

Seriously. It's like they hired every midget, dwarf, and other variety of little person in the Philippines (plus a few children thrown in to fill out their numbers)

to wrap themselves in burlap and meet Slade and Michelle in the jungle. They're a friendly sort, but they've been having awful trouble with the Mongols, so they make a deal with Slade and Michelle: you help us defeat the Mongols, we'll show you where the Venus Valley is. You know, where the spear's shaft is. That goes with the head of the spear of Longinus. That Matthew brought back from the future. I thought you'd appreciate the recap, since we've moved so far away from the initial premise that the opening scenes must seem like a distant memory.

And now? Now a full fifteen-minute digression as Slade, Michelle, and the Mighty Munchkins sneak up on the Mongol camp and attack. Here are some things you may not know about Mongols: their camps are liberally decorated with oil drums, and they buy modern chemicals in plastic containers to mix their own gunpowder for their primitive firearms. And despite their reputation as ruthless warriors, they can be easily taken on their home turf by a dozen midgets and two whiny Americans.

Fifteen irreplaceable minutes of my life later, the Mongols are wiped out, and the cave-dwarfs cheerfully point the way to the Venus Valley. Of course, before they get that far… you guessed it. Right into the hands of the Nazis again. By this time, I was about ready to slip Fielding a Jackson to just kill them and be done with it, but no; before he can do anything decisive—Amazon attack! (Filipino Amazon attack.) They kill a bunch of Nazis and take Slade and Michelle prisoner.

And when Michelle tells them what she and Slade are looking for, the Head Amazon declares that the only way to earn the right to go up to the cave at the end of the valley is single combat. Not Slade; Michelle. Boy, that'd be a real nailbiter if we cared. As it is, despite the fact that the awkward Michelle is facing the Amazons' undefeated champion, it takes little time for her to knock her opponent into the crocodile pit and earn their passage.

And in the cave, they find... well, a stick. (What were you expecting?) Oh, and Fielding, showing up for his last-ditch attempt to get the whole spear-and-accessory set for himself. Slade and Fielding fight; Fielding gets killed with the spearhead. (Oh, irony... or something.) Naturally, the cave decides to collapse into huge styrofoam boulders, but Slade and Michelle are dug out by the cave midgets. ("Hey, we've paid for the whole troupe through Thursday—maybe we should use them again!")

Michelle emerges into the sunlight, fits the spearhead to the shaft, holds it aloft, and... The end.

That's it? The spear doesn't *do* anything?

Nope. Roll credits.

This pitiful excuse for a motion picture comes to us courtesy of Cirio H. Santiago, notorious Philippines-based hack director from the Corman stable who has quite likely directed more forgettable post-apocalyptic movies than anyone before or since (with the possible exception of Albert Pyun). But even having seen several of Santiago's other movies, I still didn't anticipate that he could put his hand to such an ill-conceived—or *un-*conceived—project. It's a movie that surprises and horrifies you by hitting what you thought was bottom pretty early, then digging several sub-basements below that.

Even more horrifying is that the screenplay is by J.L. (aka "J. Lee") Thompson, director of the last two *Planet of the Apes* movies. Thank whatever you hold holy that, of all the filched crap that shows up in here, he didn't throw in any talking chimps.

And in retrospect, it's easy to see what's the best part of the movie: Richard Norton as *Mad Max* ripoff Matthew, waaaaay back there at the beginning. Sure, he's no master thespian, but his fight scenes were energetic, well-paced, and natural-looking. I could have watched ninety minutes of meaningless post-apocalyptic combat of that caliber pretty easily, relatively speaking... On the other hand, if Matthew hadn't brought the spear back in time, there's no reason to suppose that a world-cleansing freak like Fielding would have ever had a chance to get hold of it... so the only thing making the future apocalypse Matthew's trying to forestall possible is the effort of the man trying to keep the apocalypse from happening.

Well, what do you know. This whole movie is even more useless and pointless than previously supposed.

Some Notable Totables:
- body count: 82
- breasts: 3
- explosions: 33
- ominous thunderstorms: 0
- upset fruitstands: 1
- actors who've appeared on *Star Trek*: 0

PRAY For DEATH (1985)

THEY SHATTERED HIS AMERICAN DREAM. SHO KOSUGI, MASTER NINJA, REDEFINES REVENGE.

- *Directed by Gordon Hessler*
- *Written by James Booth*
- *Starring Sho Kosugi, James Booth, Donna Kei Benz, Kane Kosugi and Shane Kosugi*
- *Produced by Don Van Atta*
- *Executive produced by Moshe Barkat, Moshe Diamant and Sunil R. Shah*

There was a big difference between American ninja movies and Hong Kong ninja movies in the '80s. In Hong Kong, ninjas were the Japanese heavies being defeated by the heroic Chinese. (Jeez, get over it, will you? I mean, you don't see Americans still making movies about the war against the Nazis... oh wait, never mind.) In the U.S., the ninjas were the heroes—mysterious, disquieting heroes, but heroes nonetheless.

Of course, to turn a natural heavy into a hero, you have to do something to mitigate that bad-ass ninja mystique. The obvious solution: make him a former ninja, trying to forget his shadowy past but forced back into using his deadly skills for self-defense.

Enter Sho Kosugi.

There are plenty of great martial artists, and I'm sure some of them could whip Kosugi in a fair fight, but no one has ever been as good a movie ninja as Kosugi. Especially as a reluctant ninja; he made so many movies with his character being forced to use his ninja skills to protect his family (usually including at least one of his two real-life sons Kane and Shane Kosugi playing his movie sons), it practically became a subgenre of its own. And as for that fair fight above? Forget it; ninjas don't believe in fair fights. Ninjas play to win.

In classic form, then, Kosugi is Akira, a middle-management type at a Yokohama produce company, with a Japanese-American wife, two sons, and a secret: he was raised an orphan in a ninja shrine and became a ninja. Of course, because this is a secret even from his family, he plays the mild-mannered dad to a T, despite his children's obsession with the *Black Ninja* TV show.

At a turning point in his career, he and his wife decide to move to America, where they buy a small restaurant from its retired owner and set out to make a new life.

Naturally, trouble drops in their lap, in the form of crooked cops who have been using the unused back room of the restaurant as a drop for stolen goods. One of the cops takes this occasion to cheat on his employer and keep the big-ass necklace for himself; when the goons find it missing, they first assume that the retired restauranteur took it; the fact that he's moving out of town only confirms their suspicion. They cut him off leaving town, and show why they're not top bananas: instead of actually searching his car and luggage, they say, "Hey, this'll take too long," and blow it up. The old guy, too.

Naturally, they next come after Akira's family. Now, like I said, Kosugi's characters

always hold back. Even when the heavies kidnap his son, he shows up quietly and rescues him.

But everyone has a breaking point—and for Akira, it's when the heavies run down his wife and one son in the street, then show up in the hospital to finish the job.

Time for a ninja ass-kicking.

I'll admit that it's a hackneyed excuse for a story, but I don't care. Kosugi just exudes controlled cool. He can do double backflips and pin you with his sword. He can tell the American cops to go to hell so authoritatively that they start packing their bags. He can escape from chains and melt into the shadows. He can even forge his own sword, since he brought no ninja weapons with him to America. And he can look cool even with floppy hair that looks like he went to Jackie Chan's barber.

Alas, Kosugi disappeared from the scene after starring in roughly ten movies and appearing in supporting roles in a handful more. One can only imagine that he retired to a quiet corner of his native Japan, waiting for the occasion for the ninja to rise again... maybe with a haircut this time.

Some Notable Totables:
- body count: 23 (plus another 15 in the opening episode of *The Black Ninja*)
- breasts: 0
- explosions: 3
- ominous thunderstorms: 0
- flashbacks: 1
- trips to the cemetery: 2
- thugs named "Bubba": 1
- "homages" to *Raiders of the Lost Ark*: 1
- actors who've appeared on *Star Trek*: 3
  - Matthew Faison ("Sargeant Daley") appeared as Surmak Ren on the 1st season *DS9* episode "Babel"
  - Parley Baer (Sam Green, the unfortunate widower) played "old man" in the 3rd season *Voyager* episode "Sacred Ground"
  - Robert Ito (Kaga, Akira's adoptive priest-father) was "Tactical Officer Lt. Chang" in the *TNG* 1st season episode "Coming of Age"

TRANCERS (1985)

Jack Deth is back... and he's never even been here before.

aka *Future Cop*

- Produced and directed by Charles Band
- Written by Paul De Meo and Danny Bilson
- Starring Tim Thomerson, Helen Hunt, Michael Stefani, Art La Fleur and Telma Hopkins

Over a forty-year career with the stated goal of becoming the next Roger Corman, legendary crapmeister Charles Band has produced (or executive produced or associate produced or whatever) roughly three hundred movies. Some few, such as *Re-Animator* and *Crawlspace* and *The Pit and the Pendulum*, have become much-beloved classics among that segment of the movie-going public that pays attention to such things. Many of the rest, including much of the output of the "Full Moon Pictures" label which he created specifically for direct-to-video content, are best not mentioned in polite company.

And just like Corman, Band has directed a small proportion of the movies he's produced. Some of them feel as though production was ready to start and they didn't have a director for some reason, so Band took the chair. In any case, the movies that Band both produced and directed, like *Metalstorm: The Destruction of Jared-Syn* (1983) or *Doctor Mordrid* (1992), don't have any particular twinkle to them over the ones he produced without directing.

But if Charles Band will ever be fondly remembered as a director, it will be for this movie: *Trancers*. No one will ever mistake it for a good movie, but it's got that certain something that manages to impress only its positive qualities on the viewer's memory.

Tim Thomerson is Jack Deth, a Chandleresque cop on the Angel City PD in the 23rd century, an era which seems to delight in retro fashion and furnishings (sure makes it easy on the costumer and set dresser, doesn't it?). As he explains in the requisite *noir* voiceover, his driving mission up until now has been the apprehension of one Martin Whistler (Michael Stefani), who's used his innate psychic powers to grow a cult of mind-controlled followers called trancers; this obsession has been more than a little personal, as trancers also killed Deth's wife. Now that Whistler is supposedly dead, Deth is basically drifting around, ignoring his current assignments, mopping up stray trancers like the cook in the diner where he stops for coffee. (The cook graciously exhibits for us the features that will distinguish a trancer in full berserker mode, to wit: pasty skin, blackened eyes, and foam-flecked drool. In other words, identical to the protagonist in most Tim Burton movies.)

Deth gives up his badge, tired of the grief he gets over his personal vendetta, but re-ups when he gets a special summons from the Council, the three-person ruling body that governs this post-quake California. It seems that Whistler isn't dead after all, and he has managed to go back in time in order to kill the ancestors of the Council members. Because of Deth's intimate knowledge of Whistler, not to mention his more-than-a-paycheck motivation, he's selected to follow

Whistler back to 1985 Los Angeles, protect the ancestors of the two remaining Council members (one's already been phased out by Whistler's actions), and head Whistler off.

One of the movie's more memorable devices is a clever little reversal of the time travel rules of *The Terminator,* which posited that living tissue was the only thing that could survive time transit. Here, time machines that can send objects back in time, but in order for living people to go "down the line" they have to be pharmaceutically regressed into the body of an ancestor in the appropriate time period. Deth thus ends up in the body of a journalist progenitor, Phil, who's just finished a one-night stand with young Lena (Helen Hunt—everybody pays their dues, brother). Meanwhile, Whistler's got a leg up; his ancestor in that time period, Whysling, just happens to be a police lieutenant.

Now, the setup's designed for economy; aside from a couple of futuristic interior sets (and a matte shot of the post-quake skyscrapers of "Lost Angeles" poking out of the Pacific), the entire movie can play out in various unassuming locales around present-day L.A. Special effects are also kept to a minimum; Deth is given his own Bond-style toolkit to help him out, but one is simply a .38 special which also secretly holds two doses of the time-travel antidote to bring Deth and Whistler back to the 23rd century, and the other is a "long-second" wristwatch which can slow time for Deth, giving him ten seconds in the place of one. This technological marvel is presented for us on screen by an equally advanced cinematic technique called "slow motion."

Nonetheless, even cheap locations can be used to good effect: a department store North Pole display (complete with a trancer Santa), a tanning salon, various sections of Chinatown, and an abandoned pulpmill inhabited by homeless drunks provide enough color and variation to liven up the paltry budget, as Deth, assisted by Lena, attempts to get to the Council's ancestors

and, naturally, falls in love along the way. If you can just manage to ignore one of the worst film scores ever to saddle a movie, you'll be in good hands.

What really brings the movie to life is Tim Thomerson, having the time of his life as Jack Deth. Perfectly grizzled and square-jawed, Thomerson's early showbiz experience was in comedy, and he brings just the right light touch of self-parody to his hyperbolically hard-boiled role with his slicked-back hair, trenchcoat and retro-future lingo of "singeing trancers" and "small-minded squids" (the people weak-willed enough to be tranceable). And mention must be made of recognizable but undersung character actor Art La Fleur as Deth's superior McNulty, simply because not to mention La Fleur whenever he appears in a movie is a mortal sin.

Whatever you do, do not attempt to make sense of causality in this movie, as *Trancers* is worse than most time travel movies in that regard. (This came out in 1985, the same year that *Back to the Future* also required moviegoers to check their brains at the door and not wonder why someone in an alternate timeline would have been taking a picture of an empty hedge.) When an ancestor is killed in the past, the descendant in the 23rd century simply disappears—but nothing else in the timeline has changed; everyone remembers the person and reacts with horror, despite the fact that this person has retroactively been rendered non-existent. It's enough to make you want to kill your own grandfather.

But that's nothing compared to how the successive movies play with the series' continuity. *Trancers* was produced through Empire Pictures, Charles Band's production company that provided theatrical B-movies during the '80s. The first sequel was produced in 1991 by Band's successor company, Full Moon Pictures, which instead produced direct-to-video fare exclusively. *Trancers II* was largely a less successful retread of the premise of the first movie, with Deth and Lena still protecting the one councilman's ancestor who survived from the last movie against the trancers now created by Whistler's brother. 1992's *Trancers III* changed the origin of the trancers themselves, making then the result of a covert U.S. military experiment; it also marks the last appearance of Helen Hunt as Lena in a small role. *Trancers 4* and *5*, shot back-to-back in 1994, threw Jack Deth into a medieval "alternate universe" (one that looked a lot like Romania, which is where Full Moon was shooting the majority of their pictures by then), in which trancers were a vampire-like ruling class exploiting the human villagers. By 2002's *Trancers 6*, Full Moon's production budgets had dropped to the point that even Tim Thomerson was beyond their resources, and the story instead places the 23rd-century psyche of Jack Deth in the body of the never-before-mentioned daughter of his 20th-century marriage to Lena—a cute concept, but one which ultimately doesn't satisfy those for whom Thomerson was increasingly the only worthwhile part of the *Trancers* films.

Some Notable Totables:
- body count: 5
- breasts: 0
- explosions: 1
- ominous thunderstorms: 0
- actors who've appeared on *Star Trek*: 2
  - Richard Herd (Councilman Spencer) had a recurring rols as "Admiral Owen Paris" on *Voyager*, and also played "L'Kor" in the *TNG* two-parter "Birthright"
  - Biff Manard ("Hap Ashby," the drunk ballplayer ancestor) played "Ruffian" in the *TNG* episode "Elementary, Dear Data"

LAND of DOOM (1986)

THE LAST WARRIOR WOMAN. A DARK RAIDER OF DEATH. THE BATTLE FOR SURVIVAL BEGINS AT THE END OF THE EARTH!

- *Directed by Peter Maris*
- *Written by Craig Rand, based on the novel by Peter Kotis*
- *Starring Deborah Rennard, Garrick Dowhen, Daniel Radell, Frank Garret and Akut Duz*
- *Produced by Peter Maris and Sonny Vest*
- *Executive produced by Ken Kimura and Walter Schroetter*

We probably all remember seeing this cover on the video store rental shelves for over two decades. It's a stunner, really, and that's perversely what kept me from renting it for most of that time. The reasoning goes something like this:

- The cover kicks major ass.
- If the movie were anywhere as good as the cover, I would have heard about it.
- I have heard nary a peep about this movie.
- Therefore, the movie is nowhere as cool as the cover. In fact, it probably sucks, rather than kicks, ass.

With that kind of expectation, I am happy to report that this movie isn't as bad as I had imagined. Of course, since my expectations were as low as they could go, "not entirely rancid" is about what I mean by "pretty good."

As we all know from exposure to the standard post-apocalyptic scenario, the ravaged future is made up of scattered human settlements in an arid land, terrorized by ruthless raiders (herein officially known as "Raiders"). Our opening scene is one such raid, a night filled with burning homes and plenty of rape. The Raiders seem to be dedicated to a "scorched earth" policy, and thus it is only by craftiness and sneakiness that our blonde heroine, Harmony (Deborah Rennard), escapes them and makes her way to a nearby cave (preternaturally well-lit, too, after the town scenes) to wait out the night.

There she finds a lone stranger, Anderson (Garrick Dowhen), wounded and thirsty after being stranded there by his injuries for two days. She grudgingly gives him some water, and he shoots a snake about to bite her, so in lowest-common-denominator story mechanics, they might as well start picking out china patterns. But of course, it's going to take the male-hostile Harmony the whole movie to realize the worth of a good man. Or even of this one.

When she leaves the next morning, with no particular destination, Anderson importunes for permission to tag along, promising not to get in the way and all that. (He does keep up well for being too wounded to roll over for 48 hours.) So off they go.

But of course, Anderson has history with the Raiders. Specifically, he's one of their former organizers, trying to turn them into a force for rebuilding. (I certainly hope he called them something different back then, or else recruits were probably signing up with entirely the wrong picture.) In a power struggle, he ruined the face of the usurper, Slater (Daniel Radell), who now wears a mask not nearly as cool as the one on the box cover, and who wants Anderson taken care of permanently.

Thus, Harmony and Anderson's trail is dogged by a number of Slater's lackeys, all of whom wear the studliest studded leather harnesses you ever did see, and drive motorbikes decked out with flaps and spikes. The bad guys aren't the only scenery to be appreciated, by the way. This production apparently took place in the "Peri Bacalar" area of Turkey (though the credits decline to identify the locale—they can spend an entire screen length on who wrote/sang/produced/recorded/arranged/sang backup on the theme song, but they couldn't spare a line for "This movie was filmed here"). The locations and backdrops are full of stone homesteads, carved-out cliff dwellings, and a landscape which demonstrates that all arid futures need not look like the Australian outback or Bronson Canyon. It does lead you to wonder, though, how much time has passed since the holocaust; most of the clothing is roughed-up versions of modern (i.e., mid-'80s) fashions, but people have apparently had time to build structures and have them age a good while. (Thinking too much. Must stop. *THUMP* Better.)

Plotting, of course, is a matter of convenience, with genre conventions, already well-established in 1986, being strung together on the flimsiest of rationales. The Raiders seem to burn and pillage for no motive but sheer nastiness; they don't gather booty from the villages they destroy, nor do they keep any prisoners alive for slave labor to support their lifestyles of über-macho excess. At the very least, they need someone to attach new studs onto leather harnesses. Amidst all of this, there are a couple of touches of intelligence, such as the mention of alcohol as the motorcycles' fuel, thus removing the "Where the hell's the gasoline coming from?" elephant in the living room.

(And I notice that several of the Raider goons wear gas masks as part of their getup at their BatCave headquarters, which makes perfect sense when you consider several dozen sweaty men batching it in a desert environment without the benefit of running water...)

Naturally, Harmony and Anderson end up depending on each other, despite her implied rape trauma or somesuch that makes her suspicious of men in general. It's a pity then that the plot threw her in with such a milksop, because Anderson, frankly, is useless. He's got a square jaw, sure, but he's a wounded gimp for most of the picture; what's more, he's got a raging case of Male Answer Syndrome, acting more like a surrogate father to Harmony than an equal traveling companion, and always talking like he's got all the answers. (Anderson's best fortune-cookie line: "You can't change the world by killing everybody." I dunno, I think that would constitute a pretty significant change right there.) But despite his beatific calm and resolute moral compass, Anderson keeps getting his ass into a crack and needing Harmony to pull it out.

This is one of those "bathroom break" movies, in which any time is a good time to go potty without hitting the pause button because most of what happens really doesn't affect the story. Harmony and Anderson's adventures—encountering rag-wrapped plague victims, stumbling onto a trio of cannibal brothers, and battling a variety of incompetent Raider thugs—happen in no particular order, mostly marking time between opening and closing credits. Plotting gets so lax eventually that we have to have a new character introduced twenty minutes from the end, Orland (Akut Duz), whom Anderson and Harmony rescue from some wild dogs; he's thus close enough when Harmony and Anderson get scooped up by the Raiders that he can effect a rescue at the last minute, along with a tribe of unexplained Jawas. This kind of character is known in genre literature as a "spear-carrier," after the ubiquitous lackey characters who return a slight favor earlier by pulling the hero's fat out of the fire at the climactic moment; in Orland's case, though, the label isn't entirely accurate, as he springs out at an opportune juncture with a flamethrower on his side.

Despite the general slackness of the story, though, it's not a painful movie to sit through. Vapid, yes, and unambitious, but not painful. At least events move at a fair pace, and if your attention starts to wander, there's the pretty scenery to look at behind the performers.

All the same, though, looking at the cover illustration and imagining the movie it could have gone to is a helluva lot more fun.

Some Notable Totables:
- body count: 33, plus 1 snake
- breasts: 0
- explosions: 26
- ominous thunderstorms: 0
- actors who've appeared on *Star Trek*: 1
- Richard Allen ("Halsey") played "Kentor" in the *TNG* episode "Ensigns of Command," and "Tamarian First Officer" in "Darmok"

NIGHT of the CREEPS (1986)

The good news is your date is here. The bad news is... he's dead.

- Written and directed by Fred Dekker
- Starring Jason Lively, Steve Marshall, Jill Whitlow, Tom Atkins and Wally Taylor
- Produced by Charles Gordon
- Executive produced by William Finnegan

"Oh my God, oh my God, oh my God, oh my God, oh my God, oh my God! Do you think it's taking the Lord's name in vain to say 'oh my God' a whole bunch of times really fast like that?"

Ladies and gentlemen, I give you the quintessential B-movie. A laundry list of features should prove sufficient to whet your appetites:

- midget aliens
- brain-eating alien slugs
- zombies
- a world-weary detective
- nerdy freshmen trying to get the attention of beautiful sorority girls, who are in turn going out with Nazi frat boys
- an axe-murderer
- character actor Dick Miller

To put it all in a semblance of order for you:

We open with butt-ugly midget aliens having a rather violent dispute aboard their spaceship, with one of them managing to jettison some sort of experimental canister amidst laser fire.

The canister ends up crash-landing in 1959 America (shot in black and white), adjacent to the campus of Corman University (ha ha), where young lovers Johnny and Pam break off from their "parking" to investigate. When Johnny goes into the woods to find the canister, an alien space slug flies into his mouth; Pam waits nervously in the car until an escaped mental patient with an ax cuts the evening short.

Fast forward to 1986, where freshmen Chris (Jason Lively, smack in the middle of his underperforming career) drifts around campus with his witty friend, double-crutch cripple J.C. (Steve Marshall). You know, I learned in high school, while studying *The Catcher in the Rye*, that characters named "J.C." usually die a martyr's death. Whoops, hope that's not too much of a spoiler. Chris is instantly smitten with sorority girl Cynthia Cronenberg (can't wait to go home and meet dad!) (Jill Whitlow), but being a nervous freshman he can't bring himself to talk to her, despite J.C.'s sarcastic prodding. No, instead he tries to take the circuitous route—pledging the Beta fraternity. Of course, the facts that A) they're geeks and B) Beta president Brad is Cynthia's boyfriend kind of doom the enterprise.

Nevertheless, they're given a pledge assignment (furthering my thesis that '80s teen movies are actually fantasy quest tales in disguise) to snatch a cadaver from somewhere and deposit it on the steps of a rival frat. In search of such a thing, they sneak into the Med Center on campus and accidentally luck into something else hidden in the basement: a cryogenic chamber, complete with the prologue's Johnny in a tank (the American version of Prince Albert in a can). It being the closest corpse at hand, they try to abscond with poor Johnny, but when his eyes open, they freak and run away.

Johnny, obviously, is not terribly dead, and after killing a medical grad student and spitting a space slug into his mouth, goes on a stroll across campus, ending up at the window of the sorority house that used to be his girlfriend Pam's—and is now Cynthia's. Cynthia is treated to a view from her window of a smiling naked cadaver whose head splits open, spilling slugs into the shrubbery.

The ensuing police investigation of both the dead grad student and the ambulatory cadaver falls to Detective Cameron (Tom Atkins), world-weary and hard-boiled; he also happens to have been Patrolman Cameron, Pam's boyfriend prior to Johnny, who discovered her body after the ax murderer was finished with it, a fact that has haunted his life ever since.

It doesn't take Cameron long to track down Chris and J.C., as both were identified by the Med Center night janitor, but since they obviously didn't run from the building with the corpse under their arm, they're turned loose. But not before Cameron scares Chris poopless by relating how he had long ago tracked down the psycho, blown him away, and buried him in a vacant lot which is now occupied by the sorority house mother's cottage.

Now, let's see: there's a corpse hidden under the building right next to where there was a big spill of slugs that like to reanimate the dead. What's better than an ax murderer? A *zombie* ax murderer!

What ensues is just plain tons of mayhem, culminating in a busload of frat boys crashing and dying on the way to pick up their dates for the formal, then being reanimated and proceeding on their dates, while Cameron, Chris, and Cynthia defend the sorority house with a 12-gauge and a flamethrower. (Where's J.C.? Um, remember what I said about martyr's deaths? Yeah.)

Now, I don't know if I've said it before, but I'll say it now: any movie whose climax involves blowing the heads off slug-infested frat boys is a winner in my book. And this

movie wins in spades. There's even a lawnmower scene which could very well have inspired Peter Jackson's longer such scene in *Dead Alive* (1992).

As B-movies go, this one is just about right. Nowhere is the truncated budget visible; in fact, between the alien ship interiors and the 1959 period recreation (complete with licensed music like "Smoke Gets In Your Eyes" and "Put Your Head On My Shoulder"), we're given the impression that there was plenty of money to go around. Writer/ director Fred Dekker gives us a script chock-full of witticisms and in-jokes (though it goes a little too far in character nomenclature: in addition to the aforementioned Corman and Cronenberg references, we also have characters named Raimi and Landis), not to mention a lengthy segment of iconic so-bad-it's-good flick *Plan 9 From Outer Space* (1959) on the house mother's TV and a good cameo by Dick Miller.

With his directorial hat on, Dekker then presents said script in rare fashion, replete with comic-booky gore, engaging pacing, and just plain fun.

It's sad, therefore, to look at Dekker's career and wonder just how someone this good seems to have trouble staying on the radar. He wrote the original story for *House* (1986), made the wonderful movie under discussion, wrote and directed the well-regarded cult '80s movie *The Monster Squad* (1987), wrote and directed some episodes of *Tales From the Crypt*, co-wrote and directed *Robocop 3* (1993) (which could probably explain a lot of his career woes), and wrote a few episodes of *Enterprise* while also acting as "consulting producer" on that show; in between, he's credited with the stories of a couple of movies that no one's heard of. But despite his hot-and-cold resume, there's only one man on Earth who can have etched on his tombstone "I made *Night of the Creeps*." That's accomplishment enough right there.

Some Notable Totables:
- body count: roughly 32 (what, like I'm gonna stop and count frat boys?), plus one cat and one dog
- breasts: 4
- explosions: 3
- dream sequences: 1
- ominous thunderstorms: 0
- spring-loaded cats: 1
- actors who've appeared on *Star Trek*: 4
  - David Oliver (Steve, the unibrowed jock) played "Young Man" (what a role) in the *TNG* 5th season episode "Cost of Living"
  - Lori Lively (Lori, one of the sorority girls) was "Siana" in the *DS9* 7th season "Shadows and Symbols (she also was in *Free Enterprise*, which almost counts)
  - Todd Bryant (credited as "Informative Student") was Klingon Captain Klaa in *Star Trek 5* (and *Star Trek 6*, but you have to look fast to catch him)
  - Dick Miller (the police armorer) was "Vin" in the *DS9* 3rd-season two-parter "Past Tense" and the vendor in the *TNG* 1st-season episode "The Big Goodbye"

The RIPPER (1986)

From out of a dream, he returns to stalk the living...

- Directed by Christopher Lewis
- Written by Bill Groves
- Starring Tom Savini, Tom Schreier, Mona Van Pernis, Wade Tower and Andrea Adams
- Produced by Linda Lewis
- Executive produced by Bill F. Blair

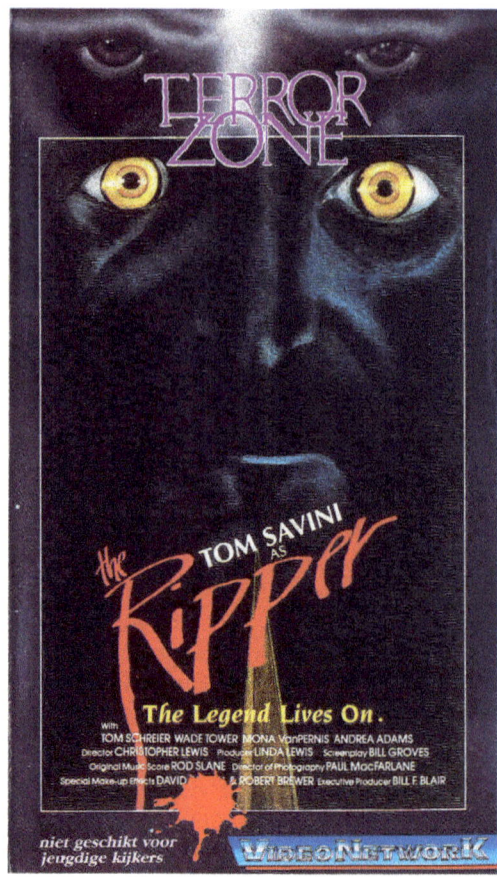

Because I am a tremendously fair individual (I'm also charming, nice-smelling, and kind to animals), I always try to grade movies on an appropriate curve. The present movie, *The Ripper*, was made as a follow-up by the same people who brought us *Blood Cult* (1985), the grandpappy of the shot-on-video, direct-to-video feature (reviewed on page 25). Wisely, those worthies realized that simply doing more of the same would not bring them the same level of success; *Blood Cult* banked hard on its publicity and novelty value, and that's a nickel that really couldn't be spent again. So they tried to make a better movie. And, honestly, they succeeded. On a comparable budget ($70,000) and shooting schedule (two weeks), they made a movie that is demonstrably better. Which does not, I hasten to add, mean that it is a "good" movie by any widely-acknowledged scale of reference. But if you, like I, were to watch these movies in relatively quick succession, you would definitely see and appreciate the improvement. It's not much, but such tiny rewards are the only things that keep me going some days.

The opening scene takes on the daunting task of a shooting location in Tulsa, Oklahoma standing in for the Whitechapel area of London, circa 1888, as a woman exits a horse-drawn cab at night, waits under a streetlamp for a few minutes, and then flees a stalking figure in cloak and top hat, only to end up on the edge of his blade. Yes, it's a clichéd scene, and that turns out to be the point: university professor Richard Harwell (Tom Schreier) has just started teaching a course on famous crimes in the movies, and he uses that scenario as a specifically "Hollywood-like" treatment of Jack the Ripper-style killings. It seems an odd sort of undergrad course, especially since it doesn't seem to be tied in to any of the conventional departments like Film Studies or History (Harwell may even be a lit professor, according to a reference to one of his other courses). In any event, he's got about a dozen students, notable among whom are Steve (Wade Tower), a horror movie maven, and his long-suffering girlfriend Cindy (Andrea Adams).

Harwell also has a significant other, Carol (Mona Van Pernis), a dance instructor on campus. That gives us an opportunity for what we all hope to see in a mid-'80s movie: A bad *Flashdance* scene! Since Carol's status as a dancer is never referenced again, the sole point of this scene is to take up as many minutes as possible.

Which means that we're seventeen

minutes in before we finally getting close to starting the plot. Harwell and Carol go to an antique store to see the brass bedframe that Carol's all ga-ga over; while she's dickering with the owner, Harwell wanders around and finds a huge gaudy gold-and-ruby ring. Bemused, he puts it on, and is overcome with hazy flashbacks of someone getting knifed. He doesn't decide to buy the ring right away, though—not until he sees a drawing in the book from which he's teaching of an identical ring that was found at the site of the Ripper's last murder. (Yes, a clue found in a book illustration was a prominent plot point in *Blood Cult*, too.)

Even before Harwell found the ring, there were reports of "Ripper-like" killings in town. And reports is all we get for the first several murders, until we see a cocktail waitress in a dark parking lot being assaulted by a shadowy figure in a cloak and top hat. Harwell's contribution to the story is mostly to fall asleep early in the evenings (while watching horror movies) and be out of sorts in class the next day. We spend plenty of "couple time" with Harwell and Carol, as well as with Steve and Cindy, though why they're of any importance is a mystery for most of the running time. It turns out that Steve becomes a full participant in the plot when A) he notices that Harwell's got a new ring and has started using his left hand far more than he used to (the Ripper was left-handed, you know), and B) a lengthy parking session with Cindy turns bad, and he ends up as the Ripper's next victim.

The more I describe this movie for you, the less supportable my above contention of improved quality seems, even to myself. So let me point out the pluses:

The acting is a full order of magnitude better than in *Blood Cult*. Tom Schreier as Harwell is the best of the lot, as befits the character with the most screen time. And the interactions between the members of our two couples, Harwell/Carol and Steve/Cindy, is surprisingly relaxed and authentic. I wouldn't be surprised to learn that either or both of these were real-life relationships off-set.

The gore FX, when we finally get to them, are pretty decent. Jack the Ripper was known for slitting throats and disemboweling his victims, both of which are effects that are often botched on productions with ten times the budget; here, both effects are pretty convincing. (Although I'm still not convinced that a pay telephone cord, when used as a tool of strangulation, would actually cut the throat wide open.)

On the other hand, our top-billed star, FX-guru-turned-cult-actor Tom Savini, only showed up for one day of shooting for those scenes which required his face to be seen (no word on whether the stand-in was a chiropractor[1]), and appears only in the last five minutes of the movie. Savini's always had a lot more screen presence than most people give him credit for, but his turn as the spirit of the Ripper is hideously mismanaged. Only with his last victim does he prattle on and on explaining (without really explaining) how his killings give him immortality, in a manner so suave and refined as to be almost fey.

And frankly, the screenplay plants a lot more seeds than it ever intends to harvest. The entire idea of the class examining the inaccuracies in cinematic depictions of crimes goes entirely unused; despite the protestation that the initial scene we were shown exemplified Hollywood's stylized take on such crimes, every "real" killing we see thereafter follows wholly in its footsteps in terms of style and staging. If there's a reality to such crimes that horror movies don't handle well, we really ought not to be informed of that in a movie which isn't going to handle them any better, or any differently.

The closing scene, in fact, is a concatenation of arbitrary B-movie writing, in which we're supposed to believe that the simple sight of three cars parked near a closed warehouse will cause a small-town policeman to call massive quantities of backup, all of whom will train their weapons on an open door and then, without any announcement or warning, open fire *en masse* on an individual who is very obviously unarmed. It makes me wonder why the local police force agreed to appear in the scene, if it was going to portray law enforcement

---

[1] That's a *Plan 9 From Outer Space* joke. We must keep ourselves amused.

procedure so poorly.

In the end, despite Harwell being the protagonist, he seems oddly self-unaware; there's never a moment in which he starts to suspect that he might have anything at all to do with the killings. Heck, there's never even a moment in which he realizes how events around him are starting to resemble the scenario of a horror movie—and if your protagonist is an academic expert in such things, it damned well ought to matter.

Some Notable Totables:
- body count: 6
- breasts: 0
- explosions: 1
- dream sequences: 1
- ominous thunderstorms: 1
- visible boom mikes: 2
- actors who've appeared on *Star Trek*: 0

The SUPERNATURALS (1986)

OUT OF THE MISTS OF TIME THEY RETURN, SEEKING REVENGE FOR THE ATROCITY THAT KILLED THEM.

- Directed by Armand Mastroianni
- Written and produced by Michael S. Murphey and Joel Soisson
- Starring Maxwell Caulfield, Nichelle Nichols, Talia Balsam, LeVar Burton and Margaret Shendal
- Executive produced by Don Levin and Mel Pearl

I'm glad that I'm not in the military. Aside from the fact that I have problems with rigid authoritarian structures and I don't like the haircuts, I'd probably react to this movie by breaking out in hives. As it is, blissfully unaware of most of the specific ignorances committed, I'm only mildly annoyed/mildly entertained.

During the Civil War, Confederate prisoners are forced by the dastardly Union forces of the 44th (division? platoon? brigade? battalion? I don't know the proper terminology) to walk across a Confederate-set minefield to clear it, made all the more cruel by the inclusion of a small boy, Jeremy (Chad Sheets), who had been dressed in a Confederate uniform. Jeremy's what an old timer has called a "special" child with some unspecified "gifts," one of which is apparently the ability to avoid the mines that kill the dozen prisoners around him, despite shuffling his feet as if her were trying to generate some static electricity. He makes it to the far side of the field… and then the Union Commander tells him to walk back…

(I'll just tell you now that, no, we never discover why the filmmakers decided to feature the Union as the bad guys. I'm guessing that all the Italian director knew about the Civil War came from watching *The Outlaw Josey Wales* (1976).)

Cut to the present, where two U.S. Army soldiers head into the country in a jeep to stake out an area, from the modern-day version of the 44th. As luck would have it, one of them is black and one is white, which means that the black one has to display his blackness by listening to his boombox loud (this is, of course, back when they were called "ghettoblasters"). The white guy is given no analogous "personality" bit, absence of melanin apparently being characterization enough. It's not like they matter much anyway; while they pound the stakes, the ground beneath them suddenly opens up, and both are dragged into the glowing fissure.

Having gone through two sets of Designated Meat players, we finally get to our main characters. Not that they're any more palatable; it's a troop (squad? unit? herd?) of eight recent recruits, being taken into the wilds for… um… some sort of training exercise or something. I guess. Ellis (Maxwell Caulfield—my wife is one of the seven living fans of *Grease 2* (1982), so this bit of casting at least got her to walk in the room for 15 seconds) qualifies for his Designated Hero status by running real fast: he drops out of the back of the truck on a bet that he couldn't catch back up and jump in. The rest of the privates range from vaguely interesting—there's the token female/love interest LeJune (Talia Balsam) and the Italian horndogger Cort (Bobby Di Cicco)—and completely uninteresting—well, that's the others. Notable among them is the token black, Osgood, as played by LeVar Burton.

But that's not the only *Star Trek* connection, as their gruff Sergeant Hawkins is played by none other than Nichelle "Uhura" Nichols! (Almost didn't recognize her without a spark plug in her ear.) I don't know who thought that Nichols was the perfect person to play the no-nonsense sarge, but I admit to taking a perverse pleasure in hearing her curse like a sailor. 'Course, if you got knocked back from Lieutenant to Sergeant, you'd probably swear too.

Frankly, I don't think she's tough enough on them. As I said, I don't know the military, but I do know discipline, and these goons don't have it. We've got whining, backtalking, lollygagging, drinking, smoking, sexual harassment, some attempted "fraternization," shooting live rounds for fun, and falling asleep on watch. This is the part that would have viewers who are also members of the U.S. Armed Forces seeing red, and it didn't impress little ol' civilian me either. Frankly, I wouldn't put up with this kind of whiny insubordination and lack of discipline from a troop of Boy Scouts. Despite my bugger-all level of knowledge on matters military, I still know more than the yahoos who wrote the script.

Hiking into their area (supposedly the one that the earlier soldiers had staked out, though they never miss the stakes—come to think of it, nobody seems to miss the soldiers themselves), they first encounter a mysterious woman (Margaret Shendal) in somewhat antiquated garb washing her face in a stream, then some spiked-log barriers such as the Confederates used to use in the Civil War (good thing there's a know-it-all along), and then a clearing (which looks just like the minefield from the prologue) where nothing grows and the ground is an odd yellow, as if some poor production assistant had hand-sprinkled sulfur all over. Opines Osgood, "Beings from an advanced world quite unlike our own landed here on Earth, shat, and left." And coming from LeVar Burton, that just sent me into the giggles.

The offensive horndogger Cort, in the middle of making gestures at LeJune, falls through the rotted ceiling of a hidden underground Confederate bunker. No, he doesn't kill himself, dammit. Ellis explores it briefly and finds a desiccated skeleton, but he doesn't think this is worth mentioning to his commanding officer. Do I need to keep pointing out that this script was written from a position of matching ignorance and stupidity?

Then the mysterious woman wanders into camp, eyeing Ellis. Her name is Melanie, and Hawkins doesn't seem terribly concerned that a civilian can mosey into an area where ill-disciplined recruits are doing some sort of training exercise with live ammo in their guns. How do we know it's live? Well, in digging a latrine, Ellis finds a skull—which Cort promptly props on a treeroot and shoots. He gets an easily ignorable talking-to from Hawkins. Ouch, watch it with those sarcastic tongue-lashings, Sarge, you just might run afoul of the Geneva Convention.

Given that Hawkins is clearly all bark and no bite, it's not surprising that Ellis and LeJune manage to share a kiss a little later, with Ellis getting only double sentry duty as a punishment (and LeJune getting no censure at all); it's also no surprise that later into the night, drunk Cort forces his way into LeJune's tent, and it's only by holding his anatomy hostage with a knife that she gets him to leave. He wanders out past the sleeping soldier now on watch (I think this these guys have now committed every military sin short of spitting on the flag and killing a four-star general), and manages to fall down another hole.

And this time… Did I ever mention this

was a zombie movie? It is, and there are undead Confederate soldiers waiting down there for him (and the body of the missing black soldier from the beginning, remember him?). Yay! Couldn't have happened to a more deserving fellow! Now get out there and take care of the rest of 'em!

Alas, it's not to happen so soon. Instead, in the morning Hawkins gives them all another one of her ineffectual dressings-down—"I ought to put you all on report," she says, though leg-irons would be more my choice—and sends three of them out to find Cort (or, in this case, his body).

And unfortunately, the radio's having supernatural trouble, and the truck's not due back to pick them up for another couple of days, so Hawkins has no choice but to rely on the world's least confidence-inspiring soldiers to try and find out who killed Cort and why.

Rehashing this movie any further might stimulate my gag reflex past the suppression point, so let me just say that, yes, Melanie is involved further, still drifting around the woods and staring beatifically whenever spoken to, though with a much more sinister agenda. And since they still haven't managed to get out of dodge by nightfall, they end up bearing the brunt of a zombie soldier attack from the midst of the standard backlit blue fog (funny how dead soldiers using hundred-year-old ball muskets can out-shoot fit young solders with modern assault rifles, ain't it?). Oddly enough, the zombies are never shown full on, always obscured by fog or shadow—an especially odd choice given that FX wizard Mark Shostrom provided the zombies, and he's always been one who delivers camera-friendly work (and the brief glimpses we get bear that out).

Other artistic choices are even more puzzling. One would certainly expect more racial issues when Confederate ghosts encounter Union troops with two African-Americans among them (with a black woman in command, no less). Exposition comes late in the game, but it muddies the water more than clears it: we've got vengeance of the South on the North, plus a briefly glimpsed and hardly significant reincarnation angle.

Rarely have I seen an American-made zombie films with characters more unsympathetic, or exhibiting such a dearth of gray matter. There are, despite appearances, things going for this movie: the story is set in such a way that a low budget doesn't show overmuch (all they really needed was two acres of woodlands, some period costumes, some army uniforms, and a few zombies), and the technical considerations really aren't too bad; this movie was in the first fledgling wave of features intended specifically for a video premiere, and compared to, say, similar offerings from the notorious Wizard Video label (like *Robot Holocaust* (1986) or *Mutant Hunt* (1987)), it's definitely a technically superior film. But none of that matters if the characters manage to alienate the entire viewing audience, either by technical inaccuracy or sheer preternatural stupidity. I wonder if some movie producers don't think zombies are really that inherently scary, and so dumb down the human protagonists to make it a fair fight.

Some Notable Totables:
- body count: 16
- breasts: 0
- explosions: 7
- ominous thunderstorms: 2
- actors who've appeared on *Star Trek*: 4
    - Nichelle Nichols (Hawkins) has played Lt. Uhura in several incarnations of the original series
    - LeVar Burton (Osgood) has likewise played Lt. La Forge in several incarnations of *The Next Generation*
    - Jessie Lawrence Ferguson (the boombox soldier) played "Lutan" in the *TNG* episode "Code of Honor"
    - Gary F. Bentley ("Union Soldier #3") was a special effects technician on *Star Trek 2*

WARRIORS of the APOCALYPSE (1986)

THEY TURNED PARADISE INTO HELL!

aka *Operation Overkill*, aka *Searchers of the Voodoo Mountain*

- Produced and directed by Bobby Suarez
- Written by Ken Metcalfe and Bobby Suarez
- Starring Michael James, Deborah Moore, Franco Guerrero, Michael Cohen and Ken Metcalfe
- Executive produced by Just Betzer

Wandering. That's what a good portion of this movie is. Our protagonists are a five-man party of scavenger-survivors who wander the post-apocalyptic desert for no given reason. They might have been kicked out of somewhere by the fashion police; their accessorized motorcycle outfits make them look like The Village People. (Wait, there's no Indian. Okay, make that Judas Priest.) Plus, they have this thing for big quilted shoulder pads; one guy looks like he's wearing saddles on each shoulder. Their leader is Trapper (Michael James, I assume—the end credits don't give character names to go with the performers), a man so stoic that he doesn't have to act. He just has to lead. As they wander.

Their wandering takes a different direction when they run across a similar band of ruffians in the desert. Well, not really similar; I mean, they do wear leather and shoulder pads and all that, but these guys are also keeping captured slaves to taunt. That makes them distinctly evil, so the somewhat gooder good guys take them out in a fist- and gun-fight. (These guns have the niftiest bullets, I tell you. Sometimes they can take out an opponent without leaving a mark, Western style. Other times, they can blow a tree in half.) But the fight almost goes against them—until a mysterious mountain man leaps out and decides things in our heroes' favor. If you can imagine an Indian with a pseudo-afro, then you can picture this new figure, who introduces himself afterward as Anook (I think—see the earlier complaint about the credits), and shares his food with them. They're amazed by quality of his vittles; fresh fruit sure beats century-old Spam! His explanation is that he's from a magical fertile mountain where people live forever in luxury. Oh, and by the way, there are scores of lonely women.

Trapper's men never question whether a colony of affluent women would want to be visited by a handful of scruffy, smelly bachelors with bad fashion sense; they just take Anook up on his offer to follow him back home. And so very soon…

…We're in a locale that's pretty uncommon for a low-budget post-apocalyptic stinker: a jungle. (Say hello to cheap Philippines shooting locations.) Not only that, but the party also manages to cross the only rope bridge suspended over a deep ravine in all of movie history which doesn't collapse under their feet. But the jungle is dangerous in other ways: they are attacked by natives! (You know, dark-skinned fellows wearing grass wigs and garish body paint. "Natives." No matter where you are in the world, that's what "natives" look like.) They manage to fight them off once, but sheer weight of numbers (plus the fact that their bullets aren't consistently exploding things anymore) leads them to capture. They are then subjected to a native dance designed to make them plead for the release of death (I think so—at least, that's the reaction I had). Death seems certain—until they're rescued, by the two slaves they rescued out on the desert! Boy, what are the odds?

It doesn't take them long before they run across *more* hostile natives, though. But these ones… If this movie has any claim to fame, it's the fact that it's got a tribe of jungle dwarfs who wear Kabuki-style face paint and speak with chipmunk voices. Somehow, I wish the movie had been about them instead of five scruffy guys in leather.

But even better—they're *immortal* Kabuki dwarfs! After they've been wasted

once, their wounds all heal and they come back to attack again, until Anook reveals they're really on his side, here to help "usher" Trapper's men into the fabled city. (And to add some Kabuki dwarfs to the movie, which is a worthy purpose in itself.) Because it's really hard to persuade five lonely men to visit a pseudo-Mayan city populated almost entirely by statuesque eternally-young blondes who really aren't turned on by Kabuki dwarfs.

Their queen, Shela or Sheba or Shira or Shiva (my kingdom for either clearly-looped dialogue or closing credits!), decked out in high heels and lamé wraps, immediately takes a fancy to Trapper, while the other girls are content to split up the three other able-bodied men. (The token old guy, Doc, isn't really in prime condition any more. But that's okay; he's a self-confessed Man of Science, and we all know they really don't mind all those lonely nights.) The only one who isn't ecstatic about the new blood is Gurik/Garak/Gorek/ whatever-the-hell, the white-haired high priest of the city's temple. (Actually, he's the only priest. And the only full-sized male resident.) He used to be the queen's squeeze, but I guess a hundred and

fifty years with the same mate can be tiring for even the most dedicated monogamist.

Trapper's men, naturally, are eager to get down to business (so much so that they don't even feel a bit silly walking around decked as they have been), but there's a catch: they have to wait for the fertility rite of the full moon. So the men walk around thinking about old nuns and dead kittens, while Gorook tries to find a way to get the men to voluntarily sneak away and escape.

Now, I know what you're thinking: the fertility ritual's got sinister overtones, and since immortal women usually need other people's lifeforce or somesuch to stay young, the poor men are going to be led by their lusts to their gruesome dooms. Right? Well, I don't think that it's too much of a spoiler to tell you that, nope, nothing bad happens. After waiting for most of the movie, the men finally get dragged off to separate huts, each with a handful of girls of their very own, and dot dot dot. The dot dot dots get spelled out even more with Trapper and the queen, who get sweaty behind gossamer curtains while the saxophone love theme from some other movie plays.

Eventually, of course, the spat between Queen and Priest will come down to blowing things up (bedding down the wandering warrior always exacerbates these rifts), plus some mutant attacks. But hey—the men are still left with a hungry bunch of women who don't know what a sharp-dressed man really is, so it's sort of a happy ending. Except for Doc.

In many cases, post-apocalyptic movies, especially those produced by Euro-exploitation auteurs, mostly recycle the old Spaghetti Western tropes with rusty metal thrown in. Here, I suppose, the innovation is that the post-apocalyptic movie has been cross-bred with the jungle adventure, another Eurotrash specialty. (We don't quite venture into the realm of the cannibal flick, though—I think cannibal Kabuki dwarfs might have been too much even for me.)

It's a pretty forgettable movie, really, despite the odd touches. The dialogue is as leaden as the actors' faces are immobile, and the plot meanders like it was made up on the spot. It's bad, but pretty unremarkable in its badness.

Some Notable Totables:
- body count: 50, plus 1 deer and 1 chicken
- breasts: 33 (coulda counted some twice, though)
- pasty white guys' butts: 1
- explosions: 47
- ominous thunderstorms: 0
- actors who've appeared on *Star Trek*: 0

BAD TASTE (1987)

WILL DO FOR VIDEO WHAT "ROCKY HORROR" DID FOR MIDNIGHT SHOWS!

- *Produced, written, and directed by Peter Jackson*
- *Starring Terry Potter, Pete O'Herne, Craig Smith, Mike Minett and Peter Jackson*

I know that some entertainment stores have put labels on recent DVD editions of *Bad Taste* that read, "From the Director of *The Lord of the Rings*!" I almost pity clueless shoppers who pick it up, thinking that they're getting something full of slow-motion battle scenes with Celtic women singing on the soundtrack. This is Jackson's first film, made on weekends over a four-year period with his friends, and it hits just the right level of over-the-top violence and gore to be an uproarious comedy.

The plot is almost too simplistic to be called that: the New Zealand government's bumbling four man anti-alien department, the Astro-Investigation and Defense Service ("A.I.D.S."), stumbles onto the wholesale slaughter of the small town of Kaihoro by an alien horde. And not just any aliens—capitalist aliens! Alien entrepreneurs! Interstellar bastards who plan to promote human flesh as the latest fast-food taste sensation, under the banner of Crumm's Crunchy Delights!

And what transpires on screen is lunacy of a magnitude not seen since *Monty Python and The Holy Grail* (1975).

By sheer dint of the hats he wears simultaneously, Peter Jackson qualifies fully for the inclusive title "filmmaker": he wrote, directed, produced and starred (in two separate roles) in *Bad Taste*. But he also qualifies for the label "comic genius" with the way he manages to translate the *Looney Toons*-style humor of complete exaggeration into live-action. Granted, *Looney Toons* were never this gory, but the inspiration is still completely visible. *Bad Taste* belongs on the same video shelf as *The Ren & Stimpy Show*.

For example: a bunch of the dimwitted "3rd class aliens" (Jackson's friends, dressed in identical jeans and work shirts) use one of their number as a live battering ram; said ram doesn't seem to mind.

For example: poor Derek (Jackson), the nerdiest of the A.I.D.S. boys, ends up on the wrong end of a cliff. But is he dead? No, he just managed to crack the back of his skull apart, so that his brains keep falling out at inopportune times, forcing Derek to don the tightest hat he can find.

For example: An alien trying to knock Derek down said cliff raises a sledgehammer. Derek shoots his shoulder, so that the hammer swings all the way back, into a fellow alien's cranium. A few more bullets cause the arm to detach completely at the shoulder, which leaves us with one alien missing an arm and one alien with a sledgehammer sticking from his head—with an arm still gripping the handle.

For example: Hapless donations collector Giles is captured to be used for the aliens' celebratory feast. He wakes up from a blow to the head to find himself naked in a huge pot of herbs and spices, with an apple in his mouth. (How much more blatant a cartoon reference do you want?)

I could go on with examples—the "clowns from the volkswagen" scene, the different-sized hammers, the vomit-eating scene, the exploding sheep, the sheer cartooniness of the Old Alien Bastard's face—but I'd end up describing every scene of the entire movie.

On top of the inspired lunacy, Peter Jackson's technical accomplishments inspire awe at his resourcefulness. Somehow, he manages to make effects that shouldn't work, work. Some incredible miniatures work is presented in the use of a rocket launcher on the house in which the aliens are reveling; it was only on my second viewing that I finally said, "Hey, wait, they couldn't have afforded to blow up half a house!" And the sound design, too often neglected by amateur filmmakers, makes the movie; it's what turns minced raw chicken breast into believable brain matter.

Lest this sound too much like hagiography, I will point out that most of the second half of the movie is taken up with an interminable assault on, and firefight with, the aliens, and even the many more moments of cartoony beauty can't keep it from dragging a bit.

But it still ranks as one of the best independent movies to come out of the '80s, as well as one of the best success stories. After *Bad Taste*, Jackson produced *Meet the Feebles* (1989), the transgressive love-it-or-hate-it sleaze version of *The Muppet Show*. Jackson's second directorial effort, along the same lines in terms of content and audience appeal as *Bad Taste*, was the over-the-top zombie cartoon *Braindead* (1992), aka *Dead Alive* in the U.S., funded in part by the New Zealand Film Commission. (Name one other semi-governmental agency anywhere that will help make a zombie movie!) He then showed his range by making *Beautiful Creatures* (1994), a psychological thriller based on the real case of two girls who conspired to kill one of their mothers. His introduction to the Hollywood movie-making machine (though he still shot in New Zealand, as with all his films) was 1996's *The Frighteners*, a popcorn horror-comedy that got a lukewarm reception. But he really came into his own with that movie trilogy that began in 2001—you know, the one about the hairy-footed midgets trying to get rid of some antique jewelry.

Some Notable Totables:
- body count: 66 (plus 3 seagulls and 1 sheep)
- breasts: 0
- explosions: 3
- ominous thunderstorms: 0
- actors who've appeared on *Star Trek*: 0

The BARBARIANS (1987)

WARRIORS. CONQUERORS. HEROES.

- *Directed by Ruggero Deodato*
- *Written by James R. Silke*
- *Starring Peter Paul, David Paul, Richard Lynch, Eva La Rue, and Virginia Bryant*
- *Produced by Yoram Globus and Menahem Golan*
- *Executive produced by John Thompson*

This is one of those movies that manages, by a fluke of the universe, to bask in the spotty sunshine (or at least, the brightish haze) of my favor. In large degree, that's because I know just how bad a barbarian movie can be and usually is. Thus, when an example of a bottom-scraping genre manages to keep its belly off the bedrock, I'm inclined to forgiveness.

The Barbarian Brothers, twin bodybuilders named Peter and David Paul, probably jumped at this chance of a starring vehicle; after all, if a movie about *one* barbarian could jumpstart the career of Arnold Schwarzenegger, then a movie about *two* barbarians should be twice as successful! Right? It's thinking like that which has probably kept the Barbarian Brothers from becoming household names (in most households, anyway), despite their obvious superiorities over Ahnuld's portrayal of Conan, such as a native command of the English language and… well, there's that, anyway.

Our stage is set by a pseudo-mythic voiceover (missing only "Know, O prince…" and "…beneath his sandaled feet" at either end), which informs us that a time of long ago and far away, the tribe of Ragniks (yes, giggle all you want) were the minstrels of the age, possessing a certain magical ruby that bestowed upon them mastery of the arts and song and all that frou-frou stuff. No sooner do we know this than we see the Ragnik caravan pursued and attacked by the *ee*-vil warriors of the tyrant Kadar (Richard Lynch, looking pretty frou-frou himself in his regalia). The queen of the Ragniks, Canary (Virginia Bryant), has one of her lieutenants slip away from the caravan with the ruby, so that it won't fall into Kadar's hands. What no one explains, or even alludes to, is why an evil overlord would be so hot for a magic gem that's all about sweetness 'n' light 'n' flowers 'n' things. It's like Darth Vader setting his heart on all of the My Little Pony collectibles on eBay. On the other hand, given Kadar's wardrobe, maybe he just had to have it because it would absolutely go with this cutest little outfit he has…

Kadar surrounds them, terrorizes them while laughing maniacally (as per Evil Overlord Union requirements), and makes the mistake of tousling the heads of twin boys Kutchek and Gore (Pasquale and Luigi Bellazecca), whom the caravan had picked up as orphans a ways back. One of them promptly bites off two of Kadar's fingers. He's ready to strike them dead, but Canary pleads for them and promises to do all of those hideous, perverse things that Kadar usually has to pay for in exchange for their lives. (She doesn't seem much devoted to the rest of the tribe in the same sense, I must note.)

Canary, the twins, and the better-looking Ragnik girls are dragged back to Kadar's capitol; the women are given to Kadar's men, Canary is sent to his harem, and the twins are dragged off to The Pit, the brutal rock-quarry prison run by the Dirtmaster (Michael Berryman), though Kadar's pet sorceress China (Sheeba Alahani) advises him to do them in. (Sorceresses. Evil overlords go to the trouble of having them on the payroll, only to ignore them completely.) He did make a promise to spare their lives, after all. But he has a plan.

The twins grow up in bondage, eventually maturing into the Paul brothers. Each is kept separate from the other, and each is ritually whipped and tortured—one by a man in a black mask, one by a man in a golden helmet. Then, when Kadar is eventually tired of how Canary won't luv him or tell him where the ruby is (how much time has gone by, anyway? the twins are fully grown, but no one else has aged a day), he arranges for the brothers to fight each other in a public spectacle—one wearing a golden mask, the other in a black mask. Why, they'll kill each other! Yet Kadar will have kept to his promise! That's ingenious! No wonder Kadar runs things!

Except that he never thought to put chin straps on the helmets, so they soon get knocked off in combat, and the brothers band together. Kadar also never thought to have the battle-to-the-death in an arena strong enough to keep the musclebound twins from escaping by pushing the wall down. Off they ride to find the Ragniks and come back to rescue Canary.

The Ragniks have lost their old joys, and their caravan is now parked permanently in the woods (sort of a Hyperborean trailer park). They've got no weapons of their own, but they do have a captured thief-girl, Ismene (Eva La Rue), who agrees to help the twins get some weapons and rescue Canary

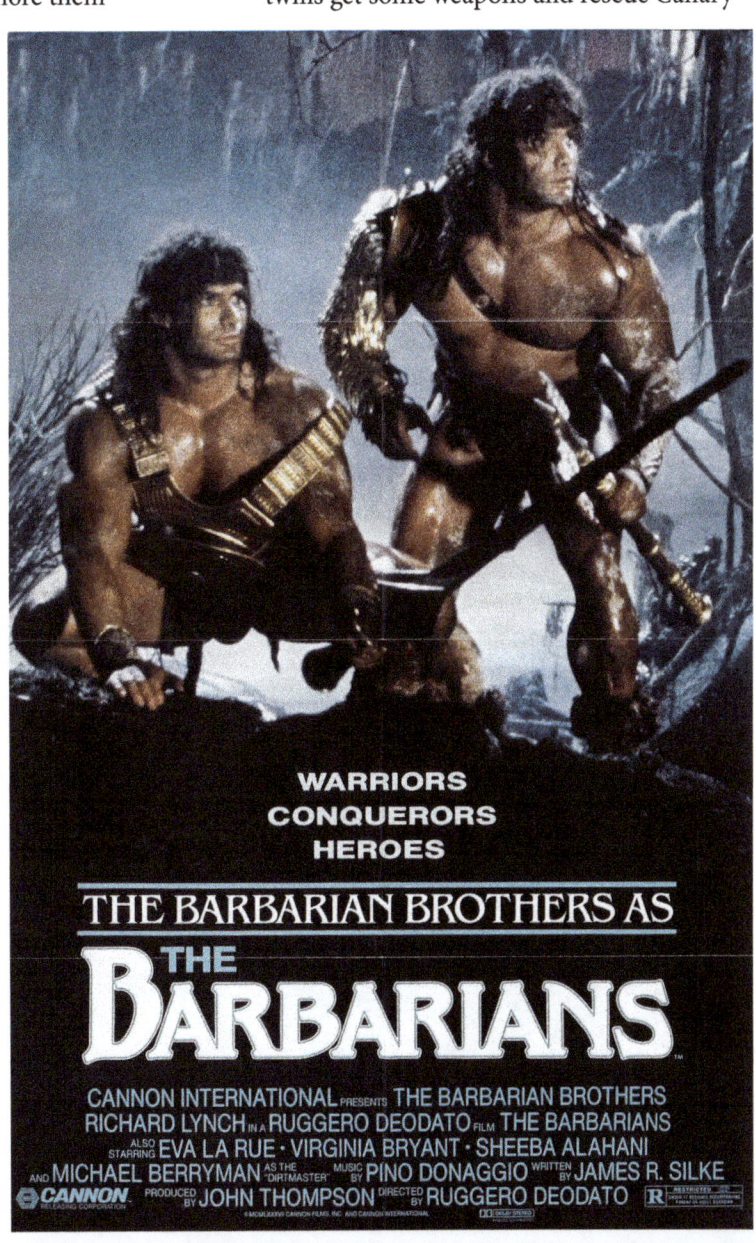

in return for her freedom. (You may notice, by the way, that I'm not even trying to differentiate Kutchek and Gore. There's a reason for that. I mean, they're twin barbarians. They've got different belt-buckles, and there are passing indications that one of them is meant to be the marginally smarter one, but since I never picked up on which one that was supposed to be, it doesn't matter.)

The path to Canary's freedom is fraught with bar brawls and loose women, naturally, and to really do the job right, they have to find the magical armor of the Ragnik king who originally acquired the ruby, then use it to fight the goofy-ass dragon who guards it where it was hidden. And they have to outrun the sorceress China, who's finally figured out where to look for it.

If I tell you that the third act gets disappointingly stupid, you might take that to mean that the movie up to that point had been intelligent. Far from it, but it was at least consistently and knowingly stupid. The twins, after all, are slavery-raised sides of beef. They're not bright, they're not subtle, and they bray like donkeys when they're enjoying themselves. In that regard, they're

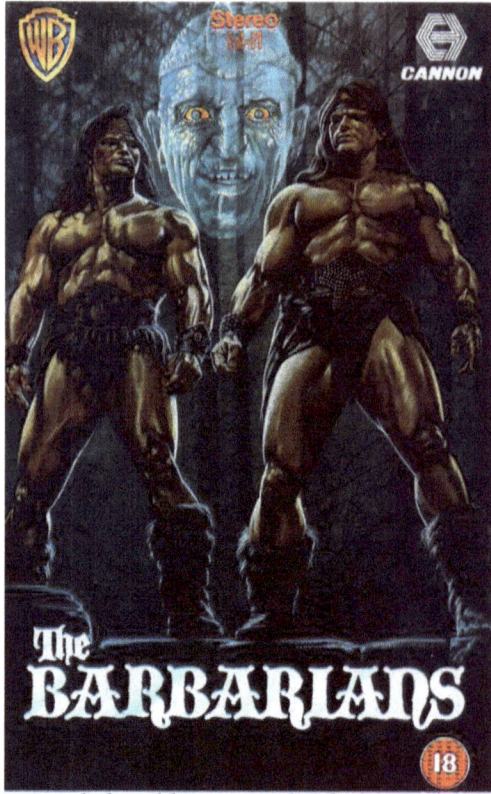

pretty believable portrayals of what musclebound barbarians would really be like (aside from the idea that The Pit has a waxing salon). There's some wit to the writing about these witless oafs—not enough to turn it into a spoof or an out-and-out comedy, but enough to keep things more lighthearted than the standard ponderous-beyond-all-proportion-of-quality barbarian movie. (Writer James Silke is, among other things, the screenwriter of *Revenge of the Ninja* (1983) and *Ninja III: The Domination* (1984), but he's also the writer of the Frank Frazetta's *Death Dealer* paperback novels, which are probably the closest thing to thoughtful sword & sorcery books out there.) At its worst, most of this movie comes across as smart people making a knowingly stupid film.

By the end, though, we're given plenty of stupid planning and "surprise" revelations that make absolutely no sense. And the ruby itself… It's referred to a couple of times as the "Bellystone," and we finally find out why: it will only fit and stay in the navel (!!) of the Ragnik girl it has chosen as the next queen. Makes our presidential elections look positively rational, doesn't it?

But again, by the standards of an undemanding genre, it still ranks in the top half. The sets and costumes, while corny, never show themselves to be impoverished. The Barbarian Brothers don't embarrass themselves with their undemanding lines (boy, that native grasp of English sure comes in handy sometimes). And we do get to see Michael Berryman doing his impression of the Grinch's dog Max, which is something you don't get to see every day. As long as you placate your brain, you might enjoy it—otherwise you'll end up asking questions like, "Would barbarian warriors *really* shave their armpits?"

Some Notable Totables:
- body count: 23
- breasts: 4
- explosions: 1
- ominous thunderstorms: 1
- actors who've appeared on *Star Trek*: 2
  - Richard Lynch (Kadar) played "Arctus Baran" in the *TNG* two-parter "Gambit"
  - Michael Berryman (the Dirtmaster) played "Starfleet Display Officer" (under tons of latex) in *Star Trek 4*, and "Captain Rixx" (under blue makeup) in the *TNG* episode "Conspiracy"

BLACK COBRA (1987)

aka *The Black Cobra*

- Directed by "Stel Mass" (Stelvio Massi)
- Written by Danilo Massi
- Starring Fred Williamson, Eva Grimaldi, Karl Landgren, Vassili Karis and Maurice Poli
- Produced by Lucciano Appignani

When *Cobra* (1986), the low-quality but high-profile action-thriller starring Sylvester Stallone, made its way out of Hollywood, I can only imagine that some Italian filmmakers (most likely director Stelvio Massi and producer Lucciano Appignani) were shooting the breeze one day over warm beer or cold tea or whatever it is that Italians drink, and chuckling about the lousy reviews. "Those Americans think *Cobra* is lousy?" one chortled to the other; "they don't know how lousy it could have been!" "Let's show them!" said the other.

And thus *Black Cobra* was born.

If you've seen *Cobra*, the opening scene of *Black Cobra* (in fact, most of the movie) will ring little bells of unsettling *déjà vu*: first, we're given close to two minutes of stock footage of New York—helicopter shots, people walking down the sidewalk, vendors hawking their wares—footage that was obviously shot years before the 1987 date on the movie. Why so much footage under the opening credits? It's a desperate attempt to convince you that the rest of this movie is actually set in New York, rather than the obviously Italian shooting location. Over this footage, we get a looped-in conversation over police radio in which the police chief explains to tough cop Malone (Fred Williamson) about a botched bank robbery from which the perps have fled to a sports club, there to have shot several patrons and grabbed some as hostages. (Why are we being told about this, instead of seeing the actual assault, as was shown in the comparable scene in *Cobra*? Because it's cheaper to talk about it, duh!)

Former football player Fred Williamson had first come to the attention of movie-going audiences through blaxploitation fare such as *Hammer* (1972), *Black Caesar* (1973), *Hell Up in Harlem* (1974), and *Boss Nigger* (1975). By the late '70s and early '80s, he had somehow become a staple of casting for Italian producers, being featured in war movies like *The Inglorious Bastards* (1978) and *Heroes in Hell* (1987) and post-apocalyptic fare like *The New Barbarians* (1982), *1990: Bronx Warriors* (1982), and *Warrior of the Lost World* (1983), reviewed on page 15. I don't think he ever changed his citizenship, and the '90s and '00s saw him return to more stateside casting, largely through the pop-cultural cachet of his early blaxploitation roles, but for a decade there in the middle, he was pretty much an honorary Italian.

Malone arrives at the health club. As I said, it's pretty obvious we're not in New York City; the grassy hills with low expansive apartment buildings are a clue. So are the police cars, with a very un-American style of light carriage on top. And then there's the clincher made visible as soon as Malone gets out of his car and begins speaking to cop-on-the-scene Walker: Williamson's lips are the only ones that do, or will for the length of the movie, move in tandem with his English dialogue. It's like watching Clint Eastwood in one of Sergio Leone's spaghetti westerns, only much, much sadder.

Since this is a cop movie, the First Law of Cops must be invoked: of any two officers shown to be of comparable rank, one must be a rule-breaker, one must be a straight arrow, and the straight arrow must have a chip on his shoulder about the rule-breaker. Walker relays the instructions from The Brass that Malone is supposed to go in there and accede to every demand (this is the Italian version of "negotiating"? I thought it was more French). Well, you know that nobody hires Fred Williamson to play a meek capitulator, so...

So Malone wanders inside to where the three robbers are holding three hostages by the pool. He doesn't announce himself, doesn't say, "Hey, negotiator coming in," nothing; he just wanders in, not looking particularly cop-like in his black leather trenchcoat, and waits to be noticed. One of the ski-masked mafia gives Malone his list of demands—two million dollars, a plane to Mexico, Twinkies for life, expanded basic cable—to which Malone says, "No." He then flips out the shotgun he's been hiding under his coat, pulls his automatic with the other hand, and blows the three away. Naturally, Walker and his uniforms promptly flood the building, and before they even get the distraught hostages out of the crime scene, Walker starts chewing ass: you were supposed to negotiate, give them everything they want, why you always gotta be the tough guy, etc. It really makes you wonder what, exactly, was the point of sending the known loose cannon into a situation where the Brass ostensibly wanted diplomacy and retreat. Is there an even less suitable person on the force for such a job? This doesn't even have the rationale of *Cobra*, in which Cobretti is sent in as a last ditch effort (in a police force that apparently doesn't have honest-to-goodness S.W.A.T. teams). Were they just trying to set Malone up to fail? I dunno.

You realize that all of the above was just in the first five-minute "set piece" scene, the events of which have absolutely no impact on the plot. Let's see: Italy masquerading (poorly) as New York, Fred Williamson as the lone English-speaking member of the cast, dumb police tactics... Yup, we've pretty much nailed down the problems that are going to be our constant companions for the rest of the movie.

All right, then. On to the story. If you've been following our progress in our *Cobra* template, you know that sooner or later we have to meet our evil gang, right? Well, here they are, a posse of leatherclad bikers, led by a smirking psychopath (Karl Landgren) with a big scar under his jawline. (The credits call him "Snake," due to the large snake tattooed on his forearm; in practice, he's never called by name. Once again, this is as in *Cobra*—hereinafter "A.I.C.") I should also let you know that despite the spike-covered *Road Warrior*-style bikes on the original movie poster (though it might be more appropriate to call them *The Cars That Ate Paris*-style), what they ride on-screen are much wimpier bikes—the kind that would get their asses kicked at any biker bar in the U.S. of A. They hang out in a big abandoned warehouse and occasionally venture forth to terrorize and pillage, such as in the ensuing scene in which the half-dozen bikers accost a young couple at the beach, kill the guy, presumably rape the girl, and steal their Jeep Camper.

We've got our kick-ass cop, we've got our terrorizing cultists—who else do we need? Why, the hapless witness girl, of course! We meet Elys (Eva Grimaldi) in a fashion photography studio, though in a stunning break from the *Cobra* template, she's not a model; no, she's the photographer! Wow! How creative! She goes home (with her camera, you know), and sees the dastardly gang murder the people in the condo next to hers. Why? Because they're a dastardly gang, dang it! What do you want them to do, bang hammers together over their heads? Snake catches sight of her and moves to catch her, but she cleverly clicks her camera at him repeatedly, blinding him with the flash. (If you want to give these Italians extra credit for having seen *Rear Window* (1954), go ahead.) Off she drives in a panic, and the gangbangers give chase—though this time, they're using their recently-acquired Jeep Camper (minus the camper shell, and repainted with flames trailing back from the hood; nothing says class like an oversized blocky vehicle with painted flames). Given that Snake is driving, and he recently got blinded, plus he insists on wearing mirrorshades at night, it's not surprising that they can't catch up with her before she finds a patrol car to scare them off.

Okay, let me know if you saw this coming: Malone is assigned to protect Elys. Actually, this has a lot more basis here than in *Cobra*—as you'll recall if you've seen that movie, Brigitte Nielsen didn't even see Brian Thompson committing a crime; she just noticed his disturbing face. In this instance, not only did Elys witness a crime, she took several pictures of Snake—although it turns out that the reflection of the flash in his mirrorshades washed out the picture, so the police can't use that to identify him.

From here on out, you can pretty much plot the movie in your sleep: the bad guys try to attack Elys in the hospital only to be thwarted by Malone (and no one else—apparently the concept of hospital security hadn't taken root in Europe by 1987); Malone protects her at his apartment, where she starts to see his human side; Malone and a goon get into a big knock-down fight when they got back to Elys' place to get some of her things; etc., etc.

Eventually, Snake has Walker's daughter kidnapped, offering to exchange her for both Malone and Elys, which leads to a big-ass battle as Malone and an erstwhile sidekick go armed for bear: knives, grenades, throwing stars (!), UZIs… Just to spit on all things American, our darling screenwriter even puts in Malone's mouth a bastardized version of the famous "*Dirty Harry*" speech, complete with "Do I have any bullets left?" and "Do you feel lucky?"

From reading my description, you may get the impression that this is a lackluster but adequate entry in the action-thriller department. However, my recap doesn't convey the tepid pacing of all of the action scenes. Nor do you get an accurate impression of the soundtrack (one part generic synth score that would be at home in any any early-'80s Italian post-apocalyptic film, one part sax-and-electric-piano improv jazz that plays inexplicably during the "tensest" scenes). Nor, really, do you truly understand the sense of despair that comes from Williamson himself, surrounded by a whole bunch of performers speaking a different language. He's a professional, and as a professional he shows up on the set, remembers his lines and performs them competently; but quite frankly, they aren't paying enough for him to muster any real enthusiasm.

And yet, after all of this lambasting, I can't quite bring myself to condemn this movie as being without any redeeming virtues. For one thing, the upper-limit of quality was imposed by the initial goal of imitating *Cobra*; the odds of surpassing the source material are pretty low. (Of course, one could blame them for taking *Cobra* as their template in the first place, but that's kind of like slapping a baby because his parents had unprotected sex.)

But the other thing is, in a real sense, these Italians did really show how to make a bad movie. Sure, this is worse than *Cobra*, but it probably cost about one-fifth of *Cobra*'s budget. And as the ultimate proof that the Italians can make bad movies better than anyone: *Black Cobra* spawned two direct sequels in 1988 and 1990, plus a semi-sequel, *Detective Malone* (1990), cobbled together from outtakes and repurposed footage from the earlier three movies. The mind reels.

Some Notable Totables:
- body count: 23
- breasts: 1 (from the "Hey, we need a breast in here somewhere" department)
- explosions: 1
- ominous thunderstorms: 0
- actors who've appeared on *Star Trek*: 1
  - Fred Williamson played "Anka" in the original episode "The Cloud Minders"

FOREVER EVIL (1987)

It is evil beyond time and imagination… forever watching… waiting… killing!

- Directed by Roger Evans
- Written by Freeman Williams
- Starring Red Mitchell, Tracey Huffman, Charles L. Trotter, Diane Johnson and Howard Jacobsen
- Produced by Jill Scott
- Executive produced by Bill F. Blair and Betty S. Scott

Forever Evil has a reputation among B-movie aficionados in far greater proportion than its distribution and viewership can justify. Why? Because the writer, one Freeman Williams, went on to become Dr. Freex, proprietor of The Bad Movie Report (*http://www.badmoviereport.com*), once a shining star in the nascent galaxy of bad movie websites, and one of bad movie fandom's great cuddly godlike figures. Freeman's even gone so far as to post an eighteen-chapter account of the genesis and production of *Forever Evil* online for all the world to see. So between that and the dozen other reviews floating around on the web, anything I have to say will either be redundant, superfluous or just plain wrong.

What can I say? That's the kind of guy I am.

Our story opens with Mr. Freeman Williams himself, wearing his acting hat. (This is the original video release version of the movie; the currently-available two-DVD set also contains the slightly longer director's cut, which doesn't open with this scene. But I decided that the more familiar version is the one I should review here. And I'm too lazy to watch two marginally-different cuts of a movie for a single review. What can I say? That's also the kind of guy I am.) Freeman here plays the role of Ben Magnus, a Tarot reader and generally occultish spooky guy. He is, however, a good guy, and his card reading, meant for his ditzy customer (Kayce Glasse), instead gives him the warning that he's been targeted by pissed-off demonic forces. Alas for both Ben and his customer, tarot card red alerts don't give much in the way of a time margin, and Ben soon finds himself on the receiving end of an animated lightning bolt being wielded by a hooded figure with glowing red eyes.

Our plot proper starts with Marc (Red Mitchell) and his girlfriend Holly (Diane Johnson) getting ready for his last weekend party at the family cabin before they toss the keys to their realtor (Howard Jacobsen). Marc and Holly are in a bit of a bind, as she's pregnant and hasn't decided what to do. But they put on a happy face and greet Marc's brother Jay, his significant other, and another couple. I'll list the actors here for form's sake—Jeffrey Lane, Susan Lunt, David Campbell, Karen Chatfield—but I'm not going to bother with the character names, because you're not going to have much chance to get to know them.

That's right, they're cannon fodder. That

evening, a mysterious something starts killing them all, starting by ripping Holly's fetus out of her stomach. The other characters react with not nearly the level of panic you'd expect, but not even their levelheadedness (or stolid non-emotiveness) saves them; by the end of the evening, everyone has either been pulled down a dark hallway by something with red glowing eyes, torn out the window by tree branches, or just plain broken by a towering zombie figure, who (we find out in the end) goes by the name of "Alfy" (Kent T. Johnson). Marc alone escapes, using the brilliant plan of running through the woods onto the highway and getting himself hit by a car.

That all happens in the first twenty minutes, because the point of the movie is to pick up the real story where the standard slasher plot ends: with the sole survivor recovering from the night of slaughter. Putting himself back together in the hospital, Marc meets two soon-to-be-important people: Lt. Ball (Charles L. Trotter), the officer investigating the deaths of his friends, and Reggie (Tracey Huffman), who is herself the "final girl" of a similar attack a couple of years back. Together, they try to discover a pattern to this and other massacres carried out over several decades, and keep similar attacks from happening again.

They're given a good lump o' clues by the now-absent Ben Magnus, who left a box of occult books upon his disappearance for his good friend Lt. Ball. Together, they point to an eldritch power known as Yog-Kothag, an exiled dark god with scattered cult followers. Bits and pieces start to fall together from the unlikeliest places, such as an archived newspaper article which notes that a mystic dagger was stolen from a museum just before the first such attack several decades back, or the report that astronomers have discovered an "irregular quasar" whose whose history of periodic pulses lines up precisely with the timing of all of the murders. It seems that it's something that happens only "when the stars are right."

There's a tidiness to the way in which pseudo-Lovecraftian mythology is woven into a slasher-zombie plot without overt reference (though, yes, Magnus' box of books does include a copy of the ubiquitous *Necronomicon*). And you have to remember that this movie was made (or at least conceived) before the Golden Age of Slasher Sequels, in which the ultimate fate and further story of both the sole survivor and the murderous nasty are routinely examined and remilked for further box-office fodder.

But there are some recurring weaknesses that keep cooling the elements of the movie before they can achieve critical mass. Just about every actor plays their role overly-phlegmatically, even in the fact of unbelievable violence; the general reaction of Marc's buddies in the opening sequence seems more appropriate to a perniciously-clogged toilet than to the grisly deaths of their compatriots in quick succession. And Reggie, introduced to the story after having spent a couple of years criss-crossing the area in search of the demons that killed her fiancé, looks and acts like a suburban soccer mom. (When not watching a game.)

And the less said about Marc's "secret weapon," his wrist-mounted grappling-hooked gimmick-on-a-stick, the better.

One of the reasons I declined to watch the director's cut in favor of the video release version (aside from the cited laziness) is that seven additional minutes of footage don't seem like the kind of thing that would raise the tension level. With so much of the movie revolving around investigation, self-recrimination, and a succession of spooky dream sequences, the last thing this movie needs is a more languid pace. (Well, actually, the last thing it needs is a scene in which the murder sites, plotted on a map, turn out to be a pentagram, but since we already have one of those…)

Having said all that, the mistakes which pepper the movie are not the result of stupidity or apathy, but those to be expected of unpracticed intelligence. There are plenty of good ideas here, just without the connecting tissue of experience among the largely-neophyte movie makers. But especially against the backdrop of the slasher-plotted movies of the early '80s, *Forever Evil* doesn't come out so bad.

Some Notable Totables:
- body count: 8
- breasts: 2
- explosions: 0
- dream sequences: 3
- ominous thunderstorms: 4
- actors who've appeared on Star Trek: 0

HELL COMES to FROGTOWN (1987)

A NEW BREED OF ENEMY HAS TAKEN OVER THE WORLD... SAM HELL HAS COME TO TAKE IT BACK.

- Directed by Donald G. Jackson and R.J. Kiser
- Written by Randall Frakes
- Starring Roddy Piper, Sandahl Bergman, Cec Verrell, William Smith and Rory Calhoun
- Produced by Randall Frakes and Donald G. Jackson

If you ask a member of the general public to name a movie starring wrestler "Rowdy" Roddy Piper, they'll most likely answer *They Live* (1988), John Carpenter's paranoid sci-fi parable about corporate Reaganomics. Ask them to name a second, and it'll probably be *Hell Comes to Frogtown*. (If they can name three or more, they're no longer members of the general public; they're fellow B-movie geeks.) The main difference will be that, while they very well many have seen *They Live* at some point (probably on cable), they'll likely only know *Frogtown* by reputation—or simply by its very memorable title.

Yes, it's a silly title. And it fits the rest of the movie: unrepentantly silly, and memorable for that.

The stage is set well by the very opening, a voice speaking against a black screen: "In the latter days of the twentieth century, there arose... a difference of opinion." Cue atomic test footage.

Now, I ask you: for those of us who have gritted our teeth and stuck it out through scores of poorly made but deadly serious post-apocalyptic flicks, isn't it refreshing to finally hit one that treats the obligatory opening mushroom cloud as a punchline?

Here's the situation. It's ten years after the Big One, and the population is dangerously unproductive. Fertile women are few and far between, and virile men are as rare as hen's teeth. (Granted, in the mutated future, hens with teeth may be the norm—what do I know?) One of them just happens to be Sam Hellman, aka "Sam Hell" (Piper), an uncouth drifter who's left a trail of pregnancies behind him. As we meet him, he's about to get the crap kicked out of him by Captain Devlin (William Smith), a standard-issue fascist law enforcement type whose daughter was Hell's most recent bed-warmer.

Fortunately for Hell, virility is more important than these petty squabbles, at least as far as the provisional government is concerned, which is why two MedTech nurses, Spangle (Sandahl Bergman of *Conan the Barbarian* (1982) in hideous square-rimmed glasses) and a big black woman whose name I didn't catch, swoop in and rescue him from Devlin. MedTech is the government agency dedicated to rebuilding the species, and since the other arms of government don't really matter if there aren't any people... MedTech offers Hell complete amnesty, provided he signs up with them to do his patriotic duty.

They outfit him with a high-tech codpiece (with "PROPERTY OF PROVISIONAL GOV'T" stenciled across the front—and I think they mean the contents, not the codpiece itself) and ship him out on his first mission. A caravan with fertile women has been captured by the "Greeners," frog-man mutants who live out on their own reservation. Relations with the amphibians have been strained of late, and there's rumors that they've even been getting illegal arms from somewhere, so simply relying on diplomacy for the women's return is out of the question. Instead, Hell, Spangle, and a beautiful and incredibly dykey gunnery corporal Centinella (Cec Verrell) set out in what looks like a bright pink Studebaker to either rescue the women and impregnate them later, or, if rescue is impossible, to impregnate them on the spot. It's a dirty job, but someone's got to do it. (Yes, the codpiece will open at the opportune moment—"SPROING-G-G!")

I'm having trouble coming up with good jokes for this review because all of the good jokes were taken by the movie itself. There are gratuitous *Planet of the Apes* references right from the start, every possible "government equipment" joke, and even a humming women's chorus rendition of "When Johnny Comes Marching Home" as the Studie heads into the wastelands. If this movie's tongue were any more firmly in its cheek it would be poking right through.

On the other hand, too many of the best nickels are spent too soon. The trek across the wasteland gives us time for the obligatory love/hate relationship to grow between the awkward (and bony) Spangle and the really-a-nice-guy-underneath-it-all Hell, including perhaps the most mechanical striptease in the history of cinema. And though you know that Spangle's glasses are so ugly that they must be a setup for a "take off the glasses and she's pretty" scene, the payoff is kind of spoiled by the fact that Sandahl Bergman here is a dead ringer for Judith Light from the TV sitcom *Who's the Boss?*—and if there's any cast member from that show that I want to see in a camouflage bikini, it's not Judith Light.

Eventually we get to Frogtown, which is naturally an abandoned industrial refinery something-or-other (everybody knows that industrial complexes are the only structures that can withstand an atom bomb), and the "plan," such as it is, is for Hell to lead Spangle in on a chain as if she's available for sale, thus getting her into the harem of the frog leader,

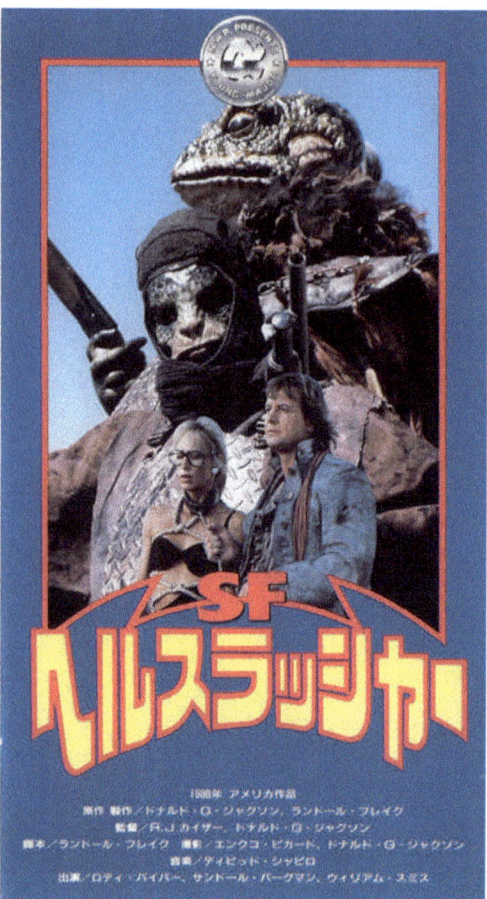

Commander Toty. I ought to remark on the frog effects here. They're not uniformly bad; the mutants run the gamut from subtly frog-like to full-blown wide-mouth. Some of the latter are pretty fakey, as they're sparsely-animated cable-controlled masks. But Toty's head is fully articulated, complete with nictating membranes for his eyes. He also likes to indulge in the "Dance of the Three Snakes"—but I really don't want to explain that, or even think about it very much.

As I said, we spend our best nickels quickly, and things lose a lot of steam as the jokes run thin. Suffice it to say that there are captures, escapes, unrequited interspecies lust, and an exploding chastity belt. There is not, however, any explanation as to how man-sized amphibians are managing to propagate in the middle of the desert.

Now, here's the moment I've really been dreading. Because I have to tell you what the biggest single anchor is around this movie's neck. And may the Cosmos (meaning the totality of the universe, not the twin singing fairies) have mercy on my soul, because the single biggest sinkhole here is… Roddy Piper.

I'm not blaming the guy, okay? I proudly proclaim him the paragon of all that is manly. But this was his first starring role, and he really hadn't figured out this whole "performing in front of the camera" thing without clotheslining his costars. He's energetic and all—you might even call him "rowdy"—but he's not that good. And even though *They Live* was released only a year later, I think that there was a greater time lag between the two shoots, because in *Frogtown* Roddy has what might be generously called "undefined facial planes" and what might more crassly called "pudgy squirrel cheeks." Add to this a haircut that was bad even by '80s standards (compare, again, to *They Live*, in which his haircut was great for the era, though laughable in hindsight), and you end up with the movie carrying Roddy, rather than the other way around.

Roddy! Don't take it personal! I still love you, man! Hey, everyone's allowed to suck their first time out the gate—it's not like this was *Hercules in New York* (1970) or anything! Please don't hate me!

Anyway. After all this bitching, I still have to say that a post-apocalyptic flick that even makes the attempt to be clever, instead of unrelentingly grim, is to be commended. There are enough high points in the first half to give the second half sufficient momentum to coast through to the closing credits. (There wasn't enough momentum to carry over to the two almost-unknown sequels, a fact which Piper undoubtedly knew, as he declined to appear in them.)

Some Notable Totables:
- body count: 9
- breasts: 2
- explosions: 10
- ominous thunderstorms: 0
- actors who've appeared on *Star Trek*: 2
    - Julius LeFlore ("SquidLips") did stunts in *Star Trek: Insurrection*
    - Nicholas Worth (Bull, the one-eyed frog) played "Alien Captain" and "Sorm" on a couple of episodes of *DS9*, and showed up as "Lonzak" on two episodes of *Voyager*

NAIL GUN MASSACRE (1987)

IT'S CHEAPER THAN A CHAINSAW!

aka *Texas Nailgun Massacre*

- Directed by Bill Leslie and Terry Lofton
- Written and produced by Terry Lofton
- Starring Rocky Patterson, Ron Queen, Michelle Meyer, Beau Leland and Sebrina Lawless
- Executive produced by Linda Bass and T.F. Lofton

No one would argue that most slasher movies aren't clichéd. But the clichéd ones are actually the middle of the bell curve. Those above the hump are those which use originality and inventiveness to create something more than a cliché. Those below the hump are made by people too stupid to use the clichés to help their godforsaken movie (also too stupid to include such things as good dialogue, an actual plot, characters, etc.). *Nail Gun Massacre* falls below the curve. Way below. Like, at the end of the long tail where the curve has gone practically flat and become one with the base line.

We start with a gang rape by a bunch of rednecks at a rural construction site, and for just these first few seconds I held out some hope for this movie. Not that I enjoy cinematic depictions of sexual assault, but this scene at least put its focus right where there's most emotional impact to be had, the woman's anguished face.

And then that ten seconds passed, and with it all hope.

We cut immediately to a camo-wearing figure traipsing through the woods, wearing what looks like a motorcycle helmet wrapped with electrician's tape, and a nail gun connected to an air bottle backpack by a bright yellow curly hose. (We find out, most of the way through the movie, that six months have elapsed between the rape and the first attack; from what we actually saw, it could have been twenty minutes.) The killer cleverly eludes the fat redneck woman hanging out clothes, enters the rundown redneck house, and kills a redneck man (I suppose he was one of the gang-rapists—it's not like they really gave us a good look at their faces) with multiple shots with the nail gun.

Repeat this scene about twelve times, and you have the movie.

The next attack is one on two woodcutters (after one foolishly leaves his naked girlfriend who is literally begging for fondling—"They're lonely! They need some attention!"). The sheriff, who apparently is the lone representative of the law in this Texas county, drives up in his non-police car, finds the woodcutters' pickup truck (again, he later says its been there a couple of days, though no passage of time is actually conveyed as we're watching the scene), discovers the bodies, and calls the only other person we will ever see at a crime scene: the doctor, who dresses in white t-shirts and denim jackets to save on the expense of a doctor costume. The doctor comes in, hems and haws, disturbs all of the evidence, and then they leave the bodies there. Apparently they just let the cycle of nature take its course in Texas.

Meanwhile, three people (and we never really find out their relationship—two brothers and a sister? a guy and his friend and a girlfriend? a free love triumvirate?) are invited to move into the empty house on Old Lady Bailey's property for free, provided they fix it up. This is the house in which the first redneck was killed. They move in, eat some Spaghettios, buy some lumber, discover the next couple of bodies —and then suddenly disappear from the film entirely at about halfway through. We've followed them for a full half of the movie, and suddenly we're apparently not interested in them anymore.

Some more people are killed, and the killer (who's got some funky reverb voicebox in that helmet) keeps trying to make Freddy Krueger-like wisecracks that are about as good as you'd expect a redneck killer to make up on his own. And the town… You've heard of *The Town That Dreaded Sundown* (1977), right? In that movie, after two killings, the entire populace was afraid to go outside. Well, apparently this is *The Town That Had Its Collective Head Up Its Butt*. Everyone still goes to make out in the woods, or traipse around alone and unarmed. We've still only got the one lawman and one doctor, examining each body (in so doing, making the makeup nail-head appliances jiggle) and then leaving, with the bodies left unattended *in situ*.

Finally, four-fifths of the way through, the sheriff makes a startling discovery: of the ten victims in the last week, six of them all worked at the same place—that house under construction! And they all happened to be among those accused by the girl at the hardware store of gang rape about six months ago (which the sheriff appears to have investigated in the usual style, i.e., doing absolutely nothing except standing around honing his bad Dan Haggerty impression).

But we already know that it's not the girl doing the killing, because the filmmakers, in an effort to prove that they thought all the viewers were as stupid as their characters, accidentally gave away the identity about twenty minutes into the film. Not only does this movie contain a character named Bubba—he's also the killer!

This doesn't even cover the full list of ineptitudes. I have to share some more:

• No one involved in the production ever learned about using a microphone to pick up sound; most scenes apparently had a single mike, so that one character is heard crystal-clear and all others are muffled and distant. Some scenes are appallingly similar to that gag scene in *Singin' in the Rain* (1952) in which the character keeps turning to and from the mike, but for real.

• What is it with hairy-backed guys? I understand why the first victim was shown in an undershirt that exhibited the dark tufts sprouting all over each shoulder; he's supposed to be a dumbass redneck. But later, a supposedly handsome young fellow is shown shirtless (making the beast with two backs with his ugly, bustless biker girlfriend), and ta-dahh! He's got a patch of dark back hair on each shoulder blade. Is there some sort of inbred gene in this town?

• If you're going to have a scene with wide-eyed corpses, make sure your "corpse" actors know not to breathe deeply. Or blink. Repeatedly.

The biggest problem here (yes, above and beyond those already listed) is that these people are all portrayed as illiterate, small-minded, ugly rednecks. Who did they think would watch this movie and give a damn about the fates of characters who were already a waste of oxygen?

I finally exploded at the end; the sheriff and the doctor (again, no other law enforcement) chase the killer to his death. Says the doctor, "At least the killings are over."

The sheriff stares as expressionlessly as he has the entire movie and says, "Are they?"

I yelled at the TV screen. "Yes, you inbred retard! The killer is dead, despite the fact that you couldn't investigate your way out of your own bathroom! The killings are over, and so is the movie! Please roll credits!"

And finally, they did something right. Credits rolled.

Small comfort though it is, it's gratifying to know that, with the exception of one girl who played something like "victim's daughter" here and ten years later played "secretary #1" in some other unknown film, no one involved behind or in front of the camera in *Nail Gun Massacre* was ever part of another movie.

Some Notable Totables:
• Couldn't be arsed

PLUTONIUM BABY (1987)

Be good to him… or he'll tell his mommy.

aka *The Mutant Kid*

- Produced and directed by Ray Hirschman
- Written by Wayne Behar
- Starring Patrick Molloy, Danny Guerra, Mary Beth Pelshaw, David Pike and Joe Viviani
- Executive produced by Richard A. Bunstein, Dale Cunningham and Clifford J. Schorer

Perseverance. That word usually evokes an admirable state of unwillingness to quit or slacken in one's efforts in the face of adversity. Let's all sing a verse of "To Dream the Impossible Dream," shall we? But there are times when perseverance isn't so laudable—specifically, when the object of pursuit or effort is simply not worth it. In those instances, when someone displays a stubborn unwillingness to give up despite all indications, we use another word instead of perseverance: idiocy.

I'm not necessarily saying that producer/director Ray Hirschman was or is an idiot. I have no idea what behind-the-scenes arrangements brought this movie to fruition; maybe he was offered an obscene amount of money to bring in the finished product, and being paid to make a godawful movie is better than being broke. I'm not saying that writer Wayne Behar was or is an idiot; we all know that writers are hired for their unique ability to craft story and character, and then the very people who hired these individuals for that ability somehow think they know better and proceed to muck things up with reckless abandon. I'm certainly not besmirching the intelligence of any of the cast; who wouldn't jump at the prospect of being credited and paid as an actor, despite a complete dearth of thespian ability?

No, I can't put the dunce cap on any particular head with any confidence. But I can tell you that somewhere, in someone attached to this movie, there was a vast reservoir of ill-focused, blind-to-quality stubborn perseverance—in other words, idiocy—brought to bear on this movie. Because otherwise, something this relentlessly pointless and inept would never have been made, and the world would be a better place for it.

The movie begins with a preamble telling us that Emily Atkins died giving birth in 1965 to a boy so contaminated by radiation that he glows in the dark. (We also have a word that describes people like that: dead.) The movie proper begins a dozen years later with said son, Danny (Danny Guerra), playing in the secluded wood near his grandfather Hank's (Joe Viviani) cabin. Near this same spot is the dumping ground from the government nuclear facility where mom Emily died. On the fateful day in question, workmen clearing the land uncover a casually-buried canister of radioactive waste; and Danny explores it once they've left. He find his mother's old locket, and his grandpa exults; this is, apparently, enough additional "evidence" to re-open the unsuccessful wrongful-death suit which Hank had lodged against Emily's employer—a shadowy government organization known as "The Organization."

The Organization is not happy about this, and the former head of the defunct nuclear facility, Dr. Drake (Patrick Molloy), is given the mop-up job. He first has his crack hitmen get rid of Grandpa Hank's two "expert witnesses" in the city, then heads out into the hinterlands with a goon squad to deal with Hank himself.

But that's not really enough people to make a movie about, especially way out in the middle of nowhere. Not to worry, though, as we've got that old standby waiting in the wings: horny campers! Yup, two couples have hiked past the "No Trespassing" signs around Hank's land to set up camp and make with the nookie. You may not care much, but for the record, the couples are Ken and Diane (David Pike and Helen Rosenthal), and Brad and Wendy (Dan Tyler and Mary Beth Penshaw).

After some city-folk-in-the-woods komedy (what? there aren't any bathrooms in the forest?), the couples get down to sweatiness. Unfortunately, Brad and Wendy get interrupted by—a mutant rabbit! It takes a chomp out of Brad's shoulder, and immediately becomes my favorite character, a status that never has reason to change by the closing credits. Ken and Diane are interrupted a little more gently by Danny spying them through the trees. Thus everyone in this tract of woodland gets to know each other. (And Danny cops a feel from Diane. Hey, he's been sheltered.)

By the next morning, Brad's bite wound is completely gone, replaced by a rash. Ominous! Even more ominous is Dr. Drake and his Evil Suits clomping through the woods like a troop of lost Boy Scouts. (Evil Boy Scouts, of course.) And want to know what's even more ominous? They run across two dead bodies, slashed and splattered up! Wait, did I say "ominous"? I meant "stupid." I'm sure we're meant to start worrying about what deadly force may lurking in the forest; I was instead trying to figure out in vain exactly who these other fresh corpses may have belonged to. Why did we spend so much time with the campers, if someone else is going to get chomped up first, and off-screen to boot?

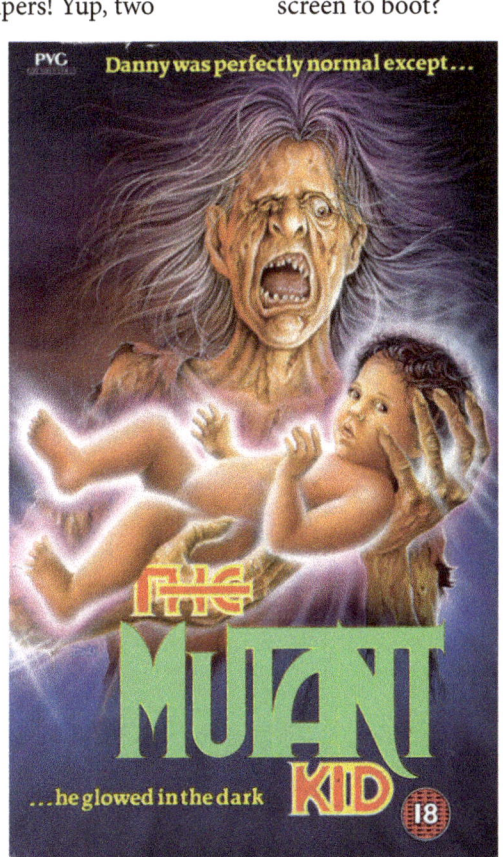

Dr. Drake finds Hank and makes him sign a release at gunpoint, which would certainly stand up in court once Hank testified that three men held him at gunpoint to sign it. Then, mainly because they're evil, they shoot him anyway and tear up the release. (Whah?) Danny, who heard the shooting, runs off through the woods, and as they pursue him—

—A mutant zombie thing attacks them! There's some slight "suspense" for about ten minutes as we wonder just who or what this is, but I'll ease the tension for you: it's Emily, Danny's mother, either reanimated or just plain kept alive by radiation or somesuch. She kills one of the goons and strings his entrails through the trees.

Danny finds the campers, and together they try to get to civilization for help. But man, this just isn't their day; once they find a road, they flag down a van—whose occupants turn out to be kung fu rapists! They beat up the men, steal the women, and drive off... until something goes "thump" on the roof. When they get out to investigate,

Zombie Mom Emily kills all the bad guys.

And wouldn't you know it, Danny and the campers give up on trying to make it to civilization. I think this is a notably extreme case of what has been dubbed the Monster Death Trap Proviso: "This stipulates that any stratagem to destroy a monster, once it has failed, may not be attempted again, even if it only failed because of some bizarre fluke. Nor can the same plan be refined and tried again. Instead, a completely other plan must be formulated."1 I mean, what are the odds that the next vehicle they flag down would also be full of kung fu rapists?

Instead, they stay there long enough for Brad's body to begin to be covered by weird scaly patches; for the mutant bunny to attack again, this time without casualties; for Brad to go into temper tantrums, accidentally kill Diane, and run off into the woods; and for Dr. Drake to make it back to civilization and back out into the woods again with replacement goons. Why? I guess the shadowy government organization called The Organization thinks that a vaguely radioactive twelve-year-old who's been raised in the woods is a serious security threat. Too bad they didn't reckon on—mutant zombie Brad! That's right, he shows up and kills most of the goons, leaving just Dr. Drake for Mutant Mom to deal with. She does so by cramming him into an empty radioactive waste container and sealing it shut; then she expires from bullet wounds. Which leaves Danny, Ken, and Wendy to finally figure out how to leave the woods and all go back to New York together.

You may think that that's a natural stopping place for the story, such as it is. But no—we're only about fifty minutes into the movie. We now fast-forward a full ten years, which actually helps explain some things, like why Emily gave birth in 1965 to a boy who is twelve in a movie made in 1987. It also explains the über-'80s fashions on the campers, especially Wendy, though why the director allowed her to look so up-to-date trendy in scenes ostensibly set in 1977 is beyond me.

Anyway. Danny, now played by Ciaran Sheehan, is reasonably well-adjusted except for nightmares which have recently begun.

But he does have a bedmate, Lauren (Julie Hays), who helps him stave them off for a while in the old-fashioned way, if you know what I mean. (Note to all you directors out there: if you're going to have a sex scene, especially an interminably-long one, how about you try to make it sexy or something? Just a thought.) He's working at a soon-to-open health club, run by ex-camper Wendy. (Cue too-long aerobics workout scene.) Yes, everyone's still all chummy; nothing like a camping trip with mutant bunnies and zombie mothers to bond you for life.

But all is not well, because two idiot hunters in the woods decide that a sealed radioactive waste container would be the perfect place to cool their beer. Out pops Dr. Drake, all zombified but surprisingly well-groomed. And now a psychic connection between him and Danny is drawing Dr. Drake to New York. Danny knows it, too; he blacked out at the moment the canister was opened, and now he's got mutant skin growing on his leg and hand.

There are still at least twenty minutes to

kill before the credits roll, so we get several long scenes of Danny pensively walking the city streets, complete with a muttered, incoherent voiceover monologue. Then we get several long scenes of Dr. Drake shuffling down the sidewalk as if he were a garden-variety homeless guy, complete with his own muttered, incoherent voiceover monologue. And at the top of our scale of inadvertent comedy, we get a, um, "tense" scene in which Wendy puts away groceries, not knowing that Drake is lurking in the house. She takes packages out of the bag… puts them in the cupboard… takes out more food… drops something… picks it up… puts food in the closet… takes more food from the bag… puts it in the fridge… takes out some more… puts it in the cupboard… *Can you stand the nail-biting suspense?!?*

Eventually, though, after all of the stalling, things end in the most unimaginative way: Danny and Dr. Drake finally meet up, fight, and kill each other. And Lauren is left pregnant with the next generation of little mutants. The end.

You know by now that I'm a story guy, which is why a movie like this—with no arc to the proceedings, with no reason for (charitably) half of the scenes to exist, with blind alleys and unpursued plot threads—is torture for me. Danny has to be the least cool mutant of all time; during the first scenes, the juvenile version shows he has the abilities to eat live fish, start very small fires when they won't help anyone, and sense the presence of Mutant Mom. But he is so inactive in the plot, he's little more than a human McGuffin, the person around whom all the stuff happens.

It's so disheartening to sit through, it's almost inconceivable that anyone would have the drive to complete the thing, instead of leaving a pile of incomplete footage sitting unclaimed in a lab somewhere. Perseverance. Or idiocy. Call it like you see it.

Some Notable Totables:
- body count: 23 (plus 1 mutant bunny)
- breasts: 1
- explosions: 0
- ominous thunderstorms: 0
- actors who've appeared on *Star Trek*: 0

REDNECK ZOMBIES (1987)

Tobacco chewin', gut chompin', cannibal kinfolk from Hell!

- Directed by Pericles Lewnes
- Written by "Fester Smellman"
- Starring Lisa DeHaven, W.E. Benson, "Zoofeet" (Pericles Lewnes), James H. Housely and Anthony Burlington-Smith
- Produced by Pericles Lewnes and George Scott
- Executive produced by Edward Bishop

You could have been forgiven for thinking that *Redneck Zombies* was the first shot-on-video feature released, before you had read the earlier entries in this book which set you straight. But while it wasn't the first, *Redneck Zombies* was certainly there in that initial batch out of the chute, and deserves more attention in the history of microbudget cinema than the pseudo-trilogy of *Blood Cult* (1985), *The Ripper* (1986), and *Revenge* (1986). Those three movies attempted to be for-real movies, shot cheaply on Sony Betacam, to be taken seriously (or at least not to be considered intentional comedies). But the lack of film only highlighted the other deficiencies—wooden acting, cheap sets, dumb dialogue—that would have made them unremarkable dreck even if shot on 16mm.

But Pericles Lewnes, director of *Redneck Zombies*, wisely realized that no one would take a shot-on-video horror flick seriously in the mid-'80s, and used that to his advantage by making a movie that no one *should* take seriously, no matter the medium. Lewnes' opus has been distributed lo these many years by Troma, the production/distribution company behind such flicks as the *Class of Nuke 'Em High* and *Toxic Avenger* franchises, and the tone of *Redneck Zombies* fits in well with the knowing camp of Troma's homegrown output, with tongue firmly in cheek and outlandishness thrown into the proceedings in huge dollops whenever the action starts to flag. You can't really say that *Redneck Zombies* was any closer to "good filmmaking" than the *Blood Cult* trilogy, but it's clear that *Redneck Zombies* doesn't *want* to be considered "good"—this is a movie made as an excuse for bad taste, and on that score, it succeeds.

The setup is spun directly from the oft-stolen premise of the *Return of the Living Dead* movies: there's this oil-barrel-sized canister, see, of extremely dangerous radioactive biowaste. It's so dangerous that it can only be transported between bases by... a single enlisted man, Robinson (Tyrone Taylor), who's got the canister slung lopsided in the back of his jeep as he cruises the ill-maintained rural roads that are the only means of transportation between military centers in this great land of ours, stoned out of his mind. It's no wonder, then, that the canister bounces off the jeep and rolls down an embankment.

It ends up in the hand of the Clemson clan —father Jed (W.E. Benson) and sons Junior, Jethro, and Billy Bob ("P. Floyd Pirana", William-Livingston Dekker and "Zoofeet" (director Lewnes himself))—the latter of whom wears a halter top and insists on being called "Elly Mae." These, as you might guess, are rednecks, although by the standards to which I subscribe governing the labeling of localized subcultures, they're closer to "hillbillies." They are, of course, both illiterate and belligerent; and as befits their station in life, they're also moonshiners. Professional moonshiners, even. Their last still has recently been shot up by rival moonshiner Ferd (Bucky Santini), and so the sudden acquisition of this brightly-painted metal barrel with the indecipherable markings on it (what you and I would call "the English language") is a lucky happenstance.

But while they're off fixing up their new apparatus, we're also introduced to—wait for it—a group of campers! Where would the horror movie genre be without family cabins, or summer camps, or simple overnight hiking trips? Fresh out of meat, that's where. Our jolly hillbillies may be too unsympathetic to be our official protagonists, but these cityfolk out roughing it aren't much better.

Here's who we've got:

• Wilbur (James H. Housely), who used to live in the area but moved away a decade ago, now leading his friends back to a primo camping spot by a pond.

• Andy (Martin J. Wolfman), nebbish white guy.

• Sally (Boo Teasedale) and Lisa (Lisa DeHaven), the two white girls. We know that Lisa will end up being "final girl," because the framing device at the beginning of the movie shows her straitjacketed in an institution.

• Bob and Theresa (Anthony Burlington-Smith and Darla Deans), the black couple.

(None of the others in the expedition seem particular attached to one another.)

• The other guy (I dunno). He's chunky and hairy, he never has a line, and every time we see him he's downing a bottle of hard liquor. Eventually, it becomes apparent that this is a running gag, but I'm not even sure whether it was intentional from the beginning or whether it simply evolved as shooting progressed.

While our fine junior outdoors-persons hike, set up camp, and smoke some grass, they interact in that format so well known to denizens of low-end cinema: they bicker. Also, they whine, make and rebuff blunt sexual references, and occasionally call into question the size of one another's genitalia. This is sophistication, see, in stark contrast to the rednecks' rural ways.

Speaking of the rednecks, it doesn't take too long for them to get their still operating, with the barrel unrinsed (and some of its contents accidentally splashed into the mash). The resulting moonshine looks like lime Kool-Aid in pint Mason jars, but they go ahead and send Billy Bob— excuse me, Elly Mae— to truck their deliveries in and around town, while the other three sample their new recipe.

Which would mean, you know, they become zombies. But only after every single cheap digital effect has played over them as they howl and cackle and writhe on the ground—afterimages, over-exposures, you name it. This movie comes closest to surrealist art when either Junior or Jethro (don't blame me for being unable to tell them apart, neither can their dad Jed) starts bellowing at the sky, "Aliens! Aliens!" in radioactive delirium.

After the campers start to wake from their cannabis-induced naps, Sally heads off into the woods to answer nature's call, accidentally discovers the still site, and also accidentally discovers a zombified redneck. Important anatomy lesson: according to *Redneck Zombies*, the weakest structural point in the human body is right across the belly; through the course of this movie, at least three people get pulled apart right at that spot. Then Theresa follows Sally, and gets more of the same. And then everybody else finds the remains, and freaks right out. (Bob, who up until now has behaved himself as a cultured and educated African-American, spends the rest of the movie in spooked Stepin Fetchit mode.)

While all of this has been going on, Elly Mae has been dutifully making deliveries, which leads one to wonder, When exactly is this supposed to be taking place? Was the pot-aftermath nap over the night, or just through part of the afternoon? Or is Elly Mae delivering clear until sunup? Apparently time of day was never a consideration during shooting, so any scene could appear to be taking place at any time of am or pm. Anyway, just to keep things interesting, Elly Mae's deliveries include a "freelance butcher" who uses people as raw material, a mother who promptly pours 'shine into her infant's bottle, and a couple of yee-haw types watching probably the worst porno video in the world. Pretty much everyone in town is a moonshine customer, in fact. Which means that presently there are plenty of gelatin- and greasepaint-smeared zombies lurching out of the woods to attack our surviving campers. No telling, though, why they all decided to lurch out of town to that particular spot in the wilderness.

What really differentiates this movie from the *Blood Cult* trilogy and makes it the true grandpappy of indie shot-on-video horror is the repeating phenomenon of Filmmakers Amusing Themselves. When you're making a movie for pocket change, having fun on the set suddenly becomes one of the most important considerations. That's how you get scenes that make their tiny leaps into inspired lunacy, to make up for having such a thin story. These include:

• The Tobacco Man (credited as "E.W. Nesneb"), the warped analogue of the Ice Cream Man who visits the backwoods with a floursack over his cancer-deformed face and distributes chew to the hillbillies.

• Elly Mae's hitchhiker (Frank Lantz), a compulsive shaver who apes the hitcher scene from *The Texas Chainsaw Massacre* (1974).

• Bob, tripping on some LSD, attempting to conduct an autopsy on a zombie and hallucinating all sorts of incongruous items among the guts. (Okay, the scene's actually not that amusing, but it's still indicative of doing whatever is fun on the set.)

• The pink-to-the-gills soldier (Jim Bellistri), one of two who come back with Robinson to retrieve the canister. Unlike Elly Mae, who's merely gender-confused, this soldier flounces and simpers and titters like an entire platoon of junior high girls. He meets his end by diving right into a throng of zombies to live out his *Deliverance* fantasy.

There is certainly gore aplenty, which is what most people remember this for: splatter and grue gets on everyone and everything, in a number of different colors and consistencies. But somehow, you can almost smell the Jell-O and cherry syrup behind it all. Considered as a motion picture made by filmmakers for an audience to watch, it's seriously lacking; considered by the genre-indie standard of a video made by some guys for some other guys to watch, it's surprisingly entertaining.

Some Notable Totables:
• body count: 23, plus 1 piglet
• breasts: 2
• explosions: 0
• ominous thunderstorms: 0
• visible boom mikes: 1
• actors who've appeared on *Star Trek*: 0

REDNECK ZOMBIES: Executive Producer Edward Bishop's Comments

We were all huge fans of Romero and Argento and had spent countless hours intently studying (also known as "toking up and watching repeatedly") the zombie genre and horror-comedies like *Evil Dead*. That said, we actually started throwing titles around without really having a specific genre in mind. Somehow the words "Redneck" and "Zombies" came up, and when we heard them together we knew beyond a doubt that would be our movie. How could anyone see a movie called "*Redneck Zombies*" on the video store shelf and not be compelled to know what the hell it is? Once we had that title, the style and tone just fell into place. We knew that with no money we were not going to be making a great "quality" film, so we decided to make the best "horrible" film ever. A few things were obvious to us from the start:

• It had to be the goriest, bloodiest, over-the-top zombie movie ever. The goal was to take Romero gore and multiply by 10. Realism was out of the question, so we went for sheer emotional "gut" response and a vast "slimy chunks and goo" factor.

• It had to have silly, slapstick humor to accompany the gore, so that people would laugh, then be disgusted with themselves for laughing. In fact, our original tagline was "The 3 Stooges Meet *Dawn of the Dead*."

• It had to have a ridiculous plot, characters, and cheezy dialogue that parodied all the horror movie clichés, and played to the quality of acting we expected to have.

• Most of all, it had to be fun to make and fun to watch. Our ultimate goal was to create something that we would enjoy hanging out and watching with friends, that could be viewed over and over, as with so many of our favorites, and you would always catch some new subtle joke or background detail.

When we started we thought it would take us six weekends to shoot. It ended up taking eleven weekends plus a few scattered days and evenings for effects shots and pickups. I started editing evenings while we were in production, then for about three months afterwards, fitting it in between a full-time production job. Meanwhile Pericles and DP Ken Davis were working with some other friends in Salisbury to create the psychedelic visual elements.

Video was instrumental in very much of what ended up in the movie. Even though videotape at the time was not cheap—it was our single biggest expense—it did give us the freedom to ad lib, to do a whole lot of re-takes and coverage that wouldn't have been possible with film. Our actors were actually very talented with improv and some of the funniest moments in the movie are ad libs or actor contributions. "Well at least I don't have to put a bag over her head this time" is my personal favorite, but there are countless others, including most of the autopsy scene and Andy attempting to put Bactine on his gaping neck wound. Videotape also allowed us to keep rolling between takes, providing a wealth of classic outtakes and behind-the-scenes material.

Peri played Elly and I played Junior (the head-blast zombie). There were a variety of reasons for the pseudonyms. Peri and I wanted to separate our production and acting personas, so we created ridiculous characters for ourselves that even had full bios and backstories. We created "Fester Smellman" simply because we thought it was funny, plus we could have someone to blame. A couple actors were working under SAG radar, others were afraid the movie would jeopardize their future careers or bring shame to their families. Oddly enough, the one person who seems truly embarrassed by his appearance to this day used his real name, and is widely regarded as one of the best performances in the movie.

We were happy and proud that Lisa DeHaven (Final Girl) never hesitated to use her real name and has enthusiastically supported the movie all along with all her heart. Lisa is the niece of B-movie/soap opera icon Gloria DeHaven, and daughter of David DeHaven, star of *Angry Red Planet* and *Beast with Five Fingers*, so she carries the family legacy like a Barrymore.

The actress who played Ma Clemson was cornered in an "Intervention" by members of her church and told she would be excommunicated if she continued to participate in "Satan's work." She told us in tears and was genuinely crushed to back out. Fortunately we had already shot her "Ma" scenes, so my good friend Jeff McKinstry, who was already taking on various crew positions as needed, stepped in to fill the role as "Ma Zombie". Unfortunately he refused to shave his Grizzly Adams beard ("It took me a year to grow that thing, I wasn't about to shave it off for my buddy's little zombie flick") so we had to triple his makeup budget to cover it.

On the first take when Peri picks up the barrel and drops it, he slammed his head so hard into the barrel we thought he was dead. He did get a pretty bad concussion, but he got up and insisted on doing another take. We used the first one, and that is the actual sound you hear of his head hitting the barrel.

Two weeks into shooting we discovered that "Theresa" was pregnant. We raced to finish her scenes before she showed too much but I think you can see how successful we were.

Due to the length of the shoot and scheduling issues there are several scenes where pickups or reverse angles were shot months apart. See if you can spot the shots where it's 30 degrees out and we're wearing t-shirts. We actually sucked on ice cubes between takes so you wouldn't see our breath.

To get to and from the farm that was our main location we had to cross a major toll bridge over the Chesapeake Bay. Many of us delighted in driving home in full gore makeup with bloody body parts scattered around the car. We got some shocked looks at the toll booth, but strangely no one ever called the cops.

The cabin we shot in was so old and dilapidated we were concerned the whole time that it would collapse on us. It survived us, but fell down in a storm a few months after we finished shooting. However, the Tobacco Man's truck is still out in the field where we left it, and if you knew where to look you could see it on Google Earth.

We had no distribution lined up, but about halfway through production we saw *The Toxic Avenger* and we immediately knew that Troma was where we belonged. We still shopped it around for a few months. I met with several small distributors in LA, and Peri and I saw a few others in New York. Responses ranged from "we like it but it doesn't fit our distribution model" to "this is the worst piece of shit I've ever seen! How could you defile our office with this vile abomination?!" We had one other offer, but when we met with Troma it was an instant mutual admiration-fest, and we pretty much had a deal by the end of the day. I think it was really inevitable, but we wanted to know our options. By the way, the legend that we just took a bus to New York and showed up on Lloyd and Michael's doorstep is a myth. We called ahead and we went by train.

Why did we not do any feature film projects between *Redneck Zombies* and *LOOP* (2007)? We couldn't find anything we thought worthy of our talents. Actually, we did two feature documentaries that have played film festivals and won numerous awards—*Fast Game Fast Money*, a tongue-in-cheek exposé of New York's Three-Card-Monte and Shell Game grifters, and *Fighter*, about the early days of Ultimate Fighting featuring the start of Randy Couture. We shopped a couple narrative scripts around looking for financing but eventually we got into music videos, documentaries, and working on other people's projects, putting our own narratives on the back burner. We didn't want to do another no-budget feature. But *LOOP* was a movie that had to be made, and now I think we'll do more soon. Meanwhile we're doing everything we can to support independent filmmaking and develop new methods of financing and distribution.

If we were to do it today, we'd shoot HD digital and plan the shooting schedule better. Otherwise we wouldn't change a thing.

I also want to clear up the question about the Unknown Hiker. He was Peri's brilliant brainchild, addressing the convention that the characters who don't say much are the first to die. Peri's idea, which I immediately loved, was to have this character that never said a word and no one ever acknowledges, who reflects the audience's disdain for our obnoxious band of campers, and in the end he's the only true survivor. The drinking started as a way to make him noticeable, but it became a running gag that was far more successful than we could have hoped, especially as he pulls infinite full bottles of liquor out of nowhere. He is the most talked about and debated character, definitely a fan favorite.

FRIDAY the 13th PART VII: The NEW BLOOD (1988)

On Friday, May 13th, Jason is back. But this time someone's waiting.

- Directed by John Carl Buechler
- Written by Manuel Fidello and Daryl Haney
- Starring Lar Park-Lincoln, Kevin Spirtas, Susan Blu, Terry Kiser and Susan Jennifer Sullivan
- Produced by Iain Paterson
- Executive produced by Frank Mancuso, Jr.

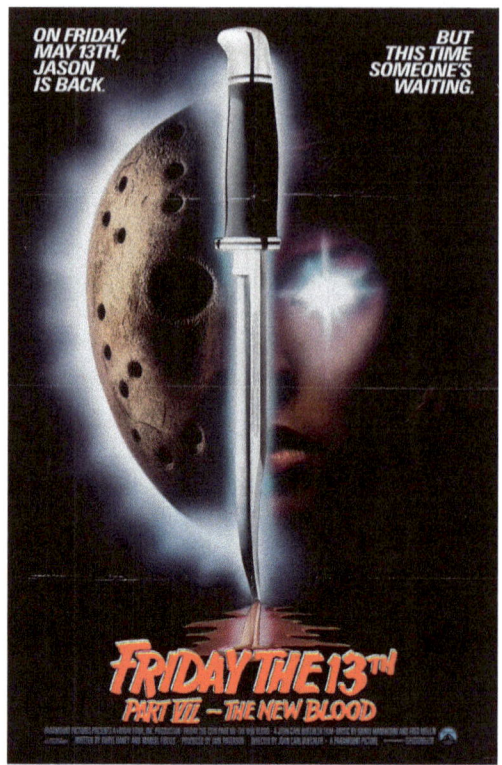

> "Rejection. Okay. Fine. I can take it. I've been rejected by some of the finest science fiction magazines in the continental United States!"

The *Friday the 13th* franchise has always been second-rate. The first installment was just another of the subgrade slasher films that clogged the early '80s in the wake of *Halloween* (1978), and after that a series inexplicably developed around Jason (rather than his mother, who was the killer in the first film—oops, I hope I didn't ruin that movie for you). All of the movies told variations the story of a group of horny teens getting mowed down by the masked killer, and they all told it adequately at best; a collection of hand-held camera shots that were meant to incite suspense, and various gory deaths by FX maestro Tom Savini or an imitator that were really the only signs of creativity on the part of anyone in the production.

Then, somewhere in the middle of the series (I mark *Part VI: Jason Lives* (1986) as the real turning point), the producers had a moment of insight. Perhaps the reins had been taken over by youngsters who had seen the first few movies as paying customers. Whatever the reason, there seems to have been a realization: "Hey, these movies are goofy!" And from that point on, they became self-consciously so. Jason had died at the end of the fourth movie, *The Final Chapter* (1984); when he was resurrected in *Part VI*, he was no longer presented simply as a *Halloween*-style boogeyman; rather, he became an unkillable zombie, chopping down human bit parts between each "plot" scene. Suddenly, the films became fun.

Right around this time, too, the movies had become such a force on home video that their obligatory theatrical run acted more as an advertisement for the coming VHS release than as an attempt to actually get audiences into the cinema. In my hometown, *Part VII* was at the multiplex for exactly one week. This sequel also marks the point in the series at which the producers began throwing novelty concepts at the tried-and-true formula to try to keep the franchise semi-fresh. *Part VII* is often described as "Jason meets Carrie."

This installment opens with a montage and a voiceover, mainly meant for anyone who'd never heard of the series before; we get to see several of Jason's earlier killings, his resurrection in *Part VI*, and his fate at the end of that movie, chained to a boulder at the bottom of Crystal Lake (oops, hope I didn't ruin *that* movie for you).

We then cut to a young girl, Tina, on the shore of the lake some time later. Upset at her father for beating her mother, she gets in a rowboat and pushes away from shore. When dad comes out to plead for her to come back, she screams, "I wish you were dead!" Unfortunately, this little girl just happens to be psychokinetic; the dock starts shaking as if it were mounted on hydraulics (which it obviously is), and Dad falls to his death in the lake.

Fast-forward roughly a decade. Tina (Lar Park-Lincoln) is now a young, nubile, and very mixed-up woman, and she's going back to the lake house with her mom and her shrink, Dr. Krews (ubiquitous character actor Terry Kiser) to confront the demons of her past and her guilt over her father's death. However, Dr. Krews' motivations aren't really so pure; recognizing her PK abilities, he's been instigating "episodes" which he catches on videotape to make himself famous.

It just so happens that the old house is isolated on the edge of the lake—right beside another cabin full of college-age kids come to celebrate a birthday. In other words, it's House O' Fodder. Since we're planning such a high body count, we go beyond the standard four or five stereotypes used in these movies; we have a full *ten* stereotypes. There's obviously Hero Boy, who befriends Tina and actually believes her when the truth comes out; the Rich Bitch, who's inexplicable cruelty can only serve to engender distrust between the classes (she also lasts for most of the movie, just so we'll really be rooting for Jason when she finally gets it); and then, with less importance, we have the Wallflower, the Stoner and the Pothead Girl, the Sci-Fi Geek, the Yuppie and his Yuppie Slut, and the Black Boy and Black Girl (apparently ethnicity is all the distinguishing characteristic they need). And to add to the body count, we also have the birthday boy and his girlfriend, who never make it to the party, and a couple of random campers thrown in.

When Dr. Krews' "therapy" upsets Tina worse, she runs away from him out to the pier. She concentrates on the lake, half-believing she can raise her father; but it isn't her father she reanimates. It's Jason, still chained to the rock, much the worse for wear. (His ribcage and backbone are showing through, some teeth are exposed along the jawline, and his fingers are meaty but skeletal —not too bad).

Let the slaughter begin.

For no logical reason, Jason starts on the campers and such who are far from the lake (the sign says "5 Miles"), using tent pegs to dispatch them until he picks up a handy machete (a camper was chopping wood with a machete? what is this, Bolivia?). All of the deaths are couched in the standard simplistic morality of this and other slasher flicks: everyone who has sex… or tries to have sex… or thinks about having sex, dies.

Jason seems to have full "off-screen teleportation"[1] qualities. He can kill someone in the house, then kill someone who's lost in the woods and can't find the house, then kill another person in the house... He eventually gets bored of his machete and apparently raids the tool shed; he attacks some fodder in the woods with a long pruning hook—and then, in the next set of attacks, still in the woods, he employs a gas-powered tree trimmer with a circular blade. I'm still trying to figure out if he went all the way back to the tool shed to change equipment and then back out into the woods, or if he has the coolest Swiss Army knife ever.

Also of note: horror aficionados know to look for at least one "spring-loaded cat"[2] scene—you know, where a cat leaps from a closet, releasing the audience's tension, and then the real killer shows up when you "least expect it," except that you do expect it if you've seen movies like this before. Not only is there a spring-loaded cat scene here, but its arbitrary nature is highlighted or "lampshaded" for us: the Pothead Girl who discovers the cat goes out of her way to say that she hasn't seen it in the house before.

I think this installment also holds the honor (to date) of Most Methods Attempted

---

1 A term coined by Ken Begg of Jabootu.net.
2 Another of Ken Begg's terms.

to Off Jason. In the last fifteen minutes Tina and Hero Boy electrocute him, throw furniture at him, drop a roof on him, drop him through a staircase, try to crush his skull with his own mask straps, strangle him, drop him through the floor, shoot nails into his head, cover him in gasoline and set him alight, explode a house around him, and finally empty the requisite six shots into him. I'd be lying if I said he looked no worse for wear after that, but still…

After this, *Part VIII* was *Jason Takes Manhattan* (1989), which the man in the mask got aboard a boat hosting a high school graduation party that was heading for the Big Apple (further confusing the geography of where, exactly, Crystal Lake is). And after that, the producers really got creative/desperate, with *Jason Goes to Hell* (1993) injecting more supernatural elements than had been seen in the series previously, *Jason X* (2001) transplanting the story to space and turning it into an *Alien* imitation after a long lacuna in production, and *Freddy vs. Jason* (2003) throwing him into the mix with another '80s horror icon running out of steam, before finally rebooting the whole franchise in 2009.

Some Notable Totables:
- body count: 15
- breasts: 4
- explosions: 2
- dream sequences: 1
- ominous thunderstorms: 2 (well, sorta—there are random lightning bolts throughout the night of the climax)
- actors who've appeared on *Star Trek*: 1
  - Craig Thomas ("Ben"—I think he was the black kid) was a Klingon crewman in *Star Trek: The Motion Picture*

KILLER KLOWNS FROM OUTER SPACE (1988)

IN SPACE NO ONE CAN EAT ICE CREAM!

- Directed by Stephen Chiodo
- Written and produced by Charles, Edward, and Stephen Chiodo
- Starring Grant Cramer, Suzanne Snyder, John Allen Nelson, John Vernon and Michael Siegel
- Executive produced by Paul Mason and Helen Sarlui-Tucker

Clowns are evil. That's no surprise. It may be a little more surprising that they're actually from outer space, and they drink human blood. Beyond that, though, *Killer Klowns From Outer Space* doesn't try to surprise. This is intentional camp, following the plot structure of a million B-movies in the service of a wonderfully ludicrous premise, and the fun comes more from seeing the devious ways in which the Chiodo Brothers use carnival buffoonery as springboards for carnage than from any dramatic suspense.

In fact, the plot could best be described in its obligatories. As we all know, any mysterious shooting star must fall in such a way that it attracts the attention of either A) teens necking at the lookout point over the town, or B) a crazy old coot. Here, we get both! The old coot (Royal Dano), being closer, ventures out into the woods and finds a mysterious carnival tent at the crash site. He and his dog disappear in quick succession, at the hands of… a clown!

Meanwhile, the only two lovebirds at Lookout Point who bother to pay attention to the shooting star are college kids Mike (Grant Cramer) and Debbie (Suzanne Snyder), who decide that going off to look for it is more exciting than whatever they were about to get up to. (At Deb's insistence, actually. Given that Mike has an inflatable raft in the back of his 4x4, I think it's a good choice.) They venture out into the woods, and discover… a carnival tent!

Well, it'd be a short movie if our protagonist pair met the same end as our throwaway coot, so instead they find the entrance and wander around the brightly striped corridors. The engine room they find (complete with warp core) convinces them that they're actually on a UFO; the storage room, in which they find the coot's body cocooned in cotton candy, lets them know that these aliens aren't cuddly New Age space brothers. After a close encounter with one of the clowns' popcorn gun, they escape to make it back to town and warn the populace.

Which works about as well as you'd expect. Especially when, after discussing with each other how insane their story sounds, they still spill it forth complete with spaceships, killer alien clowns, cotton-candy cocoons, and popcorn firearms. One would think that a moment's reflection would tell them that simplifying it to "somebody dressed like a clown is killing people" would garner a lot more respect. After all, by 1988 everyone had seen at least one slasher flick featuring an unstoppable killer in a garish disguise, and a town with a name like

"Crescent Cove" seems ready-made for its own local serial killer. But no, Mike and Deb insist on sounding like complete lunatics to the police.

Fortunately, the increasingly unpleasant Officer Mooney (John Vernon) isn't the only cop on duty; in fact, young and cleancut Officer Dave (John Allen Nelson) is Debbie's ex-boyfriend who still carries a torch for her, so there's at least one listening ear. After insisting that they drop Debbie off at home, Dave and Mike head back up into the woods to check out their story. Of course, the carnival tent is no longer there, and Dave's ready to haul Mike's ass back to sit the weekend in the cooler, but on the way back down to town they pass Lookout Point, now strewn with abandoned vehicles… and traces of cotton candy…

There's much running back and forth, trying to warn the populace and get back to Debbie before the clowns capture the entire town. (Meanwhile, Mooney sits self-righteously in the cop shop, convinced that the scores of calls he's getting about surly pierrots are all some elaborate hoax aimed at him personally.) In the end, all the right people are dead, all the right people are alive, and the world is set to rights with the obligatory "shocker" tacked on.

But the plot is mostly an excuse on which to hang all of the killer clown gags the Chiodos could come up with. You've got the cotton-candy guns and the popcorn guns (and the popcorn itself grows into clown-faced creatures), ferocious hand puppets, bloodhound balloon animals, carnivorous shadow puppets, flesh-eating cream pies, and the classic "clowns from a small car" shtick. The clowns show up on doorsteps under any number of pretexts—pizza delivery, candy-grams—in order to wrap the unsuspecting locals in cotton candy and hoover them up into a big garish parade float rolling down the street. Mooney gets grabbed by a party razzer with fingers and ends up a flesh-and-blood ventriloquist dummy. And my favorite gag? Debbie runs from a clown in her apartment, throws open the window to jump… and there below are five clowns in fireman hats, holding one of those trampoliney things to catch her.

Technically, the whole thing's well-realized; the clowns themselves are accomplished with nicely articulated and textured cable-controlled masks. And those effects in which realism breaks down are instantly forgiven—after all, clowns and

circus hoopla are supposed to look garish and fake.

The movie stops short of being a full-fledged classic simply because that's one of the limits of intentional camp; there's always that winking knowledge that someone went to a lot of trouble to make things look this goofy and outrageous. But *Killer Klowns* offends a lot less in that regard than, say, every single movie ever produced by Troma Studios.

Some Notable Totables:
- body count: 23 (plus tons more implied), and 1 dog)
- breasts: 0
- explosions: 5
- ominous thunderstorms: 0
- protestations that there has to be a logical explanation: 1
- longest shower ever: 1
- actors who've appeared on *Star Trek*: 0

NIGHTFALL (1988)

THE GREATEST SCIENCE-FICTION STORY OF ALL TIME.

- *Written and directed by Paul Mayersberg, based (ostensibly) on the short story by Isaac Asimov*
- *Starring David Birney, Sarah Douglas, Alexis Kanner, Andra Millian and Starr Andreef*
- *Produced by Julie Corman*

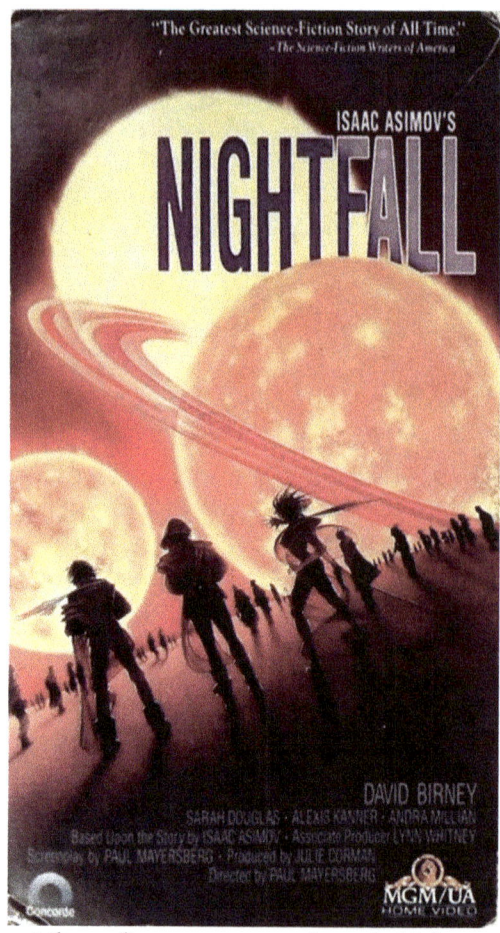

Here's the thing about different media: they're different. You can do things in one medium that you can't in another. That's patently obvious if you compare, say, landscape painting with dance choreography. But sometimes people forget that even the narrative media—short fiction, novels, poetry, theater, film—each exist for a reason; each can do things the others can't. Sometimes you can't translate a narrative from one medium to another and have it retain what made it noteworthy originally. And sometimes, when you technically could translate from one medium to another, it still isn't done with enough skill or horse sense to make the exercise worthwhile.

The original "Nightfall" by Isaac Asimov is a short story, which necessarily means that it's short on plot. At best, one might be able to stretch it out to the length of, say, an *Outer Limits* episode by dramatizing the embedded exposition. Any longer than that—for instance, if someone were to attempt to make a full-length motion picture out of it—and you're going to end up adding a lot of plot to take up the running time.

In this case, though, writer/director Paul Mayersberg, couldn't confine himself to adding to the core plot; instead, he grafted in enough ephemeral subplots that they manage to completely eclipse any main storyline, as well as the core idea that has kept the original short story popular for (at the time of production) almost fifty years.

If a movie starts with a long voiceover to get the audience up to speed on a half-dozen plot threads, there probably isn't enough of a focused story to hold their interest to the finish line. Such a voiceover begins this movie, informing us of a planet with three suns keeping it in perpetual daylight (instead of the six in the original story—what a place for a budgetary cutback!), and a city run by Aton (David Birney), astronomer/statesman. He's been derelict in his duties of late (whatever those might be—is staring at the suns really an 8-to-5 job?), thanks to a mysterious desert woman named Ana (Andra Millian), who's bewitched him with the standard feminine wiles to the point of utter distraction and obsession. Meanwhile, the followers of blind prophet Sor (Alexis Kanner) are spreading around a prophecy of "nightfall," a coming time of doom in which the planet's three suns will all vanish and darkness will spread. Aton, naturally, poo-poohs the idea when he isn't busy sucking face. His ex-wife Roa (Sarah Douglas), though, is as much a believer as Aton is a skeptic, and has gone off to join the cultists in their doomsdaying.

Lotta background to absorb at once, isn't it? It'd be best if you took notes, because coming up there are long stretches in which nothing in particular happens, and you'll have plenty of time to go back and mull over this expository blob.

In fact, so little happens for so long that it's difficult to recap the plot and not have it sound like a half-hour short. Aton spends far too much time drinking and nuzzling Ana, so his own people kidnap her and drag her back to the desert where she belongs. Sor's followers spend a lot of time chanting. Aton's son-in-law, Kin (Charles Hayward), a professional bell-forger and bell-player, spends a lot of time playing his bells. (Gripping cinema, I tell you.) Aton and Sor visit one another and trade barbs phrased in a manner that's supposed to sound all deep and philosophical but which really reminds of that friend you had in high school who thought he was getting in touch with Cosmic Truth whenever he was stoned and thus regaled you with inane observations in serious tones. (I hope you remember that friend, because if you don't, odds are you *were* that friend.)

Then one of the suns disappears! (I'm assuming it dips below the horizon, or fails to come up again, or something. It's only referred to obliquely. Who needs story details when we've got bell-ringing to watch?) Aton has to come to grips with the idea that Sor might actually be on to something. Sor's followers, meanwhile, chant and mumble with renewed vigor.

Right about here is the movie's sole memorable scene. Roa, determined to progress to the next level of "illumination" (an odd expression for a blind prophet to use) through voluntary blindness. So she lies in a coffin, and a metal mask is placed over her face on which two hawks perch. The hawks proceed to cheerfully peck out her eyes for lunch. It's a haunting image. Too bad it was wasted in such a lame movie.

What else happens? Aton sends Kin out into the desert to find Ana again, while Aton tries to come up with some way for the people of his city (who seem to number maybe two dozen) to survive the coming nonspecific doom. Over the course of several scenes (interspersed with Aton and Sor separately pontificating), Kin finds Ana among her people, doing what desert nomads do best, i.e., interpretive dance. Then he and she go through a cutesy scene of falling in love while playing with a variety of burlap facemasks, and end up rutting beside the campfire. (And then Kin gets bitten in the groin by a snake. But Ana helpfully sucks the poison out. And if you think I'm going for any of the obvious jokes, you're crazy.) Eventually, he persuades her to come back to the city for Aton's sake. (And, I suppose, so that his wife, Aton's daughter, can take care of his laundry.)

Dear lord, is there still more of this movie? Unfortunately, yes. Somewhere along the way they lose another sun (check the couch cushions), an assassin tries to kill Aton, the city people build an underground bunker lit by wind power, and as night finally falls, people start lighting fires. No, not big city-destroying ones like in the short story; there isn't the budget for that kind of thing. Just a few bonfires here and there. That frustrates Sor, as he was expecting big apocalyptic destruction to make that whole fanatical belief deal worthwhile for his followers.

Oh, and Aton discovers Kin and Ana playing kissyface, so they have a duel to the death with the crystal swords that everyone uses (even though they show many metal implements, no one on this planet has apparently had the bright idea of forging a blade). Oh, and Aton also throws Sor off a cliff. Did I mention that this is our noble protagonist?

The ending could well be termed "anti-climactic" if what comes before had been any kind of build-up. As it is, well, it's just kind of there. The suns disappear, the stars come out, and Aton's people all look up and say, "Huh. Stars. Nifty. Is that it?" Aton gives a little speech (the last of many, thank goodness) about how maybe, in the fact of such cosmic cosmicness, no one on their planet had ever done or said or thought anything truly significant to that point. I'm sure when Mayersberg was penning those words, he wasn't thinking of how appropriately they fit this movie, but I couldn't have summed it up better myself.

Among the many sleepwalking performances here, Alexis Kanner as Sor brings a dash of talent to his part. Instead of being the normal ethereal prophet intoning Words Of Wisdom, he delivers his lines in a very matter-of-fact, understated tone. In fact, the actor brings so much more appeal to the character than Birney brings to Aton that one almost wishes that the arbitrary "protagonist" and "antagonist" labels had been reversed.

Of all the people to blame for this one, though, don't blame the good Dr. Asimov. He knew, wisely, that film was a very different medium, and one in which he had very little experience or interest, and so he let the producers who paid for the rights do as they pleased. If he ever saw the movie that resulted, I'm sure he drew some comfort from the fact that the people who had and have read his original story still outnumber the people who saw this dumped-to-video movie by a sizable margin.

Some Notable Totables:
- body count: 4, plus 1 snake
- breasts: 2
- explosions: 0
- ominous thunderstorms: 1
- actors who've appeared on *Star Trek*: 2
    - David Birney (Aton) played "Senator Letant" in the *DS9* episode "Tears of the Prophets"
    - Larry Hankin ("Desert King") played "Gaunt Gary" in the *Voyager* episode "The Cloud"

PHANTASM II (1988)

For ten years the secret of Perigold Cemetery has remained a mystery. Now the ultimate evil is about to be revealed.

"You think that when you die, you go to heaven? You come to US!"

- Written and directed by Don Coscarelli
- Starring James LeGros, Reggie Bannister, Angus Scrimm, Paula Irvine and Samantha Phillips
- Produced by Robert A. Quezada
- Executive produced by Dac Coscarelli

Plot descriptions are fairly useless when describing this series, which is one of the best examples of the "rubber reality" horror movie, in which at least one protagonist sees things that other people don't and often can't tell which is the dream and which is reality. Granted, horror movies have relied this trick for ages, but most of them use it as a crutch to add spooky value to long stretches of story in which nothing really happens. In this movie, though, and in the *Phantasm* movies generally, the whole rubber reality adds to the stylized, atmospheric mood of the story, giving us a masterpiece of ambiance above all. (The fact that some of the scenes in this movie were originally shot as dream sequences and then made a part of the "real world" narrative only adds to that wonderful confusion.)

Knowledge of the original *Phantasm* (1979) is unnecessary to appreciate the sequel, but I'll fill you in a little anyway: adolescent Michael (Michael Baldwin) loses his brother to a car accident, and discovers in mid-mourning that the strange mortician, whom he dubs "The Tall Man" (Angus Scrimm), has been putting corpses to nefarious use after their death, though his ultimate goal remains unexplained. With some prodding, Michael ropes his adult friend Reggie (Reggie Bannister), an ice cream vendor, into helping him investigate. The Tall Man has dwarf minions in monks' robes to help him in whatever he's doing, as well as softball-sized metallic spheres which fly under their own power and kill their victims with an assortment of Swiss Army knife attachments. *Phantasm* isn't a great movie—the most common complaint is the slow pacing—but it is notable for working with the paranoia which can be part of the coping mechanism, especially in a bereaved adolescent.

The original's success was significant for an independent film, but even though it ends inconclusively, nothing about it really cried out for as sequel; even stranger was that the franchise was picked up by Universal Pictures, who bankrolled writer/director Coscarelli into revisiting the premise. Because of Michael's continued insistence on his outlandish claims about the Tall Man, he's been in a mental institution for the last seven years (i.e., since the events of the first movie)—long enough for original actor Baldwin to be replaced by James LeGros at the studio's insistence, LeGros being seen then as an up-and-comer. (When the third and fourth movies were made independently like the original, Baldwin got his old role back) For some reason, the LeGros version of Michael seems to be much more an active, take-charge character than Baldwin's version in any of the other movies, and it's interesting to speculate as to the reason—a character rewrite (more studio interference), or possibly a simple matter of how LeGros plays the character.

Getting out of the institution, Michael teams up with Reggie, the only "family" he has left; and with Reggie's family then killed by the Tall Man, the two set out on a quest for vengeance, tracking the Tall Man across the Northwest with a trunk full of weapons and tools, guided only by Michael's vague dreams and hunches.

Adding another layer is Liz (Paula Irvine), a young woman who has been haunted by dreams of Michael and the Tall Man for years, and who knows that, sometime soon, the Tall Man will be coming to her small town, and hopes that Michael will arrive before things come to a head.

Beyond this, a plot description is of little use. The disjointed narrative adds to the wonderful dreamlike narrative; the Tall Man is never truly explained, except for the fact that his mere presence somehow drains the life from small towns, allowing him to then reanimate the cemetery's corpses as malevolent dwarfs and ship them off to Somewhere Else. In this movie, Angus Scrimm's age works perfectly, portraying the Tall Man as a being of ancient evil; in later movies, he tends more towards plain old and tired.

While I tout the dreaminess of this movie, such would obviously be dreary if it were the main defining characteristic of a movie; in fact, I think that the original *Phantasm* suffers from too much languid unreality, so dreamlike that it sometimes *induces* sleep. Here, Coscarelli has added the elements of a male-bonding road trip (enhanced by wonderful well-considered cinematography, which gives the movie a visual richness that disguises its low budget), as well as more comic-booky action scenes involving the dwarfs, the "graver" minions (silent figures in camouflage and gas masks), and the trademark flying spheres which cruise the hallways of the Tall Man's mausoleum, using a variety of new accessories to slice and dice their victims.

Also wonderfully macabre is the inclusion of actual embalming techniques. If there's anything spookier than the assistant mortician pounding to dust the bone fragments left over after a cremation, it's that same mortician sewing shut the lips of Liz's dead grandfather with a curved needle—a scene made all the more striking when Grandpa comes back later to claim Grandma, and his lips bear the tiny tears where he opened his mouth and pulled the stitches through the flesh.

It's not a perfect movie—the actors are comfortable but not stellar, and there's a little too much roaming the mausoleum halls encountering the next spooky obstacle—but it is a dang good one, worth watching and remembering. The first film is ponderously slow and dated by late '70s fashions and music; the third one veers too far into camp territory; and the fourth one, while recapturing much of the mood of the second movie, relies far too much on familiarity with the rest of the series to give it meaning. (The fifth and final movie, made a full eighteen years after the previous one and released just after Scrimm's death, only had Coscarelli in a producing role and ended up being more of a fan film than anything.) But this one, as far as I'm concerned, is a terrific combination of all of the positive elements in the rest of the series. It's also the reason that I've never trusted Roger Ebert; he hated it.

Some Notable Totables:
- body count: 22 (plus 1 rat)
- breasts: 2
- explosions: 3
- dream sequences: 2 for certain, and possibly many more
- ominous thunderstorms: 0
- attacks on the male crotch: 2
- characters who get to do voice-overs: 4
- actors who've appeared on *Star Trek*: 2
    - Kenneth Tigar (Father Meyers) played "Dammar" in the *Voyager* episode "Displaced"
    - J. Patrick McNamara (Michael's psychologist) played "Captain Taggert" in the *TNG* episode "Unnatural Selection"

PUMPKINHEAD (1988)

Cruel, devious, pure as venom. All Hell's broken loose.

aka *Vengeance: The Demon*

- Directed by Stan Winston
- Written by Mark Patrick Carducci and Gary Gerani
- Starring Lance Henriksen, Cynthia Bain, Jeff East, John D'Aquino and Kimberly Ross
- Produced by Bill Blake, Alex Howard and Richard C. Weinman
- Executive produced by Alex De Benedetti

Despite appearances, horror films as a whole can be pretty emotionless stories. Sure, you've got plenty of screaming and cowering, but without a feel for the individual characters, such expressions of fear really only qualify as demonstrations of the "fight or flight" instinct, present in just about every form of life. And odds are, aside from fear symptoms, the only pseudo-emotions in nine out of ten horror flicks are horniness (and I'm not sure if that really qualifies as an emotion so much as another instinct) and the grating irritation caused by the pointless bickering that characterizes far too much of the dialogue.

That's probably why *Pumpkinhead* has managed to maintain a healthy following since its release. The story may not be the most original, but the movie manages to evoke some true emotion from and about its characters, and video audiences have responded to that with a respectable level of fandom for the last two decades.

Not that fear doesn't have a significant presence—this is a horror film, after all, and the first thing we see is young Ed Harley (Chance Corbitt Jr.) cowering in his bed in his redneck parents' backwoods cabin as, outside, a neighbor is hunted and mauled by a tall, gaunt something.

Thirty years later, the adult Harley (Lance Henriksen) still lives in the hinterlands of Appalachia (for which, admittedly, the Californian shooting locations make a poor substitute) with his young son Billy (Matthew Hurley), supporting them from his small grocery store/vegetable stand. It's here that other emotions make their presence known, as the scenes with Harley and Billy have a genuine affection to them, beyond the normal "mark the person as doomed by declaring your love for them" screenwriting crutch seen so often.

Whoops, I hope I didn't spoil anything for you there, because Billy isn't long for this world. A sixpack of trouble shows up in the form of a half-dozen college kids, off for a weekend in a mountain cabin. You may think it a flaw that the six pretty much blur together for most of the movie; however, when you consider that most attempts to differentiate such a crowd usually degenerate into slapping each with a stereotype label (the Jock, the Brain, the Slut, etc.), resulting in such diversity that you can't imagine all of them ever interacting socially, somehow their uniformity in this case is refreshing.

The only one you really need to know right now is Joel (John D'Aquino), the designated bad boy who drinks beer while driving and looks upon the locals with derision. It's his idea to take the dirtbikes out of the trailer for a spin when they make a pit stop at Harley Grocery. And while Harley's back up at the house on an errand for a local customer, it's Joel's bike which manages to come over a hill, land on little Billy and kill him.

While Joel is hightailing it to the cabin in a panic and preventing the others forcibly from calling for help (he's already on probation for a previous injury/accident), Harley discovers his boy and reacts with understandable rage. He approaches the patriarch of a redneck family, Wallace (Buck Flower), for help finding the old witch woman who's fabled to live somewhere in the mountains—the only one with power to help him get revenge. Wallace refuses to help, even in the face of such tragedy, but his grandson Bunt (Brian Bremer) agrees to point him on the right road to where the old conjurer Haggis (Florence Schauffler) lives in a mist-enshrouded bog.

Harley gives his all to Haggis, not for resurrection, which is beyond her power, but for vengeance—for the summoning of the fabled Pumpkinhead, whispered about for generations in the mountains as a demon of revenge. She has him retrieve a misshapen, worm-eaten body from a neglected graveyard and, with Harley's and Billy's blood, brings it to life.

And Pumpkinhead is on the job.

Because Stan Winston, the director here, was the award-winning FX man on *Alien* among his many credits, some people are quick to point out similarities between the titular creatures of these two movies. In reality, the correspondences are less than they may seem at first glance; both are tall critters with elongated heads, but the unstoppable alien is designed for sleekness and a personality-less efficiency at killing. In contrast, Pumpkinhead is as personalitied as the Appalachian settlements themselves, and its face reflects a personality of cruelty and sadistic playfulness—not in the sense of bad one-liners *a la* Freddy Krueger, but like an intelligent cat playing with its catch out of sheer malice.

And even though Harley is looking for

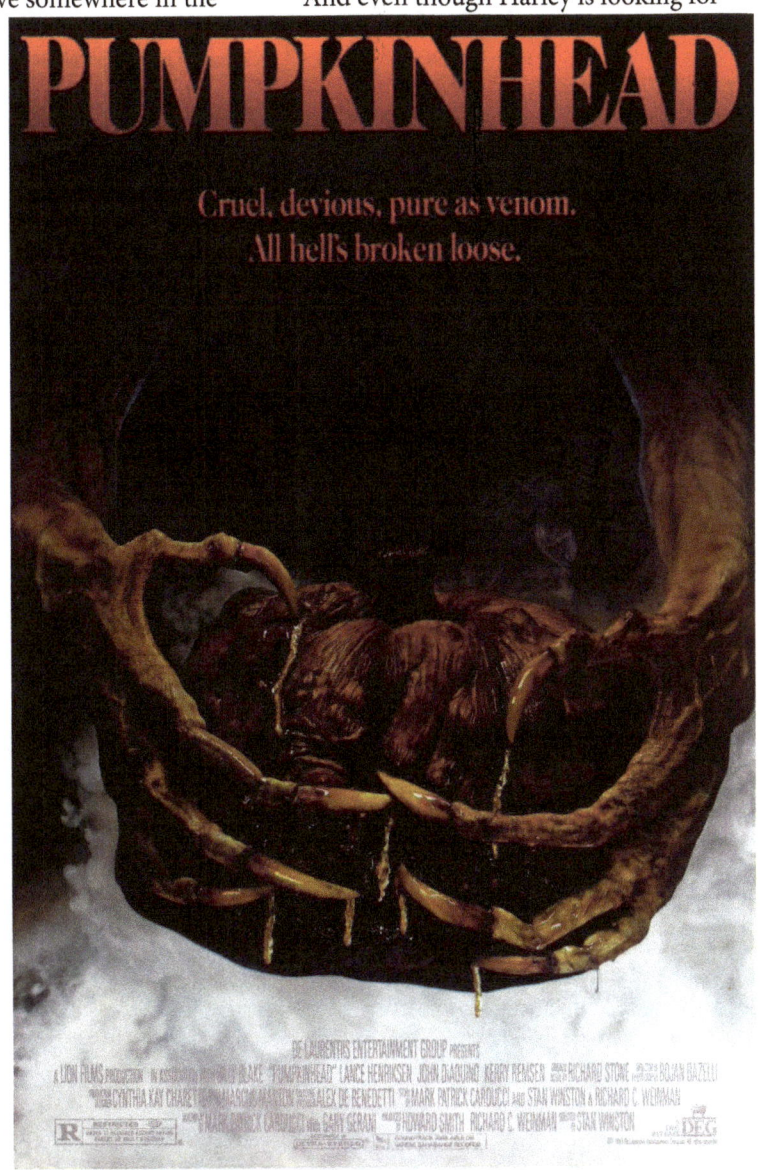

revenge for his son's death, sympathy for the kids isn't hard to come by. It was, after all, an accident; and after holding his friends hostage for hours, even Joel comes around and decides to do the right thing by turning himself in. Not that that matters to Pumpkinhead; he's on the clock, and picks the friends off one by one, guilty and innocent alike, making sure the deaths are witnessed by the others to work them into a state of panic.

And the enormity of what he's done is driven home to Harley—first by the grief that assaults him once his rage is exhausted, second by a waking dream he has of his son's corpse sitting up and asking, "What did you do, Daddy?" and third by the visions and tremors that assault him as Pumpkinhead kills each of his targets. He sees their deaths; he feels their pain; and when he confronts Haggis (boy, everything's sure within easy commuting distance in the back country) and tries to call it off, she ridicules his naiveté. "What did you think—that it'd be easy? Neat and clean and painless?" she cackles.

This is what sets *Pumpkinhead* above other revenge-horror movies: an awareness that revenge can breed more problems and poison the soul worse than the offense being avenged. It's not a new idea, but even the fact of its presence puts the movie head and shoulders over most of its compatriots on the horror rental shelf. It certainly elevates it above the level of a simple morality play, which is the best face most killing-machine movies can put on their proceedings.

Of course, none of that could be effectively conveyed without the actors' performances, and Lance Henriksen distinguishes himself well here. Most of his filmography is filled with roles in which he was called upon to portray (at most) one emotion; here, he plays the range of feelings, good and bad, and his deepening conflict and disgust at what he's done, inciting him finally to attempt to save the surviving kids from the demon he's unleashed, is more compelling to watch than the seven-foot foam latex creature. (Not that the creature's bad to look at—no, you have to wait until the vastly inferior first sequel before you see the figurative zippers on the suit. In fact, the entire movie's visually beautiful—or ugly in a

beautifully-realized way—with just enough overt stylization to heighten the impression of fairy tale-like archetypes at work.)

You want spoilers? Tough. All that I'll tell you is that the method of final defeat of the demon isn't as gimmicky as is often seen, and ties directly into Pumpkinhead's power as the unstoppable avatar of Harley's own rage. In many ways, the tale is a tragedy in the proper sense—the story of an admirable man, Ed Harley, whose downfall stems from his own flaws, and the catharsis to which can't legitimately have a happy ending. It's a movie that tends to stick with viewers a little while, and thus has stayed a sleeper hit among horror fans.

Some Notable Totables:
- body count: 7
- breasts: 0
- explosions: 0
- dream sequences: 1
- ominous thunderstorms: 2
- spring-loaded dogs: 1
- actors who've appeared on *Star Trek*: 1
  - Jandi Swanson (one of the Wallace grandchildren) played "Katie" in the *TNG* episode "When the Bough Breaks"

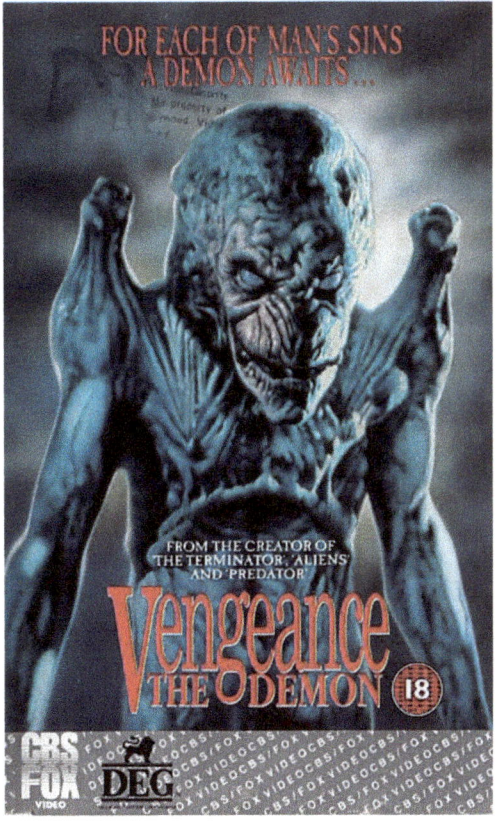

VICE ACADEMY (1988)

WHERE NICE GIRLS BECOME VICE GIRLS.

- Produced, written and directed by Rick Sloane
- Starring Linnea Quigley, Ginger Lynn Allen, Karen Russell, Jayne Hamil and Ken Abraham

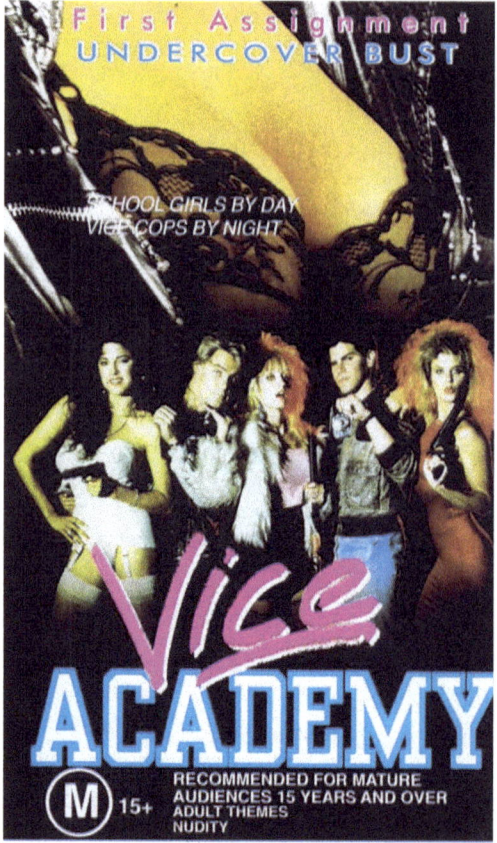

Whenever B-movie aficionados and reviewers chat, we eventually come around to our hobby-specific version of the fisherman's oneupmanship contest: "Oh, yeah? Well, I once saw a movie that was *so* bad…" In this case, Chad of the sadly departed website *The Good, the Bad, the Ugly* and I were taking a break from our normal sociopolitical debates and instead were trying to outdo one another with psyche-scarring cinema. It came down to an exchange; I sent him a tape of *Bangers* (1997), an obscure zombie rapist horror flick so bad it causes brain lesions. In return, Chad sent me his brand-spanking-new DVD of *Vice Academy*.

I gotta tell you, it feels good every once in a while to get the sweet end of the deal.

Not that *Vice Academy* isn't a truly bad movie. It's knowingly insipid to the point of being grotesque, but it isn't the kind of lingering badness that places an indelible shadow on your soul, in contrast to some of the other movies reviewed in this book (or to the movie I sent Chad). If you build up a resistance by watching enough bad movies, something lightweight like *Vice Academy* can be laughed off without a backward glance. Ha! Ha ha!

The trick, really, is to realize from the outset of the movie that none of this is going to make a lick of sense. It takes place in a parallel universe in which everything in society—heck, everything right down to the basic laws of physics—is senseless and inconsistent. As soon as you're free of such mental constraints as cause, effect, logic, and quality, it goes down quite easily.

As you may surmise from the title, a vice academy is central to the story, i.e., a police academy focused on turning out vice cops. Not general-purpose police officers who may well end up working in vice, mind you. Nor are the students currently cops going in for a special course to qualify them for vice work. No, in this academy, you enter as a brainless aerobicized bimbo, and leave as a brainless aerobicized bimbo with a badge. Unless you're Dwayne (Ken Abraham), the lone male in a class of thirty-odd women. But his main purpose is to be the practice dummy when the cadets are taught the most effective way to paralyze a male assailant (let's just say that his chances for having children in the future are slim).

Our story, or semblance thereof, centers on a few of the students. On the one side, we've got Didi (Linnea Quigley), Shawnee (Karen Russell), and the aforementioned Dwayne—a trio of well-meaning slackers who arrive late for class and stuff. This means, of course, that they're our heroes. There's also their arch-nemesis Holly (prolific '80s porn queen Ginger Lynn Allen in her short-lived attempt at a non-XXX career), daughter of the police chief, who's at the top of the class and loves to point it out. She's the pet of the one and only teacher of this fine institution, the harpyish Miss Devonshire (Jayne Hamil), who reports directly to the police chief and has it in for our heroic trio.

The plot engine is that there are only a few days to go before graduation, and each of the cadets needs to make a quota of ten arrests to graduate and earn a place on the force. Let's repeat that: despite the fact that they are not yet peace officers, they still are expected to go out there and hunt up their own arrests with no backup save each other. This despite the fact that they are, this close to graduation, just being taught how to disarm an opponent and how to fire a gun. Is anyone feeling safer yet? I didn't think so.

In one of those bizarre (but momentary) changes of tone more usually expected in Asian cinema, Didi and Shawnee on their night off (but dressed like they're on duty, if you know what I mean) meet a battered underage pornstar who's afraid to rat on her producers for fear they'll kill her. Didi takes this personally, and makes it her goal to bust the porn ring to make her graduation quota.

Okay, the heavy social conscience segment is over. Dressed even more skankily than before, Didi auditions at the porn studio and becomes twitter-pated with the leading man, Chucky Long (Stephen Steward). She even maintains her cover through an entire sex scene (what a trooper!) before backups Shawnee and Dwayne come to her rescue and cart the porn crew away, along with the convenient evidence of their illegal activities. (More proof of a parallel universe: who, in our reality, would force an underage starlet to sign a contract that specifically references her real age?)

But here, is seems, producer-writer-director Rick Sloane decided he'd rather already be making a sequel, because the plot abruptly changes. Since Didi's, um, dedication to her task has compromised the respectability of the case against the pornmeisters, those ten arrests don't count for them, so now the threesome has one night before graduation in which to round up the requisite number of hookers and johns. This is helped by the fact that the hookers and johns are all exceedingly stupid. At least it's an equitable universe—everyone's an idiot!

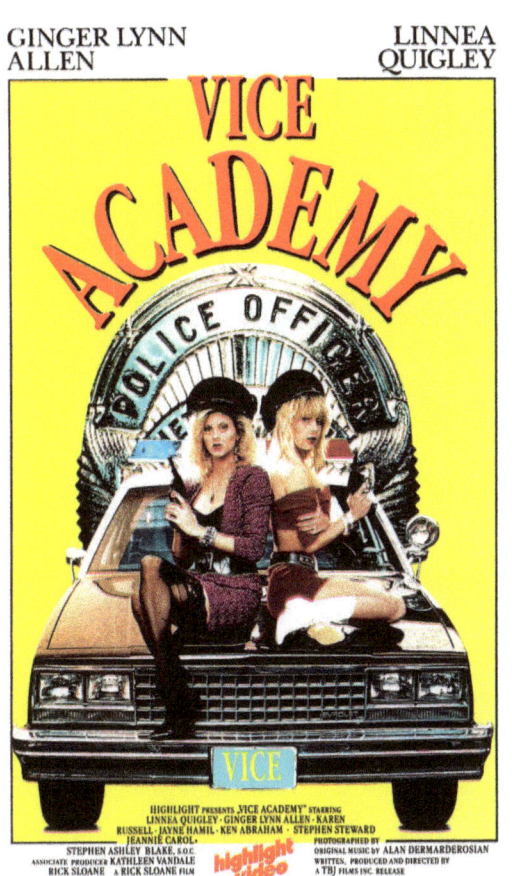

That puts them on the hit list of the local crime lord, the Queen Bee, who has managed to elude even the police chief's finest. When you consider that said finest probably graduated from this very academy, it's really not that surprising. And in desperation, Didi calls the only person she can think of for backup. If you're like me, you're expecting that person to be Holly, so that they can bury their hatchet and join together against the bad guys… but no. The person at the top of Didi's list is Chucky Long the porn star, whom she's kept handcuffed in her apartment since the porn bust the previous day.

[tap tap] Is anyone paying attention anymore? No, I didn't think so.

The concluding scene, I think, best exemplifies the poverty of this movie—not only in terms of budget (though that's certainly in evidence), but also of real comedy or quality. The academy graduation takes place in an empty municipal park, with only the police chief and Miss Devonshire in attendance—no parents, no significant others, nothing. Just a bunch of academy cadets in blue gowns, sitting on park benches arranged on the grass in front of a bare park amphitheater. Oh, and Holly, who has remained fully clothed this whole time (did I mention she was played by '80s porn queen Ginger Lynn Allen?) accidentally has revealed that the only thing she's wearing under her graduation gown is an unlikely thong lingerie ensemble.

It's a bad, bad, stupid movie, but somehow it fails to grossly offend, mainly because it doesn't try that hard; even pissing viewers off takes a modicum of effort. Instead, we get the laziest excuses for humor and sexiness, as if the screenplay had a lot of placeholder notes—"Think of something funny here when we film it"—that no one ever followed up on. If you've ever wondered what a movie would be like if its only ambition were to be adequate filler on the old *USA Up All Night* when nothing better was available, well, you've found your answer.

And yes, as much as I like to poke fun at the pointless parallel universe, I feel duty-bound to point out that this movie spawned five—that's right, five—sequels. Maybe *this* is the parallel universe.

Some Notable Totables:
- body count: 0
- breasts: 4
- explosions: 0
- ominous thunderstorms: 0
- actors who've appeared on *Star Trek*: 0

ZOMBIE 4: AFTER DEATH (1988)

aka *Oltre la Morte*, aka *After Death*, aka *Return of the Living Dead Part 3*, aka *Zombie Flesh Eaters 3*

- Directed by "Clyde Anderson" (Claudio Fragasso)
- Written by Rossella Drudi
- Starring Chuck Peyton, Candice Daly, "Alex McBride" (Massimo Vanni), Jim Gaines and Don Wilson (not to be confused with kickboxer-turned-actor Don "The Dragon" Wilson)
- Produced by Franco Gaudenzi

It's not just that Italian zombie flicks are uniformly bad movies, although heaven knows that's an unassailable matter of fact; they also manage to be some of the least classy movies ever. It's like a pall of cheapness hanging over a production that you know must have been adequately funded. There's an endomonetary reaction: more money goes in the front end than comes out on the screen.

In this case, the biggest waste of money seems to have been the paycheck to the credited screenwriter, Rossella Drudi, as she appears to have only turned in random scenes from the completed script. Either that, or editor Maurizio Baglivo too zealously excised anything containing forward momentum, meaningful exposition, or a level of quality above the lowest common denominator.

By this stage in the *Zombie* non-franchise (from the re-edited version of *Dawn of the Dead* (1978) released as *"Zombie"* in Italy, to Lucio Fulci's non-sequel *Zombie 2* (1979) which was retitled *"Zombie"* in the States just to muddy the pedigree, to Fulci's bastard stepchild *Zombie 3* (1988), notably written by none other than—Claudio Fragasso!), you really have to step back in apprehension at any film that would willingly adopt the free-for-anyone-who-wants-it *"Zombie #"* title. I mean, if your movie sucks so badly that association with *Zombie 3* would help its profitability…

To ratchet us into the plot, a helpful narrator tells us all about a group of scientists who believed that (in his words) "they could solve the mystery of mysteries." That's death, you know. So they do what scientists always do when they want to bring incredible research resources to bear on a problem that literally affects everyone alive: they set up shop on a remote tropical island with a suspicious and superstitious native population.

The movie proper starts with that hallmark of horror cinema, a disco dance scene. No, my mistake; it's actually a voodoo ritual, with the voodoo priest chanting while his wife gyrates and throbs all around the cave. (The disco vibe is accentuated by the, um, "interesting" lighting; could no one convince the lighting guy that the candles that supposedly illuminate the cave simply don't give off green and purple glows?) At the apex of the ritual, pink lights fly out of the priest's sacred book, and the wife swallows them! Then she gets pulled down into a sinkhole that opens in the floor! Pretty cool way to start a movie, huh? Seriously, this is as good as it gets.

The priest is soon confronted by a bunch

of the scientists from the lab, who've come down with semiautomatic weapons to gently persuade the priest to call off the army of vengeful zombies he's called up. He's peeved because his daughter had cancer, and the scientists weren't able to cure her. One of the scientist lets his itchy trigger finger get the best of him, but not before the priest pronounces a curse upon all of the scientists and their families and household pets. Then the zombie wife leaps out of the floor and chases the scientists through the tunnels, in a sequence that takes much longer to play out than to describe.

Meanwhile, a little family consisting of father, mother and little blonde girl stumbles through the jungle, trying to keep away from the black-clad zombies that keep popping up. Once Dad wanders off to find a way to get himself killed (I swear, they're just breeding the survival instinct out of white folks these days), Mom tells the girl to run on through the jungle by herself to get away. Because, you know, a three-year-old can pick her way through the undergrowth so much faster than if Mom had just tucked her under one arm and ran a steeplechase. And just to scar her daughter emotionally for life, Mom adds, "And if you're obedient, Mother will join you later." Oh, great; so now it's your *kid's* fault that you stupidly hung back and waited for zombies to pull you to pieces? "And if Mommy lets herself be eaten by the living dead, it's because you're naughty!" And she gives her daughter a little voodoo amulet, which will serve its most important purpose…

…Right now, because suddenly we've jumped twenty years into the future, where a small speedboat full of people just happens to be cruising among those very same islands. And the little blonde girl has become a big blonde girl (Candice Daly), as evidenced by the same voodoo amulet around her neck, which she's playing with in a very conspicuous "See? See? It's me, all grown up!" fashion. No, they haven't given her a name; we'll get to that later. Otherwise, the boat is occupied by four men who were in 'Nam together and have since gone into private practice as mercenaries, and one other woman. None have names at this point, nor is it clear how the two women hooked up with the four men, or why in the world the blonde is back in this part of the world. She does mention that the island they're passing reminds her of one she used to know when she was little. Except there were more zombies, of course.

The boat motor then starts acting up, and the steering quits; they've got no choice but to run her to a convenient wharf and go looking for help. (Because instead of simply trying to fix the boat while docked, it's much easier to wander a deserted-looking island looking for a boat shop.) The straggler of the group sees someone dressed in black skulking through the woods, so he gives chase, and ends up in hand-to-hand combat with a surprisingly spry zombie. (Good thing it turned out to be a zombie, because whomping on the first local you meet is not usually the best way to finagle some mechanical assistance out of the natives.) The others start calling for him, which finally gives us a character name: the one whomping on the zombie is Tommy (Don Wilson). But no sooner does he get named than he gets bitten good by the zombie. This, you should know, is going to be a recurring motif in our beloved screenplay: whenever a character is finally referred to by name, odds are better than even that that character is about to meet an ugly end.

Everyone helps Tommy along as they reach a rundown jungle hospital, completely deserted. Even the graves are empty. (Memo to self: If ever in a similar situation, find something to use as an impromptu paddle and get the hell off the island.) They let Tommy lie down on a bed while the rest of them explore the place. One of them finds a bottle of IV blood connected to a tube, still dripping on the floor. Another finds a whole ring of lit candles on a table. No one makes the awfully tough intuitive leap that there might be someone around in the hospital. (Memo to self: If ever in a similar situation, be prepared to dive in, start swimming, and get the hell off the island.) Oh, and a third finds a cache of M-16s, which might conceivably come in handy.

While all of this has been going on, there are three other characters hiking across the island, two men and a woman. Naturally, they have no names yet—after all, they're not in imminent danger of death—but I'll skip ahead and tell you that one of them is played by Chuck Peyton, whom you may know better (though if you do, I really don't want to hear about it) as gay pornstar Jeff Stryker. What did I say about the classiness quotient of these Italian zombie flicks? This threesome is here to find out what happened to all of the researchers. I guess twenty years without results or so much as a postcard finally aroused someone's curiosity.

They find what they were looking for: not the hospital, but the entrance to the voodoo priest's underground lair. (Why were they looking for that? Damned if I know.) They discover their own circle of lit candles, plus a book which they say is "The Book of the Dead," though the cover clearly reads "The Book of Death." They discover in it the four-word spell for opening the gate of hell and summoning the dead, and one of them forgets to use his "inside voice" and reads it aloud. Next thing you know… Well, let's put it this way: They start shouting each other's names. The only one that survives the ensuing zombie onslaught is our pornstar friend, whose character is Chuck. The names of the other two… well, it's kind of moot now, isn't it?

Meanwhile, back at the hospital, the rest of our fodder has bedded down for the night. The girl who isn't the blonde demonstrates her continued lack of survival instincts by coming up behind the 'Nam vet standing guard and placing her hand on his shoulder. (Maybe she didn't know his name either.) They almost share a moment, when—zombies! Everywhere! The front lawn is full of zombies! While the menfolk starts shooting, the non-blonde sits down on the edge of Tommy's bed. Uh-oh… somebody called her by name. She's Louise (Adrianne Joseph). Good-bye, Louise, courtesy of the newly-zombified Tommy. (Voodoo curses are contagious via bites? Who knew?)

Now, every zombie movie needs a way to distinguish its zombies from all other zombies in all other movies, and this movie has found its formula. Not only do these walking corpses wear ratty black pajamas and shrouds (quite a fetching ensemble, really), but they're ninja zombies! They don't just lurch onto the scene; their favorite mode of attack is to pounce as if they just bounced off a springboard.

Meanwhile, the blonde—and, breaking the pattern, her name is finally given as Jenny, but she'll be here until the end of the movie—runs back upstairs to the circle of candles, which the blond mercenary had earlier blown out. See, she knows that the circle is a gate to hell, and if the candles are lit and her amulet is sitting in the middle, it will close the gate to hell, and the zombies will all become docile and—

Bzzzt! Sorry, my bullshit-o-meter just buried the needle. Let's apply a minimal ten braincells to that, shall we? First up, are you telling me that the candles have been kept burning for the past twenty years to keep the zombies in check, until whatshisface decided to read the spell? By whom? I mean, we never do see another living person on the island. And secondly, um, there already were zombies roaming the island, even with the candles burning and "The Book of Death/the Dead" unread! Remember that ugly smelly guy who bit your friend Tommy? Yeah, him!

And thirdly, Jenny girl, howcome you have only vague memories of the way in which your parents died, but you know chapter and verse about the amulet that your mother hung around your neck right before she got chomped?

A stray breeze blows out all of Jenny's candles (so much for the "lit for two decades" hypothesis), so the zombies attack again. Two of the mercs plus Captain Porno (who's shown up here by this time) keep shooting and setting fire to them, but with Tommy gone zombie inside, they're fighting on two fronts. The blond mercenary gets a name—Rod (Nick Nicholson)—just in time to decide on a "blaze of glory" instead of getting bitten and going like Tommy did, so he rushes out of the house, shoots a lot of zombies, and gets himself bitten by zombie Louise. Meanwhile, the mustachioed merc gets a name—he's Mad (Jim Moss)—and gets bitten by Tommy. The remaining merc, Dan (Jim Gaines), decides to let Mad die peacefully before putting a bullet in his brain. Unfortunately, he also let the corpse keep ahold of its M-16 until it revived. Alas, Dan, we hardly knew ye.

So now there's only Chuck and Jenny left. (And this is where knowing that Chuck is played by a gay pornstar becomes a great punchline—there's only one man and woman left, and he's gay!) And from here…

I think there's a point at which your brain refuses to cycle down any further into stupidity, because a certain number of mental RPMs are necessary to maintain basic bodily functions. This movie had stupided itself below my ability to follow it toward the end. There was more falderall about the amulet, and closing the door to hell with one's soul, and in the end everyone dies.

At least (and believe me, this is the very least), *Zombie 4* is in something like the same vein as the far superior *Zombie/Zombie 2*, keeping itself confined to voodoo junk instead of a secret government bio-chem project *a la Zombie 3* (although this one was, like *Zombie 3*, shot in the Philippines). Later entries in the non-franchise would often be nothing more than an appropriation of the *"Zombie"* name, attached to movies with no actual zombies in them. I think *Zombie 4* is the point at which that's a good thing; as bizarre as it is to label an unrelated movie as *"Zombie #,"* it couldn't help but to plaster the box with the message, "Bearing absolutely no resemblance to previous *Zombie* movies!"

Some Notable Totables:
- body count: 18
- breast: 0
- explosions: 2
- dreams sequences: 1
- ominous thunderstorms: 0
- number of times we have to sit through that "Living After Death" theme song: 3
- actors who've appeared on *Star Trek*: 0

CHOPPER CHICKS in ZOMBIE TOWN (1989)

THEY'RE LOOKING FOR A FEW GOOD MEN.

- Written and directed by Dan Hoskins
- Starring Jamie Rose, Catherine Carlen, Lycia Naff, Vicki Frederick and Don Calfa
- Produced by Nancy Paloian and Maria Snyder
- Executive produced by Arthur M. Sarkissian

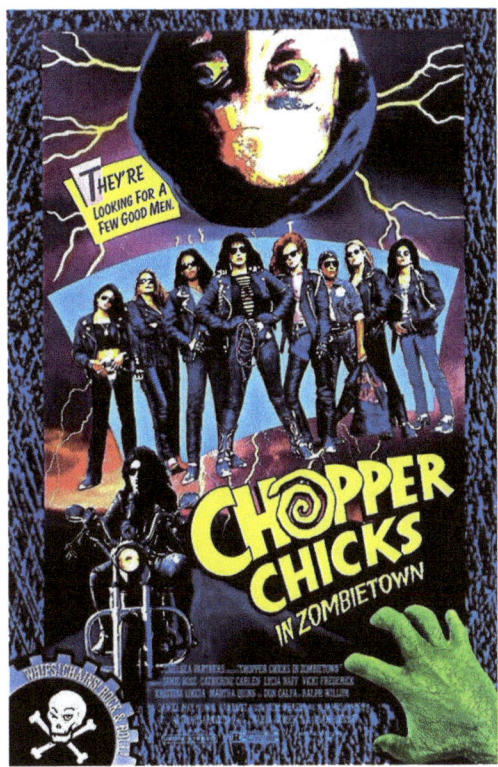

Because it's distributed by Troma DVD, you can rightly assume that *Chopper Chicks in Zombie Town* is a silly movie. (That's if the sound of the title didn't clue you in.) But independent productions picked up for distribution by Troma are often a different breed of silly from Troma's home-grown productions like *The Toxic Avenger* (1984). In other words, this is not a movie in which everything is "gratuitous" (sex and nudity, over-the-top gore, fart and effluvium jokes, general intentional campiness). It's certainly not a serious film, and most of the elements of Troma films listed above are present in some degree (though I don't recall any fart jokes). Maybe you could call it "Troma-lite"—and depending on your comfort level and patience with the sophomoric excess of Troma's in-house productions, that may be a good or bad thing.

The first sign that we've dialed back from the extremes is the chopper chicks of the title, an all-girl motorcycle gang called the Cycle Sluts, who are to a woman fit and aerobicized, permed and hairsprayed. There's not a garish tattoo or stretch mark among them; they look like cross between The Go-Go's and a Whitesnake video. They don't even put on their denim vests with "Cycle Sluts" painted across the back until they're ready to roll into town—in this case, Zariah, California, population 128. Excuse me, 127; right after the gang zooms by the sign, a dwarf (Ed Gale) in a natty suit comes and changes the count.

In what's made itself apparent to me as a distressingly common pattern in zombie films, the story is split in two tracks—we'll call them the "zombie" track and the "main characters" track—for a third to a half of the movie, until the dead finally impinge upon whatever drama our protagonists have gotten themselves embroiled in. Since just about everyone who watches this movie does so for the zombies more than the biker chicks, let's take a look at that track first:

There's a mine outside town which is boarded up in the haphazard balsa-wood fashion is that is the standard for contractors who deal with such things. A young boy on his bike enters between the slats and discovers that, a dozen feet inside, there's a wall of concrete blocks with a reinforced door and a padlock. The fact that the padlock is there, though, doesn't necessarily imply that it is locked; the boy lifts the padlock off the hasp, opens the door, and hey—zombies in their best burial dress! (Also, hey—end of little boy!) The undead shuffle their way out of the mine, demolishing in the process the boards securely obstructing their entrance, and begin lurching toward town. As that's a good five miles, we can leave them there as we catch up with the rest of the movie.

The zombies are the handiwork of the undertaker Willum (Don Calfa) and Bob the dwarf, Willum's indentured servant. The scheme, as it comes to light throughout the course of the movie, is this: the mine was closed because mining radioactive ore became too dangerous for the locals. Then Willum moved in and started engineering the string of "accidental" deaths which have plagued the town for the last two years, using Bob to do most of the dirty work. Willem then reanimates the corpses by planting an electrode in their skulls, and locks them in the mine to continue mining. I don't know how much useful ore gets mined out by workers who just barely know that they shouldn't eat their own feet, but I obviously haven't put as much thought into this plan as Willem.

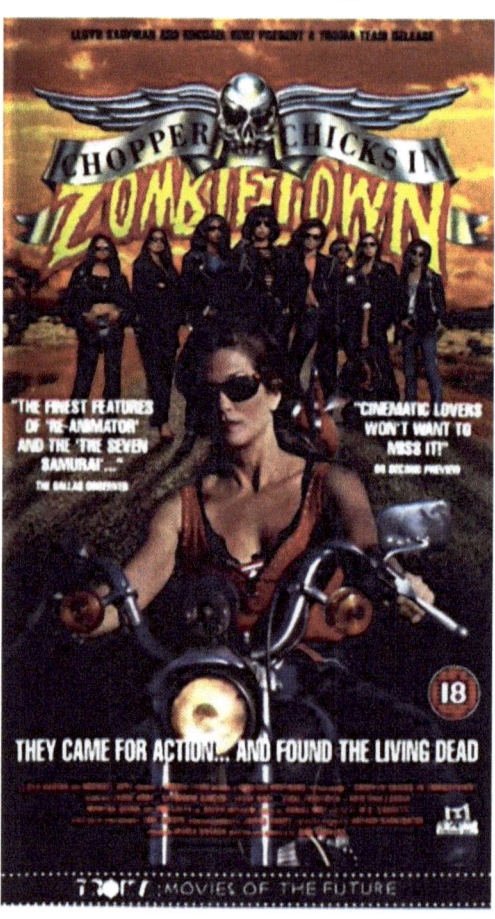

And now, the dramatic storyline: once the Sluts have made their presence known in town, they split up for a little R&R, which for several of them means finding a temporary boy-toy. This gives each of them an occasion for "characterization," i.e., "Why I'm so broken inside that I think that riding around aimlessly is a viable lifestyle." I guess I haven't watched enough biker movies; do male bikers blowing into town immediately find willing women who are intrigued by their free-spiritedness? The main Slut who abstains is their leader, Rox (Catherine Carlen), who proudly proclaims herself a bulldyke and enjoys discomfiting the locals more than seeking any personal perks. This includes interrupting a wake being held at the local bar with a nasty bump'n'grind routine to what she can find on the jukebox.

Dede (Jamie Rose, the de facto second-in-command of the Sluts and possessor of a crest of spiral permed red hair that gives her the silhouette of Gossamer from the Warner Brothers cartoons, has more than a random interest to this town. She in fact grew up here, was homecoming queen (heaven only knows where they found enough students for a high school), and even has an abandoned husband, Tommy (an early role for Billy Bob Thornton), who's happy to have her back after a six-year absence. No particular answer is ever given to Donny's question of why Dede left in the first place, a question which I think quite reasonable.

It's only once we've met our quotient of melodrama that things start happening. Mostly because of Rox's actions at the wake, the locals gang up to drive the Sluts out of town. Rox makes it a point to leave Dede behind when she finds out about Dede's connections to the locals. But that abandonment, plus the absence of another of their members (who has been purposely run down by Willem and turned into a zombie), creates a lot of friction among the Sluts, who don't get very far.

Meanwhile, Dede, caught between the world that rejected her and the world she doesn't want back into, discovers the bike of the missing Slut and stumbles onto Willem's whole reanimating scheme. So she goes for help to the only people she knows have the balls for this kind of thing: the Cycle Sluts.

There's plenty of back-and-forth and

shallow "human drama" stuff, so let's answer some important questions:

Q) *Do the zombies look good?*

A) Not too shabby. They're all dressed in their good burial clothes, too, which gives them an edge on the "victim of contagion" zombies who too often look like the college extras that they are.

Q) *Do the zombies eat flesh?*

A) Yes, though not consistently; some of them are a little preoccupied (they all get out of the mine groaning, "Home!"). And while many do gnaw on the living, they don't spend time fondling entrails.

Q) *Headshots?*

A) Well, yeah, since an electrode implanted in the head is what reanimates them, disabling their heads is kind of important. However, thanks to a lack of firearms, what we get is mostly baseball-bat beheadings, garrotings, and blowtorches to the face. And by not wasting their efforts on the torso once the head damage rule is discovered, the Sluts prove themselves smarter than 95% of zombie movie protagonists.

Q) *Are they contagious?*

A) I would love to think that this questions is stupid; after all, the dead are raised via an electronic device inserted in the skull—how could one be infected by that? But stupider things have been done in zombie films, so… No.

Q) *Are there blind orphans in this movie?*

A) Why, yes, and thanks for asking, since otherwise I would have had trouble working them into this review. Near Zariah is St. Peter's Home For Blind Orphans (talk about niche marketing!), and a busload of them is stranded on the road by engine trouble during all of this. However, thanks to the hobby of one of their counselors (who presumably succumbs to the zombie menace off-screen), they are blind orphans in possession of a UZI.

It's a cheap little movie, and I'm sure that a more highbrow critic, if forced to watch, would lambaste the whole enterprise as being unworthy of the effort it took to make it. But it holds a certain endearing charm for me. Maybe it's the fact that the protagonists are actually sort of likable (and this from someone with no preexisting affinity toward biker gangs). Maybe it's the fact that the villain Willum announces, "I didn't do it for science, and I didn't do it for glory—I'm just mean!" Maybe it's the inclusion of a dwarf who says, in his best Lou Costello impression, "I've been a baaad boy!" Maybe it's the use of cheesy arrangements of "Danse Macabre" in the score, including one scene in which it's plinked out by an ice cream truck. Maybe it's the climactic plan which involved blowing up a church, with the blind orphans acting as bait inside singing "O Holy Night" at the top of their lungs. Or maybe, just maybe, it's the realization that all of us, even unrepentant Cycle Sluts, are just looking for love.

Okay, maybe not that. (Although they are.)

Some Notable Totables:
- body count: 9
- breasts: 0
- pasty male butts: 1
- explosions: 0
- ominous thunderstorms: 0
- dwarfs: 1

- actors who've appeared on *Star Trek*: 3
  - Lycia Naff (T.C., the Cycle Slut who used to be a groupie) played "Ensign Sonya Gomez" in two *TNG* episodes
  - Earl Boen (the butcher—I think he gets one line, and that's after he'd dead) played "Nagilum" in the *TNG* episode "Where Silence Has Lease" (plus voicework in a whole bunch of *Star Trek* videogames)
  - Rob King ("Vince") performed stunts in *Star Trek 6*

DEADLY REACTOR (1989)

The good... the bad... and the **DEADLY.**

- *Written and directed by David Heavener*
- *Starring David Heavener, Stuart Whitman, Darwyn Swalve, Allyson Davis and Barbara Kerek*
- *Produced by Fritz Matthews*
- *Executive produced by Bruce Lewin, David Winters and Marc Winters*

Poor David Heavener. He's tried so hard. Since the mid-'80s, he's been trying desperately to make himself into an action star. The number of independent action/adventure films he's written and/or directed to star himself is staggering (to say nothing of other indie films he's appeared in)—in addition to our current punching bag, there's *Outlaw Force* (1987), *Twisted Justice* (1990), *Kill Crazy* (1990), *Prime Target* (1991), *Eye of the Stranger* (1993), *Fugitive X* (1996), *Outlaw Prophet* (1999), *Death Force* (2000), *Angel Blade* (2002), *Dawn of the Living Dead* (2004), *Costa Chica* (2006), and *Psycho Weene* (2006). And I've probably missed a couple.

And yet, after all that... Well, try this experiment. Go up to a friend who's a "normal" movie watcher, and ask:

"Seen the latest David Heavener movie?"

And wait for the blank stare.

Then say, "Seen *anything* with David Heavener?"

And watch the mute incomprehension intensify.

And your friend will be the luckier for that ignorance. Because this movie, like just about every one of Heavener's movies, is just plain bad. Really, really bad. So bad it's not even funny. So bad it made my fillings ache. And I'm going to make you experience every staggering minute.

This is a post-apocalyptic movie, so we have to open with that staple of such movies, the Explanation Of How Things Got This Way—an inexplicable convention, since if there's anything that moviegoers have figured out in the past sixty years, it's how atomic weapons work and what the world looks like after. In this case, according to Heavener's narration, there were only two kinds of people left afterward: "The good kind—and the bad." Apparently, then, all of the people in the middle were the ones who got toasted.

What he fails to mention in this oh-so-enlightening intro is that both types, good and bad, have one uniting characteristic: they're all as dumb as rocks.

The movie proper starts with gunshot-wounded Cody (Heavener) flashing back to how he got said gunshot (with the help of the ever-present narration): a gang of outlaws interrupted his guitar-playing with his sister, niece, and nephew. They killed the kids, raped the sister, and shot Cody, leaving him for dead. Now, I know you're used to to the standard post-apoc goons. These are not they. No studded leather. No painted football pads. No extra grills and spikes on their late-model sedans. No tattoos or warpaint. No, they look like your standard mid-'80s street punks, with their denim and bandannas and occasional leather jacket, and their leader is a huge, fat, bald, scruffy, slow-moving lardass named Hog (Darwyn Swalve). He's even missing one of his front teeth. I saw this guy, and said, "You gotta be kidding me." This is the great menace of the wasteland? This is the charismatic leader who gathers tough thugs around him and bends them to his will? Even the back of the video box calls him a "cretin." How in the hell would he gain and hold onto power? How stupid and weak must everyone else be for that to happen? (Prophetic question, that.)

Cody is found and nursed back to health by old Duke (character actor Stuart Whitman, the only recognizable face in the whole movie) in his mountain cabin. Meanwhile…

There's this rundown town inhabited by the Agopy people, who are apparently the future descendants of the Amish. The women all wear long black dresses; the men all wear white shirts, black pants (with suspenders) and wide-brimmed black hats. They're a pacifist people, though they're not above having a non-Agopy sheriff to deal with lowlife wanderers who come through, like the ex-soldier who tries to hold up the café for a meal. That's right, a small post-apocalyptic Amish-style town of maybe forty citizens has a restaurant. Whatever. It's important, though, because working with her father and mother in the café is Shauna (Allyson Davis), the young hot blonde Agopy girl who will undoubtedly become not only Cody's love interest, but the object of Hog's lust. How's that for prescience?

Because Hog has found out about the town and its café, and rightly surmises that where there's a café, there's food (ooh, good deduction), and so goes after it. So they invade, raping and generally acting like louses.

Meanwhile, Duke, who makes his own guns and shells (in a little cabin without any metalworking facilities), recognizes Cody as being one of the Agopys himself. (Agopys? Agopies? Whatever.) But now, with revenge on his mind, Duke teaches him to shoot, which Cody can't do straight even though it's revealed that, before the Big One, he used to be a cop. (Completely useless information, that.) But a two-minute lesson in Gunfighter Zen improves Cody's aim dramatically, as does a lesson in drinking and smoking (without which you jes' cain't shoot, I reckon). He also introduces the phrase that becomes the basis for the title: "Always let [the other guy] act first. It's always better to be the reactor." And I bet you thought the title referred to, I dunno, a nuclear reactor or something, right? (This scene is also notable in that apparently Whitman was unavailable for looping in post-production, because his dialogue is pervaded by the click-click-click of an improperly-muffled camera picked up on location. Heavener's dialogue, meanwhile, is crystal-clear. Similar looping funnies occur throughout the entire movie.)

Later, while Cody's out wandering the hills (just, you know, wandering), Duke is attacked at the cabin by a couple of incredibly stupid bandits. How stupid? Here's how stupid. They club Duke across the head with a shovel on his front porch, then explore the cabin and discover some of his guns — and then do that Western movie routine, "Dance, sucker!" and shoot at his feet. Note: he's still lying on the ground. Jeez Louise… Cody stumbles back on them and pulls a gun, but hesitates in shooting until after they shoot Duke. Then he blows them away. Way to be reactive.

Oh, and by the way, Hog is still chasing the Agopy folks around. (Wait a sec. The former scenes with Duke and Cody seemed to cover several hours, if not days—and now it's ten minutes later in the Agopy town? Who edited this mess?) His eye falls upon Shauna, so after he dispatches the sheriff, he starts pawing and groping her—until an underling reminds him that they need to make a 20-hour drive to get some more guns. (And some more gas, one assumes, though nobody so much as mentions it at any time.) You'd think they would have taken care of such business before an assault on a new town, but whatever. Hog leaves a handful of men in town to keep the locals in line, with explicit instructions that Shauna not be touched—she's his personal property.

Once Duke dies in Cody's arms, Cody buries him in a pile of rocks before riding off, guns strapped on under his duster and a cigarillo in his mouth, to find Hog and get some revenge.

Of course, it'll take several hours to get to town, so in the meantime we're treated to scenes of the locals being maltreated by Hog's men, including one girl being forced to strip to her underwear and play the guitar while standing on a table. We also get a glimpse (as does a goon who's got the hots for Shauna) of Shauna bathing naked in the nearby pond. All together now: Huh? This is the closest water source? I mean, we've seen very clearly that there's electricity in town; isn't there a working pump? Or maybe just a bucket-filled bathtub somewhere a little less exposed? Anyway, after what seems like hours of browbeating and sexual assault (yuk, yuk, that's always good clean entertainment, right?), Cody arrives in town.

And here, folks, is the single good(ish) scene in the movie. Cody walks into the church, where a couple of goons are hassling the locals. They mistake him for a preacher-man, and push him up to the pulpit for preaching. He instantly opens the Bible to an appropriate verse which I've been unable to locate, but which basically says, "Watch out for the minister of the Lord or you'll get a divine ass-kicking," and then he blows them away.

I didn't say it was a good scene *per se*; it's slow, clichéd, and predictable. But it's still the best scene in the whole movie.

Cody then lures out the second group of baddies into the street and shoots them down from the rooftops (did you know that a single shot to the crotch will kill a man instantly?), earning the gratitude of the townsfolk. Especially Shauna—you can tell from they way she sets a plate of food in front of him in the cafe and asks, "Is there anything else you want?" He's offered the job of sheriff, and accepts once he finds out that Hog will be on his way back. (By the way, I was expecting the townspeople to recognize him, seeing that he was Agopy, too. Apparently he's from another town or something, which leads to further questions: why the hell don't the Agopy all pick one town to live in for strength in numbers, rather than spreading out forty to a town where they can get tromped so easily? Or is the competition between Amish Cafés that fierce?)

Next morning, he deputizes the ex-soldier in the jail, and then he heads out to bathe. Yes, to that same swimming hole where Shauna was the day before. So, does everyone in town stop to bathe at the same place? Is there a sign-up schedule in the town hall to guarantee privacy and avoid embarrassing accidental encounters? In any event, while he's washing with his back to the shore, Shauna walks up quietly and then, without a word, drops her dress and wades naked out into the water with him (I guess not every Amish chick wears underwear). This, mind you, is after she's spoken maybe ten words to him, and he's never said anything back to her. Man, once word gets out how easy Amish chicks are, Hog'll have some stiff competition (did I just type that?).

Cody greets this with the same reaction he's had for everything: a stony stare. You'd think that David Heavener was afflicted with a stroke early in life, because his face changes expression about as often as the third guy from the left on Mount Rushmore. Learning to shoot to take vengeance on murderous bastards? Stony stare. Burying your one friend in the world? Blank stare. Shooting cretins in a church? Stony stare. Offered the job of sheriff? Stony stare. Easy-on-the-eyes Mennonite babe shucks it and wades in for some bathtime lovin'? Stony stare. It's almost shocking when his lips move enough to deliver his lines.

Meanwhile, the sole goon survivor of Cody's rampage makes it out of town and informs Hog of the sharp-shootin' hero, so Hog decides to go back to the main camp to gather the rest of the gang and stomp the town into the ground. That gives Cody enough time to get cleaned up, find the five (count 'em, five) handguns in town and do exactly what you've got to do in these movies: arm the locals. Granted, these Agopies have never held a weapon in their lives, and they don't have enough ammo to waste on practice, but what other plan is there? Shauna's father, who's been notably against this drinking/smoking sheriff since the beginning, refuses to take a gun, so Shauna takes it. (Bet he'd change his mind if he knew that sheriff was making "the Agopy with two backs" with his daughter.)

After a tense night of waiting for the baddies to show (and the requisite "Oh Mother, I love him" talk), the showdown finally comes at dawn, with Cody mysteriously absent. And it comes down exactly like you'd expect with guns being wielded by until-yesterday pacifists: they don't hit a thing. Not a damned thing. For ten minutes, they shoot down from rooftops and upper-story windows at Hog's goons, and not a single bullet hits. The bad guys don't even bother ducking for cover; they just stand there as the bullets hit the blacktop around them—or rather, the embarrassingly obvious piles of dirt that are hiding the squibs. And they fire back half-heartedly, just to make the Agopy shooters duck, and don't hit them either. Ten whole minutes of people firing and nobody hitting anything. Boy, the excitement just drips off the screen and pools on the floor, doesn't it?

Finally, Cody shows up as if this was all part of his plan, and plays his trump card: grenades. A shitload of grenades. Where did he get them? I dunno. Were they back in Duke's cabin? I dunno. Maybe. They had to come from somewhere, right? So Cody works his way through the town at a leisurely pace, shooting and blowing up bad guys.

He manages to kill just about all of the ruffians and rescue the townspeople who were being held in the open outside (even though Hog had stated that he planned to wipe out every living person, so why the hell are they holding them? just so Cody will have someone to rescue?) and also investigate the gunfire from the church, where Shauna's father finally picked up a gun that Cody left there just in case (the one and only townsperson to manage to hit what he aimed at—hell, even the ex-soldier didn't bag anyone), and then he asks, "Where's Shauna?" At which point, the ex-soldier finally tells him, Oh yeah, Hog dragged her off thataway to rape her about ten minutes ago.

Apparently "thataway" is a precise address in this town, because Cody immediately runs across the street, between two buildings, around the corner, and directly to the run-down building to which Hog has dragged her for absolutely no good reason. I mean, there are plenty of similar abandoned buildings on both sides of the main street, and Hog has never really shown an obsession with privacy before, so there's simply no reason that he should drag her to yet another crumbling building—a distance which takes him ten minutes, and takes Cody two. And don't worry, Hog doesn't get very far in that extra two minutes; he spends it all forcibly slobbering on Shauna's neck. (Hog. You're raping her. I don't think any attempts at foreplay will be well-received, do you?)

When Cody arrives on the scene, he doesn't just shoot Hog through the door, no. He creeps up on him slowly, trying to get the gun right behind his head—giving the last hidden henchman a chance to club him into unconsciousness. And what does Hog do? Why, decides to drag Shauna another ten minutes to finish the job! So that in the time that it takes our tubby antagonist to get to his new Designated Spot (out by the train yards this time, in case you care), Cody regains consciousness, gets shot at by the henchman (again, the "dancing" thing, again with someone prone on the ground), and shoots the henchman with the hidden one-shot up his sleeve. He then stumbles out to the train yard without a weapon, where Hog hasn't gotten any farther, and shouts Shauna's name. He gets a bullet in the shoulder for his trouble (actually in the upper left side of his chest, so he should be out for the count, but he's the hero, so he keeps on going). Hog decides it'll be more fun to shoot the hero than rape the heroine (and he'll probably get farther), so he chases him across the train yard—until Cody pulls a pair of shotguns out of frigging nowhere and shoots him dead.

A couple of quick winding-up scenes, and then the most blessed moment: the credits roll.

I haven't mentioned the musical score, which includes Cody's synthesized cowboy theme; I also haven't dwelt on the pointless subplot about the ex-soldier's conflict with another guy who used to be in his unit, who's been making a living selling cocaine. Cocaine? How the hell do they have a distribution network for cocaine? As far as I can tell, the only difference shown between the post-apocalyptic world and a heavy garden-variety economic depression is that there aren't any cops or telephones.

And as detailed as I've been in my description, I still have not given you the scene-by-scene, shot-by-shot, line-by-line analysis which would demonstrate that the mediocrity descends uniformly to that level, like a fractal design which keeps reproducing itself at greater and greater magnifications. There are exactly two things in this movie which don't cause pain: that aforementioned scene in the church (not good, but at least not painful), and naked Shauna, who is at least fit and good-looking, as opposed to Hog's pet skanks that we see during the opening credits—saggy and with tattoos in all the wrong places.

Watching this I couldn't help but feel, in all honesty, embarrassed for David Heavener. I'm sure he knows it's not a good movie—he can speak intelligibly and walk without tipping over, so I'm pretty certain he's at least that much brainpower—but does he have any idea how gut-wrenchingly bad it is? And here it is, available on the occasional video shelf for all the world to see. It's like watching someone humiliate himself in public, someone so oblivious that he doesn't even realize how badly he's embarrassing himself, and you have to cringe for him because he can't do it for himself.

And then, most inexplicably of all, Heavener keeps making more movies! How the sweet hell does he get financing? How does he persuade anyone to let him within twenty feet of a camera or a typewriter again? Do the people who put up money for later projects never bother to see his previous output? Or does he show *Deadly Reactor* to them, and they (not having the bad cinema endurance that some of us have built up) simply lapse into bludgeoned unconsciousness, allowing him to steal their wallets?

Some Notable Totables:
- body count: 29
- breasts: 10
- explosions: 4
- dream sequences: 1
- ominous thunderstorms: 0
- actors who've appeared on *Star Trek*: 0

MOONTRAP (1989)

FOR FOURTEEN THOUSAND YEARS... IT WAITED.

- Produced and directed by Robert Dyke
- Written by Tex Ragsdale
- Starring Walter Koenig, Bruce Campbell, Leigh Lombardi, Robert Kurcz and John J. Saunders
- Executive produced by James A. Courtney, Brian C. Manoogian and Alan N. Solomon

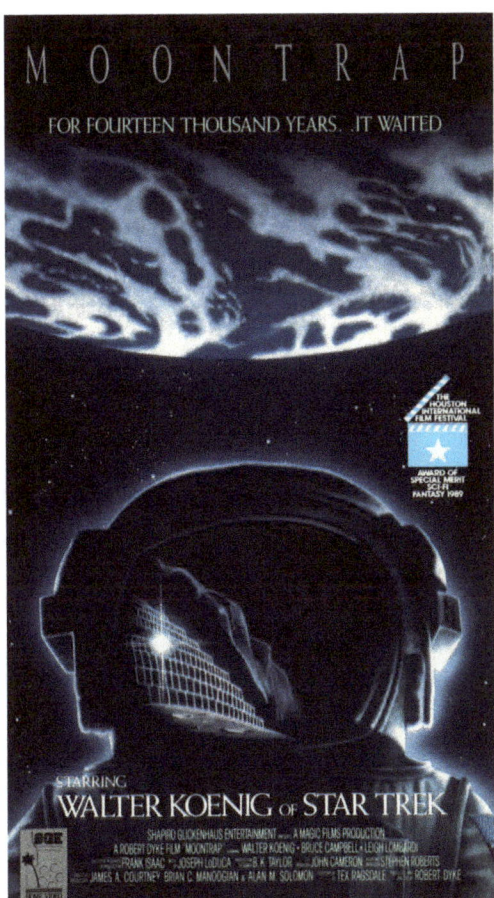

I'm surprised at the lack of respect for *Moontrap*. Not that it's a great movie by any stretch—it only qualifies as "good" by some severely bracketed criteria—but so many decades before an official DVD release? This is a movie available in every single rental outlet for more than a decade before VHS finally vanished! This a movie that pits Walter "Chekov" Koenig and Bruce "Ash" Campbell against killer robots on the frickin' moon! Where is the love?

And yes, that's the right order: Walter Koenig, then Bruce Campbell. Koenig is Colonel Jason Grant, shuttle pilot, and Campbell is Ray Tanner, copilot and sidekick. Koenig is the leading man in this one, even if he's a little long in the tooth. (Fun fact: it's been longer since *Moontrap* was produced than it was between the end of the original *Star Trek* show and the production of *Moontrap*.) He even gets the girl in the end; how's that for Chekov's final triumph? But I'm getting ahead of myself.

Grant and Tanner are on a routine 1990 shuttle mission when they pick up signs of a huge body entering orbit. (I missed the dialogue where mission control made excuses for not having picked it up before, but I believe it amounts to "Duuuuhhhrrr!") It is in fact a huge alien ship, but it's adrift and caught in Earth's gravity well. Grants suits up and spacewalks over to find some handy artifact they can salvage to take back to Earth. He finds a rupture in the hull, and a hard mechanical pod just larger than a basketball that looks like a beetle shell. Oh, and he also finds a desiccated human corpse. That's all he can grab before orbital decay gets too dangerous.

Back on Earth, of course, it's all kept hush-hush. (Gee, I wonder how they kept a lid on that *huge fireball in the sky* that the ship must have made as it descended into the atmosphere?) The pod proves unopenable; the corpse is that of a human, but carbon-14 dating shows it to be 14,000 years old. And dust on both shows that, at one point, the ship was on the moon. The government liaison, Mr. Haskell (Reavis Graham), half-suspects that it's all a hoax to up NASA's funding, but it still gets filed under "National Security."

I'm glad that national security's a concern, but local security leaves a lot to be desired. As soon as everyone leaves the examination room to discuss the find over a cup of coffee, the pod opens up revealing a mechanical eye on a stalk and various metallic tentacles. It pulls apart the room until it constructs for itself a robot body made of computer components and the 14,000-year-old corpse. And because there's no security outside or around the room holding what could be the first ever extraterrestrial artifacts, it manages to leave the room and situate itself in one of the sub-basements before security forces respond.

Along with the security forces, everyone getting coffee comes along too. There's a firefight in the corridor downstairs, with the robot proving impervious to gunfire and the security guys proving all too pervious to animated electrical bolts. (The robot itself is not too shabby, with hydraulic arm and neck motion, but it's pretty clear that it stays standing in one place because the prop wasn't built to be mobile.) Finally, Grant gets the bright idea to grab a shotgun from one of the fallen soldiers and climb up a ladder into—yes—an air duct! The overhead ductwork puts him right above the robot, and with one well-aimed blast accompanied by the robot's willingness to sustain damage when The Hero wills it, it blows up and collapses.

Well, the robot attack clinches it. An old but functional Saturn 5 is pulled out of mothballs, and Grant and Tanner, with a third man in the capsule, are sent up top check out the moon. It's a fulfillment of Grant's dream because he just missed being on the original moon landings and blah blah blah. The moon, in case you're wondering, was realized by a set covered with powdered QuikCrete. Word is that there were signs for the crew that read, "No liquids on the set!"

Grant and Tanner find some sort of base or citadel built into the side of a lunar hill, surrounded by human skeletons. From a wide and spacious atrium (hello, matte painting!), they enter a smaller chamber which seals itself and pressurizes. In the middle of the chamber is a dust-covered capsule bearing a single female occupant. Bzing! The capsule activates, and Grant's love interest is revealed! (I think she's the only female member of the cast, aside from the administrative assistant slaughtered by the robot, and the stripper in the tittie bar in which the astronauts hang out.) Her name is Mera (Leigh Lombardi), and names are really all they can communicate. But she's also got a fully-functioning space suit, so she follows them back out.

Unfortunately, something has been watching them. Several somethings, really; the pods can burrow and travel beneath the lunar landscape, sticking their electric eyes up like periscopes, and they make off with the lander before the rover can get back to it. They're stuck on the moon… with killer robots!

Now, there's quite a bit more that happens, but it's right here that the movie starts to lose cohesion, mainly because it refuses to answer any of the mysteries which were why we got into this in the first place. For instance, the robots—Mera calls them "Kylium"—have their own crash-landed ship not far away. Grant says, "Now we know what they've been doing since they got here." Oh, really? And what would that be? Simply sitting on the lunar surface, waiting for the people below to develop lunar vehicles and come up to futz around?

Or did the people below already develop that technology? No one ever wonders aloud where Mera's people came from. Were they part of an "ancient astronaut" race which seeded the Earth with humanity? Were they from an incredibly advanced prehistoric terrestrial civilization? Or were they aliens who just happened to be entirely human? When the mystery is introduced with a 14,000-year-old human corpse in space, I think it's a requirement to pay us off and tell us finally where it came from.

And the Kylium: scavengers, yes, but why? Are they an entirely robotic civilization, or are they the invasion/colonization force for another culture? How did they end up crash-landed on on the moon? For that matter, how did the ship that Grant and Tanner first encountered (I think it was one from Mera's people, but the design bears a lot of similarity to the Kylium ship) get off the moon and into orbit if it's been a derelict for fourteen millennia?

About the only question that *is* answered here is, "What kind of closures do 14,000-year-old humans have on their jumpsuits?" The answer is, None. When things look dire enough that it's time for some comfort-lovin', all it takes is one gentle pull on the front and the entire back opens. Convenient, no?

As it stands, the movie as originally released had a lot of problems (many of them created by the excision of scenes cut out to bring the movie's running time down). On the other hand, the special effects are surprisingly accomplished for a non-studio feature. The miniature work is impressive, and the replicated NASA props do justice to the originals. The set for the lunar landscape is pretty convincing, if you can ignore the swirls of dust that hang in the air whenever the surface is disturbed. (Alas, the actors can't quite replicate the effect of movement in zero gravity, even though *Space: 1999* did it well a decade and a half earlier: just slow down the footage!)

I don't know what the budget was, but I'm guessing that somebody lost a lot of money, since this seems like something that had theatrical aspirations (back in the day when an independent production had a chance of ending up in a cinema) rather than an intentional direct-to-video release. Instead, after the film festival premiere, this movie kicked around for several years, scoring video releases in half a dozen countries before finally ending up on video domestically in 1993 without a theatrical run. It's really Walter Koenig's only starring role, and it didn't do great things for the careers of anyone else involved (though at least you could say that it didn't hold Bruce Campbell back any).

Because this is the Age Of Plentiful Media And Then Some, we finally have official DVD and Blu-Ray releases, restored and remastered and uncut. But there will always be a fondness among those of us who first discovered *Moontrap* on fading ex-rental VHS tapes trading for increasingly exorbitant prices on Ebay.

Some Notable Totables:
- body count: 11
- breasts: 2
- explosions: 22
- ominous thunderstorms: 0
- actors who've appeared on *Star Trek*: 2
  - Walter Koenig, obviously
  - Judy Levitt ("Intrepid Commander") played "Doctor #2" in *Star Trek 4*, "Military Aide" in *Star Trek 6*, and "El Aurian Survivor" in *Generations*

The DEAD NEXT DOOR (1989)

How do you kill something that won't die? Where do you run when they're everywhere?

- Written, produced and directed by J.R. Bookwalter
- Starring Pete Ferry, Bogdan Pecic, Michael Grossi, Jolie Jackunas and Robert Kokai
- Executive produced by "The Master Cylinder" (Sam Raimi)

Among do-it-yourself horror aficionados, this movie has a reputation and mystique that almost approaches legendary status. The zombie epic filmed in Super-8mm! The jumping-off point for microbudget auteur J.R. Bookwalter, then only eighteen! Unofficially executive-produced by Sam Raimi, who cut bait when production costs spiraled to $100,000! The film that put Akron, Ohio on the map! (It's there, I swear. I saw it once.)

When a movie has been played up so much in the minds of its potential audience, honestly, could it possibly be as good as it's cracked up to be?

In this case, as with most others, the answer is, "Well… no." But it's still one of the better independent zombie movies to come out of the '80s.

In an obvious homage to Romero's *Dead* trilogy (in fact, huge chunks of this movie are such homages, if not the entire thing), the dead inexplicably start rising in Akron, Ohio, including a handful of zombies in a video store—renting *Dawn of the Dead* (1978), of course.

Five years later, the nation is still awash in the living dead, barely being held back by various units of the government-sponsored Zombie Squad, one of whom we meet in Virginia as they explore a zombie-overrun farmhouse. You've got stony-jawed Raimi (Pete Ferry), designated female Kuller (Jolie Jackunas), young stud Mercer (Michael Grossi), portly Kline (Floyd Ewing Jr.), and Richards (Scott Spiegel), whom you shouldn't bother getting to know well, as he foolishly gets his fingers bitten off by a decapitated zombie head and ends up infected.

After their little hunting expedition, the Squad heads back to Washington, where they're given a new assignment: accompany the stereotypically driven scientist Dr. Moulssen (Bogdan Pecic) back to Akron, where the zombie apocalypse apparently got its start with the viral research of one Dr. Bow (Lester Clark, whom we saw briefly in the prologue). Apparently, if they can determine what [technobabble technobabble] Bow used in the original virus, they can [technobabble] a [technobabble] that will [technobabble] the virus and end the reign of the zombies once and for all. The mission becomes that much more urgent when Mercer, in an unguarded moment, gets bitten by a zombie strapped down to Moulssen's examination table. If they can't find a cure soon, he'll become one of the living dead.

It doesn't take long for the Squad, accompanied by Moelsson and Dr. Franklin (Roger Graham), to locate Bow's old house and his corpse in the basement. It also doesn't take long for them to discover young Vincent (Jon Killough) skulking around—a supposedly harmless member of a supposedly harmless local church. Well, we all know that all post-zombie religions are dangerously insane, so it comes as no surprise when Vincent starts protesting the Squad's plan to eradicate the zombies, proclaims, "My religion is right!" (normally such a declaration is either preceded or followed by a delineation of some sort of doctrinal distinction, but not here), and chops Kline with a machete.

The oh-so-harmless church is led by Reverend Jones (Robert Kokai), and you know he's evil because he wears sunglasses at night. You might also get that impression from the fact that he keeps scores of zombies in outdoor cages and locked in the basement, feeding them regularly.

Despite being evil, though, Jones is also stupid, as it takes maybe another fifteen minutes for the Zombie Squad to find Bow's old notes and start working on an anti-serum. You'd think that, if Jones was so enamored of the zombies and unwilling to permit their destruction, he would have cleaned out the papers from Bow's lab and destroyed them five years ago when he killed Bow.

In between the ongoing conflict with the cultists, Moulsson comes up with a version of the anti-serum, and sends Raimi and Kuller out to get him a specimen to try it on; but being impatient in their absence, he goes ahead and injects Mercer. Then, when the cultists storm the lab, Mercer falls into their hands, where he completes the transformation into a zombie—but thanks to the serum, he remains fully conscious, and wants revenge on Dr. Moulsson for doing that to him.

The final twenty minutes is just chock full of escapes, rescues, secrets revealed, schemes unleashed, and a whole bunch of intestines being pulled from torsos and chewed on.

Now, before I start pointing out flaws, as is my wont, let's remember what we're dealing with here. Bookwalter was eighteen when he wrote and directed this in 1985 (it took another four years before editing, dialogue looping, etc., were completed and the finished product was available to consumers). Remember when you were eighteen? I do, just barely, and I'm glad that none of my artistic endeavors of the period are available for public heckling at this late date. By those standards, then, we've got a rousing success on our hands.

On the other hand, when we consider the movie apart from its production backstory and mystique, we can see a whole bunch of things that could have been done better. I'm not talking about the technical aspects; the finished product looks about as good as you can expect 8mm to ever look, and the special effects are both creative and charmingly hokey. No, I'm talking about the story being told.

The Romero trilogy to which this is a

paean is so memorable not because of the level of gore—there were certainly gorier films before, and zombie films since have kept trying to outdo one another—but because there's a depth, a level of maturity that can reach right into the viewer and rattle his bones. There are capital-I Issues dealt with. Here, though, the issues are sketched in and left as caricatures. To wit:

Religion. As soon as we find out the church leader is "Reverend Jones," we know exactly what to expect: rubberstamped brainwashed cultists willing to die for a vague religious conviction. All fine and good, but look what a fertile field this could have been. Christianity is all about the resurrection of the dead; a movie that delved into that material, showing its permutation in the face of the undead walking the earth, could be truly chilling. It could be the informing theme of such a movie, in the way that testosterone poisoning informed *Night of the Living Dead* (1968) and consumer culture-informed *Dawn of the Dead*. Here, it's given a moment's lip service; cultists are simply convenient bad guys.

AIDS. Vincent makes reference to the zombies being a punishment from God, very clearly mimicking the language used by fundamentalist pundits to explain the scourge of AIDS upon the unrighteous (back before heterosexual infectees started outnumbering homosexual ones by a ridiculous margin). But that's all it is, a single-line reference. If there's a parallel here, a statement being made, it's certainly well hidden.

Military vs. scientists. Romero dealt with this familiar (to sci-fi fans, anyway) conflict in *Day of the Dead* (1985), and did a wonderful job of it, even if he did plant the black hat firmly on the military's head; the science contingent wasn't infallible, either, and it turns out to be a single scientist's myopic pursuit of narrow goals which destroys the fragile truce between the two camps. The situation here is almost a refutation of Romero's scenario, and it goes overboard in differentiating the camps. Moulsson, personifying Science, is egotistical, overconfident, and casual in his assumption of moral superiority. The Squad members, on the other hand, are fine and upstanding and just about always right. It's a knee-jerk characterization, and its application keeps the characters (especially the Zombie Squad soldiers) from becoming well-developed, because rounded characters have, you know, flaws. These guys have none; they're content to fight for Truth, Justice, and the American Way.

The point is not to bag on the movie, or call it names. The point is that chewing what's been bitten off here requires a level of maturity that the eighteen-year-old director didn't have, despite many strengths. It's a fanboy production, albeit an unusually capable one, and it demonstrates it at every turn by referencing and mirroring Romero, instead of taking the ball Romero held and running with it.

J.R. Bookwalter directed several microbudget features before moving on to low-budget digital effects on the one hand, and DVD distribution on the other. Rumors of a sequel to *The Dead Next Door* have bobbed to the surface for years, and as unlikely as such a production may be, I would love to see how Bookwalter would revisit and delve into the deeper matters that he didn't have enough growth-rings to truly deal with the first time out. Given how far ahead of the game he was at eighteen, I think the matured version would end up being all that the original is supposed to be.

Some Notable Totables:
- body count: 56
- breasts: 0
- explosions: 8
- ominous thunderstorms: 1
- homages to *Raiders of the Lost Ark*: 1
- actors who've appeared on *Star Trek*: 0

The DEAD NEXT DOOR: Writer-Director J.R. Bookwalter's Comments

After eight or nine years of making nearly 50 Super-8mm short films between junior high and college, *The Dead Next Door* was my first time at bat on something feature length (my longest short film had been a college piece called *Go Insane*, which clocked in around 20 minutes). And as often happens with these things, it happened quite by accident. I didn't set out to make my first feature like most people do that opportunity just landed in my lap and I jumped on it, hanging on tight for the next four years!

Never in my wildest dreams could I have imagined how my first feature project mushroomed into something that over 1,500 Northeast Ohio residents wound up participating in. Closing down Main Street in downtown Akron, putting zombies on the raceway of the Soap Box Derby and hell, even having them climb the White House fence! It was a good time to be young and foolish, to be making something without the limits of time, money or energy, never listening to anyone who said it couldn't be done. Even though I was younger than most of the people who joined me in this great misadventure, they all went right along in following my dream, and to that I thank them, then and now. People often cite the "epic" nature of the movie, but you know what? I never viewed it that way, as a naive kid barely out of high school. I had my crazy ideas and by God, one way or another we were gonna put them on film. More filmmakers these days should have such conviction... people are too obsessed with "Action" and "Cut" and getting on to the ego-puffing promotion, none of which I gave much of a spit about to begin with.

I doubt anyone will ever challenge the movie's dubious reputation as "the most expensive Super-8mm feature ever made" but the ironic reality is that a lot of that money was wasted on bad film transfers, weeks of footage ruined by broken cameras and any number of other "learning curve" mistakes that were thankfully forgiven by a patient executive producer who had the courage to see the stupid thing through to completion. Weaker men would have abandoned the project, and I couldn't have blamed them.

Of course, nothing ever turns out quite the way you expect it to, no matter how you try. That was my biggest lesson on *The Dead Next Door*: despite six screenplay drafts over nine months of prep, a never-ending host of reshoots and a laborious post-production process, it was still never exactly what I hoped it would be. I spent nearly 15 years mostly dismissing the movie, until the awesome chance to remaster it for a DVD release came along from Anchor Bay. It finally took that experience for me to see it through the eyes of the people who dig it—no, it's not perfect (and far from it!), but it shows what a kid from Ohio can do if he puts his mind to it and doesn't let life kick him in the nuts. I was surprised that people embraced the movie in the '90s, and I'm still stunned to this day. It might not have been exactly what I set out to make, but folks mostly liked it anyway. (And those that didn't... hey, I'm right there with you, pal.)

The Dead Next Door seems like a lifetime ago for me... I guess it should since it's coming up on 25 years this summer since I embarked on that journey. If you've seen it and liked it, I thank you from the bottom of my little black heart. If you saw it and hated it, hey, thanks to you too... at least you gave it a shot. And if you haven't seen it yet, what are you waiting for? (Ha!)

The DEAD PIT (1989)

WHEN THE DEAD START WALKING YOU'D BETTER START RUNNING...

- Directed by Brett Leonard
- Written by Gimel Everett and Brett Leonard
- Starring Jeremy Slate, Cheryl Lawson, Stephen Gregory Foster, Danny Gochnauer and Geha Getz
- Produced by Gimel Everett

*"You're a doctor! You're supposed to be **saving** lives!"*
"I've done life. Now I'm doing death."

If you had seen this movie when it first got a video rental release, you'd remember. It had an embossed plastic cover showing a zombie crawling out of a pit toward you. And the coolest part was that his eyes were two red LED lights. A spot on the box said, "PRESS HERE," and when you did—his eyes flashed! Cool!

Of course, that was two decades ago, and there are very few of those embossed boxes intact, and even fewer with lights that still work; in fact, there may be none. (Subsequent sell-through VHS editions and the DVD release used the same cover graphic, but forewent both the embossing and the LEDs.) And there are those who will tell you that, following the Inverse Box/Movie Law (i.e., that the coolness and gimmickry of the box is inversely related to the quality of the movie contained therein), the movie ain't worth the time of day.

Those people may bite me.

I know it's not a great movie. I know it's got terrible flaws, and a whole collection of genre clichés. But I never fail to enjoy it any time I watch it.

The eponymous pit is one filled with formaldehyde and the bodies of the failed experiments (or successful ones, considering) of Dr. Sam Ramzi (Danny Gochnauer), a brilliant psychiatrist/surgeon who's been looking into the biological causes of insanity and kind of gets sidetracked into death for its own sake. Said pit is located at the bottom of a spiral staircase in the basement of one of the buildings of the State Institute For the Mentally Ill, accessed by a secret passage through a broom closet. (Do contractors making mental hospitals routinely build in such features, just in case one of the doctors goes all whack-a-mole and needs a hidden lair?) Alas, such a Mad-Sci paradise cannot last, and Ramzi's colleague Dr. Swan (Jeremy Slate) finally decides to stop covering for him and put an end to the madness. Despite Ramzi's maniacal "You can't kill me" stance, Swan refutes him with a bullet square in the center of the forehead (nice shootin', Tex). He then seals up the closet entrance with drywall compound—though if it were me, I'd have turned off the eerie green light leaking through the cracks first; those things can run up a power bill when left on.

Fast-forward twenty years. To that same

institution (now operating with several of its buildings closed up) is brought a pretty young amnesiac in her early twenties (Cheryl Lawson), known only as "Jane Doe." She's fairly stable, at least compared to the total whackjobs wandering the grounds; but despite having no memory, she holds to the fierce conviction that she didn't "lose" her memory; it was taken from her in a surgical operation. This does not endear her to designated head bitch Nurse Kygar (Joan Bechtel), who would certainly give her a tongue-lashing if not interrupted by an earthquake. Said earthquake, unbeknownst to all, pops open the sealed closet door in one of the unused buildings; it also sends Jane into a full-blown episode, screaming that the people in "the basement" need help and want out.

When she wakes from sedation, she's given the "Welcome to the Wonderful World of Institutionalization" talk by the cute Nurse Robbins (Mara Everett), and has her first meeting with Dr. Swan, who's still here but, you know, twenty years older (as evidenced by the fact that the brown dye in his hair in the prologue has been washed out). He starts a program of hypnosis to try to get to her memories, uncovering some kind of trauma from her early childhood in which she was taken away from her father by her mother.

Later in the common room, she meets the roguish Chris Meyers (Stephen Gregory Foster), who apparently thinks he's Sean Connery, right down to the accent. Why's he here? Oh, just because he likes to blow things up—which still makes him one of the sanest in the joint. And there's also a crazy nun. Don't think she won't come in handy, because she will.

Now that I've given you the setup, I can actually describe the entire center section of the movie in broad general terms, since what makes up the middle is the sort of broad general spookiness that you're familiar with. Jane has plenty of nightmares: some about Nurse Kygar, and some about a mysterious surgeon who she also sees fleetingly in her waking moments, waving at her

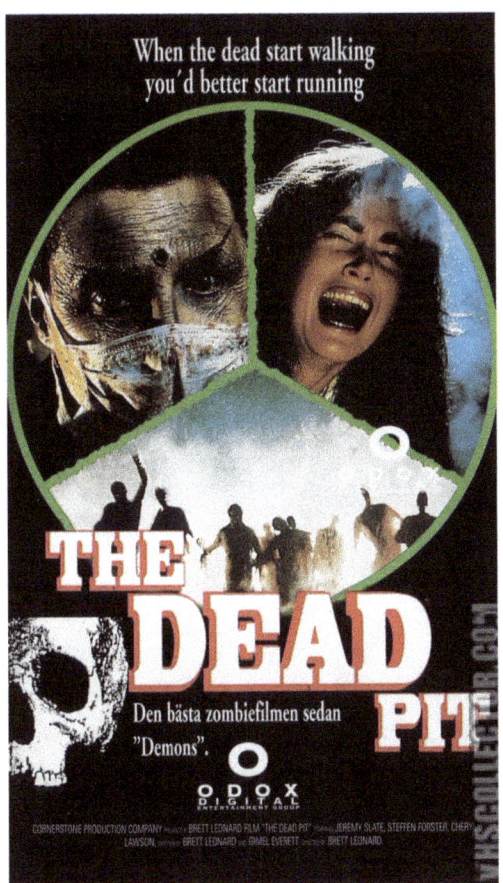

from the front of one of the unused buildings in the hospital complex. The nightmare episodes also give plenty of opportunity for the pleasantly "husky" (or "strapping") Cheryl Lawson to wander the hallways clad only in a babydoll undershirt and some really narrow exercise briefs.

There are also the usual creative killings—Nurse Robbins gets a lobotomy pick through her eyesocket, a twitchy inmate named Bud gets a dental drill through his eye, an orderly, a security guy, another orderly, etc.—all accomplished by the reanimated Dr. Ramzi, who has been released from his own pit by the earthquake. (Funny, I never attributed any specific mystical quality to drywall compound, but it apparently was an insurmountable necromantic barrier.) Under hypnosis, Jane suddenly starts speaking to Swan in Ramzi's voice, promising to "save him for later." This, needless to say, freaks Swan right out.

Desperate to get to the bottom of her nightmares and daytime visions, as well as the mysterious disappearances, Jane enlists Meyers to help her sneak out at night and get over to the other building. He does so, getting himself captured in the process, and Jane spends the next twenty minutes running around the empty building, chased by the offscreen-teleporting form of Dr. Ramzi, as well as the dead bodies of Nurse Robbins and Bud.

After playing with Jane for a while, Ramzi captures her and takes her to the dead pit (and for some reason, he changes her into a nurse's dress—apparently he didn't approve of her babydoll and sweatpants). And she gets to watch as, with a green light shining up, he reanimates his dead.

And I have to say, they're pretty cool zombies, all slimy and blood-streaked, many of them bald (brain surgery, remember?), in mildew-spotted hospital gowns. They shuffle and twitch their way up the spiral staircase to wreak havoc.

Fortunately, Meyers arrives to rescue her and together they make it back to the main building to find out all about Dr. Ramzi and his nefarious past from Dr. Swan. Then, while Swan thinks he can go and plant another bullet in his nemesis and accomplish something, Meyers and Jane encounter the

mad nun, who melts a zombie with a little paper cup of holy water. And then Meyers looks out the window at the big old water tower, looming over the empty building.

Let's see. A nun who can make holy water, a water tower, a basement lair next to the water tower… and an explosives expert. I think you can see the finale coming, can't you?

I'll admit, there are flaws aplenty. Front and center is Cheryl Lawson as Jane—easy on the eyes, and far from being the worst actress here (that distinction would have to go to Nurse Robbins), but she's not exactly a take-charge heroine; while I don't mind her *de rigueur* screaming (this is a horror flick, after all), the whiny sound she makes when when under duress or doubting her sanity isn't all that endearing.

Then there's that whole cliché of the spook that only the main character can see (including the "look, look away, look back" vanishing act). Dr. Ramzi even gets to give a couple of the standard horror-guy one-liners —not a lot of them, but what they lack in quantity they make up for in groanability. (Ramzi appears outside Jane's window at night, holding the severed head of an unlucky orderly. "*I'm* the head surgeon here!")

In between the clichés, you've got the story, which really makes no sense. By the time you get to the end, you've figured out the relationship between Jane and Ramzi long before they reveal it, but it still doesn't explain the whole "surgical removal of memory" thing.

But once you've reined in your expectations, there are some nice touches here. The presence of scads and oodles of certifiably insane people gives a great ambiance. The zombies themselves, while only present for the last twenty minutes, are nicely disturbing, and not so slow that they don't pose a credible threat. And the music,

while much less than subtle, is fiercely unsettling (although it has been known to irritate some people, such as one of the roommates I showed this to back in my college days)—and it kind of has to be loud, to be heard over the continuous shrieking and gibbering.

Bottom line: even though there are no more flashing LED eyes, it's still worth keeping.

Some Notable Totables:
- body count: 11 (plus a few others implied)
- breasts: 2
- explosions: 1
- dream sequences: 3 (plus 3 hypnotic sessions)
- ominous thunderstorms: 0
- actors who've appeared on *Star Trek*: 0

The LAUGHING DEAD (1989)

THOUSANDS OF YEARS AGO, THE AZTEC GOD OF DEATH FED OF HUMAN SACRIFICE. NOW HE'S BACK... AND HE'S WORKED UP A BIG APPETITE.

- *Written and directed by "S.P. Somtow" (Somtow Sucharitkul)*
- *Starring Tim Sullivan, Wendy Webb, S.P. Somtow, Patrick Roskowick and Larry Kagen*
- *Produced by Lex Nakashima*

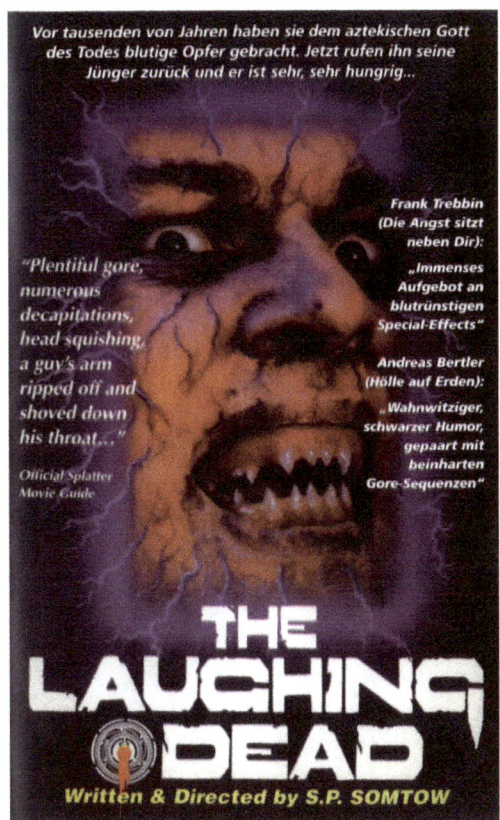

It took me more than a decade to see this movie after I started watching for it. I'd read a first-person behind-the-scenes piece in the horror movie magazine *Fangoria* by the director, S.P. Somtow (aka Somtow Sucharitkul), and it was a pretty interesting little saga. Somtow, who had become a respected genre novelist during the '80s, ended up in Hollywood with a vague plan to change his career and make movies. As luck would have it, he ran into low-budget creature effects guru John Carl Buechler in a supermarket line, and the two got to talking. Buechler's advice was, if you want people to let you make movies, get a movie made. He suggested a low-budget (a couple hundred thousand dollars) horror movie as something that would be easily marketable, and the two agreed to collaborate. Somtow went off and put together a story revolving around the Mexican Day of the Dead festival, and—in a stroke of genius—recruited a lot of friends from his circle of up-and-coming authors to get killed in his movie.

So I waited to see this movie in the video store. And I waited. And I waited.

The second part of the story, the reason *The Laughing Dead* has never had a U.S. release, was explained to me roughly thus years later: the backer who financed the production was a rich kid, with a grotesquely decadent living allowance out of his father's money. Once the movie was completed, he suddenly realized that, if it was successful, Daddy might expect him to go out and make himself useful on a regular basis, and to that end might cut off the gravy train. So the rich kid nixed the possibility of domestic distribution. Even today, the movie has had VHS and DVD releases in Britain, but nothing on this side of the Atlantic.

So it took me a full dozen years between reading about *The Laughing Dead* and finally seeing it. And... let me put it this way. I don't think that the living allowance was really in that much danger.

The romance of the "living the Hollywood dream" story aside, what you've got here is someone who came to Tinseltown with no previous screenwriting or directing experience who then proceeded to write, direct, and co-star in his first feature. (He also provided the score, having had another previous career as an avant-garde composer.) When you take that genesis into account, then, I guess it's not half bad. And it certainly doesn't look rock-bottom cheap, I'll say that for it.

Things get off to a bang with an unusual gambit: child sacrifice. Money changes hands, a little girl leaves home in the back of a banged-up pickup, and the next thing you know, she's lying on a stone altar having an obsidian dagger plunged into her. The plunger, in full feathered regalia, is the evil (obviously) Dr. Um-Tzec (Somtow, quite possibly the only Aztec high priest of Thai descent ever). Dr. Um-Tzec then changes from his ceremonial garb into a white suit reminiscent of that of Col. Sanders.

Meanwhile, in Tuscon, Father O'Sullivan (Tim Sullivan) is preparing for his annual archeology tour to Oaxaca for the Day of the Dead festival. O'Sullivan's got some strong points to his character; he plays basketball with the local youth, and is always ready to arrange shelter for battered women and such. But he's got a terrible stain on his past; a few years ago, he and a nun caused something of a stir for using the confessional for activities frowned upon by the Vatican, if you know what I mean. He's also near the end of his faith. And he's stupid enough to leave all of the newspaper clippings and a photo of the nun all over his desk for parishioner Laurie (Premika Eaton) to find.

He's also the sucking point of the movie, because Tim Sullivan manages to convey all of the emotional intensity of a straight-backed Shaker chair. In every scene, he looks like he's straining all of his thespian abilities to blink convincingly. That's Neophyte Director Error #1: give out all the supporting roles to your friends if you want, but make sure your lead is a competent actor.

Not that he's alone in the bad acting department. His early scenes with Laurie are an amusing exercise in contrasts, since Eaton delivers every line with full-bore histrionics ("**WHAT ARE WE HAVING FOR LUNCH???**"), while Sullivan, well… (blink)

Anyway. The tour group this year has a few colorful oddballs in it, including Wilbur and Clarisse Lemming (Larry Kagen and Krista Keim), a geeky-but-trendy New Age couple, and a pair of arguing and ill-dressed friends, Dozois (Raymond Ridenour, and yes, his character's name is an in-joke) and Frost (SF novelist Gregory Frost). Oh, and Laurie stows away for the trip to get away from an argument with her sick father at home.

But wait, there's one more stop—and the two other members of their company prove to be Tessie (Wendy Webb), who once upon a time was the nun that O'Sullivan knew, and her—*their*—ten-year-old son Ivan (Patrick Roskowick). (blink) Ivan's a little snot (even his mother calls him "Ivan the Terrible"), and the implication is that he would have turned out better if he had ever had a real father. He also manages to drop more F-bombs in the next ninety minutes than any other child actor I've ever seen. Ever. Isn't there, you know, a law against that sort of thing?

After some spooky happenings on the road, they arrive in the village for the festival, where Dr. Um-Tzec is still cheerily murdering children on cue. And just to make matters worse, he's got a little shrine in his house, centering on a picture of—Ivan!

Dr. Um-Tzec lures Father O'Sullivan into his house with a message that Um-Tzec's daughter is possessed, and even though O'Sullivan's faith tank is running on fumes (and he half-recognizes Dr. Um-Tzec's face from some disturbing dreams), he consents to go ahead with the exorcism. At least the doctor wasn't lying; his grown daughter definitely is possessed, and after showing the priest some dirty dancing, she rips open her chest, pulls out her heart, pulls O'Sullivan's heart from his chest, and exchanges them. So now O'Sullivan is possessed too, by the spirit of the great Death-God Um-Tzec (for whom Dr. Um-Tzec's family has borne its name all these generations).

And hoo-boy, there are few giggles in this movie better than watching O'Sullivan act possessed. Because, with his glassy stare, his monotone voice, his wooden demeanor… there's really not much change! Except, of course, for those moments in which O'Sullivan's soul is struggling to get out, when he jerks around like he had too many habaneros for lunch. (Let's just gently remind of Neophyte Director Error #1, shall we?)

Of course, to fill the time before the grand finale, we have to have some miscellaneous killings. Dozois gets his head knocked off and used for a basketball; Dr. Um-Tzec's henchmen kill the innkeeper and the busdriver; and O'Sullivan goes wild and starts punching straight through people before disappearing into the catacombs beneath the inn, where Ivan is being prepared as a final sacrifice to usher in the reign of Um-Tzec, the Death-God.

Thankfully, Cal (Ryan Effner), a kid from a local archaeological dig, has the hots for Laurie, so he just happens to be around for the finale, when he summons Kukulkan to fight Um-Tzec. Well, "summon" might not be the word; Cal actually transforms into a huge saurian critter, and Dr. Um-Tzec becomes his namesake, looking very much like a stereotypical Buechler creature.* Talk about *deus ex machina*… Meanwhile, in the background, the living good guys have to play against a group of zombies in one of those Mayan ballgames… to the death!

So. Aside from some lamentable acting, what else can I say? The story's not nearly as professional as one would expect from an experienced novelist. Characterizations are a combination of sketchy clichés. (Actually, the only character who really gets any character development is O'Sullivan. (blink)) The showdown at the end really comes down to the scenery-chewing ee-vil of Dr. Um-Tzec (Somtow's performance is actually the most fun to watch) and the maudlin familial sentiment of O'Sullivan's sudden family situation, despite the fact that Ivan swears like a sailor and makes fun of the priest for wearing a skirt.

On the other hand, if you read a lot of *Isaac Asimov's Science Fiction Magazine* during the '80s, you just might want to watch the credits first, so you'll know who to pick out. Edward Bryant as the busdriver! Arthur Byron Cover as Zombie #1! Tim Powers as Zombie #2! Brynne Stephens as Zombie #3! William Wu as Zombie #4! Bill Warren as Corpse #2! Len Wein as Corpse #3! (Not exactly a SF novelist, but comic book writers are cool on their own.) And of course, professional fanboy Forrest J. Ackerman in a masterful turn as Corpse #1!

Not exactly the kind of audience appeal on which filmmaking careers are made (and this one wasn't—Somtow only directed one other movie, five years later), but I probably wouldn't judge it harshly compared to other horror movies in its budget range if it weren't for that *Fangoria* article that's been stuck in my head for so long.

Some Notable Totables:
- body count: 12
- breasts: 2
- explosions: 3
- dream sequences: 3
- ominous thunderstorms: 1
- actors who've appeared on *Star Trek*: 0

---

* Somehow, Buechler's creatures all have a facial similarity to them—and I think that they all actually resemble Buechler himself. There's not necessarily anything sinister about that; he probably used his own face in the mirror as a convenient model when sculpting.

DARK HERITAGE: The FINAL DESCENDANT (1990)

SOMEONE OR SOMETHING HAS AN APPETITE FOR DEATH...

- Produced and directed by David McCormick
- No writer credited (based, uncredited, on "The Lurking Fear" by H.P. Lovecraft)
- Starring Mark LaCour, Tim Verkaik, Eddie Moore, Joan Parmalee and David Hatcher

Of the three movies based on or inspired by H.P. Lovecraft's story "The Lurking Fear" (the other two being 1994's *The Lurking Fear* and 1997's *Bleeders*), this one proves most faithful in terms of story events and structure, despite no credit being given not only to Lovecraft for the original story, but even to whoever adapted and wrote the screenplay. Yet despite the fact that it follows most closely one of Lovecraft's most cinematic short stories, it's no more successful than the other two at making the adaptation work as a piece of cinema. In fact, once you factor in the problems inherent in it being a cheap independent production (a restrictive budget and an amateur cast), this version might prove the most inferior of the three. And that's even more of an insult than it seems if you haven't seen the other two movies.

From the outset, it's clear that we're going to be blending a healthy respect for the original short story with a grasp of human behavioral psychology gleaned almost entirely from other bad horror films. Take, for example, the initial scene, set in a camper trailer in a public though secluded Louisiana campground at night as a thunderstorm rolls in. While the man cooks over the camper stove, the woman utters the line you never want to hear as the first words of dialogue in a movie: "I thought I heard something." To keep his woman happy, the man sticks his head out the camper door, then declares that there's nothing. When the woman retroactively becomes more and more sure that she heard something, the man does not very sensibly point out to her that there are other campers around and a storm is rolling in so there's no reason she shouldn't hear something; no, he reluctantly grabs the flashlight and opens the door wider. Given the lead-up, it's almost unfair to the man that she turns out to be right: a hideous something (seen only as a blue hand) guts him, then comes after her.

According to the next day's news report, the occupants of the entire campground were killed by parties unknown, with fewer than half of the thirty-seven registered campers accounted for bodily. Armed with this information, newspaper editor Mr. Daniels (Eddie Moore), on orders from the publisher Mr. Jordan (whom we never see), gives the case to their crack investigative reporter, Clint Harrison (Mark LaCour). Mr. Jordan's a man of many crackpot ideas, and his current one is that this massacre may have something to do with the abandoned Dansen estate, five miles from the campground, and that Clint should begin his investigation by spending the night at the old mansion. Above Mr. Daniels' own misgivings, Clint happily accepts the assignment, along with two compatriots, Roger (Joe Jennings) and Daryl (Todd Leger) from the production department.

(Join me for a moment in pondering the reaction of Mr. Howard Philip Lovecraft, he of the bookish diction and a general disdain for all things degenerate and backwoodsy, to an adaptation of one of his stories that features a cadre of Deep South good ol' boys as protagonists.)

Clint and his compatriots drive and then hike to the old mansion, which is spooky and old and colonnaded but, I'm sorry, it ain't been abandoned for a hundred years as everyone says. If you've ever seen a house that's been abandoned even for twenty years, you can imagine what a century of neglect would do to a building, especially in the moist South. This place has no animal spoor, no broken windows, no sagging floors, no flaked paint or crumbling plaster… in fact, none of the details which Lovecraft would have used to describe such a derelict mansion. Instead, there are a few pieces of serviceable furniture, some still with pristine sheets draped over them. At least when the three see a bed in one of the rooms, they don't immediately decide to sleep on it; that's one of my pet peeves in movies.

The three pick an empty room and set up, playing poker until the wee hours, at which point they take turns on watch for whatever, with a videocamera running to capture the whatever should it appear. And when thunder awakens Clint later in the night, he sees A) the absence of both of his friends, B) the tipped-over videocamera, and C) a mysterious silhouette thrown on the wall by the lightning. He doesn't stop to investigate the shadow; instead, he grabs the videotape that's lying half-out of the smashed machine and runs for the hills.

Subsequent police investigation not only fails to uncover any sign of the two missing fellows, but can't even find their gear or anything to indicate that the three had ever visited the house. The videotape only shows one of the missing men being dragged away in front of the upended camera by something we can't see. Mr. Daniels decides that this would be a good time for Clint to take a couple of weeks off and stew at home to try to forget all about things. Because that always works, right? Instead, Clint starts going through the special collections at the university library for clues about the old Dansen place. That's where he meets a couple of parapsychology grad students, Jack (Tim Verkaik) and Greg (David Hatcher), who are themselves looking into the old place as a basis for local folklore. Time to compare notes! It seems that the Dansen clan, after establishing themselves in the area a couple of centuries earlier, had become progressively more aloof from the locals until they cut themselves off sometime in the mid-1800s; it wasn't until a decade or two later that someone realized they hadn't seen any lights in the windows of the mansion for a while, and when they investigated, the place was empty. The Dansens had disappeared.

And then, time for a field trip! Out they go to the ill-fated campground. Only one sign of the tragedy hasn't yet been hauled away by the police, a single camper trailer (in fact, the one from the prologue). The three men use it as a base of operations as they putter around with no idea what they're looking for. When the evening brings yet another lightning storm, the three take shelter in the camper, watching out the windows and open door just in case whatever cast the silhouette that Clint saw at the house likes to caper about in the storm. But when the rain abates, they find that Greg, who was watching with his face out the door the whole time, is dead—his face gashed open!

This is, by the way, one of the most effective moments in the original short story; it's not a technique Lovecraft ever mastered, but here at least he keeps the reader in the moment of the story, rather than always looking forward to the end with anticipation. So it's good that these filmmakers retain the scene, even engineering things like the leftover camper in order to set it up. On the other hand, the following scene, also taken from the story, doesn't work nearly so well in the modified context: Clint and Jack decide to bury Greg out there to avoid inquiry. That kind of thing works when your setting is a backwoods community sixty years in the past and the individuals in question had only met as their separate investigations of the matter brought them together; it's a lot harder to swallow when it's the present day, the location is a public campground, and one of the people doing the burying is the deceased's best friend. I don't think any questions are going to be avoided.

After a night of nightmares back in town, Clint and Jack meet up again to go after whatever got Greg. Jack's idea is to find the gravesite of Eric Dansen, the fabled son who had left the family enclave for college and returned, not long before the disappearance, only to be killed by his kin with whom he didn't reintegrate so well. Since the wronged ghost of Eric Dansen has been a figure in local folklore, Jack's idea is that his gravesite might have some connection to whatever killed Greg. So they locate the overgrown family plot in the woods, dig up an empty (though surprisingly intact) coffin, and discover beneath it a mysterious tunnel. (If I were feeling really snarky, I could say that the most mysterious thing about it was where its diggers had found the chickenwire to use as the visible

structure under the paper-mache tunnel walls. But I'm feeling magnanimous today, so forget I said anything.)

And in the tunnel, as yet another thunderstorm rages overhead, they meet… a something. A white-haired, blue-skinned something that is wisely kept barely seen (though not as barely seen as the characters let on). And as it backs away from them in the narrow tunnel, a lightning strike directly above them breaks the tunnel inward, and they have to crawl out to avoid being buried in the rain-driven mud. And once they see the mound left over where a tunnel breaks out, they realize that the small mounds of earth which they had taken to be "badger holes" all over the campground and forest are all signs of miles and miles of tunnels.

Since they are now stuck in the middle of the woods on a rainy night, they find a spot under a tree for shelter, and in the morning go about presaging *The Blair Witch Project* (1999) right down to crossing a stream instead of following it. Finally, by late in the day, they find a familiar landmark: the Dansen mansion. Shucks, might as well go in, especially because they've come to suspect that the tunnel system somehow converges on the mansion. And it's here, finally, that we get a little bit of information that comes awfully late in the game, when they walk in and see the old painting of one of the Dansens still hanging on the wall. Jack points out the dissimilarly-colored eyes, which were a Dansen family trait. Um, could someone have thought of a way to introduce this tidbit sometime earlier than right before it's supposed to lead to a shocking revelation?

That withheld fact is the reason that I've kept my synopsis going to this point, which is about twenty minutes from the end of the movie. Although despite the general faithfulness to the original story displayed thus far, the ending of the movie is not the ending from the story. "The Lurking Fear" is, as I've said, one of Lovecraft's better tales, and much more tempting to adapt (repeatedly) to the big screen. But it still relies on one of Lovecraft's favorite literary tricks: revealing some withheld detail in the final paragraph, the last piece of the Big Picture, even though the narrator or protagonist is aware of it earlier. That's a lot harder to do in a movie, where we largely see what the characters see, and so some other climax needed to be devised here, one which involves adding a whole other branch to the Dansen family and having our "crack investigative reporter" be completely oblivious to his surroundings. I don't want to spell it out further, not because of any respect for spoiling a hard-to-find movie that you'll probably never see, but because they payoff in the end simply isn't worth the effort to get there.

While not intensely horrible, every element in this movie seems as if it's trying to hang back from appearing any better than any other element. The acting is uniformly wooden and unskilled, as if *"Because the director told me to"* was the primary motivation for every actor in every scene. The omission of any credited screenwriter is doubly counterintuitive, because this movie is far from ad-libbed; it's very, very scripted, using diction and speech patterns which few people would ever let come from their mouths naturally. The cinematography is unimaginative and murky, and the editing seems to have forgotten how to get from A to B.

In other words, it's a movie entirely made by well-meaning amateurs, who wanted to draw from and dramatize "The Lurking Fear" but had no idea how to do it well.

Some Notable Totables:
- body count: 7 (plus the other unseen casualties at the campground)
- breasts: 0
- explosions: 0
- dream sequences: 1
- ominous thunderstorms: 5
- actors who've appeared on *Star Trek*: 0

EVIL SPIRITS (1990)

SCARY, DISTURBING, FRIGHTENING, BLOODY FUN!

- Directed by Gary Graver
- Written by Mikel Angel
- Starring Karen Black, Arte Johnson, Virginia Mayo, Michael Berryman and Martine Beswick
- Produced by Sidney Niekirk

In one of those funny little happenstances, Karen Black and Michael Berryman shared the screen in three movies made between 1990 and 1993: Fred Olen Ray's *Haunting Fear* (1991), *Auntie Lee's Meat Pies* (1993) (reviewed on page 176), and this one. (They both also starred in 1985's *Cut and Run*, directed by Ruggero Deodato, but their scenes were shot in different locations and their characters never interacted.) Seeing both of these well-known visages on screen at once is more than a little disconcerting. You may not know Michael Berryman's name, but you definitely know his face, which is probably most famous from the poster for the original *The Hills Have Eyes* (1977) and its sequel. (Or you might recognize him from the video for Mötley Crüe's "Smokin' in the Boys' Room.") Berryman was born with a prematurely fused skull as well as Hypohidrotic Ectodermal Dysplasia, a condition which prevented him from developing sweat glands, body hair, fingernails or teeth. The result is... not pretty, but it's definitely recognizable. Karen Black, on the other hand, is just plain ugly. (Yes, I know. Karen Black has feelings too, and she very well may drift across this book one day and see me calling her names like an insensitive playground bully and burst forth into tears at my cruelty. Boy, you just take all the fun out of being a hatchetman critic, don't you?)

After the brief spate of insanity in Tinseltown that had Karen Black appearing as a sultry seductress, she immediately joined the ranks of slumming former stars who paid the rent by appearing in anything at all. There's something about her close-set eyes (and her willingness to genteelly chew scenery) that makes her a natural for semi-crazed roles, so much of her work has been in low-budget horror films, appearing as a matronly but less-than-balanced individual. Here we have a movie which, I can freely tell you up front, is a *Psycho* (1960) ripoff.

Evil Spirits certainly doesn't dawdle in getting things started. As soon as the credits are over, a hapless fellow opens his front door and BAM! gets a knife shoved into his eye. Then Karen Black shovels dirt on top of his corpse in a hastily-dug grave in the backyard, and immediately comes inside to wash her hands and quench her thirst by hauling a big ol' gallon of product-placed Gatorade from the refrigerator. Black is Mrs. Purdy, proprietor of this here boarding house full of the requisite odd individuals (according to Hollywood, no boarding house is filled with boring people), all of whom are receiving some kind of welfare, disability, or Social Security check. She also talks quite frequently to her husband, Mr. Purdy, even when he's not present. And when he is present (in her private apartment), he's in his dress Marine uniform in a wheelchair facing into the corner. And his voice always has an unreal reverb effect to it. If you've figured out that Mr. Purdy is dead and Mrs. Purdy is more than a little crazy… well, give yourself no points, because it's pretty obvious.

The poor corpse just planted was Mr. Stevens, one of her boarders. The remaining tenants are Willie (Mikel Adams, who also wrote the script), a perpetual drunkard; Mr. Balzac (Michael Berryman in a cravat), a hungry and frustrated novelist; Vanya (former Bond girl Martine Beswick), the resident New Age mystic; and Tina (Debra Lamb), the mute ballerina who dances all over the house. It's a jolly bunch, who are more than a little disconcerted by Mr. Stevens' abrupt "departure." And well they should be, because part of Mrs. Purdy's standard rental agreement is that her boarders sign over to her their maintenance checks. (I missed one other resident—Hans (Sam Menning), the skinny rag-clad cannibal chained to a wall in the basement, but I don't know if he's an official tenant.)

In fact, according to Mr. Potts (Arte Johnson), the Social Security caseworker who starts nosing about in Stevens' disappearance, there are at least fourteen other checks she's collecting monthly for those who've "moved on." Vanya also starts causing trouble, having "visions" of the deceased Mr. Stevens, and insists on having a séance with all of the residents, including the newcomers Mr. and Mrs. Wilson (Bert Remsen and Virginia Mayo), who are quite freaked out by the spectacle. Mr. Wilson, refreshingly, is completely sane. Mrs. Wilson, on the other hand, appears to believe that she's on a first-name basis with the cream of Hollywood royalty. The general character of the boarding house community doesn't seem to be the kind of place that Zsa-Zsa or the Matthaus would drop in to visit, so they decide to cut their contract short and move. Wanna lay bets on whether they make it out the front door?

With the Social Security snoop not giving up, grave portents and offers of exorcism from Vanya, and a nosy neighbor (Yvette Vickers) complaining at the smell coming from the Purdy backyard, Mrs. Purdy starts getting desperate and ramping up her efforts to do in anyone with suspicions. Mysteriously, we never see Mrs. Purdy directly kill anyone; we just get flashes of someone done up in a dress Marine uniform. Could Mr. Purdy still be alive? Or could someone else be committing the actual murders?

It's a slight movie, which fortunately tempers its derivative nature with lightheartedness. Balzac has a peephole into Tina's room, which serves him well when she gets her frequent urges to dance around her room topless. Watching Michael Berryman press his face against a wall and blink excitedly through a peephole is a form of entertainment all to itself. (He's also got a peephole into Mrs. Purdy's room. Yes, that's fully as horrifying as you might think.) There's also a low-key running gag about how Willie the drunk keeps avoiding death —either because his pickled guts have built up such a resistance that he's immune to poison, or because he believes that Hans in the basement is an hallucination and offers him a friendly drink. And of course there's Tina, who will dance with, around, and against anybody at all with a combination of ballet and stripshow grind.

I had a sneaking suspicion that credited director Gary Graver was actually schlockmeister supreme Fred Olen Ray under a pseudonym, merely based on the names in the cast; aside from the headliners already mentioned, the cast features small roles for other Ray regulars like Hoke Howell and Robert Quarry. In this I proved close, but misguided; Graver is indeed a real person, who has been cinematographer on close to thirty of Ray's films, explaining both his access to Ray's habitual cast and the visual similarities. (Graver is also otherwise known as porn director Robert McCallum, credited with over seventy-five adult films. This is a very busy man.)

I can't in good conscience give this movie a high recommendation, but I can credit it with not doing too much damage to my psyche (aside from that inflicted by seeing Karen Black show waaaaay too much leg—can anything erase that image from my memory?). Of course, my movie-watching brain is approaching a state not unlike that of Willie's ironbound innards, capable of shrugging off films that might kill a normal person. So, as always, consider the source.

Some Notable Totables:
- body count: 6
- breasts: 2
- explosions: 0
- ominous thunderstorms: 2
- actors who've appeared on *Star Trek*: 2
  - Michael Berryman (Balzac) played "Starfleet Display Officer" (under tons of latex) in *Star Trek 4*, and "Captain Rixx" (under blue makeup) in the *TNG* episode "Conspiracy"
  - Bert Remsen (Mr. Wilson) played "Kubus" in the *DS9* episode "The Collaborator"

MINDWARP (1990)

In the future life will be a dream. And reality, a nightmare.

aka *Brainslasher*, aka *Dream System*

- Directed by Steve Barnett
- Written by "Henry Dominick" (John D. Brancato and Michael Ferris)
- Starring Bruce Campbell, Angus Scrimm, Marta Alicia, Elizabeth Kent and Mary Becker
- Produced by Christopher Webster
- Executive produced by Norman and Steven Jacobs

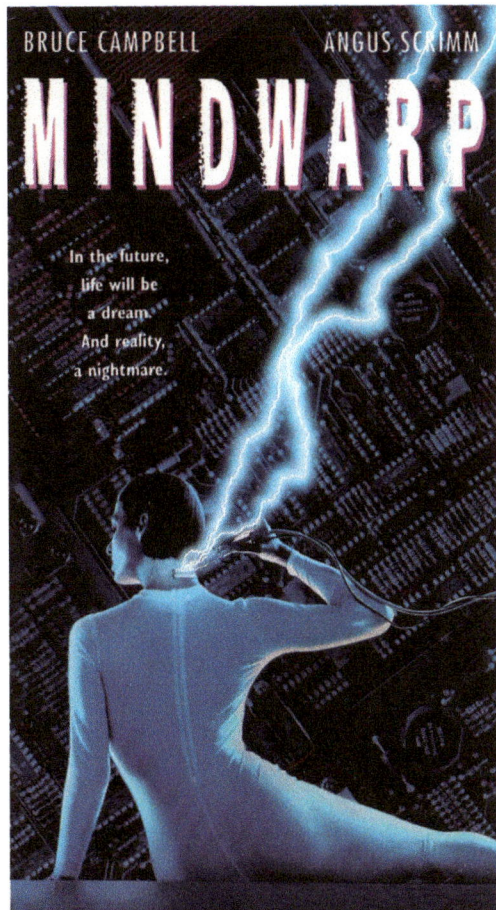

Years ago, when I was a single student, there was a pizza-and-video store across the parking lot from my apartment complex. Not even across the road; just across the parking lot. Given my general laziness, there were plenty of days when I came home from school, looked at the boring food in my cupboard, and then went to the student paper to get the "Personal Pepperoni Pizza for $1.99" coupon, or even the one that gave me a large one-topping for just over five bucks. And off across the parking lot I scampered.

And, because the store featured pizza and videos, there was nothing better to do while waiting for my pizza than browse the video boxes. Crafty business model, that. And since it was a small collection with absolutely no rotation (the powers-that-be had determined that this outlet would be closing at the end of the school year, so no new titles were brought in), I sometimes ended up taking home the same movie several times.

I think I took home *Mindwarp* six times. I couldn't help it; something about the movie kept pulling me back to it.

In general terms it's a post-apocalyptic movie, but if you want a more precise sub-genre, it's a "pre-*Matrix*" movie. Once the world blew itself up (cue stock nuclear test footage), people went underground and found something better than reality: Infinisynth, an individualized virtual reality setup that plugs into the back of your neck via a nine-pin connection (just imagine the superior bandwidth if they had used USB!). It's the complete solution for the suckiness of reality, and it works fine for everyone…

…Except Judy (Marta Alicia), a young hothead with an incurable lust for "reality." Somehow, the virtual stuff doesn't satisfy her, and she's tired of having her physical world bounded by a 9'x9' room shared with her mother (Mary Becker), who only unplugs from her private reality for biological imperatives like eating green nutrient glop and going potty. She also wonders desperately what happened to her father, who disappeared suddenly years ago; when the rest of the family unplugged one day, he was simply gone.

Judy spends most of her plugged-in time battling wits with the SysOp, a shadowy figure who forcefully tries to get her to conform. Finally, in an effort to wake someone else up, Judy finds a way to enter her mother's simulation (singing in an opera—boy, give some people unlimited fantasies and look what lame stuff they come up with) and knocks her off the stage in the middle of her performance. When Judy unplugs, she finds out to her horror that Mom is really and truly dead. Then two black-helmeted soldiers enter, wrestle Judy into a cloth bag, drug her… and when she wakes up, she's Outside.

Kudos to the producers for going with something other than the standard Southern Utah/ Australian Outback/ Bronson Canyon-lookalike post-apocalyptic setting. Instead, it's the flat ashen grayness of the stamp sand dumping grounds outside of Gay, Michigan—and unlike the sweltering desert we normally see, it's damnably cold. And the only signs of civilization she finds are three crucified skeletons, one of whom has a nine-pinned jack dangling from his desiccated neck.

But she's not quite alone, as she discovers when she almost falls down a sinkhole; the "Samaritans" who rescue her are actually cannibal mutants—driving a tractor! They're decked out in the best post-nuke manner, all car parts and military surplus, and their faces are all gnarly and pocked. (The makeup effects are by KNB EFX, a makeup FX house which built an impressive resume in B-movies through the '80s, and even though a large number of the mutants we see throughout the movie are done with over-the-head masks, they still look cool.) She would be the main course for lunch if it weren't for a fur-bedecked trapper who rescues her with a combination of crossbow bolts and broadsword fighting. He's quite possibly the last unmutated man on earth… and he's Bruce Campbell. Rock on.

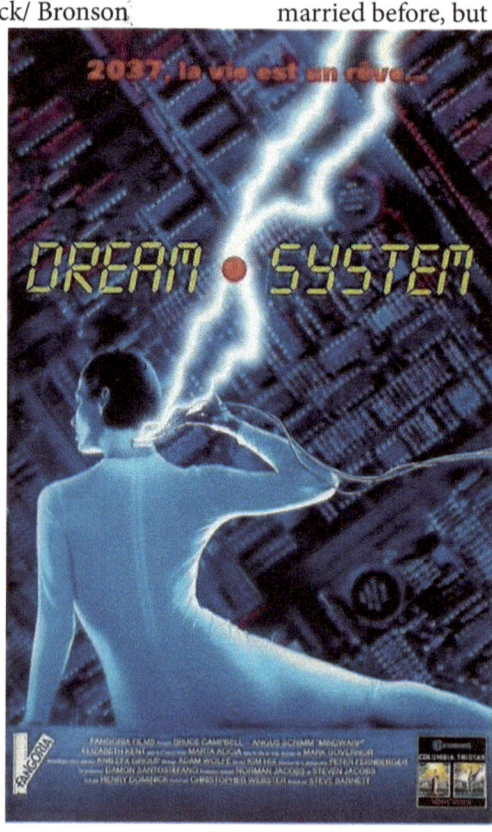

His name is Stover, and he takes her back to his one-room cabin and starts teaching her how to survive in this barren, re-Ice Aged world. He shows her how to avoid the mutants, "crawlers," who inhabit the landfills beneath the radioactive Badlands where he found her. And naturally, since they're the last two of their kind, they teach each other about This Thing Called Love. (Well, he didn't need much teaching; he had been married before, but his wife died. And Judy's not too naive, having "used" the Infinisynth simulations many times.)

That's when the crawlers decide to take them down, digging a tunnel right under Stover's cabin and dragging them off to their underground domain, which is where things start getting really interesting. Stover is hauled off and forced to mine the landfill for usable junk, and Judy is taken to Cornelia (Elizabeth Kent), the consort of the Crawler's leader: the Seer. Cornelia gets her dander up that Judy's got no radiation sores or anything, and is about to do her in out of jealousy, but the Seer has other plans. He's a well-spoken former "inworlder" himself, now bedecked in a mask decorated with the eyes he plucks from those he sacrifices in the community's sacramental ceremony, which purees the victim into a gory drink that all consume in cups made from human crania.

Oh, and just to make matters worse, the Seer is Judy's long-lost, exiled father—and even worse than that, it's Angus "*Phantasm*" Scrimm!

The underground is where this movie

really shines; not only is it gory, but it's a convincingly gritty, caked-with-filth gore. There's a perverse, mealy grime to everything that I hadn't seen since the sets of *The Texas Chainsaw Massacre 2* (1986—silly movie, but terrific art direction) and wouldn't see again until the advent of "torture porn." You have to respect creative visual nightmare fodder here, from the Seer's pointy-fingered eyeball-plucking gloves to brain-devouring minnows to the lobotomized "bloaters" placidly churning out huge broods of mutant infants. In other words, my wife is really glad she didn't watch this with me.

And there are nice bits of conceptual creativity here, too, like the discussion between Stover and Judy on the concept of "God," which she can't take seriously thanks to her upbringing in a plastic reality, or the fact that the crucified corpses were really put up there as a sign of respect to protect them from the Crawlers that could have tunneled up underneath a grave and eaten them. And the Seer's explanation of the purpose of these sacramental rites he's initiated among the crawlers make a strange sort of sense if you listen to him long enough. Screenwriters John Broncato and Michael Ferris (here both under the pseudonym "Henry Dominick") obviously have affection for post-apocalyptic settings, as evidenced by their partnership later on *Terminator 3: Rise of the Machines* (2003) and *Terminator: Salvation* (2009).

On the other hand, there are throwaway absurdities, like the bathrobe and granny glasses that Judy's mother wears in their 9'x9' room, or the fact that there doesn't seem to be much for the Crawlers to eat except each other (I don't care how much you loved *Soylent Green* (1973), it's just not a sustainable food economy). But somehow, when a bloody and minnow-crazed Bruce Campbell gets to lurch around the murky sets doing his "I'm crazed Bruce Campbell!" shtick, it really doesn't seem so bad.

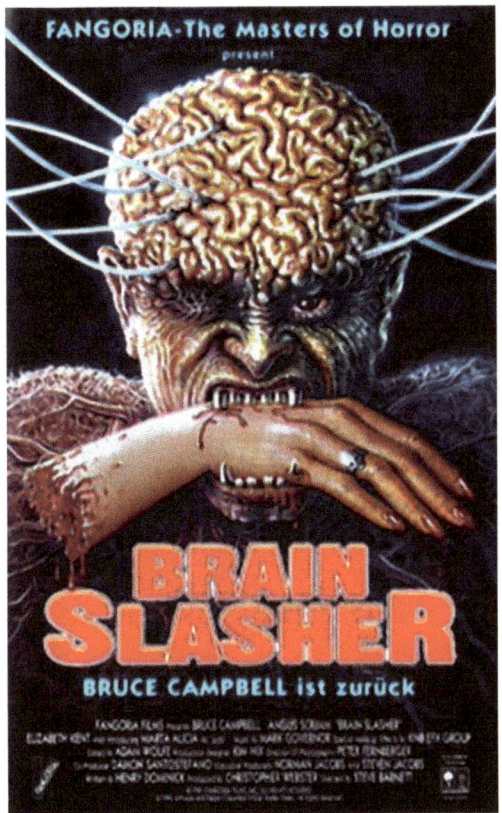

In fact, it seems great. Well, maybe not great. But between the cast, the setting, the costumes, and the gore, I've always been amazed that *Mindwarp* hasn't attracted more of a cult following (especially when compared to the other production released under the Fangoria Films label in that same period, *Severed Ties* (1992)). When I call something a "great B-movie," *Mindwarp* is the standard of comparison I use.

Some Notable Totables:
- body count: 15
- breasts: 0
- explosions: 2
- dream sequences: ain't going there
- ominous thunderstorms: 0
- actors who've appeared on *Star Trek*: 0

ROBOT NINJA (1990)

THE ULTIMATE SUPER-HERO OF THE FUTURE HAS ARRIVED!

- *Produced, written and directed by J.R. Bookwalter*
- *Starring Michael Todd, Bogdan Pecic, Maria Markovic, Floyd Ewing Jr., Burt Ward and Linnea Quigley*
- *Executive produced by David DeCoteau*

You should recognize the name of producer/writer/ director J.R. Bookwalter from the review of *The Dead Next Door* (1989) on page 124. Among the people who sat up and took notice of that Super-8mm zombie epic was director David DeCoteau, who had with several films (*Dreamaniac* (1986), *Nightmare Sisters* (1987), *Creepozoids* (1987), *Sorority Babes in the Slimeball Bowl-O-Rama* (1988), *Dr. Alien* (1989)) established himself as a fixture in low-budget genre flicks through the middle of the '80s. Those pictures had been directed as work-for-hire expressly for distribution by Charles Band, the prolific B-movie producer whose Empire Pictures and Full Moon Entertainment provided prodigious amounts of genre product through the '80s and '90s. Toward the end of the '80s, DeCoteau decided to branch out into producing and start his own line of direct-to-video cheapies under the label of Cinema Home Video. He brought Bookwalter on board to crank out the made-to-order product, and functioned as executive producer on Bookwalter's next project: *Robot Ninja*.

Robot Ninja was shot on 16mm (a step up from the Super-8 used on *The Dead Next Door*), but with a budget of only $15,000—which seems impossibly low until you realize that subsequent Cinema Home Video titles Bookwalter would direct (such as *Zombie Cop* (1991), *Humanoids From Atlantis* (1992) and *Kingdom of the Vampire* (1991), the latter of which is reviewed on page 169) had budgets reduced by a full decimal point.

Robot Ninja is a fanboy response to comics, just as *The Dead Next Door* was a fanboy response to Romero's zombie movies. Unfortunately, it's not as successful a movie as Bookwalter's first one. To tell the truth, it's got a pretty high suckiness quotient; it plays just like the movie version of a little independent black-&-white comic book.

Lenny Miller (Michael Todd) is a comic book creator who's hit the big time. His series, *Robot Ninja*, is one of the big bestsellers, and that's created one of his worst headaches: it's been translated to TV, and the series intentionally harks back to the campiness of old *Batman* TV show, despite the grittiness of the comic. (We get to see his pubisher Stanley Kane (Burt Ward, "Robin" of said *Batman* show) and his secretary (scream queen Linnea Quigley) chuckling away as they watch an episode on TV.)

Unfortunately, the publisher has complete control in this arena, so Lenny can only grit his teeth and bear it. I found that kind of puzzling, given that the 1990 release date puts this movie's production right in the middle of the first wave of creator-owned characters that followed the success of *Teenage Mutant Ninja Turtles*, a fact explicitly referenced here in the script. So how did the publisher manage to get so much control?

After whining at the TV production facility (the new darling of Must-See TV is produced in Ridgway, Ohio?), Lenny drives home, only to encounter along the way a phenomenally ill-conceived rape. I mean on the part of the rapists. Two guys (James L. Edwards and Bill Morrison), lead by heterodyke Sanchez (Maria Markovic), grab a couple and throw them in their van right outside a restaurant, then drive them off somewhere and rape them. Lenny stumbles onto the scene and tries to play the hero; he gets roughed up and left for dead. (The guy and girl are also left for dead, the big difference being that they actually *are* dead.)

Recovering rather easily, Lenny decides that these events would make a good storyline for *Robot Ninja*, and draws it. Time for a sidenote on the artwork, because I have to at some point: David Lange did the art (and gets a credit for creating the character), and what he's produced is exactly what you'd expect from an independently-published black-&-white comic book in the late '80s. In other words, it's pretty amateurish, with very little sense of perspective, anatomy, or any of those other basics. It's been a while since I've had my hand in the comic-illustration field, but I coulda whupped this fella hands down when I was trying to make a go of it. (And I gave up because I wasn't good enough to do it for real.) He's gotten better since (for a while, Bookwalter's Tempe Entertainment was distributing copies of his self-published series *Sybil War* from 1999), but at this stage of the game he was just another generic not-ready-for-prime-time self-taught wanna-be. The point is not to rag on Lange, but to state that it's hard to accept Miller being the "hottest thing" on the market when the art we see so blatantly contradicts this.

Anyway. When Lenny turns in the rape storyline, Kane chides him for not going with their agreed-upon plan to make the comic more an adaptation of the TV series, rejects the artwork, and threatens not to renew his contract. Between this rejection and seeing on the news that there's been another rape assault (bringing the total up to five attacks), Lenny decides instead to become the Robot Ninja for real.

And this is where I've got real problems. Obviously we're going for something in the vein of the dark, Batmanesque vigilantes who all got a big boost since Frank Miller gave the world the graphic novel *Batman: The Dark Knight Returns* in 1987. True to form, there's usually an inciting incident that drives the tortured hero to don a getup and patrol the night streets for evildoers. In this case, the incident was supposedly the double rape-murder, even though Lenny knew neither of the victims. Okay, I thought, that's a misstep not having him be emotionally attached to the victims, but not a fatal error. But then it turns out that Lenny's almost happy to have had the whole thing happen, just for the story fodder. It's only when his artwork is rejected that he decides to put on a costume. Anyone besides me find that to be a less-than-compelling motivation, and not terribly sympathetic to boot?

Lenny persuades his reluctant friend, "inventor" Dr. Goodknight (Bogdan Pecic), to create the suit for him; "I figure the costume alone'll freak 'em out," he says. It's like "Criminals are a superstitious, cowardly lot," but dumber. But here's the next problem. Raise your hand if you'd be freaked by someone in a somber, dangerous costume in a dark alley. All right, that's most of you. Now keep your hand up if you'd be as frightened once you realized that it was a Batman costume. Nah, you'd assume he was off to a masquerade or a supermarket opening or something, not out on the prowl fighting crime. Same thing if you met a costumed crimefighter dressed exactly like the campy superhero on TV Wednesdays at 8pm. Pop-culture familiarity's going to work against the whole fear response.

Goodknight macgyvers together some stuff from the hardware store based on Lenny's drawings, and at the end of the day, Ta-dah! Lenny has in a suit appropriate for a cosplay convention appearance. Which leads to another question: what, exactly, are the Robot Ninja's powers? ("Robot Ninja" is at best a cyborg, being shown in both the comics and the TV series as a guy in a black suit and metallic mask.) Lenny certainly seems pleased with the suit and its protection, but frankly, the only thing it has going for it is a pair of claw-blades extending from one wrist. That, and a metallic mask with a red visor and a voice modulator. In other words, it looks like Lenny's bringing a knife to a gunfight.

Lenny goes off into the night in his Camaro, looking for trouble, and discovers the same vanful of criminals knocking over a suburban video store. (Because, you know, video stores just rake in the dough. Plus you could steal a tape or two.) Lenny manages to get in the way of the getaway and slash a rapist to death, but not before the thugs' twelve-year-old hostage gets knocked to the ground and dies (!) from hitting his head on the pavement.

So Robot Ninja's being blamed for the kid's death as well as the thief's, and Goodknight goes ballistic on Lenny the next day. (Um, Goodknight, you knew he wanted to play superhero, and the only weapon you gave him was twin ten-inch blades. You thought maybe he'd hit with the flat?)

But that doesn't stop Lenny from going out again the next night. As far as he's concerned, hunting down and killing these rapists is the most exhilarating way to spend a weeknight. He drives out again, hits the right place at the right time (again), meets Sanchez and her new half-dozen thugs—and gets the robotic snot beaten out of him. Even without shooting him (which, you have to admit, is what any half-decent gangbanger would have done in the first five seconds), they overpower him and, with only a couple of casualties on their side, beat dents into his mask; Sanchez also carves a deep hole into his forearm. It's only through the gangbangers' own stupidity (they decide to take him home to finish off, instead of doing him in right there) that he manages to get away, taking a couple of bullets in the process.

Something to be said about the conceits of the fight scenes: in between his escapades, Lenny chronicles his encounters in comic-book form. During the fights, there are edited-in comic panels that mirror the combat going on. It's a nifty idea, in theory… except that the real-life fight choreography is substandard, and so is the art, so that in switching back and forth, you're only reminded that both are pretty lame.

Being smarter than the average bear, Sanchez easily follows Lenny's car back to Goodknight's place; she immediately assumes that Goodknight is in fact Robot Ninja, and therefore they plan to come back in the morning and do some damage. Goodknight's not actually home when Lenny gets there, though, so Lenny remove the bullets on his own using Goodknight's tools and does a little bit of reparative surgery on himself. For instance, he takes a length of rubber tubing and inserts it into the bloody gap in his forearm to replace a severed vein, then shoves a metal plate under the edges of the skin to close the wound.

Which is just cool enough to be really, really annoying. Because if they did anything with this idea—that Lenny is in a sense becoming a real robot (or cyborg)—then the movie would experience a quantum leap forward in coolness. Is Lenny truly becoming the Robot Ninja?

Well, it never comes up again, so let's just pretend the scene didn't exist. And remember, we wouldn't know if Lenny's becoming like the fictional Robot Ninja anyway, because we have no idea of the Robot Ninja's powers anyway.

So. While Lenny's home drawing with his bad hand and sleeping the night off, Goodknight comes home to his place and gets accosted by Sanchez and her little helper. Miffed that he's only the techie, not the actual guy in a suit, they blow his brains out and leave him strung up from the ceiling struts for Lenny to find when he limps in that night, a note attached to the corpse instructing Robot Ninja to meet them in the junkyard.

Sooner or later I ought to mention the police officer. Apparently in Ridgway, Ohio, there are all of two cops, and one is Officer Hickox (Floyd Ewing Jr.). Since Ewing also played an ex-cop named Hickox in the previous year's *Skinned Alive* (produced, though not directed, by Bookwalter), I can only assume that the character cleaned up his life and got back on the force. He spends most of the running time here showing up too late to catch the bad guys, arriving in time to find bodies and look around morosely. Except for the time that he got to Lenny's apartment before Lenny got home from Goodknight's, when means he showed up too early and looked at the locked door morosely.

And naturally, he finds Goodknight's body and the note about the junkyard too late, so Robot Ninja takes on the baddies alone armed only with his blades, his red visor (which gives him night vision, via the trick of filming his POV shots during daylight through a red filter), and enough painkillers that he could probably impersonate Pacino in *Scarface* (1983). There's some ass-kicking and face-slashing, Robot Ninja vanquishes the last of the bad guys, and then goes home and blows his own brains out. Just in time for Hickox to arrive too late and gaze on the corpse morosely.

Oh, and the final unfinished issue of the *Robot Ninja* comic book is published and becomes a bestseller. The end.

It's really not that inspiring a movie; the dialogue is pedestrian, and the acting rarely rises to community theater standards. And it's pretty generic as comic book stories go. As I mentioned way back at the beginning, it reminds me of nothing so much as all the half-baked black-&-white limited series that were self-published at the tail end of the '80s by a bunch of fanboys who hoped that the *Teenage Mutant Ninja Turtles* lightning would strike again.

Nevertheless, remember that J.R. Bookwalter is really one of the progenitors of the microbudget film movement. It's easy to critique now, but back in the day there wasn't a thriving internet community supporting pocket-change filmmakers. He may have stumbled while making this movie, but one might say that it is only by standing on his prone figure that today's microbudgeters have reached as high. (That's absolutely the worst metaphor I've come up with in ages.)

And as I pointed out, there were some good ideas here, even though they were never developed. The fight scenes intercut with comic panels (with a slight intimation that maybe fighting crime isn't quite as easy as they make it look in the funnypages), the concept of becoming a makeshift cyborg... Both still have potential.

In fact, since somehow Bookwalter's early flicks are now fodder for the second generation of microbudget filmmakers to remake (a topic we'll cover in greater depth when we get to *Kingdom of the Vampire*), what I'd really like to see is a couple of the current generation of extra-low-budget action filmmakers draw inspiration from Grandpa Bookwalter's *Robot Ninja* and make their own costumed cyborg crimefighter flick, one that plays up those ideas and brings the energy level of the fight choreography up to cartoony levels (in a good sense).

Some Notable Totables:
- body count: 13
- breasts: 0
- explosions: 0
- dream sequences: 2
- ominous thunderstorms: 0
- actors who've appeared on *Star Trek*: 0

ROBOT NINJA: Writer-Director J.R. Bookwalter's Comments

"Be careful what you wish for," as the saying goes. After being chained to the same movie for four long years, I was eager to spread my wings and fly away to something—anything!—else. My journey to complete *The Dead Next Door* had landed me in Hollyweird, California, where I went from a mentor whose star was rising to one whose work was barely noticed outside of B-movie circles. But at the time, I didn't care. I had initially set out to produce a couple films for friends, but when my new benefactor lost interest in them, I salvaged any kind of deal I could by making *Robot Ninja*... and no, to set the record straight, that was not my title. At the time, I didn't want to deign to do any of my own projects for a paltry $15,000 budget, so when said benefactor blurted out, "I have this title: *Robot Ninja*," I didn't hesitate to say yes, even as one half of my brain was screaming, "Noooooo!"

That said, I've always risen to any challenge put before me, and truth be told, I was just happy to have somebody willing to hire me to make any movie at that point, just to get away from the specter of *The Dead Next Door*. It was actually an exciting time to be making a movie, with Tim Burton's *Batman* about to hit theatres and here we were, making our own superhero movie. But as it turns out, neither one of them would actually be very fulfilling experiences. Hey, it happens.

Robot Ninja was conceived on a Greyhound bus from Los Angeles back to Akron, Ohio. I had come to L.A. with cohort David Lange a couple months earlier just for fun (he was working on the ill-fated *Murder Weapon* with our mutual friend David Barton) and wound up staying to score and do post sound on *Dead*. Anyway, a three-day bus trip back to Ohio is no kind of fun, and I blame that trip for a lot of the negative energy on screen in *Robot Ninja*. It was the same bus trip that spawned the character of "Hubert Goodknight," the garage inventor in *Robot Ninja*, because it was the name of one of the bus drivers. (Likewise, the "female thug" Gody Sanchez was the manager of a hardware store in Pasadena, California... I used to collect amusing names as a hobby to use in these early movies.)

Still, on a positive note, we were shooting and editing in 16mm for the first time and it was quite a thrill to get to do another movie so soon after (finally) putting the first one to bed (*The Dead Next Door* was finished in March or April, 1989 and we were shooting *Robot Ninja* by June). The biggest lesson I learned from that movie was not to do everything myself—I went a little "power mad" after *The Dead Next Door* and insisted on producing it completely alone on top of writing, directing, editing, composing and "performing" the music score, doing squibs and even doing a cameo. It was too much, and the movie suffered as a result.

While it's apparent to anyone who watches it, I actually didn't realize just how bad *Robot Ninja* was until I sat down to watch the VHS for the first time after opening the shrink wrap. I guess doing so much of the post work had insulated me from realizing it was a stinker, but there was no denying it. I don't think I've sat through the entire movie again since that fateful day in early 1990... with the possible exception of a German-dubbed DVD that came out years ago, which is infinitely more entertaining since you don't know what the (poorly-written) dialogue is.

Robot Ninja was my sophomore slump, even though it technically came out months before

The Dead Next Door, which thankfully made most people forget about *Robot Ninja*. But it was a slump that would last another few years, a "creative curse" that was only finally broken by *Ozone* in 1994.

SOLAR CRISIS (1990)

IN THE YEAR 2050, THE BATTLE TO SAVE THE EARTH WILL BE FOUGHT ON THE SUN.

- Directed by "Alan Smithee" (Richard C. Serafian)
- Written by Joe Gannon and Crispan Bolt, based on the novel by Takeshi Kawata
- Starring Tim Matheson, Charlton Heston, Peter Boyle, Annabel Schofield, Corin Nemec and Jack Palance
- Produced by Richard Edlund, James Nelson and Morris Morishima
- Executive produced by Furuoka Hideto, Takeshi Kawata and Takehito Sademura

Solar Crisis has the dubious honor of being the most expensive movie reviewed in this book. $55 million isn't exactly chump change; I wouldn't turn up my nose at it if it were thrown at me. And back in 1990, it was even more money in a movie industry yet to really feel the pressure of the coming rampant production inflation. (Some figures for perspective: The top-grossing movie of 1990, *Home Alone*, cost $15 million. The Academy Award winner for Best Picture, *Dances With Wolves*, cost $15 million. The biggest budget of any of the year's top ten grossing features was $70 million for *Die Hard 2*, and the average budget for the top ten was a hair over $30 million.) With a budget of $55 million, then, *Solar Crisis* certainly lost someone a lot of money when it was given a truncated theatrical release and then dumped to video. In fact, for the longest time I believed it had *no* theatrical release, until someone volunteered to me that he had indeed seen it on the big screen.

It's easy to see where the money went: extensive space station and spaceship sets, beautifully-done external space shots (both of which incorporated production design by Syd Mead), complex desert location shoots, and a fair stable of name actors. It's just as easy to see why it gained no fans upon theatrical release, and why director Richard Serafian (who had certainly never shied away from less-than-stellar projects) went so far as to remove his name from it. In a word, it stinks.

A Japanese/American co-production instigated and financed by the Japanese half, *Solar Crisis* is based on a novel by Takeshi Kawata. I'm betting it's a pretty thick novel. And every last bit of it is here. Unlike some other more successful novel-to-screen adaptations of recent years (like, say, The *Lord of the Rings* trilogy), nobody involved in the production seemed to care about adapting it, i.e., changing it in ways designed to take advantages of the strengths of the cinematic medium. Instead, one gets the impression after watching *Solar Crisis* that someone has just read the entire damned novel to you in under two hours. It's a huge collection of subplots composed largely of expository speeches, rendered in some of the clunkiest dialogue ever forced on an actor.

As explained in not one but two screen crawls (complete with a narrator to read them for you), the sun has begun acting up in the middle of the 21st century, and the Earth is overheated and parched. Now some predict a dangerous solar flare of huge proportions, possibly powerful enough to end life on Earth entirely. So a plan has been put together to send the spaceship Helios to the far side of the sun, armed with an antimatter bomb to trigger a solar flare far from the Earth and defuse the situation.

Our mission commander is Captain Kelso (Tim Matheson, probably best known for his recurring role on TV's *The West Wing*), a man troubled by his past, notably the death of his wife—so much so that he neglects his teenage son Mike (Corin Nemec, who went on to TV's *Parker Lewis Can't Lose* and *Stargate SG-1* and a metric crapload of Sci-Fi Channel Originals), now enrolled in a military academy. How do we know this? Why, his Executive Officer, Commander Borg (Dorian Harewood) tells the crew all about it, in a scene in which every crewmember tells all about himself and explains the entire mission to other crewmembers who already know what the mission is. Then, when Borg leaves the scene, some other crewmember takes it upon himself to explain the competitive backstory between Kelso and Borg. We've also got a bio-genetically enhanced crewmember, Alex Noffe (Annabel Schofield), and a character who hits on other characters (as he cheerfully explains), and Dr. Minami (Tetsuya Bessho), who helped design the smart bomb they're using and fully expects to sacrifice himself for the mission.

Ah, the smart bomb. I don't know why, but somebody decided that a bomb containing five tons of antimatter needs to have artificial intelligence. It's named Freddy (voice of Paul Williams—yes, the singer/songwriter who worked with the Muppets), and it's slightly neurotic. I waited all movie for someone to attempt to teach it phenomenology;* in this, as in so many things, I was disappointed. I also don't understand how complicated it must be to pilot a bomb into the sun from close orbit—are you expecting to miss or something?—but the plan calls for an expendable pilot to go along, just in case something goes wrong with Freddy and he finds he just can't manage to fall down an inescapable gravity well.

Back on Earth, meanwhile, there's an evil corporation called IXL which owns just about all of the world, and has its eye on the remainder. In fact, from a long expository dialogue sequence by corporate hard-ass Teague (Peter Boyle of *Young Frankenstein* (1974) and TV's *Everybody Loves Raymond*), icy yes-woman Claire (Brenda Bakke), and naively moral scientist Dr. Haas (Paul Koslo), we learn two things: 1) IXL can make a killing on futures if the Helios mission fails, and 2) Peter Boyle just cannot play a corporate hard-ass. Teague sets things in motion for the Helios mission to be sabotaged by a blond Frank Sagarino-lookalike (never caught his name, so I don't know what actor he was).

But wait! In yet another corner of the rich tapestry of our plot, we have Captain Kelso's father, Admiral Kelso (Charlton Heston), who berates Kelso for ignoring Mike to the point that Mike has stolen an aircraft and gone AWOL from the academy. Unknown to them, Mike has crash-landed said aircraft in the desert, where it promptly exploded once he was out; he manages to stumble across a crazy desert hermit (Jack Palance), who has

---

* That's a reference to John Carpenter's first film, *Dark Star* (1974). If you don't get the joke you really shouldn't admit it.

a long and complicated backstory himself, but jeez louise, I'm getting really tired of shovelfuls of exposition by this point. Let me do something for you that the production team never did for me: let me attempt to summarize.

Kelso and Alex develop the least believable Instant Attraction for each other in cinematic history (and considering the movies I've seen, you should take that claim seriously). But Alex is soon compromised before their ship leaves spacedock, as the Fake Zagarino sedates her in her shower and uses a laser to… um… I dunno. It beams in her eye, and has something to do with her being bio-enhanced, and basically programs her to sabotage the mission.

Meanwhile, Admiral Kelso has co-opted far more military equipment and manpower than he can probably justify to find his missing grandson.

Meanwhile, Teague leaves the still-protesting Dr. Haas in the desert to die.

Meanwhile, hermit Palance tries to help Mike get to Red Sands so he can catch a shuttle up to the space station to say goodbye to his dad.

Meanwhile, Alex starts having a breakdown aboard the station, thanks to her new programming.

Meanwhile, we're given tons of exposition on the formation of sunspots and possible repercussions (heat sufficient to turn the surface of the Earth to glass would only inflict 50% casualties? You mean we're going to be able to grow crops in the glass or something?) and the electromagnetic shielding on the ship. We're also given some moments of false tension when a ship docking almost goes wrong but not quite; after all, exposition is plenty exciting, but some people might want a change of pace, right?

Meanwhile, Dr. Haas is rescued in the desert (by Michael Berryman, of all people) and taken to a desert bar which just happens to be where Mike and the hermit end up.

Meanwhile, IXL spooks are searching for Haas, and end up also looking for Mike.

Meanwhile, Heston gives a big speech about possibly losing his son and his grandson at the same time, and how he never did all those things he always wanted to, etc.

Meanwhile meanwhile meanwhile…

Of the many problems here, the most consistent is what screenwriters call "on-the-nose" dialogue. People in the real world don't walk into a room and immediately explain what's bothering them and what they need while recapping the entire situation even though their companion already knows it. Yet every character here does that, explaining who they are and why they do what they do at every conceivable opportunity. We don't have time for clever or natural dialogue here; how the hell else do you expect to touch on every single subplot and theme in an bazillion-page novel in 111 minutes?

Every once in a while, there's a glimmer of hope for the movie. At one point, some part of the Helios' engine gets stuck, and Kelso has to choose a crewmember for a guaranteed suicide mission; then he forces himself to listen over the intercom as the crewmember burns up with radiation while he repairs the problem. But such rare moments of honest drama are defused by compensatory scenes such as Teague and the captive Mike Kelso, discussing the applicability of the prophecies of

Nostradamus to the current crisis. And the entire project becomes a write-off when Mike looks at a television showing continuous images of famine, rioting, and other signs of discord and deprivation all over the world, and say, "This solar crisis has brought the whole world together." The mind boggles.

Eventually, of course, it all works out for the best: it ends. The movie, I mean, not the world. Though the latter might not be a bad thing, if it's what it took to bring about the former.

Some Notable Totables:
- body count: 8
- breasts: 2
- explosions: 6
- ominous thunderstorms: 1
- actors who've appeared on *Star Trek*: 11
  - Dan Shor ("Harvard") played the Ferengi "Dr. Arridor" in the *TNG* episode "The Price and the *Voyager* episode "False Profits"
  - Brenda Bakke ("Claire") played "Rivan" in the *TNG* episode "Justice"
  - Paul Williams (the voice of Freddy) played "Koru" in the *Voyager* episode "Virtuoso"
  - Michael Berryman ("Matthew") played "Starfleet Display Officer" (under tons of latex) in *Star Trek 4,* and "Captain Rixx" (under blue makeup) in the *TNG* episode "Conspiracy"
  - Roy Jenson ("Bartender") played "Cloud William" in the classic episode "The Omega Glory"
  - Jimmie F. Skaggs ("Biker") played "Glinn Boheeka" in the *DS9* episode "The Wire"
  - Paul Carr ("IXL Executive #2") played "Lt. Lee Kelso" in the classic episode "Where No Man Has Gone Before"
  - Louie Elias ("IXL Man #4") played "Technician #1" in the original episode "And a Little Child Shall Lead" and "Troglodyte #2" in "The Cloud Minders"
  - Terrence Beasor (the narrator) has done voiceover work in most of the *Star Trek* films and the modern series
  - John Deadrick ("Bandit"), aka Vince Deadrick, played "Matthews" in the original episode "What Are Little Girls Made Of?", "Romulan crewman" in the original episode "Balance of Terror," and was the stunt coordinator on *Enterprise*
  - Eurlyne Epper ("Bandit") did stunts in *Insurrection*

The INVISIBLE MANIAC (1990)

The new physics professor has a disappearing act that's a real scream.

aka *The Invisible Sex Maniac*

- *Written and directed by "Rif Coogan" (Adam Rifkin)*
- *Starring Noel Peters, Shannon Wilsey, Melissa Moore, Stella Blalack and Robert R. Ross Jr.*
- *Produced by Anthony Marks*

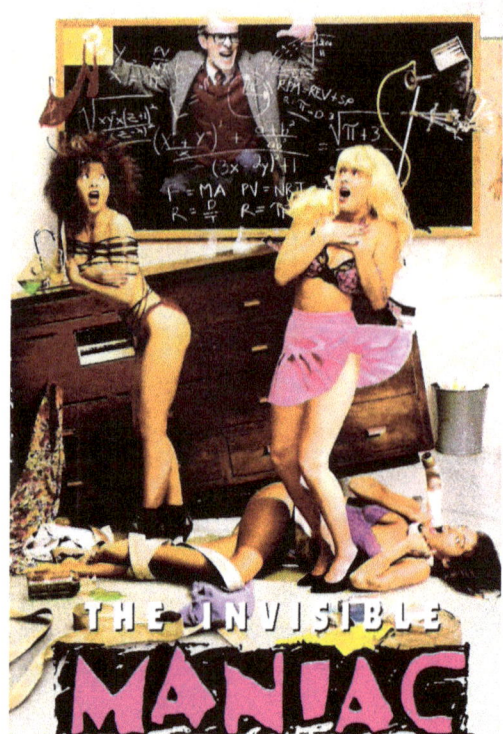

It's been said before, and by people much smarter than me, that a failed comedy is about the most pathetic thing in the universe. A bad action or horror or sci-fi movie can be inadvertently funny, but if a movie that tries to be funny fails, there ain't nothing left. Even if you load it up with breasts.

Even if you start off with a naked girl dancing during the opening credits. Specifically, the girl next door to young Kevin Dornwinkle, a confused young man on the cusp of puberty. Being of a scientific bent, young Kevin is watching his teenage neighbor undress and dance around her bedroom, but such a worthy scientific endeavor is interrupted by his ugly-as-sin mother who uses the occasion to instill in Kevin (insomuch as possible) a pathological distrust of women, in addition to a negative self esteem. Let's see—a maternally-instilled love/hate attitude toward women… I'm sure I've seen that somewhere before…

Twenty years later, Kevin (Noel Peters) is presenting his scientific breakthrough to an international physics symposium—and this must be the best of the best of the best in the scientific community, because this entire international symposium is comprised of maybe a dozen people who didn't even bother to take off their labcoats. Kevin's specialty is "molecular reorganization," which I suppose is meant to mean something other than plain ol' chemistry. As he explains through pseudoscientific technobabble that wouldn't hold water to anyone with a junior-high science education, Kevin has supposedly discovered how to turn living organisms invisible. To demonstrate, he injects himself with his serum; but, as always happens under pressure, nothing happens. These physicist types, meanwhile, must not get out much, since they think Kevin's failure is more hilarious than a Carrot Top marathon, and laugh uproariously at him; perhaps they should have checked the presenter bio: "Kevin Dornwinkle is an eccentric physicist with a deeply disturbed self-image and a homicidal reaction to being laughed at." He manages to kill four of them as they run from his sudden rampage. (Hey, that's like a third of the symposium attendees!)

He's sent to the state institution for the criminally insane (that's what the sign says: State Institution for the Criminally Insane), but naturally he escapes six months later.

Two weeks later still. A summer school classroom, populated by a dozen people that you wish would be removed from the gene pool. As we meet them, they're laughing because the scheduled physics teacher choked to death on a sandwich. Ha! Ha! Maybe they'll get out of having to take physics, right? No, because the principal (Stella Blalack) has found a last minute replacement: Dr. Kevin Do–, uh, Smith.

The kids immediately start treating him like dirt, including Bunny (Melissa Moore), the girl who I assume is supposed to be something like a protagonist. After all, the camera lingers on her a little more often, and she is awfully cute. But no, she's just as into persecuting the teacher as everyone else. (They act like Kevin's an incredible geek. Granted, he's not exactly socially adept, but compared to most of the physics teachers I had in high school—and college, for that matter—he's pretty near the top of the barrel. He even makes sense in the short teaching segments we see here. The students don't know how good they've got it.)

Kevin has apparently taken the position (without any credentials, somehow) because it affords him a perfect cover to continue his invisibility experiments. Yeah, because grading tests really helps unwind after a night of "molecular reorganization." In the meantime, the students subtly torture him and disdain him, in between cheerleading practice and—wait a sec. Apparently, all five or so girls in the physics class (which appears to be the only summer school course running) are cheerleaders. I suppose that isn't that remarkable, but why the hell are they practicing their cheers during the summer? Are they planning on having a game between their summer school team and some other school's summer school team? Oh, well, at least it affords them a chance to hit the showers. Frequently. And since the school was designed by a complete moron, there's an air grill right there in the gym which provides clear visual access to the shower, a fact that hasn't escaped either the male students or the mute janitor. Or Kevin, for that matter.

With all this sexual tension in the air, it's no surprise what Kevin's mind turns to as soon as he perfects the invisibility serum: he immediately spies on the sleeping Bunny in her bedroom. (It's pretty sad that Paul Verhoeven chose this scene—and really, this whole movie—to draw inspiration from for *Hollow Man* (2000).) By the way, in an incredibly convenient chemical side-effect, the injected serum not only makes Kevin instantly invisible, but it also causes his clothing to vanish! Wow! How about that! I guess anything to save on the cost of putting the actor in a bluescreen hood and doing any actual picture compositing, hmm?

And for the rest of the movie, we get more of the same. Kevin spies on the girls in the showers; the students torment him; the principal seduces Bunny's boyfriend (he's something of a pushover, admittedly); etc., etc., etc. Finally, the principal tries to seduce Kevin, blackmailing him with one of the hypos she found in his desk, which she assumes to be evidence of illicit drug use (which it is, after a fashion). So he kills her. And then, what the hey. He locks all the school doors and starts killing everyone invisibly.

In one incredibly inept scene, Bunny and boyfriend Chet (Robert R. Ross, Jr.) sneak into the principal's office to have sex. We're treated to the whole scene, accompanied by a standard-issue '80s love ballad—and cutaway shots to the principal's corpse lying on the other side of the desk. They get sweaty, enjoy the afterglow, and leave. Nope, they don't even discover the body. Um, point of this scene? Hello?

Remember what I said earlier about Bunny being an unimpressive heroine? That goes double for Chet, who apparently is supposed to be a hero in the final scenes. This after being the ringleader of the persecutors, after very willingly having sex with his principal, after spying on all the girls in the shower (these latter two actions after swearing his devotion to Bunny), and after rebuffing Bunny's questions about their future together. Yup, that's hero material, right there. I mean, it's not like Kevin's a very sympathetic character either, but once he starts killing teens there's nothing to do but wish him well and root for him.

Director Adam Rifkin has gone on to greater success since this, his first credit in the big chair; before the '90s were done, he wrote *Mouse Hunt* (1997), co-wrote *Small Soldiers* (1998), and directed *Detroit Rock City* (1999), among other things. In other words, he's made his living from comedy, so it comes as a disappointment to see that this earlier ostensible comedy is about as funny as a beehive up the butt. In hindsight, it was a great move on his part to direct this one under a pseudonym.

Some Notable Totables:
- body count: 13
- breasts: 19
- explosions: 0
- dream sequences: 2
- ominous thunderstorms: 0
- characters named Bubba: 1
- actors who've appeared on *Star Trek*: 1
  - Clement Von Franckenstein ("Dr. McWaters," and yes, that is his real name) played a gentleman in the *TNG* episode "Ship in a Bottle")

AMERICA'S DEADLIEST HOME VIDEO (1991)

A KILLER ROAD MOVIE.

- Written and directed by Jack Perez
- Starring Danny Bonaduce, Mick Wynhoff, Mollena Williams, Melora Walters and Gretchen Bonaduce
- Produced by Michael L. Wynhoff

There are two basic philosophies behind shooting a movie on video. The first, and most common, is simply to shoot a movie as if it were film and hope that no one minds that it's on video. *Blood Cult* (page 25) and *Redneck Zombies* (page 82) rely on this philosophy. The only thing that would really be different if these had been done on film (all other things being equal, such as budget) would be that, well, they would look like film. They're movies; the medium is is supposed to be as transparent as possible in order not to detract from the story.

The other philosophy was practically unknown to the general public until a certain surprise hit in the summer of 1999: *The Blair Witch Project*. In this darling little flick (which was imaginative, if not completely original, and which never should have been shown on a big screen), the fact that a large portion of it is shot on video is made germane to the plot; the footage was produced as part of the story, and thus has a reason to be there. No need to pretend that the video isn't readily recognizable as such; it's supposed to be obvious video. Whatever your opinion or intestinal reaction to The Blair Witch Project, you should admit that it was an ingenious device to create a movie partially on video without having the attendant stigma.

Since that time, the opportunities for shot-on-video features have widened somewhat. Unfortunately, because that very idea of the filming being integral to the plot (rather than some kind of omniscient viewpoint) is what made it possible, too many videomakers have been unable to come up with a story that didn't also imitate the conceit of *The Blair Witch Project*. In fact, most of those projects have been either direct ripoffs or parodies of *The Blair Witch Project*, which managed to use up any residual goodwill really damned fast.

America's Deadliest Home Video uses that same basic device as *The Blair Witch Project*: the filming is part of the narrative, with the camera being operated by a character. It wasn't an original idea in 1991, either—heck, it wasn't new when Ruggero Deodato used it in *Cannibal Holocaust* in 1980—but writer/director Jack Perez also manages to tell an incredible story here, one which doesn't rely solely on the novelty of the medium (as some have charged of *The Blair Witch Project*) but of which the medium is an integral part of the story.

Gee, is that enough pretentious verbiage? On to the movie itself.

The tape starts as Doug (former child star Danny Bonaduce!) sets up his new videocamera to tape his anniversary, though the reaction of spouse Debbie (real-life spouse Gretchen Bonaduce) shows that we're not exactly witnessing marital bliss here. Doug's a bit of a garden-variety jerk, and putting a camera in his hands doesn't make him any more likable; he continually gets in Debbie's face and, like every other male, somehow thinks that he'll be able to persuade her to, ahem, "perform" on camera.

Things change course when Doug hears rumors that Debbie hasn't been spending her evenings at the bartending course she's supposedly taking. How do we know this? Because Doug records it on the same tape, talking to the camera as an introduction to an excursion to Debbie's actual whereabouts, catching her tryst on video.

As revenge, he takes her minivan from the driveway and simply leaves— him, the van, and the camera, a Kerouac-esque road trip (at least, that's what he wants to believe). He uses the tripod to catch small travelogue scenes of himself as he meanders across country (and it's some pretty damned fast meandering; he manages to hit Utah, Iowa, Illinois, Nebraska, Indiana, and Wisconsin—in that order—in four days). While filming a small segment of himself standing in front of a Wisconsin gravel quarry, he also manages to catch some suspicious people pushing a car off the edge to crash into the pit; and then those suspicious people capture him and put guns up his nose.

His captors are the three members of the Clint Dryer gang: Clint himself (Mick Wynhoff), a personable and manipulative fellow who's a walking definition of "sociopathic personality"; Gloria (Melora Walters), his blonde gunmoll; and Vezna (Mollena Williams), a solid black woman with a chip on her shoulder the size of the *Queen Elizabeth II* (she's the one who always says, "Let me kill him! Can I kill him?"). They take Doug and his minivan prisoner; Clint is instantly enamored of the idea of taping their "exploits," and wants to keep Doug around as their official recorder (no, he didn't ask if Doug likes the idea).

A captive to the gang, Doug becomes the unwilling eye on their crimes, recording both their convenience store robberies (and the inadvertent but frequent deaths that accompany them) and Clint's post-robbery wind-down. And because Doug's eye is usually the camera's eye (with some notable exceptions), we follow exactly what he finds himself looking at—and too often it's Gloria, whose relationship with Clint is a love/hate one.

One senses that, even as a prisoner, Doug finds some kind of safety behind the lens; as long as he's only filming the proceedings, he's a designated voyeur, not an actual accomplice—a self-deception that takes him right up to his own first armed robbery and, later, his own first bullet wound. Will he, armed only with his camera, ever get the gumption and the opportunity to stand up to his armed captors? Can he help Gloria escape the life that she has been—quite literally, in some scenes—roped into?

The brilliance here is that the entire story quite naturally fills a normal videotape, told in the sequence in which it would naturally be shot, in scenes which are just as long as they would be in normal amateur shooting. *The Blair Witch Project* gave itself a safety net by having multiple cameras and an editing team to piece the "found footage" into a concise story (a feature which makes it the direct ancestor of *Survivor* and other "reality TV"—not an heritage of which one should be proud). This movie has no such escape hatch; each scene ends when the camera is turned off, and the next begins when the camera is turned back on. This leads to some ingenious transitions, such as when the gang forces Doug to see a dead body they buried on the beach at night: Doug turns to run, the camera bobs wildly and topples to the sand —and the next thing we see is Doug tied to a chair in a motel room and Clint staring into the lens, saying, "The red light means it's going, right, Dougie?"

Given that we can't cut away from distasteful action, nor can we use conventional editing tricks to convey meaning, director Perez uses more than his share of brilliance in finding alternate ways to give his scenes impact. At one point, Clint borrows a camera to record a night's activities alone with the semi-willing Gloria (an interesting counterpoint to Doug's own earlier attempts with Gretchen). After tying her up on the bed and taunting her with his switchblade, he cuts her bra free and removes his tighty-whities— at which point, right when I started wondering if the ensuing scene would be legal by local community standards, the "Low Battery" icon flashes and the picture fades… The next shot is the breakfast table at a restaurant, where Clint is complaining to Dougie that the camera went out last night. Gloria, meanwhile, is sitting stony-faced to the side, flicking a lighter repeatedly. That's just damned good storytelling.

(Another noteworthy workaround is the death of a video store clerk. With the camera swinging around as various shots are fired, the actress playing the clerk is substituted for her identical twin, made up already with a bullet wound. I knew to look for the switch, thanks to a long-ago film magazine article that originally put me on the path to track down this movie, and it still worked beautifully.)

The only complaint I have is the final ingenious workaround. In the climactic chase and getaway, part of the action is shown from the point of view of a camera crew riding with the highway patrolman, *COPS*-style. While this is a clever way to show events that logically can't show up on Doug's camcorder, it does effectively puncture the conceit we've been building up this whole time that the entire movie is simply what was in the tape in Doug's camera.

Despite that, it still doesn't lessen my admiration for the video as a whole: a brilliant fusion of content and form that allows the videocamera to be a natural participant in the events it records. Add to that deep character interactions and an actual storyline, and you have a movie that should have enjoyed much more success than it did, even though I don't think a camcorder movie would have looked right on the big screen. As I write this, *America's Deadliest Home Video* has finally been released on DVD, after full decades of being mostly unavailable after a limited VHS release. I'm thankful, because I can recommend that people see this movie without having to offer to lend my copy.

Some Notable Totables:
- body count: 9
- breasts: 4
- explosions: 0
- ominous thunderstorms: 0
- actors who've appeared on *Star Trek*: 0

GODZILLA vs. KING GHIDORA (1991)

GODZILLA IS BACK. THIS TIME, IT'S FOR GOOD!

aka *Gojira vs. Kingu Gidoraa*

- Written and directed by Kasuki Omori
- Starring Megumi Odaka, Kosuke Toyohara, Anna Nakagama, Chuck Wilson and Kenpachiro Satsuma
- Produced by Shogo Tomiyama
- Executive produced by Tomoyuki Tanaka

In 1990 to 1992, I was a Mormon missionary in Japan. During the summer of 1991 I lived in a small house with my companion (missionaries always travel in pairs) and two other missionaries. One day, the other two took off early in the morning without a word, and were gone until at least nine that night. They wouldn't say where they had been; they just acted mysterious about it until we finally threatened them with physical violence, missionaries or no.

"We were extras in a movie," they said with a shame-faced snicker.

"No way," I said.

"A *Godzilla* movie," they said.

My jaw hit the floor.

Thus began my long love affair with *Godzilla vs. King Ghidora*. It's an indefensibly goofy movie, but dammit, it's a *good* indefensibly goofy movie.

We open in 2204 AD, as a submersible drifts along the deep sea, examining the sunken form of a monster identified for us (for those who don't have comprehensive knowledge of *Godzilla* films) as King Ghidora, a giant golden dragon with bat wings and three heads on serpentine necks, although the undersea carcass we see is minus one head. The dialogue of the submersible's occupants informs us that Ghidora got his head-removing whuppage back in the 20th century, at the hands of— Godzilla!

Cue credits.

buzzes Tokyo repeatedly, prompting great crowds to stand and point, and inciting sensational headlines in the otherwise staid Japanese press. All of this is brought to the attention of Terasawa (Kosuke Toyohara), a young but successful science fiction writer who's trying to get away from paranormal subjects and into respectable nonfiction; his former cutie editor at *Super Mystery Magazine Mu* wants him to investigate and write a story on the UFO for them. Terasawa's more interested in a much smaller article in the paper about a crazy old man (Koichi Ueda) at Dinosaur World museum who claims to have seen dinosaurs.

He's a crazy old fella, all right; he walks around Dinosaur World with a megaphone, proclaiming that a dinosaur saved his garrison in the Pacific during World War II, and that it's like their guardian angel. After the coot is thrown out of the museum, Terasawa questions him at the little food stand he runs. The geezer explains that their unit was trapped on Lagos Island in the Pacific with the Americans surrounding them and blowing their butts off, when suddenly the dinosaur emerged and chased the Americans away, saving the Japanese soldiers.

Meanwhile, we're introduced to all the government muckamucks whose job it is to say terribly obvious and not very helpful things about the UFO. The saucer has landed in a remote part of Japan, and is just waiting for someone to come a-knockin'. This scene also reintroduces us to some of the long-time players in the Heisei (1985-1998) *Godzilla* series: Defense Minister Segawa (Kenji Sahara, the old guy), Takehito Fujio (Tokuma Nishioka, the younger guy), and Miki Saegusa of the ESP Research Institute (Megumi Odaka, the cute but jug-eared girl —I'm not being mean, I just call 'em as I see 'em).

Terasawa goes to visit Professor Mazaki (Katsuhiko Sasaki), who believes that saurian extinction may not be as complete as everyone thinks. But alas, it's impossible to go back to Lagos to check on the current status of the dinosaur, as the island was used for H-bomb testing in 1954. That leads to Terasawa's hypothesis (more like an unsupported flight of fancy, but since it proves correct, he's allowed to smirk) that the radiation from the nuclear testing turned the dinosaur into—Godzilla!

Then the cutie editor comes up with another interesting fact. Guess who else was on Lagos island? Businessman Yasuaki Shindo (Yoshio Tsuchiya), formerly Major Shindo, who was one of the main figures in the post-war reconstruction, and who also owns Dinosaur World.

That same morning, two helicopters on routine patrol explode as they reach the vicinity of the UFO. The army naturally surrounds the area.

When Terasawa visits Shindo and puts the question to him, Shindo flatly denies that there were dinosaurs on Lagos Island, but changes his story when Terasawa mentions his idea that the dinosaur became Godzilla. (Apparently, being reminded that a two-hundred-foot fire-breathing monster exists soothed his fears that he'd be ridiculed.) He even provides some old photographs that he'd had the presence of mind to snap at the time, which Terasawa goes over with the professor and the cutie editor. (Is it wrong of me to continually refer to the editor as a cutie? I know it seems terribly sexist, but she doesn't really contribute much to the story except her pretty face.)

Meanwhile, at UFO central, three figures emerge from the underbelly of the craft. Segawa and Fujio go out to meet with them. They are Wilson (Chuck Wilson), an American; Grenchinko (Richard Berger), supposedly a Russian, though nobody bothered to tell the guy doing the English dubbing; and Emi (Anna Nakagawa), a Japanese girl. (Unlike Nick Adams in some earlier *kaiju* movies, both Wilson and Grenchinko speak fluent Japanese in the Japanese-language version. My own Japanese was never good enough to tell whether Grenchinko was speaking Japanese with a Russian accent, though.) They explain to the befuddled locals that they're from the 23rd century, and that the UFO is actually a time machine. No apologies are made for the two exploded helicopters.

An aside: in English, the dialogue in this movie and many other Japanese films sounds especially ludicrous because every character apparently feels the need to repeat already established facts several minutes after we've passed that point in the conversation. "So it's a time machine!" "So you're from the future!" "A hologram, huh?" etc. While I will agree that it's silly, I will defend writer/director Kazuki Omori by stating that it's also completely natural in Japanese conversation. Repetition and meaningless confirmations are an integral part of speaking Japanese, and it often drives Westerners crazy. No, that doesn't make the English version sound any less ludicrous.

Anyway, Wilson asks them to arrange a meeting with the Prime Minister and the other heads of government for the next day. When the appointed time arrives, the future folk use a teleporter to arrive at the meeting and finally explain their presence.

Here's their story: In the future, Japan no longer exists. Sometime between now and then, Godzilla awakens once again (after naps like that, you'd think he'd be a little less cranky) and destroys some nuclear plants, and the resulting radiation destroys the country. The futurians' solution? Well, they have a book, written some years hence by a certain writer named Terasawa, about the origin of Godzilla…

So Segawa and friends bring Terasawa and Professor Mazaki (who wrote/will write the intro to Terasawa's as-yet unwritten book) in for a meeting. The time travelers' plan is to go back in time, before Godzilla was created, and move the dinosaur from Lagos to prevent it from getting exposed to radiation. Thus, no Godzilla. (Mazaki's comment: "Our history will no longer include Godzilla." No, but we'll all be able to console ourselves with Gamera, won't we?)

The futurians ask for Terasawa, the professor, and jug-eared Miki to accompany them on their expedition to the past, guided by Emi and M-11 (Robert Scott Field), the futurians' pet android with much better table manners than the Terminator. Why? Uh… We'll talk about that later.

From the mother ship, the expedition members enter the smaller shuttle ship, where Emi has a trio of Doraks—biotech-created pets from the future, which resemble little golden cat puppets with bat wings. M-11 sets the controls, and *zzzzooom* they're off through a time warp that resembles the wormhole from *Star Trek: The Motion Picture*.

Welcome to 1944! The shuttle streaks over the U.S. boat off the coast of Lagos at night, inspiring some cutesy dialog between the Captain and "Major Spielberg," who says he's gonna tell his son about this. (Get it? Get it? This was just before *Jurassic Park*, too.) The Captain, by the way, is played by Kent Gilbert, a celebrity American in Japan who also runs his own chain of English language schools. From his performance here, I'll wager that a string of drama schools did not rapidly follow.

M-11 goes and looks in on the Japanese troops, huddled in a cave, waiting for the American assault tomorrow. His six-million-dollar eye manages to pick out both the crazy old guy and Shindo, or at least their ostensibly younger versions. (One of the bigger sticking points for suspension of disbelief in this movie —and that's saying something—is the ages of these characters,

since they're played by the same actors in both 1944 and 1992. There's only so much that hair dye will do to reverse the signs of aging, you know.)

Next morning, the U.S. troops attack, and it goes poorly for the Japanese, until *thump... thump... thump...* A ponderous carnosaur-type dinosaur trudges through the jungle. (If you look really close, you can see the itty-bitty ears on the sides of its head. Yup, this is definitely the origin of Godzilla.) While the Japanese wisely retreat, the Americans insist on shooting it; but that only riles it, and a score of servicemen lose their lives under its big feet or beneath the trees it knocks over. (It was in this scene that my fellow missionaries performed, dressed as G.I.s and shooting firearms. I've yet to be able to pick them out reliably in the background.)

When the dinosaur follows them onto the beach, though, the ship has a clear shot at it, and bombards it pretty thoroughly (comment from the ship: "Take that, you dinosaur!"), but not until every single American on the beach is dead. Finally, the wounded dinosaur stumbles off into the jungle, and the captain decides that they should just plain leave the area. (Footage of his subsequent disciplinary hearing is not included.)

We fast-forward a couple of days (hey, we can do that, we've got a time machine), when the Japanese troops are ready to leave the island. Major Shindo and his troops pay their respects to their feeble saurian savior, whom they don't expect to survive his injuries. Once they're gone, M-11 sets the big teleporting lamp on top of the shuttle to transport the dinosaur off to the deep sea of the Bering Strait.

Right before they leave, Emi mysteriously leaves the Doraks outside. And then *zzzzip*, back to the future (or rather, the present), and let the paradoxes begin.

See, the people in the present confirm that Godzilla is gone. Wait! How would they know? There's never been a Godzilla, right? So howcome everyone still knows about him?

But no one has time to worry about that, because almost immediately, a new monster shows up on the scene—King Ghidora, the radiation-induced amalgam of the three Doraks! And he's controlled from the UFO! Ghidora lands at Fukuoka and performs the standard *kaiju* urban renovation project.

(You really gotta love the evacuation scenes in these movies. Watch the running people closely; half of them are smiling. They're just jazzed to be in a *Godzilla* movie.)

Emi gets mad at Wilson and Grenchiko because, hey, they're stomping her homeland! But the men ignore her and, having decimated Fukuoka, then set King Ghidora on Hokkaido.

Now, let's take a gander at the map:

As you can see, Fukuoka is on the island of Kyushu, down in the southwest corner, right by the East China Sea. Hokkaido, on the other hand, is the northernmost island—as far from Fukuoka as you can get and still be in Japan. This is an attack plan?

Well, Emi sneaks out with a jetpack and visits Terasawa, and this is where the exposition comes in. The time travelers are not representatives of the future world government, as they originally claimed; instead, they're from the more radical Equal Environment Earth Union, and stole the time machine. It seems that, far from being destroyed, the Japan of the future is far too powerful, having used its economic might to buy up whole continents (South America and Africa are explicitly mentioned) and generally lording over the whole earth. So these three had come back to use the Doraks to create a monster they could control, and use it to knock Japan down a peg so it wouldn't have the wherewithal to become such a world power. Only now Wilson and Grenchiko have decided that it's more fun to blow Japan clear back to the Stone Age.

Normally, the perfect weapon against one building-stomping *kaiju* is a second building-stomping *kaiju*—but Godzilla ain't around any more! Or has never been around at all! So why is everyone talking about him? My head hurts. Anyway, is there any way we can recreate Godzilla? Say, by exposing the dinosaur to radiation? Gee, the drowned corpse of the dinosaur has been languishing in the waters of the Bering Strait for almost fifty years now; shoot, why not? But who's got the nuke they can use?

Shindo does, it turns out; he has a single private sub with nukes, designed to protect Japan in an extreme emergency. It's currently in the vicinity of South America, but he's certainly willing to turn it around.

Apparently we don't need to wait that long, though; Miki starts harping about how she can "feel Godzilla." (This, apparently, is the extent to which her psychic powers will benefit this movie.) How could that be? Could some other source of radiation have caused the dinosaur to become Godzilla? (This conversation, by the way, is taking place in a room whose door proudly proclaims it the "Super Scientific Play-Room." Scientists need downtime too, right?) Apparently, yes, as the cutie editor is able to find out from their back issue files; a nuclear sub went down in the Bering Strait in the mid-'70s and was never recovered. So, if the dinosaur's been slowly absorbing radiation for almost twenty years, it's only natural that it's about to emerge as Godzilla! I'd really love to read a biology textbook from this parallel universe.

Well, gosh! We'd better tell Shindo to call off his sub; we don't want overkill! But Shindo's not answering his phone, so Terasawa and Emi set off to find him. But someone else has found them—M-11, on a mission to bring Emi back. A car chase ensues, in which M-11's vehicle rolls and explodes. But he merely steps from the flames, his burnt false skin exposing metallic parts in his face and shoulder. M-11 six-million-dollar-mans his way in front of them and stops Terasawa's jeep with his bare hands, then lifts the front end off the ground.(In the Japanese release, the jack which is really holding up the jeep is clearly visible entering the frame at the end of the shot; in the American release, that fraction of a second has been snipped out. Party-poopers. At least the ludicrous science has been left intact.)

Dragged back to the UFO, Emi unloads her foul mouth on Wilson and Grenchiko: "You disgusting men are filled with deceit!" Oddly enough, the disgusting men are unfazed; their reply falls more along the lines of "No one can defeat us, bwah-ha-ha" etc.

Deceit they may be filled with, but apparently not intelligence, as they give Emi the run of the ship again. Her first project, then, is to reprogram the reupholstered M-11 to obey only her commands. And you know what they say: "One person and an indestructible android is a majority."

Meanwhile, undersea, Shindo's sub is dutifully making it's way to the Bering Strait, when—what's that ahead? That, huge, bipedal, corduroyed thing? It's Godzilla! And he's in the mood for a good sub sandwich!

Terasawa, having gone home after Emi's capture, then gets picked up by the new friendly version of M-11 and snuck into the UFO. Emi has changed out of her futuristic granola clothes into her action outfit—a short black skirt, thigh-high black boots, and her hair in a tail off the top of her head. They come up with a plan…

An army chopper with most of the other characters (Miki, the professor, etc.) hovers over the spot where the sub disappeared. And with a flourish of bubbles, and a ridiculous harp run (I wish I were kidding), Godzilla surfaces! And off he goes, heading unerringly toward Japan.

Meanwhile, King Ghidora is finally arriving on Hokkaido; he easily dispatches the stock footage fighters that try to annoy him. But then Godzilla reaches Hokkaido from the Bering Straight (in less that fifteen minutes?! He may look clumsy on land, but

Godzilla must swim like a sumbitch!). He ignores the field of cows and instead starts wrecking power stations and the like.

Wilson, incensed that Godzilla has reappeared, sets King Ghidora after him. The expected *kaiju* whupass ensues, as each decks the other with its own energy-laden breath. But though Godzilla is bigger than before (and meaner thanks to the double dose of radiation, as signified by his red eyes), the battle does not go well for him…

…Until Emi's plan comes to fruition. She, Terasawa, and M-11 set explosive charges around the UFO's main computer. Terasawa declares, "Make my day!" (yes, he says this in English in both the Japanese and American versions) and *Boom!* Suddenly Wilson can no longer control King Ghidora, and Godzilla gains the upper hand.

We all know from *Star Trek* that there are no circuit breakers in the 23rd century, so the entire UFO begins showering sparks from instrument panels. But Wilson and Grenchiko are unworried because A) the new Godzilla is antisocial enough that, even if he beats Ghidora, he'll go on to destroy Japan himself, and B) the UFO has a time homing device; if there's a major power interruption, it will automatically return to its own time in 20 minutes. Bwah-ha-ha!

The good guys knock out the bad guys and escape in the shuttle. They then turn on the teleporter and aim it at the UFO…

Back up in Hokkaido, Godzilla's kicking King Ghidora's heinie. When Ghidora loses his middle head, he finally decides to turn tail(s) and run, but Godzilla doesn't give up so easily; he blows a hole in Ghidora's wing as he flies over the ocean, and Ghidora plummets into the deep. That's about when the UFO teleports into his field of vision, and the last thing Wilson and Grenchiko see is a big fiery belch coming their way.

But now… Godzilla's on a rampage. And those are notoriously hard to curtail. So onward to Sapporo, the major city of Hokkaido. (Cue evacuating crowds.) The anti-Godzilla laser cannons roll onto the scene, and do about as much good as the anti-Godzilla weapons do in every other *Godzilla* movie. Godzilla leaves Sapporo a smoking pit, and proceeds south.

All those with hair are pulling it out. Now that Ghidora's gone, what other force can

stand against Godzilla? Then the brainstorm: Emi and M-11 can go back to the future in the shuttle and find some way to repair Ghidora and bring him back to 1992. It's a long shot, but hey—you got a better idea? Off they go.

So now we're back at that scene that began the movie in 2204, with Emi, M-11, and some other guy in the submersible. M-11 detects life signs in Ghidora (after all, if the dinosaur can stay viable at the bottom of the ocean, why not Ghidora?), and Emi convinces the guy to help her reconstruct Ghidora and send him back.

Meanwhile in 1992 (can you say "meanwhile" about something happening two hundred years earlier?), Godzilla enters Tokyo Bay. Fortunately, all of Tokyo has been evacuated—except Shindo, who watches the destruction from his penthouse office window. Ah, what poetic justice, he muses; it was the dinosaur who saved him and allowed him to reconstruct Japan after the war, and now it is that same dinosaur who is stomping it all to kindling. Shindo gives Godzilla a final salute before Godzilla fries his entire building.

Many more buildings fall before Godzilla's unfocused rage before the sky crackles, and there it is! The new, improved, Mecha-Ghidora! Gleaming chrome covers its torso (from which Emi controls it in an onboard cockpit), reinforces its wings, strengthens its shins, and comprises the whole of the new mechanical head in the middle.

Kaiju whupass round two.

After flattening most of the city (and having been knocked down a couple of times), Emi releases Mecha-Ghidora's secret weapon: a set of four grabbing clamps which grip Godzilla's limbs, and a mega-clamp which grabs Godzilla's midriff. Then Ghidora takes off, flying Godzilla out over the ocean before Godzilla manages to fry Ghidora again and send them both to the bottom of the sea; at the last minute, the shuttle, which was part of that whole torso panel, pops back out of the ocean safely.

Emi makes her farewells, including revealing to Terasawa that he's actually her distant ancestor, and pops back into her own time.

The end.

It's a whiz-bang show while it's running, but it only takes ten minutes of half-conscious thought afterward to see that the plot makes absolutely not one lick of sense. In fact, it raises more questions than Socrates himself:

Why does the UFO buzz Tokyo a full day before making contact? Why do they bother to reveal themselves and get help from the present-day folk, when they already have the book, which tells them more than the present-day Terasawa knows? And what's the point of having Miki along? Why do they linger in the past and watch the whole drama instead of efficiently zipping in after the fact and removing the dinosaur? Why didn't they check first to see where there were downed nuclear subs? What's with that massive frigging paradox? Why do they blithely let Emi sneak out and help the others? Why do they let her reprogram M-11? How can Godzilla get to Hokkaido so quickly?

Thinking about all this will kill brain cells. On the other hand, there are many things which raise this movie above the rest of the *Godzilla* corpus. I mean, it's got UFOs! Time travelers! WWII battles! Surviving dinosaurs! *Gaijin* who speak Japanese! A Terminator-style android! Nuclear subs! Cows!

And just as notably, it doesn't follow the pattern of "Another monster happens to appear on the scene just as Godzilla is waking up, so they fight" that they resort to in so many of these movies.

And plus, there's just the fact that I have a personal connection to this one. I was there when it was being made; I got to see firsthand the marketing blitz and the love that the Japanese public have for their own worst cinematic enemy. I've been in buildings that Godzilla later smashed.

In fact, aside from being pissed still that I didn't get to be an extra, this is a great big warm fuzzy for me.

Some Notable Totables:
- body count: 71 (plus various pilots, crew, and stragglers in the evacuated cities)
- breasts: 0
- explosions: 157 (give or take)
- ominous thunderstorms: 0
- actors who've appeared on *Star Trek*: 0

KINGDOM of the VAMPIRE (1991)

SUBURBAN NEIGHBORHOODS ARE HER KINGDOM... AND DEATH IS HER DOMAIN!

- Directed by J.R. Bookwalter
- Written by Matthew Jason Walsh
- Starring Matthew Jason Walsh, Cherie Petry, Shannon Doyle, Tom Stephan and Jo Norcia
- Produced by Scott P. Plummer

While all microbudget productions have a particular lack in common (that of money, naturally), most of them also lack plenty of other attributes: skill behind the camera, witty or insightful scripts, acting ability, or just plain ambition. Too many independent shot-on-video flicks, especially those in the horror genre, seem eager to betray that their only goal all along was to deliberately make a sow's ear. *Kingdom of the Vampire,* J.R. Bookwalter's first "camcorder movie," isn't going to make anyone's Top Ten list by any criteria, but it's still head-and-shoulders above so many of its microbudget brethren, simply by virtue of the attempt to accomplish something of greater depth than a bottom-of-the-barrel slasher flick. From time to time, it even succeeds in that attempt. Not too bad for a budget under $3,000.

The "kingdom" of the title is more irony than anything else. Our protagonist is Jeff (scriptwriter and score composer Matthew Jason Walsh, who's had considerable work in the ensuing years writing low-budget features), a sallow-faced introvert who works the closing shift at a small-town convenience store. He's out of high school, and his life has pretty much stopped: no friends, no hobbies, no job skills, no romance, no prospects. All he has is his elderly mother (Cherie Petry), who sits at home napping and watching TV until Jeff comes home. Occasionally she buys and eats some Girl Scout cookies. Right after she eats the Girl Scout.

Because Mom is a vampire. So was Dad, who disappeared when Jeff was little. And so, naturally, is Jeff, though he resists it; so cripplingly shy is he that he can't even conceive of hunting and killing humans for blood. Instead, he simply cleans up his mother's occasional bloody messes, and very occasionally takes a quick lick from one of his mother's recent kills before guilt pulls him back. He sleeps all day and he works at night. This is not the romantic ennui of an Anne Rice-style bloodsucker; his life simply sucks.

And it isn't going to get better. Mom regularly regales him with tales of the ancient vampire kingdom, which was a power to be reckoned with up through the Middle Ages; alas, as far as they know, the two of them are the last of their kind, hiding out in Midwestern suburbia, sneaking kills when they can (or when Mom can, anyway). And Mom's such a domineering, demanding old hag that Jeff's spirit is a broken little thing; she beats him and demeans him, she demands his presence whenever he's not working, and she consistently grinds into him a sense of his own worthlessness. This movie ranks right up there with *Psycho* on the scale of bad mother/son relationships.

The one bright spot in his life, which he doesn't even dare recognize, is Nina (Shannon Doyle), a young truck-stop waitress who knows Jeff peripherally and wants to know him better. It takes so much work for her to draw him even marginally out of his shell that one starts to wonder if Jeff is Nina's intended paramour or her charity social case; on the other hand, when she contrasts him to the ass-grabbing customers she deals with all day, her attraction to someone quiet and reserved like Jeff makes a little more sense.

Of course, the two women in Jeff's life are bound to end up in conflict. It does take a long time to get there, though. The entire middle section of the movie deals instead with the Halloween enticement of a mother and child into the vampire home, and the aftermath. I guess it's just the rotten luck that the mother and child were the sister-in-law and nephew of Sheriff Blake (Tom Stephan), the homespun but intelligent lawman who remembers a certain other vampire which that town had put down twenty years back…

It's a small movie, and in some ways it stays far too understated; the "romance" between Jeff and Nina never gets past a couple of walks home and a chaste kiss or two, and the final conflict between mother and lover owes more to happenstance than inevitability. I appreciate that Jeff is beaten, broken and passive, which gives us scenes like him trying desperately to bring himself to stake his mother, but losing nerve with the point against her heart. But he's such an inactive character that most of the movie is a string of things that happen either to him or around him; very little that he actually does has any effect on the flow of the story. (And I question whether a vampire who hates the life apart that he's forced to lead would wear *Night of the Living Dead* T-shirts or paper his room with posters for *Evil Dead 2* and *Creepshow* and *I Spit on Your Grave*.)

On the other hand, much of the movie's success comes from attention to detail. Little things like the all-day time lapse that runs under the opening credits. Or the blank medicine cabinet door where a mirror should be. Or Mom beating Jeff with a crucifix (that's gotta sting). The music's good, though it suffers from overscoring, as so many indie flicks do; the performances hovers between underacting and overacting, with the occasional scene right on the mark.

I guess the crowning virtue is that it's a sincere movie, not a slavish pastiche or winking camp. J.R. Bookwalter's always been one to take his filmmaking seriously, and that kind of attention shows. In fact, *Kingdom of the Vampire* garnered enough respect among the second generation of microbudget filmmakers, despite it being incredibly hard to find, that Ottawa independent filmmaker Brett Kelly sought for and received permission to remake it in 2007, with Bookwalter as executive producer and eventual distributor.

Some Notable Totables:
- body count: 7
- breasts: 0
- explosions: 0
- ominous thunderstorms: 0
- actors who've appeared on *Star Trek*: 0

KINGDOM of the VAMPIRE: Writer-Director J.R. Bookwalter's Comments

After producing a couple more 16mm disasters for Cinema Home Video, moving to Los Angeles for a year and a half and then coming back to Ohio, *Kingdom of the Vampire* was my next chance at bat. The problem is, it was the first of two movies being made back-to-back (the other one being *Zombie Cop*, which speaks for itself). Despite the insanity of trying to shoot two Super-VHS-C features over a couple weeks for a grand total of $5,000, I did pour some extra effort into *Kingdom*, which was certainly the closest to my heart since *The Dead Next Door* and for sure the best effort prior to *Ozone* a few years later.

Kingdom marked the first time I had directed a script that someone else had written—in this case, Matthew Jason Walsh, who also wound up starring in the flick. At first we totally didn't connect on what the movie should be about... I recall in the first paragraph of Matt's original treatment he had coffins flying through basement walls and all kinds of other crazy shit we'd never be able to pull off. So, I sat down and scribbled up the first part of a story idea about a dominating mother vampire and her meek son, inspired by watching too much *Dark Shadows* and maybe even a little bit from George Romero's excellent *Martin*. Matt connected with the idea and for the most part, his script was something we were both excited about doing.

Unfortunately, toward the latter part of the first night of shooting, I busted my knee and had to finish the movie in a wheelchair. This was a problem since I was supposed to light and shoot the movie. Thankfully it was video, so I could sit at a monitor and have my co-producer, Scott P. Plummer, tweak lights and run the camera and still get mostly the results I wanted. But it was slow going, and we ultimately had to pull pages out of the script as the deadline loomed to start shooting *Zombie Cop*.

The result was a movie that was only 45 minutes long in the first cut! That meant we had to go back out and shoot more footage, not only putting back the pages I had yanked but actually coming up with a lengthy exchange at the police station between the sheriff and a new secretary character. Not the ideal solution, but it got done and delivered on schedule and on budget. The same cannot be said for the next four movies we did the same way, and by the end of that experience six months later I was ready to throw in the towel for the first time in my short career. (It took the script for *Ozone* falling in my lap shortly after that for me to change my mind.)

The biggest problem with *Kingdom* was some of the acting—I wanted it to be a little hammy and boy, did I get more than I asked for. Where Matthew Jason Walsh and I were on the same page about the script, when he stepped onto set to act, he decided he wouldn't listen to a damn thing I said. He later admitted that wasn't the smartest idea he'd ever had, but by then it was too late. In discussing the possibility of remastering the movie someday for a DVD release, Walsh always joked, "There's no After Effects filter for bad acting." 'Nuff said.

I did finally get to remaster *Kingdom* for a 2007 DVD release, tweaking the movie a bit here and there and beefing up the sound and visuals. It's still far from a perfect movie, but despite many negative reviews, I like it just fine for what it is. In fact, I gave another filmmaker, Canadian Brett Kelly, the money to do a far superior remake (also featured on the same disc), actually made for a little less money than the original. So, at least that demon was exorcised as best it could be.

NIGHT of the DAY of the DAWN of the SON of the BRIDE of the RETURN of the REVENGE of the TERROR of the ATTACK of the EVIL MUTANT HELLBOUND FLESH EATING SUBHUMANOID LIVING DEAD, PART 2 (1991)

It doesn't get any better than this.

- *Produced, written and directed by Lowell Mason*
- *Starring Duane Jones, Judith O'Dea, Karl Hardman, Marilyn Eastman and Keith Wayne*

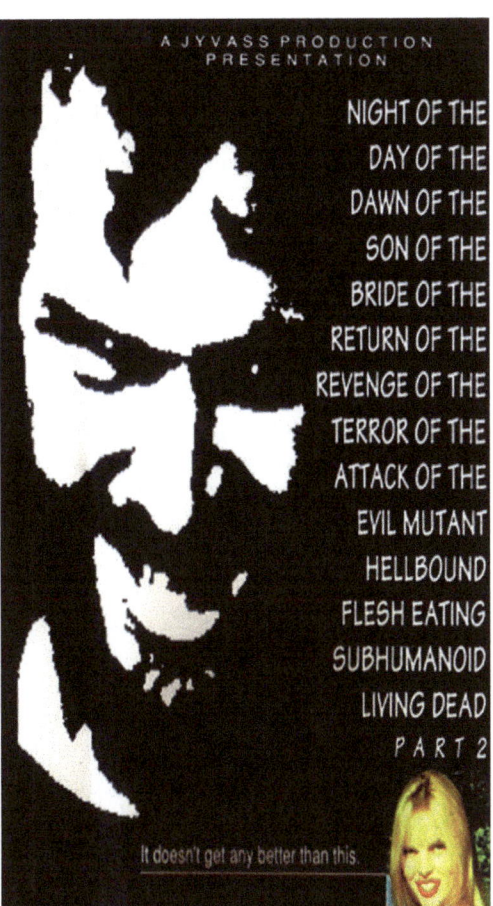

Actually, according to the title card (which is literally what it is—a woman holds a piece of artboard with Magic-Markered text up for the camera), the full title is *Night of the Day of the Dawn of the Son of the Bride of the Return of the Revenge of the Terror of the Attack of the Evil, Mutant, Alien, Flesh-Eating, Hellbound, Crawling, Zombified, Living-Dead Part II in Shocking 2-D.*

And you might as well stop right there, because the title's probably the funniest part of the whole exercise.

You've heard the shtick before. Woody Allen did it in 1966 with *Kokusai Himitsu Keisatsu* (1964) aka *International Secret Police: Key of Keys*, re-editing and redubbing it into a comedy called *What's Up, Tiger Lily?* A troupe of Californian comedians (including an unknown Jay Leno) did the same thing in 1983 with *The Hideous Sun Demon* (1959), ending up with a movie known alternately as *What's Up, Hideous Sun Demon?* or *Revenge of the Sun Demon*. This time out, Lowell Mason applied the same gimmick to George Romero's *Night of the Living Dead* (1968).

Now, please note a couple of dissimilarities between the former two and the latter. For one thing, both *Kokusai Himitsu Keisatsu* and *The Hideous Sun Demon* were fairly obscure movies; one could bet that the audience for the spoofs had never seen the original. (Of course, things have changed since; I doubt there are many people who seek out *Revenge of the Sun Demon* these days without having seen the original. But who knew, in 1983, how the video revolution would transform the viewing habits of movie geeks?) By contrast, you just have to assume that every single viewer of *Night of the Day of the Dawn of the Son of the Bride of the Return of the Revenge of the Terror of the Attack of the Evil, Mutant, Alien, Flesh-Eating, Hellbound, Crawling, Zombified, Living-Dead Part II in Shocking 2-D* has seen the original *Night of the Living Dead* any number of times, and rightfully admires it as being a thoroughly stunning piece of cinema.

There's another big difference. Woody Allen is known as a comedian. He's made a career of being funny, at least sporadically. Jay Leno? Big-time funnyman too.

Heard the name "Lowell Mason" bandied around in the big comedy arenas lately? (Or the name "James Riffel," which is apparently his real name?) Me, neither.

I can understand a bunch of drunk friends thinking that recording a humorous vocal and sound effects track to *Night of the Living Dead* would be a good idea. It would be doable, too; with the well-known copyright difficulties Romero has had with his opus, Mason and friends would be pretty much bulletproof no matter how they modified the movie.

But for a movie with as great a cult following as *Night of the Living Dead*, a movie which has won the hearts of both underground genre fans and academic critics, a half-assed spoof attempt will earn that half an ass a severe kicking. And *Night of the Day of the Dawn of the Son of the Bride of the Return of the Revenge of the Terror of the Attack of the Evil, Mutant, Alien, Flesh-Eating, Hellbound, Crawling, Zombified, Living-Dead Part II in Shocking 2-D* can only be considered "half-assed" if you're rounding upward. (There's a joke to be made in there involving "cheekiness," but I'll let you work on that one yourself.)

I'll assume your familiarity with the original *Night of the Living Dead* here. John and Barbara travel to the cemetery to place some flowers on a friend's grave. And John has gas. Ha! And talks about the pleasures of a good crap. Ha ha! And Barbara is voiced by a male in falsetto. Ha ha ha!

What, you're not laughing yet? These are the jokes, folks.

The cemetery zombie isn't a reanimated corpse so much as a blue-collar worker driven into a trance-like state by his mind-numbing gas station job—although, in his muttering, he reveals that he's gay, and the best part of his job is sticking the long hard nozzle into that tight little hole. Fag jokes! Ha ha ha!

Barbara runs to the farmhouse, making little muttering noises because there's not really a lot of dialogue through here to rewrite. There's a running gag about a duck somewhere in the house, which is why Barbara's always looking around so sharply.

Then Ben arrives. Wait for it—what zany character trait will he have? Why, he's black, of course! Which means he calls Barbara a "stupid white bitch" and talks in rhyming jive all the time! Plus, he came to the house looking for a bathroom, 'cause he's got to drop a log! Wow, black jokes and more poop jokes at the same time! Ha!

You may have run across the term "komedy" before. It bears the same relationship to genuine comedy that "krab" (as in the "krab salad" at the supermarket deli) bears to genuine crab. But this is a movie that makes komedy look like comedy.

Harry and Tom eventually show up—Tom with a surfer accent—and they argue for about ten minutes about who's going to go get the pizza, or if it should be Mexican, or maybe Chinese. And…

Dear heavens, are you still paying attention? Aren't you bored to tears? I know I was. There are few "thrills" in the world less thrilling than wondering whether the next swath of time-filling dialogue is going to be another of Ben's raps, more argument about where to get take-out, or maybe another fun-filled poop reference. Maybe someone will say "motherf___er" again—after all, it's been a whole forty seconds since the last time. Or maybe Ben will have another conversation with Tommy, the Talking Shotgun. All interspersed with a musical score heavy on the calliope music. Ha ha ha ha…

You may be thinking, "How could Lowell Mason and his partners in crime have been unaware of the unfunniness of their endeavor?" My theory is, they knew. Maybe not right at the start—they were still drunk, after all, and thus it seemed like a good idea—but at some point, they came to understand just how bad their attempts at humor were. So they did the only thing they could to try and punch it up:

They added parts that were even less funny.

Interspersed throughout the movie (about every five minutes or so) are unrelated clips, bits of (mostly) original footage shot for this very purpose. Chunks of random historical knowledge about George Bernard Shaw and Calvin Coolidge. A locally-produced music video. And bits that try for the "so unfunny it's funny" gag. A man eats a donut slowly. Another man waits at a train station for a train that never comes. All of these serve to remind us that at least the main portion of the movie contains the visuals of a good movie, if not the dialogue.

You may have heard of this title before. You may have even been tempted to track down a copy. You don't have to now, because I did it for you. Whatever comedic potential there is in this movie is entirely in your optimistic imaginings. Give me four friends who've seen *Night of the Living Dead* before and sit them in front of *Night of the Living Dead* with the sound turned off, and I guarantee that whatever they improvise on the first try will be head and shoulders above *Night of the Day of the Dawn of the Son of the Bride of the Return of the Revenge of the Terror of the Attack of the Evil, Mutant, Alien, Flesh-Eating, Hellbound, Crawling, Zombified, Living-Dead Part II in Shocking 2-D*.

And just to shock your sensibilities further: James Riffel (using his real name this time) also wrote and produced *Night of the Day of the Dawn of the Son of the Bride of the Return of the Revenge of the Terror of the Attack of the Evil, Mutant, Hellbound, Flesh-Eating Subhumanoid Zombified Living Dead, Part 3* in 2005, giving the same treatment to *The Brain That Wouldn't Die* (1962). Odds of me checking it out? Pretty damned poor.

Some Notable Totables:
- body count: 9
- breasts: 0
- explosions: 1
- ominous thunderstorms: 1
- actors who've appeared on *Star Trek*: 0

AUNTIE LEE'S MEAT PIES (1992)

A BLACK COMEDY ABOUT CANNIBALISM... DONE TASTEFULLY.

- Directed by Joseph F. Robertson
- Written by Joseph F. Robertson and Gerald Stein
- Starring Karen Black, Pat Morita, Kristine Anne Rose, Michael Berryman and Pat Paulsen
- Produced by Gerald Stein

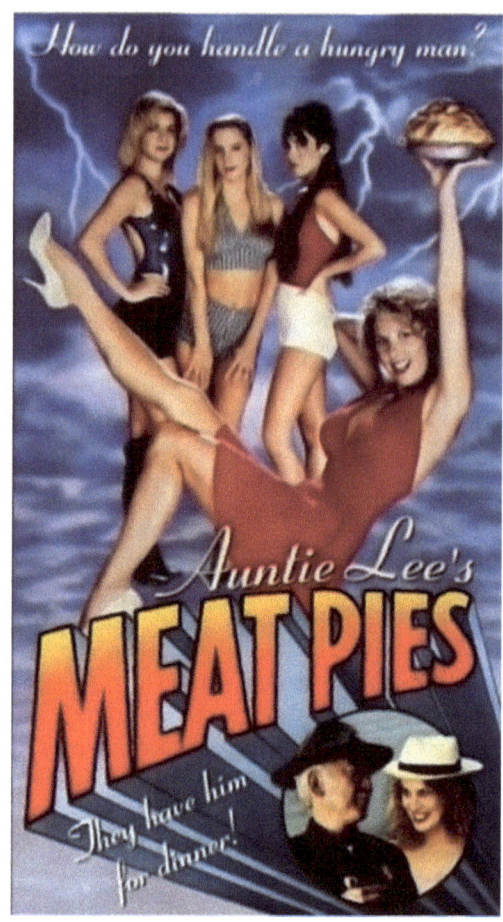

> "Utah's Mormon country. Auntie says Mormons been inbreeding with each other for such a long time, their brains are salty mush!"

As I remarked before (in my review of *Evil Spirits*, page 140), Karen Black used to get roles written for attractive women. You may think I'm talking about way back, like 1978 when she appeared in *Capricorn One*. But at least as late as 1985, when she did an episode of *The Hitchiker*, she was regularly cast as a good looking woman—in some cases even as a seductress. Then somewhere along the way, it dawned on the good people of Hollywood that Karen Black is actually one of the most incredibly unattractive women of all time. (Those showbiz types don't miss a thing, I tell you.) And from then on out, she ended up playing the roles of evil stepmothers, witches, harpy bosses, etc. From the gusto with which she attacks these roles, she's apparently comfortable with being as ugly as sin, and plays it up. In this movie, she even plays opposite Michael Berryman again, and still comes off as the uglier of the two.

Black is Auntie Lee, proprietor of Auntie Lee's Meat Pies. Since meat pies ain't exactly popular cuisine here in the U.S. of A. (I'm not sure where this story's supposed to take place, since I don't know if all of the California plates are supposed to be ignored or noticed—all I know, thanks to the quote above, is that it doesn't take place in Utah), you can pretty much guess that whenever they're featured prominently in an American movie (prominently like in the title), you're watching a cannibalism movie.

We start out with an unlikable criminal lowlife ditching a stolen car with a dying motor in it on the side of the road and hitching a ride with a priest (comedian/perpetual Presidential candidate Pat Paulsen!), then blowing the priest away, crashing that car, and stealing the priest's collar and shirt. At this rate, he's getting maybe three-quarters of a mile per vehicle. The next car he flags down is driven by short-skirted hottie Magnolia (former playmate Ava Fabian), and naturally he stops behaving like a man of the cloth pretty quick. He gets her to park in a secluded spot, tosses her on the ground, and... I'm unsure if there's supposed to be a rape indicated here. If there is, it's probably one of the least coherent bits of storytelling in movie history, but if not, then I'm not sure what Ugly is grunting about. In any case, she quickly stabs him in the head with a pick, zips him into a bodybag she conveniently keeps in her trunk, and takes him home to Auntie Lee.

Magnolia, you see, is one of Auntie Lee's four drop-dead gorgeous nieces; the others are Fawn (Kristine Anne Rose), Coral (former playmate Teri Weigel—and thanks to everyone's affected drawl, I honestly thought her name was "Carl" until the closing credits), and Sky (former playmate Pia Reyes, the token Asian). There's also Baby (former playmate—are we sensing a trend?—Petra Verkaik), just as gorgeous as the others, but mentally at the level of an infant and confined to a huge playpen upstairs. And rounding out the family is Auntie Lee's well-meaning but cretinous brother Larry (Michael Berryman), whom the others use as the general gopher and manservant. (Berryman looks even more bizarre than usual because he plays the role without his dentures.) As part of their standard business practices, the girls pick up hitchhikers and other "strays" and bring them home for a quick butchering (usually on the pretense of a tryst—if you've gotta go, I suppose anticipatory excitement is a pretty good final sensation) and inclusion in those meat pies which are so popular all over the rural county.

And now that you've gotten the setup, what else can I tell you about the movie? The story is thinner than the fabric of the girls' outfits, unless you use "plot" to mean "stuff that happens, followed by other stuff that happens."

Part of our running time is taken up with the search for one Bob Evans (Stephen Quadros), one of Fawn's victims being sought on behalf of his wealthy father by private eye Harold Ivars (David Parry). Harold hails from New York City, and proclaims it at every conceivable juncture ("I'm not the kind of guy you want to push around, I'm from New York!"); I'm surprised that the producers weren't hit with a class-action lawsuit from the City, County, and State of New York for portraying them as being witless losers with incredibly bad fashion sense.

The good news is that he's not the only representative of the Big Apple; the bad news is that the other New Yorkers are a three-man rock band and their manager, traveling

to L.A. in a convertible. The girls shoot out their tires and the foursome gets invited back to the ranch for dinner. It's incredible how much time they spend on this, with each of the girls getting to know her designated guy, the serving of hors d'oeuvres and dinner (with Auntie Lee saying a beautiful prayer to the Lord of Darkness), and then each of the four getting sliced and diced separately and with extensive, um, foreplay. At least it's not completely boring, but since the four rockers have proven themselves to be stupid, self-obsessed, and generally unsympathetic, it's not like we cringe as each is dispatched with increasing novelty. One gets the idea that the production crew was getting a little bored by this point as well, since the last half hour is characterized more and more by colored gels, moving shadows, and blacklight glows on increasingly surreal sets.

The only two characters who even manage to come off as halfway sympathetic are poor, beset-upon Larry, and the town's lone police officer, Chief Koal (Pat Morita—I guess rent was due that week). Larry's got a hankering to be a policeman, and Koal lets him consider himself a "volunteer deputy"—until Koal finds Larry's stash of human bones in the back of Coral's car and assumes that brain-damaged Larry's been killing hitchhikers on his own.

Holding all of these elements together loosely are a few interesting cameos (in addition to Pat Paulsen, we've got Huntz Hall as a crotchety farmer), running gags dissing New Yorkers and pretentious rockers, a fair number of cheesecake shots (though a surprisingly low level of nudity), and of course the double-entendres which are to be expected when half of your cast is Playboy playmates. (Fawn to hitchhiker: "How far are you going?" Hitchhiker, looking her up and down: "All the way, if I can.")

Really, aside from the opportunity to see Michael Berryman play a hapless gomer without his choppers, there's very little here that hasn't been done several times at least as well, and usually better, in previous cannibal movies. I mean, there are only so many gags to be made about "inviting someone home for dinner."

Some Notable Totables:
- body count: 9, plus 1 chicken
- breasts: 4
- explosions: 3
- ominous thunderstorms: 0
- actors who've appeared on *Star Trek*: 1
    - Michael Berryman (Larry) played "Captain Rixx" in the *TNG* episode "Conspiracy, and "Starfleet Display Officer" in *Star Trek 4*

EXCESSIVE FORCE (1992)

FINALLY THE PUNISHMENT FITS THE CRIME.

- Directed by Jon Hess
- Written by Thomas Ian Griffith
- Starring Thomas Ian Griffith, Lance Henriksen, James Earl Jones, Tony Todd and Burt Young
- Produced by Oscar L. Costo, Thomas Ian Griffith and Erwin Stoff
- Executive produced by Michael Harpster

The '80s were the golden age of the Unbeatable Action Hero movie. I'm not just talking about normal action stars, I mean the mighty muscled ones who could take out entire enemy platoons with no injuries save a couple of artfully placed and easily ignored flesh wounds. Stallone. Schwarzenegger. Norris. Seagal. All of them larger than life, indomitable in a fight, comic-booky to the extreme.

That Unbeatable Hero burned out in the wake of *Die Hard* (1988), in which Bruce Willis portrayed a normal guy who gets the snot beaten out of him and still doesn't give up. Within a very few years, and for most of the '90s, underdog everyman heroes became the norm, and Willis and Cruise and even Hanks were playing much more mortal protagonists who survived because of their pluck, their luck, and their ability to stand back up after having the crap kicked out of their hides.

It was right during that transition that *Excessive Force* came along, with Thomas Ian Griffith performing very much in the spirit of the wish-fulfillment Unbeatable Hero mold. The tag line for the movie posits Griffith as the '90s answer to Seagal in the '80s and Norris in the '70s. A pity for him that it's so darned true.

Griffith plays Terry McCain, one of a trio of Chicago police detectives, along with Dylan (Tom Hodges) and Frankie (Tony Todd), who've got a grudge against mob boss Sal DiMarco (Burt Young). Being the badged bad-asses that they are, they take it upon themselves, without any backup, to break up a drug deal between DiMarco's underlings and some Irish gangsters. Things don't go smoothly, and guns start a-poppin' on all sides. We get quite a bit of action eye-candy as Terry punches, chops, and high-kicks seemingly dozens of armed thugs, all without mussing his preppy clothes or delicately coiffed hair.

When the smoke clears, only the three cops and two of DiMarco's men are left alive (one gets away, the other's in traction after a fling through a barroom window that lands him on a visible cushion pad). Terry then takes it upon himself to lean on—literally—the injured one in his hospital room to get a confession incriminating DiMarco. At which point, I wondered if Griffith (who also wrote the screenplay) had ever met a real cop. Does the phrase "under duress" ring a bell? How about "right to an attorney"?

As was obvious to me (but not to Terry

and his cronies), the judge immediately throws out the forced confession and the entire case with it. This doesn't sit well with Devlin (Lance Henriksen), Terry's superior, who tosses all of the "loose cannon" clichés into a single berating. Not that Devlin's actually got it in for Terry; he simply wants to see DiMarco go down, and Terry's asinine antics sure aren't helping.

Terry naturally fumes, but let's not forget that he's got a life outside his obsession with DiMarco. For instance, he often hangs at the jazz club on the ground floor of his apartment building—run by James Earl Jones, no less—sitting in on the piano with the band. And until recently, he'd been romantically involved with prestigious supermodel Anna (Charlotte Lewis). Did I mention that Griffith wrote this screenplay for himself to star?

Of course, if Terry were left alone to fume about DiMarco and tickle the ivories, it wouldn't be much of a movie, would it? But DiMarco's got a major grievance; in the course of the bust, $3,000,000 went missing. So first he kills the single escaping henchman (for bungling it), then starts after the three cops, one of whom must have it.

Dylan buys it first, after having his kneecaps broken by DiMarco's son Vinnie (W. Earl Brown) during questioning. Then Frankie gets exploded along with his apartment. With only Terry still walking around in one piece, Devlin lets him know that there are sometimes when you have to break the rules to save your skin, and that Devlin will cover for whatever Terry thinks is necessary.

Terry's vendetta gives him an opportunity to beat the hell out of a private club composed entirely of the employees of Italian-American businessmen, then go mope at his ex-girlfriend's place (nothing like a little bit of bereavement to reawaken old passions), and then finally to DiMarco's after-hours restaurant, which is so ridiculously under-guarded—unguarded, really—that one wonders how DiMarco managed to stay alive so long. After beating up two henchmen without breaking a sweat, Terry pulls a gun on DiMarco… but can't bring himself to shoot a frightened, crying, pathetic gangster.

So if Terry didn't kill him, then why does the next morning's newspaper proudly proclaim "DiMarco Found Dead"?

Obviously, there are double-crosses, duplicity, and various schemes afoot, all of which engenders a strong sense of déjà vu. I've already mentioned the strong vanity element of the story—hey, if you're going to write a screenplay to show off your martial arts prowess, you're going to make yourself ultra-cool, right? But this actually isn't the worst flaw, being eclipsed by both cliché and convenience.

As examples of cliché… Well, did you catch that DiMarco's son's name is Vinnie? It seems that Griffith's inspiration was more or less a whole big stack of other cops-and-mobsters movies, all at least a few iterations removed from real police work. (Would it have hurt to read a couple of Ed McBain novels? Or even watch a few episodes of *Law & Order*?) Terry's at least as stylin' a detective (and as improbably young) as *Miami Vice*'s Sonny Crockett, and no one else is any more original. DiMarco spends all of his time eating in his own Italian restaurants (made me hungry, but didn't get high marks for originality).

The convenience factor is even worse. Even I, Captain Suburban himself, would have better instincts for self-preservation, including having damned good locks on my doors, and not trying to hide out in a farmhouse owned in my name (it's no big secret, Terry, that that stuff's a matter of public record). Not a one of the various thugs and goons on Terry's tail has the least idea of tactics or strategy; surrounding a location is apparently never an option. We've even got the hackneyed device of an intruder hearing a message being left on someone's answering machine—twice. And apparently a wanted felon, who also happens to be a former police officer known by sight to everyone else on the force, can lie in wait in his car right outside police headquarters without any threat of being seen.

Griffith's managed to make a living for himself since that first couple of superheroic films, largely in the roles of charismatic bad guys. But he tried to bust into a subgenre already on the wane, in a vehicle frankensteined out of pieces of other, better movies. It's no surprise that he never really became the '90s answer to Chuck Norris.

Some Notable Totables:
- body count: 22
- breasts: 4
- explosions: 1
- ominous thunderstorms: 0
- actors who've appeared on *Star Trek*: 5
  - Tony Todd (Frankie) played Worf's brother Kurn on several episodes of *TNG* and *DS9*, as well as the grown-up Jake Sisko in the *DS9* episode "The Visitor," and "Alpha Hirogen" in the *Voyager* episode "Prey"
  - Tony Epper (the delivery man) played "Drunken Klingon" in the *DS9* episode "Apocalypse Rising"
  - Danny Goldring (Lieutenant Landry) played "Legate Kell" in the *DS9* episode "Civil Defense," "Burke" in the *DS9* episode "Nor the Battle to the Strong," "Alpha Hirogen/Nazi Commandant" in the *Voyager* two-parter "The Killing Game," and the Nausicaan Captain in the *Enterprise* episode "Fortunate Son"
  - Bobby Bass (the limo driver) played a guard in the classic episode "Space Seed"
  - Tom Hodges (Dylan) played "Pechetti" in the *DS9* episode "Empok Nor"

FORTRESS (1992)

IN THE YEAR 2017, ONE CORPORATION IS BUILDING A FORTRESS FOR THE ULTIMATE TAKEOVER... YOUR MIND.

- *Directed by Stuart Gordon*
- *Written by Steven Feinberg, Terry Curtis Fox, and David Venable*
- *Starring Christopher Lambert, Kurtwood Smith, Loryn Locklin, Lincoln Kilpatrick and Jeffrey Combs*
- *Produced by John Davis and John Flock*
- *Executive produced by Graham Burke, Greg Coote and Terry Ryan*

This movie comes to us from director Stuart Gordon, to whom the phrase "wildly uneven" applies perfectly. Gordon has given the horror genre some of its modern classics, including *Re-Animator* (1985), *From Beyond* (1986), *The Pit and the Pendulum* (1991), and *Castle Freak* (1995); but when he turns his hand to sci-fi, it seems like he relinquishes the director's chair to his evil twin, inflicting the likes of *Robot Jox* (1990) upon us. Fortress occupies the middle ground; it's solidly sci-fi, and corny sci-fi at that, but it's energetic and fun and not so bad that you feel embarrassed for having enjoyed it.

In the (cough, cough) near future, ex-Army Captain John Brennick (Christopher Lambert) and his wife and former fellow soldier Karen (Loryn Locklin, best known from commercials as the perky minivan lady) are trying desperately to cross the border into Canada, because Karen is pregnant for a second time—a no-no under oppressive population laws, even though their first child died at birth. Caught at the border, John sacrifices himself to the police to give Karen a chance to get across the bridge into freedom. This is the only satisfaction he can hold to as he is sentenced to thirty-one years of incarceration in "the Fortress." He is now effectively the property of the MenTel Corporation, the private company to which the government has outsourced the prison system.

The Fortress a big-ass underground prison, thirty-three stories deep. As an added control measure, the prisoners are outfitted with "Intestinators," little devices the size of an egg yolk forcibly inserted down their throats into their abdomens, with which the central computer can zap them. (Oddly enough, we are first shown the "pain" penalty for crossing yellow-lined zones, and "death" for entering red-lined zones. Then, for the rest of the movie, there isn't a single yellow- or red-lined zone. Must have been entirely meant as an object lesson; I pity the poor claustrophobic prisoner who decided to demonstrate it for his comrades.)

Brennick soon meets his bunkmates: Gomez (Clifton Collins Jr.), who entered the Fortress with Brennick; myopic computer geek D-Day (Jeffrey Combs); shaven-headed bad-ass Stiggs (Tom Towles, from *Henry: Portrait of a Serial Killer* (1986) and the remade *Night of the Living Dead* (1990)), and steward Abraham (Lincoln Kilpatrick, the poor man's Morgan Freeman). The five of them are crowded into a two-bunk cell with a laser perimeter, guarded by a roving computer eye which can also monitor and interrupt your dreams (a fact Brennick finds out the first night).

Brennick's just fine with this—fine with standing up to bully Stiggs and his psycho friend Maddox (Vernon Wells from *The Road Warrior* (1981)), fine with defending diminutive Gomez from Maddox's attempted rape, fine with visiting with Prison Director Poe (Kurtwood Smith, who went on to become very recognizable from TV's *That '70s Show*) about the resulting altercation—but everything becomes very not fine very quickly when Poe shows him that Karen did not escape after all; she's incarcerated in the women's section of the Fortress. And her baby, when it's born, will be the permanent property of the MenTel Corporation.

So naturally Brennick is going to try to escape, and take Karen with him.

It's a good little film, kept very interesting by a multitude of plot twists: Director Poe, a nasty little voyeur hanging on to what little shreds of humanity he has, takes a fancy to Karen and has her move into his apartments, not for sex, but for companionship. Her presence here is the only thing that saves Brennick when, after a deadly fight with Maddox, he's sent to the Mind Wipe chamber, where a huge gyroscoping brain controller drives him mad.

There are fights, escapes, bio-engineered soldiers, revelations as to the fate of appropriated babies (hint: Director Poe ain't exactly normal), the requisite ingenious prison break, and just about the most difficult delivery I've ever seen.

The beauty of this movie is that it's not terribly ambitious; Gordon knew that it was not meant to be this generation's defining science fiction film, and so instead had fun with it. The characters are colorful and engaging, and the actors are B-movie all-stars; the story moves along at a fair clip; and the prison itself is a novel setting, with plenty of inconsistencies in future technology but none that sit up and insist that you notice them.

I don't know if it's art, but it's fun.

Some Notable Totables:
- body count: 21
- breasts: 2
- explosions: 2

- dream sequences: 4
- ominous thunderstorms: 0
- actors who've appeared on *Star Trek*: 3
  - Jeffrey Combs is obviously a regular in the *ST* universe, with two recurring roles (Weyoun and Brunt the Ferengi, including one episode in which he was both) plus two other guest shots on *DS9*, a guest role on *Voyager*, and a recurring role on *Enterprise*
  - Kurtwood Smith (Poe) was Federation President (under a long white hairpiece) in *Star Trek 6*, also playing Annorax on the *Voyager* two-parter "Year in Hell," plus a guest shot on DS9
  - Tom Towles (Stiggs) had guest shots on both *Voyager* and *DS9* (the latter as a Klingon)

KNIGHTS (1992)

He said its takes a cyborg to kill a cyborg. She's going to prove him dead wrong.

- *Written and directed by Albert Pyun*
- *Starring Kathy Long, Kris Kristofferson, Lance Henriksen, Scott Paulin and Gary Daniels*
- *Produced by Tom Karnowski*

Albert Pyun directed his first film in 1982, the minor cult favorite *The Sword and the Sorcerer*. Since that time, he has amassed over fifty directorial credits, almost all of them in the sci-fi or action fields. Pyun has, for many people, supplanted Alfred Hitchcock as the best evidence of the "auteur theory," the idea that it is the director's artistic vision which determines the tenor of a movie more than the contributions of anyone else who collaborates on that movie. Pyun's movies certain to have a distinctive quality to them: they all suck. And what's more, they all suck in the same way; despite elements which should fire a genre cinema fan's blood—robots and aliens and gunfights and explosions—they all end up being strangely unengaging, and even dead boring. It's Albert Pyun's signature style.

Between 1989 and 1996, Pyun made no fewer than eight movies focusing on robots or androids of some kind or other, most of which were erroneously called "cyborgs" despite having no biological component. At least in *Knights* (which he both wrote and directed), the cyborgs are actually cyborgs, flesh and metal grafted together. And what are the cyborgs doing this time around? Well, let's see if I can piece together the backstory for you:

Sometime in the future, when humanity has ruined the planet and left it looking a lot like Southern Utah (exactly like Southern Utah, in fact, as evidenced by some landmarks familiar from John Wayne movies), some deadly cyborgs arrive from… I dunno. Apparently they were part of a government assassin project, although there's also mention of place called "Genesis," which

may or may not be off-planet. These cyborgs were built by someone called "the Creator," now dead, who made them with finite power sources; but then a second entity came along, called "the Master Builder," who converted the cyborgs so that they could run on human blood, extracted through hypos that the cyborgs can extend from their fingertips. Now thralls to the Master Builder, the twenty evil cyborgs roam the wasteland looking like Borg Bedouins, under the leadership of Job (Lane Henriksen), who has a huge mechanical arm and drools on himself a lot.

If these cyborgs were as smart as your average VIC-20, the remnants of humanity would be in deep trouble, especially because the cataclysms that wiped out civilization, as usual, appear to have preserved only the shallow end of the gene pool, leaving the world to be repopulated by microcephalic dullards. Fortunately, the cyborgs are no smarter, just a little meaner. For example, our first scene has a troop of cyborgs on horseback confronting some wandering farmer refugees in the desert, demanding their surrender in return for a painless death, and the lives of the children among them. Otherwise they'll kill the children first in front of their parents' eyes. Given that strategy, it would behoove the cyborgs not to let a mother hand her infant to her young daughter Nea and let the two of them trot off to safety in full view of the aggressors. But I guess Job is too busy exchanging sparkling dialogue with the lead farmer, to wit:

Farmer: They say you are the devil!
Job: I am the prophet, farmer, of things to come.
Farmer: All you bring is death!
Job: Death… is the future.

I find that last comment disturbing, because I'm very interested in the future. It is, after all, where you and I are going to spend the rest of our lives.

Ten years later (wow! it's the future already!), Nea (Kathy Long) is living with another bunch of squatter farmers, in what looks like maybe a half-dozen tents held up with rickety, unsecured poles. Which proves convenient, because it makes them easy to knock down when… the cyborgs attack!

Actually, it's mostly human collaborators under the direction of a single cyborg, Simon (Scott Paulin), who isn't terribly successful in getting his men to understand the whole "capture them alive" directive. In fact, it turns out that Nea is the only survivor, thanks to getting knocked out early on (that happens to movie heroes a lot). Thanks to the resulting slim pickings, Simon is just about to puncture her and fingerslurp

her blood when a mysterious stranger appears on horseback. Who could it be?

Well, in close-up shots, it's Kris Kristofferson. In action scenes (all shot from a distance, or with his back to the camera, or just with strong sunlight overhead to put his face in shadow), it's a stunt double who appears on screen often enough to deserve a co-starring credit. In either case, the character is Gabriel, the cyborg who kills cyborgs. Seems he was the final creation of the Creator, built out of spare parts, who was never compromised by the Master Builder, and whose hardwired mission is to wipe out all of the evil cyborgs before his internal power supply runs out in a year. All clear?

Gabriel ends up destroying Simon after some painfully "witty" dialogue (which disturbingly mirrors the Westley/Inigo banter in *The Princess Bride* (1987)), and rescues the injured Nea. Although he plans simply to leave her somewhere to heal, she wants to go with him to kick some cyborg ass, and makes him a deal. She overheard that the cyborg army with one thousand humans (and no, you're never going to see them all on screen at one time) is on its way to Taos, a city of 10,000 inhabitants a few weeks away, to suck oodles of blood for the Master Builder. She knows a shortcut that the two of them can take in order to catch up to the army, and all he has to do over the next five weeks is teach her how to kill cyborgs.

Which, despite his protestations and the cyborg reputation, is pretty darned easy. The cyborgs have this reputation for being unkillable, but Gabriel reveals that a direct strike to the "kill zone" in the center of the forehead will "take their systems offline" (and often cause their heads to smoke and melt) with a sound like the Millennium Falcon's hyperdrive giving up the ghost. Let's see—a poke with a pointy object right between the eyes is the secret Achilles' Heel of the supposedly unbeatable enemy? I'd file that under "Helluva Design Flaw."

So in what amounts to two parallel montages, the cyborg army marches, twenty extras at a time, while Gabriel trains Nea and makes her run behind the horse. It's here that you'll probably notice that Albert Pyun likes colored camera filters. Really, really likes them. Red ones, blue ones, green ones, yellow ones, it's all good. One of his favorite tricks is putting a filter on only the upper half of the lens when shooting landscapes and panoramas, which gives the impression of lowering skies. Or would, if it were used competently; on the other hand, when a mounted figure rides into the frame, his head high enough that the filter turns him black against the dark green sky, then it just gives the impression that there's something dark on the upper half of the lens. And just to give the right atmosphere to it all, the musical soundtrack is sharply divided between the generic staccato action riff that has besieged action cinema ever since *Predator* (1987), and a peppy, upbeat keyboard melody that sounds like it was rejected as theme music for the Special Olympics.

Killing time in unheard-of amounts, Gabriel feeds Nea (and us) bits of that whole Creator/Master Builder backstory that I gave you at the beginning—just enough to be annoying instead of intriguing. They also talk about being human, dreaming, and other subjects that humans and robots just have to explore whenever stuck together. Eventually, though, a team of cyborgs trailing them catches up, blows Gabriel in half, and leaves Nea with a slaver. But since she's studied ass-kicking so well, she escapes and infiltrates the cyborg army camp the day before the attack on Taos.

Well, of course! You didn't think they'd have the budget to show an actual town, did you? No, we get to see a matte painting from a fair distance, but the day before the attack, Job proclaims some gladiatorial combat with prisoners as a morale-builder, and Nea eagerly steps up, defeats the champion, and then proceeds to decimate the entire army as they attack her in twos and threes.

Come to think of it, an attack by the army on Taos would have been something to

see. Given that this "formidable army," and the combined might of the remaining cyborgs, is unable to stop a single girl armed with whatever pointy sticks are close at hand, it would have been the height of comedy to see them attempt to attack a fortified city which outnumbered them ten-to-one. And the cyborgs go down so easily it's embarrassing, as if their foreheads are made of Silly Putty. It's sort of like watching one of the later Hammer *Dracula* films, in which any time a vampire stumbled over a chair, you just knew that it would break apart in such a way that a flesh-piercing wooden stake would conveniently stick straight up.

Oh, and there's also a stupid subplot about Nea wondering where her baby brother is (remember, the infant she carried away in the prologue?), after she left him at a village which was soon torched by the cyborgs. I only mention it because she finally meets up with him by pure dumb luck, only to have him carted off by the Master Builder himself—a guy in a mechanical skull mask who shows up just long enough to grab the tyke and escape by hang glider. To make sure this is as anticlimactic as humanly possible, this unknown skullguy isn't even identified as the Master Builder until he's gone. "Oh, that was him—you just missed him!"

Given that the entire ending is left open with the Master Builder stuff, we have no choice but to end up at a supposed cliffhanger, where Nea's voiceover proclaims that their pursuit of the Master Builder would eventually take them to the "Cyborg City," to Genesis (again—where or what that is, we don't know), and even to the edge of the universe, none of which is easily filmable in the environs of Moab, Utah. I say "supposed" because Pyun must have known that there's no way in God's green earth he'd ever get the budget to continue this series with more than a handful of low-rent Borg running around the buttes; instead, it seems more the ending of desperation, as he realized that his story really had no ending. If he'd realized that it also had no beginning or middle, we could have been spared the entire sorry spectacle.

Kathy Long, according to the back of the box, is a "five-time kickboxing champion" (she was also Michelle Pfeiffer's fight double in *Batman Returns* (1992), so that must count for something). I rarely expect Oscar-winning actors to be martial arts experts, so it would be unfair for me to rag on Long's thespian shortcomings, knowing that she was hired solely for her taut buttocks. With everyone else, though, it seems like a criminal case of under-direction (yes, I will lay this too at Pyun's feet). Kristofferson squints into the sun and drawls his lines in that emotive style which I refer to as "reading the Taco Bell menu." Henriksen, in extreme contrast, puts his heart into it and comes across as the Dirty Old Cyborg, constantly growling, rasping, mugging, and of course drooling. While watching the staged combats, he sits in his pavilion, rocking back and forth as he makes little growling noises in his throat; he seems to be, um, enjoying himself so much that I was grateful the camera doesn't show what he's doing with his hand. (Or his hook.)

Not that anyone could do anything with his script. Most of it is in such leaden pretentious tones that even James Earl Jones would sound embarrassed, punctuated by brief moments of "wit" that sound like they were made up on the set once heatstroke had set in. Brief, vague messianic allusions blend with intimations that "there's something profound about all of this, but we're not going to let you in on it." All of it proof that Albert Pyun is as dangerous behind a keyboard as he is behind a camera.

Some Notable Totables:
- body count (including the cyborgs, as they're not significantly less lifelike than the rest of the cast): 77
- breasts: 0
- explosions: 3
- ominous thunderstorms: 0
- actors who've appeared on *Star Trek*: 1
    - Nicholas Guest (the outspoken farmer) was the dying cadet in *Star Trek 2*

PROTOTYPE X29A (1992)

PART MAN. PART MACHINE. ALL KILLER.
MANKIND DOESN'T STAND A CHANCE.

aka *Prototype*, aka *Final Experiment*

- Directed by Phillip Roth
- Written by Phillip Roth and George Temple
- Starring Lane Lenhart, Robert Tossberg, Sebastian Scandiuzzi, Brenda Swanson and Paul Coulj
- Produced by Talaat Captan, Phillip Roth, and Gian-Carlo Scandiuzzi

This is more than just a very bad movie, though it definitely is that; it's a *puzzling* very bad movie. Most movies, no matter how bad, have a certain spark at the core that you can recognize as the reason someone originally wanted to make the movie. Even the worst of movies have an identifiable something-or-other that lets the astute viewer know what it is that the moviemaker was trying to make a movie about, no matter how bungled the final execution was. (This doesn't mean that the inciting idea had any merit whatsoever, but at least you can discover what first seized someone's imagination.)

This one, though… I'm stumped. What, exactly, was writer/director Phillip Roth trying to accomplish? What story was he trying to tell? Whatever it was, he bungled it so badly that not only did he fail to accomplish his storytelling goal, I can't even discern what that goal was.

According to the onscreen textual exposition, in the mid-21st century there arises a group of humans called "Omegas" who have been cybernetically altered. They gain the ability to change their programming and implants, so in 2057 the government creates a line of cyborgs called "Prototypes" to hunt down the Omegas. In other words, the Prototypes aren't actually prototypes; they're a done deal. When an entire movie is focused around a misused word, you know you're in for 90 minutes of pain.

Actually, the first twelve minutes aren't terribly painful, mostly because they're an action setpiece. In the futuristic landscape of destroyed Los Angeles, represented by a semi-demolished industrial yard (shot through a yellow filter, as are all of the exteriors and most interiors in this movie), a few rebel Omegas (watch for Kato Kaelin in a small speaking role) are guarding against the onslaught of a single Prototype with a big-ass gun. The Prototype has several features characteristic of cheap robot suits: huge square metallic pecs, a dozen cables connecting the clavicle area to the jawline, and a built-in protective cup.

Inside the building being guarded, an Omega scientist is jacking into a computer via an I/O port on the back of his neck. He then hands his toddler daughter, Chandra, off to a Bedouin-wrapped woman along with a medallion that will "tell her when it's time" or somesuch. The daughter's Raggedy Ann doll is significantly left behind as the woman heads with the child toward "the outskirts." Meanwhile, the Prototype breaks in and offs the scientist.

That part wasn't too bad. Then we fast-forward twenty years, and everything goes to hell.

Yes, it's all still shot with a yellow filter, and apparently it's being shot in the same demolished factory. Everyone's dressed alike in *Road Warrior* castoffs, and apparently they spend their days sitting around in the ruins like homeless people. Look, folks, the city's been knocked down. There's no industry; there's no food source. There's no reason to stick around. I know Los Angelenos have this idea that the world outside L.A. doesn't exist, but come on.

The notable people in this yellow world are grown-up Chandra (Lane Lenhart), a beret-wearing bad-ass girl; her teenage foster brother Sebastian (Sebastian Scandiuzzi), and wheelchair-bound veteran of something-or-other Hawkins (Robert Tossberg). Hawkins, being paraplegic, is necessarily a tech wizard; he also demonstrates that, despite all of the worthwhile things the world has lost, the mullet has tenaciously survived, not unlike the cockroach. These three form a little unit: Sebastian leeches off his sister and gets tech favors from Hawkins, Hawkins pines for Chandra despite feelings of inadequacy, and Chandra basically acts surly and petulant and unsympathetic and not at all like the savior figure her father had intended her to become.

There's also Dr. Alexis Zalazny (Brenda Swanson), the young, sweaty, tank-top-clad science hottie who's gotten government permission to enter the city and reopen the sealed Prototype project to rediscover some of the medical benefits associated with it. Which means she's going to spend the lion's share of her screentime typing, staring at computer screens with one eyebrow cocked, and perspiring into her cleavage.

And here's where my synopsis breaks down, because for so much of the rest of the movie, nothing happens. That is, things happen, but they're uninteresting things which don't move forward anything resembling a story. Hawkins has cybersex with a VR Chandra. Dr. Zalazny types some and exchanges pointless dialogue with Taurence (Paul Coulj), the caretaker of the old Prototype facility. Some zen-like fighters wander the city, wordlessly beating up antisocial punks. Sebastian pisses off Hawkins' preacher landlord. Chandra apparently turns tricks as a post-apocalyptic hooker. Hawkins has his insensate ass handed to him by some more young punks, despite his impressive wheelchair fu. Zalazny types some more, and tries to revive one of the original Prototype subjects from a suspended animation tube (she fails). Chandra plays "come here/go away" with Hawkins far past the point at which I would have cut bait and told her to go to hell.

Finally, close to an hour into the movie, something resembling a plot drags itself from the primordial ooze. Zalazny checks old veterans' records and finds Hawkins living nearby. For reasons that escaped me (not that I had the will to pay close attention by this point), his veteran-ness makes him a perfect candidate subject for the Prototype project, so Zalazny visits him and offers him, essentially, the use of his legs again by being made into a Prototype (which, this time, is really a test case, so he'd be a prototype Prototype).

Aha, you say. There's finally a story here. Hawkins will get made into a Prototype, but the Prototype's mission is to wipe out Omegas, and Chandra is the last Omega. And you'd be right, but hold your horses. There's still a lot of meaningless filler in the pipeline. Sebastian almost gets killed while "processing" (which, after mentioning it without explanation for most of the movie, turns out to be using a lipbalm-sized computer to count cards), and he and Chandra are rescued by the silent toughs, who turn out to be the "Protectors"— devoted only to protecting the Omega, and called into action when the Prototype computer got turned on.

Which, I suppose, is as good a place to rant as any. The prologue almost paints Chandra in messianic terms, rocketed from the dying planet Krypton to rally and lead a people. She does none of that; in fact, she's the least active person in the story. She exhibits none of the enhancement and leadership ability that her father expected of her; she's not even remotely worth having four bruisers devote their lives to protecting her. Yet they do, dragging her off to her father's old lab, cutting through the skin on the back of her neck which hides her implant, and jacking her in to speak to her VR father. She responds by whimpering and running scared.

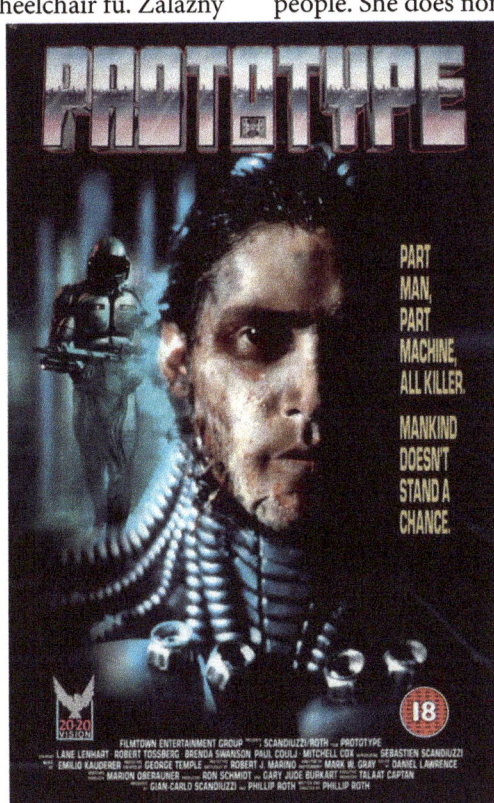

Meanwhile, among all of this, Hawkins has gone in and gotten transformed into a Prototype, with his memories recorded and reimplanted so he can do that "searching memory" thing every time he sees someone's face. He goes and visits Chandra, who's understandably freaked by his transformation. And then the evil Taurence, who turns out to have been the originator of the Prototype program in the first place (does that mean we get to blame him for calling them "Prototypes?"), kills Dr. Zalazny and turns on "Level 3" of the Prototype programming, which is the "kill all Omegas" part.

Which, you may think, will finally ratchet the story into high gear. But no. ProtoHawkins goes out, homed in on Chandra's signal, and runs into the Protectors, who make great strides against what's supposed to be an unstoppable, indestructible cyborg; one of them manages to judo-flip him twice. Then Chandra shows up and tells her Protectors, "No! Don't kill him!", giving ProtoHawkins a change to slaughter all of the Protectors. Yay, Chandra. Way to exhibit those enhanced leadership skills.

ProtoHawkins chases Chandra down and has his hands around her throat when Sebastian shows up and starts shooting at him. ProtoHawkins breaks off and grabs Sebastian around the throat—but then his memory banks dredge up Sebastian's image, and ProtoHawkins drops him and wanders off to tear away his protective helmet and die. The end. Catch that? Hawkins was completely prepared to kill Chandra; it was remembering the supporting character that reasserted his personality and control over his programming. Even here, at the very climax of the movie, Chandra's presence amounts to "no big whup."

And still, as the closing credits roll, we have no idea what the point of the Omegas was in the first place (I suppose I could posit, "Considering how clueless and ineffectual she is with her implants, imagine how bad she'd be without them!"), nor what they were doing that caused the government to start the Prototype program. Or, notably, what the medallion from the prologue has to do with anything. There's no indication of why the world's gone to hell. All in all, there's nothing here to tell me why somebody thought that this movie was a good idea.

If, however, I had done a little research before viewing, I wouldn't have been at all surprised at how pointless the entire exercise was. Phillip Roth's next film was *A.P.E.X.* (1994), which is an even more horrendously bad sci-fi film (also involving cyborg suits). And the pain doesn't stop there; Roth's filmography spans a dozen movies over a decade and a half (including such largely unseen stinkers as *Boa* (2001) and *Interceptor Force* (1999)) before finally confining his energies to producing, not directing. Being one more step removed from the camera is a good thing, in his case.

Some Notable Totables:
- body count: 16
- breasts: 2
- explosions: 20
- dream sequences: 1
- ominous thunderstorms: 0
- actors who've appeared on *Star Trek*: 0

SPLIT SECOND (1992)

He's seen the future... Now he has to kill it.

- Directed by Tony Maylam (and Ian Sharp)
- Written by Gary Scott Thompson
- Starring Rutger Hauer, Kim Cattrall, Neil Duncan, Michael J. Pollard and Alun Armstrong
- Produced by Laura Gregory
- Executive produced by Kevin Cavele and Chris Hanley

There's no way I can call this a good movie. It's a frankensteined patchwork of better films, held together with a puzzling setting and a bunch of explanatory gibberish that sounds like the aftermath of an explosion in an occult bookstore. It's patently silly in spots. But if approached in the right frame of mind, it can be a considerable amount of fun. when I first saw it, I was in the wrong frame of mind; I watched it at the insistence of a friend whose enthusiasm set me up with the expectation of a much better movie. When I it a decade later, it went down much easier because I know what to expect. (Plus, my standards had plummeted in the intervening years.)

Director Tony Maylam knew what to put front and center: Rutger Hauer. A very, very tough-looking Rutger Hauer: big black motorcycle boots to his knees, black fingerless gloves, a huge black trenchcoat, round sunglasses after dark, big-ass guns, and an ever-present cigar. He's like an amalgam of every fanboy's delusion of what they look like in their own black trenchcoats. Just ignore the fact that Hauer's wearing shoulderpads under his (black) shirt to distract from the fact that his torso is responding to the inexorable pull of gravity; that slump is balanced out by Hauer's facial appearance at this age—tired and worn, but still tough enough to chew nails. It's the perfect version of Hauer for this role.

The role in question is that of Harley Stone, an American cop working in London in the far-flung future of 2008, after eco-disasters have flooded the city and clouded the atmosphere to a permanent pseudo-night. (The intro material makes sure to blame this on the U.S. dragging their feet on environmental treaties, naturally.) What does this contribute to the movie? Not a lot, really, except plenty of puddles for people to splash through, and an excuse for all the moody night shooting. Why's Stone in London? Also murky, but best explained by the following exchange between Detective Dick Durkin (Neil Duncan), soon to be Stone's new partner, and Lieutenant Thrasher (Alun Armstrong), their commanding officer:

Durkin: If you ask me, he's nuts!
Thrasher: That's what the doctors say. Here, read the file. He's worked in every hellhole in the world, and been fired from all of them.

Durkin: They say he's the best.
Thrasher: He is.

In other words, he's a Loose Cannon Who Works Alone And Plays By His Own Rules™. You may have encountered his type in the movies once or twice. He's also Tortured By Guilt™: his old partner, Foster, was slaughtered by a serial killer three years, while Stone was having an affair with Foster's wife. Things like this are guaranteed to drive an otherwise straight-shooting police officer to wear fingerless gloves and sunglasses at night.

Stone's still on the trail of the serial killer who killed his partner, despite the fact that he's suspended. As we discover when Stone strong-arms his way into a nightclub with bondage-costumed strippers (might as well get the requisite strip club scene out of the way), he's got some sort of connection to the killer; he can vaguely sense his presence, as indicated by a heartbeat in the sound mix. Unfortunately, he's always a wee bit too late, as he is here for a blonde who has her heart torn out in the bathroom. (The editing here is unintentionally humorous, as it really looks like Stone, hyperventilating from sensing the killer, is about to, um, hit the "Big Relax" while watching the stripper shake.)

Lt. Thrasher immediately hauls him in and fulfills his duty as commanding officer to a Loose Cannon Who Etc. by shouting at him and demanding to know what he was doing there and such. And then he takes him off suspension. Because hey, what else can you do with a suspended police officer who keeps on waving his badge and Gatling-sized gun in the faces of citizens, right? The caveat, of course, is that straitlaced Durkin, the well-educated and field-green detective, is to be his partner. It's time for buddy-cop shenanigans! (And no, you get no extra points for guessing that Stone greets this directive by growling, "I work alone!")

The killer then helpfully makes sure the entire department takes him seriously by sending Stone a chilled case with a half-eaten heart in it. In fact, the killer goes out of his way to be helpful. At his

next killing, he paints a huge sigil of Scorpio and some other arcana on the ceiling in the victim's blood. I dunno; is there such thing as a "Riddler syndrome" which forces serial killers and other baddies to taunt the police and give plenty of hints? There are, I suppose, situations in which that kind of behavior makes sense (a killer who's conflicted by self-loathing, for instance, or one for whom half the thrill is derived from making the cops look like monkeys), but as will be shown later, this isn't really one of those situations. Oh, and Thrasher has a tooth mold made from the bitten heart, and the teeth in the resulting mold are huge and non-human.

Despite this, Stone and Durkin are really the only people actively working on the case —if by "working on," we mean "wandering around waiting for Stone to get one of those premonitions accompanied by the heartbeat sound." And even they have enough time for some extra-curriculars; at Foster's slot in the mausoleum, Stone runs into Foster's widow Michelle (Kim Cattrall, still wearing her haircut from shooting *Star Trek 6* (1991), right down to the shaved temples), and she comes with him back to his apartment, though more to commiserate than to restart the affair they used to have going.

Stone's apartment fits the character perfectly: it's a cluttered loft in a half-abandoned highrise, decorated in "late industrial"—motorcycle parts and other mechanical doodads take up most of the space. (There's also a ton of Harley-Davidson memorabilia all over the place, because Stone's first name is Harley. Good thing his mother didn't name him Edsel.) The kitchen contains almost nothing but coffee and chocolates, because Stone is driven to denying himself sleep to catch the killer. And sleep deprivation-induced psychosis is good for such things. (There are also pigeons all over. Unless he's got the rare housebroken kind, I'm thinking that this place smells even worse than it looks on screen.)

From here, it's a bunch of events strung together. Durkin makes himself an instant expert on astrology and the occult, and together they deduce from the fact that the killer only attacks at high tide during the new moon and from the water-related Scorpio sign that the killer has something to do with water. Maybe. Good thing they put the sharp knives on this case. And the connection between the killer and Stone? It's because Stone got slashed in the arm by its talons when it killed his partner, and because the lab report on the saliva on the heart bears "polymorphic DNA," encompassing the genetic code of all of his victims, as well as the sewer rats that are infesting the flooded city. Does that make any sense? No, it does not.

The single funniest scene (unintentionally so) puts Stone and Durkin outside Stone's apartment building while Michelle is upstairs having a shower. Suddenly, a bloodcurdling scream rings out! They race upstairs, Stone runs into the bathroom—and gets his face slapped by naked Michelle for his trouble. But why did she scream? "The water got colder!"

As the dynamic duo starts piecing together the whats and wherefores of the killer's patterns, it seems more and more like a creature with a bizarre form of obsessive-compulsive behavior than one following any sort of ritual or plan. Case in point: He gets interrupted before he can yank the heart from one victim, so Stone and Durkin show up in the morgue to keep him from finishing his business. Really? Firstly, it's not like there are no other potential victims in all of London with which the creature can keep up its quota. Secondly, Stone and Durkin don't have any more information than we do, which means there's no reason that they should suspect that the creature will come back to the morgue for that specific, particular heart.

But the shootout in the morgue ramps us up to the final confrontations; Durkin, seeing the creature (fleetingly) for the first time as he empties his gun in its direction, makes the

transformation from bookish nebbish to gung-ho gunwielder. ("We're gonna need bigger guns!") They also make the intuitive flash that the pattern of the killings is a geographic one—he's killing people across the city to draw a huge dot-to-dot version of the sigil he drew on the ceiling. (See former comment about Riddler syndrome.) Since he killed someone in Stone's own building, does that mean that coincidentally Stone lives right in a convenient spot for the pattern? Sure, what the heck. Further mumbo-jumbo has the creature gaining power from the souls of his victims, and of course the new moon/high tide/Scorpio connection means… well, something.

Surprisingly, the killer is never shown to be a were-creature of any sort. One half-expects there to be a shocking revelation that the creature is someone we've met—Durkin, Michelle, or maybe Poulsen (Pete Postlethwaite!), the cop who's got it in for Stone—but no. Apparently he's a full-time creature with polymorphic DNA and delusions of Satanic grandeur.

One also might suppose that the final showdown, in the blocked-off metro tunnels beneath the city (shown to them by Michael J. Pollard), would require some mystical awareness or gimmick to defeat a creature who had thus far proved invulnerable. But no; their (eventually) successful strategy simply revolves around shooting and blowing up the creature until it shows some damage. Bigger guns prove themselves sufficient.

It's all really a hopeless mishmash, held tenuously together by the unusual choice of The Moody Blues' "Nights in White Satin" as a theme song (not only playing in the background, but incorporated into the score). That, and Hauer looking like all of the toughest characters from all first-person shooter games combined.

Some Notable Totables:
- body count: 7, plus 2 rats
- breasts: 4
- explosions: 10
- dream sequences: 2
- ominous thunderstorms: 0
- actors who've appeared on *Star Trek*: 2
    - Kim Catrall (Michelle) played "Valeris" in *Star Trek 6*
    - Michael J. Pollard (the Rat Catcher) played "Jahn" in the classic episode "Miri"

CARNOSAUR (1993)

DRIVEN TO EXTINCTION. BACK FOR REVENGE.

- *Written and directed by Adam Simon, based on the novel by "Harry Adam Knight" (John Brosnan)*
- *Starring Diane Ladd, Raphael Sbarge, Jennifer Runyon, Harrison Page and Clint Howard*
- *Produced by Mike Elliott*
- *Executive produced by Roger Corman*

> *"So you're going to give the earth back to the dinosaurs?"*
> *"Well, you might say that."*
> *"That's really fabulous. It'd make a great theme park."*

Roger Corman has carved out a successful niche for himself in Hollywood by following one simple principle: give the audience what they want (or at least, what they'll pay money for). Westerns are popular? He'll give you Westerns! War movies? War movies it is! Teen monster movies? You got it! So in the lead-up to Steven Spielberg's adaptation of Michael Crichton's *Jurassic Park* (1993), when all of America was ramping up its dino-mania, Corman found a property, produced this movie, and released it to "limited theatrical release" three weeks before *Jurassic Park* hit the multiplexes.

The productions which have come out of Corman's various companies have generally been competent low-budget iterations of large-budget themes, usually trading ambition for entertainment value. In this case, however, entertainment value was traded for ambition, and everything falls flat on its face.

The opening is promising enough; in fact, the opening credits are the most arresting part of the film, inasmuch as they run over documentary footage of chickens in a poultry slaughterhouse. Along with the credits are cryptic superimposed messages relating it to genetics stuff—enough to let us know vaguely that Something Is Going On.

We go directly to our necessary exposition: genetics wunderkind Dr. Jane Tiptree (Diane Ladd) has been working in silence for Eunice Foods of late in their poultry division. A certain representative of Our Government is suspicious; why would an award-winning genetic engineer be working on building a better chicken?

Then something hatches in the poultry farm and starts terrorizing the personnel. Should be a simple monster-on-the-loose film, right?

Wrong. From here on out, we're going to be exposed to more underdeveloped plot threads than you normally find in a full dozen normal B-movies. Let's see if we can catalog them:

First up, we've got "Doc" Smith (Raphael Sbarge), the drunk and underachieving night watchman of a construction site which may or may not be connected to the Eunice factory (it's never really made clear). His nickname is a reference to the fact that he couldn't wait to finish med school before becoming a drunken sot. He begins a love/hate relationship with the Gaians, an enviro-communal group who want to sabotage the heavy equipment, most especially with beautiful but belligerent member Thrush (Jennifer Runyon, best known from TV's *Charles in Charge* and the clairvoyance experiment at the beginning of *Ghostbusters* (1984); this film was apparently the final nail in her career's coffin).

We've also got the guards searching for the escaped dino-thingie, which grows at a rate that's incredible for a mammal, and flat-out impossible for a reptile: from chicken-sized to full man-in-suit-sized in 72 hours. It manages to take out a delivery truck driver, three joy-riding teens, a Mexican who apparently just wandered into it, the two guards hunting it... Again, quite a voracious appetite for a reptile.

We've also got Sheriff Fowler (Harrison Page), who takes up far too much screen time for the little he contributes here; he discovers some bodies, trades ignorance with the medical examiner, and is the first to discover that the locally-produced chicken eggs have gone weird, yielding either green goo (no ham is in evidence) or, in one case, an embryonic dinosaur, still alive despite having sat in the refrigerator with the other groceries for several hours.

Oh yeah, there's also the big-ass carnosaur that Tiptree keeps in her basement and to which she feeds the occasional employee.

Eventually, with all of this going on, Doc makes his way into Dr. Tiptree's lab and spends a good forty-five minutes of the movie simply talking to her (she cements her Mad Scientist status, as if there were any doubt, with the line: "Young man, I doubt you could possibly understand"). Dr. Tiptree despises what man is doing to the earth, so she's made a two-pronged attack on the human problem. First up, she's got the whole chicken-egg thing going. Next, she's engineered and released a virus that causes all fertile women to become both sick and pregnant with little tyrannosaurs, the delivery of which naturally kills the mother. This, she says, will put everything back the way it should be.

I tell you, there are some days it doesn't pay to visit the video store. This is ludicrous on so many levels, it's almost not worth it to enunciate them, but here are the big ones:

- Isn't it simpler to just wipe out humans, without all the dinosaur rigmarole? *Homo sapiens* is responsible for a lot of extinctions, but not that of the dinosaurs, so it's not like there's any poetic justice to be had here. (She was probably just one of those girls who loved dinosaurs as a kid, so any scheme she had to destroy the world would have to include dinosaurs. That or giant spiders.)
- · The massive re-introduction of a single predatory species is supposed to somehow create a new, stable eco-system? Seems to me that a gazillion hungry carnosaurs roaming the landscape is going to decrease the spotted owl more than the encroachment of logging. After all, it only took one critter to decrease the population of pro-environmental Gaians to exactly one (the pretty one, naturally).

Meanwhile, as Doc and Tiptree are having their insufferable philosophical conversation, the government catches on to what's going on here—so what do they do?

The same thing the government does in every one of these movies: comes goose-stepping in wearing environmental suits, quarantines the town, holds women in giant birthing tents, and shoots their husbands down in the ditch. While I know several people in the Armed Forces and none of them seem like the type to fall back on the "just following orders" crutch, I also used to live in the downwinder belt of Southern Utah, so I know even We American Good Guys have a government that's not above draconian measures for "the greater good." (The one honestly disturbing image in the entire movie is of an impregnated woman screaming, "Get it out of me!!" while the (male) brass stand around, examining her and mulling her over as if she were a fascinating bug. The only other scene that comes close is the nearly ten-minute scene of Clint Howard eating messily.)

It all ends not a moment too soon, with a conclusion that tries to be both *Dr. Strangelove* (1964) and *Night of the Living Dead* (or, more accurately, *The Crazies* (1973)), but which just comes off as lame.

Where does the fault lie? I assume it partly lies with the underlying material, the novel by "Harry Adam Knight" (*aka* John Brosnan), though I have not read it to be sure. Two of his other novels have been adapted for the low-budget screen (*Beyond Bedlam* in 1994 and *Proteus* in 1995), and the uniformity with which the adaptations become not-terribly-memorable cheese leads one to believe that it must be carried over from the source material.

Another huge slice of culpability pie must land on the plate of FX man John Carl Buechler. His effects are usually cheap but

effective, but in this outing his reliance on hokey hand puppets, hokey cable puppets and hokey rod puppets completely destroys even the suspension of disbelief that a hard-core dino fan brings to the table. This on top of the fact that "carnosaur" is really vaguely used as the title, "carnosauria" being an underused classification for larger theropods (allosaurus, megalosaurus, etc.); one would expect the dinosaurs in question to be T-Rex-style thingies, but the majority are definitely cast in the raptor mode. Yeah, I know, it's a nitpick beyond those for which I normally award demerits; I'm in a particularly vindictive mood.

But a large part of the blame must be placed on Roger Corman's production style; while serviceable for "frothy" direct-to-video fare, it simply isn't adequate for a serious, multi-threaded storyline like this. For a good contrast, look at the sequel *Carnosaur 2* (1995), which jettisons the solemn theme for a standard but well-executed *Alien* ripoff. It's far less ambitious, but because its reach doesn't so far exceed its grasp, it's vastly more enjoyable.

And I must add: the insufferable "cutesy" factor in character names here only adds one more insult to injury. They're all bird names, see. In addition to Thrush and Sheriff Fowler, mentioned earlier, we've also got characters named Dr. Raven, Swanson, Peregrine, Mallard, Wren, Siegel ("seagull"—get it?), Jay, Downey, Heckel (without Jeckyl) … It's an annoying little bit of self-indulgent cleverness, and it probably wouldn't irritate me so badly except I can only think that someone sat around thinking these up when he should have been constructing a story that wasn't a chore to sit through.

Some Notable Totables:
- body count: 26
- breasts: 0
- explosions: 0
- ominous thunderstorms: 0
- actors who've appeared on *Star Trek*: 5
  - Raphael Sbarge (Doc Smith) played "Michael Jonas" on a string of second-season *Voyager* episodes
  - Clint Howard (Friar) was the little alien kid "Balok" in the classic episode "The Corbomite Maneuver", and "Grady" on the *DS9* episode "Past Tense Part 2"
  - Frank Novak (Jesse Paloma) was "businessman" on the *DS9* episode "Babel"
  - Lisa Moncure (Mallard) was "Latia" in the *DS9* episode "The Quickening"
  - Martha Hackett (Kroghe) played "Seska" in a long string of *Voyager* episodes, a Terrellian in a *TNG* episode, the Klingon "T'Rul" in the *DS9* two-parter "The Search," and Pok's mother in the video game *Star Trek: Klingon*
  -

RETURN to FROGTOWN (1993)

MANKIND VS. FROGKIND!

- *Written and directed by Donald G. Jackson*
- *Starring Robert Z'Dar, Denise Duff, Charles Napier, Brion James and Lou Ferrigno*
- *Produced by Scott Pfeiffer*
- *Executive produced by Tanya York*

Just looking at the cover for *Return to Frogtown* informs the ardent viewer (like you or me) that this sequel is inferior in at least two notable ways to the first movie, *Hell Comes to Frogtown* (1987), reviewed on page 72.

In the first place, this movie is rated PG-13, compared to the original's R rating. As I'm sure you remember, *Hell Comes to Frogtown* derived all of its best gags from the premise that Sam Hell, as played by the inestimable Rowdy Roddy Piper, was one of the last fertile men in the post-apocalyptic future, and that his wedding tackle was declared the property of the provisional U.S. Government. Strip away the jokes about fertility, virility, and the "SPROING-G-G!" sound his protective codpiece made whenever it opened for business, and you're missing most of the fun.

In the second place, after making *Hell Comes to Frogtown*, Rowdy Roddy Piper (paragon of masculinity and manliness) starred in John Carpenter's paranoid sci-fi/action flick *They Live* (1988) and banked that added thespian visibility into a string of successful direct-to-video action vehicles for most of the '90s. That put him out of financial range for a sequel to his first starring role, and so the part of Sam Hell is here filled by Robert D'Zar, a cult supporting actor whose main claim to fame is a chin that starts at his temples. Robert Z'Dar may be a fine actor (I wouldn't know, I've never seen him in a role that required him to act— zing!), but he's certainly no Rowdy Roddy Piper.

I will admit, though, that the second shortcoming helps take the sting out of the first one, as there is no joke in the world worth the image of a tumescent Robert D'Zar. And I apologize for introducing that image to your brain.

In fact, the Sam Hell in this movie bears very little resemblance to the Sam Hell we knew (and loved) in the previous one. Despite a little bit of dialogue two-thirds of the way through the sequel that attempts to harmonize the portrayals, it's much easier simply to think of this movie as concerning a wholly different character named Sam Hell who also has to deal with the amphibious mutants of Frogtown.

This time out, Sam Hell is a Rocket Ranger for New Texas. Imagine the rocket suits from the old serial *King of the Rocket Men* (1949) (or the old serial *Radar Men From the Moon* (1952), or the old serial

Zombies of the Stratosphere (1952), as they all used the same costumes) and you'll have almost the right idea, though I guarantee that your imagination is giving the budget too much credit. The rocket-packs are undisguised cardboard, the helmets are paper-mache over motorcycle helmets with only the barest nods to aerodynamics, and nobody can even springboard their way off camera convincingly. And these are our only defense against the menace of the "greeners."

The first Rocket Ranger we see is not in fact Sam Hell; no, Rocket Ranger Jones is played by the one and only Lou Ferrigno. Shot from the sky by evil frog mutants while on routine patrol, Jones lets his rocket-pack sink into a pond rather than let the froggers get it when he's captured.

Soon after, Captain Delano of the Rocket Rangers (Charles Napier) sends Sam Hell on a reconnoiter-and-rescue mission. But because no mission can proceed without deadwood, Captain Delano also assigns Sam a new partner, shapely and waifish Dr. Spangle (Denice Duff), who has even less to do with the character of the same name from the first movie; nobody even pretends they're supposed to be the same person. Sam naturally doesn't want her along (really, Jones would probably rather die than be rescued from a greener jail by a sorority babe) and Spangle's assurances that her medical training will come in handy when they find Jones is undercut by the fact that she doesn't take a first aid kit along or anything. But I guess this is how Captain Delano gets his jollies, because they're stuck together.

They "fly" into frog territory (a process

which mixes action figures sliding down a fishing line with shots of the helmeted actors leaning into a wind machine) to meet up with Brandy (Don Stroud), a former Rocket Ranger turned blacksmith just beyond the borders of Frogtown who still reports information to the Rangers. His main contribution to the plot is a dune buggy, with which Sam and Spangle drive themselves towards Frogtown… with no real plan that I can see. Heck, they're both still wearing their Rocket Ranger uniforms (though they've ditched and hidden their rocket-packs); it's not like they're going to sneak into hostile territory. They get ambushed in the middle of nowhere, because middle management frogs have nothing better to do than hang out in random spots hoping the ambushable humans mosey along; the dune buggy is blown up, and Spangle gets captured and driven back to Frogtown tied to the hood of the "frogmobile," all the while straining against her ropes and saying things like, "Let me go!" and "What do you want of me?" This is the point at which Spangle surrenders any future relevance in the plot except as a hostage.

Meanwhile, Ranger Jones has been receiving injections prepared by the insane Dr. Tanzer (Brion James), and seriously—Rowdy Roddy didn't want to act with this cast? Lou Ferrigno, Charles Napier, Denice Duff, Don Stroud, and Brion James? It's like the autograph table at a Fangoria Weekend of Horrors! Anyway, the point of the injections is to change Jones into a frog himself, and its main effect is to turn his skin green with spots. (Only in those areas that it's convenient to wear greasepaint, of course, and never on the ears.) That's right, Lou "Incredible Hulk" Ferrigno was cast in this role only for the sake of an extended sight gag.

I probably ought to make some note here of the other makeup FX. There are three basic types of frog mutants. The fully frogged-out ones, comprising most of the speaking frog parts, are full cable-controlled headpieces. Most of the extras, guards, etc., wear much more humanlike masks, with turbanesque head wrappings to hide the edges. And then there are a few mutant greeners who are done up in nothing but full-body greasepaint with some patterns and mottling. Oddly enough, these are always the females (or the only females we can identify as such), such as a couple of skanky dancers in the Frogtown nightclub, as well as Nurse Cloris (Linda Singer), Ranger Jones' nurse who's got a thing for mammal men.

So Sam easily beats up a couple of froggy guards, takes their wraps and stuff, sneaks into Frogtown (which, by the way, is a generic standing Western town movie set, right down to the livery stable and the Wells Fargo office), and then embarks on a series of captures and escapes that lasts for the rest of the movie. I know that's supposed to be suspenseful and stuff, but really, it's tedious. If Sam's captured, don't get worked up; he'll escape within five minutes. If he escapes, don't get too used to it; he'll be captured again in five minutes.

Part of what's supposed to drive the tension for the second half of the movie is the "mystery" identity of Czar Frogmeister, the mysterious ruler who has installed himself in Frogtown in the last three years. It's the kind of "mystery" that completely fails to deliver when the answer is revealed, since Czar Frogmeister is shown to be a character we never knew existed, related to one of the other characters in a way which wasn't even hinted at anywhere in the movie leading up to the reveal. A mystery has to be more than something the audience doesn't know; it should be something the audience will care about knowing.

The whole movie seems like the kind of second-string production that was financed entirely because so many of the surviving frog masks and costumes from the first movie remained in storage. It's mind-boggling that the writer/director/cinematographer here, Donald G. Jackson, was the co-director/producer/cinematographer on the first movie, as he seems to have no idea what made *Hell Comes to Frogtown* tick. The whole winking subversive attitude of the original is missing this time around, replaced only by leaden attempt at intentional camp. Sure, watching mutant frogs run around is great fun, but even that loses its appeal after the first full hour.

There is one more loose sequel in this franchise, *Toad Warrior* (1996), aka *Hell Comes to Frogtown 3*, also released as the re-edited *Max Hell Comes to Frogtown* (2002), aka *Max Hell Frog Warrior*. It stars Scott Shaw as Max Hell (brother? son? completely unrelated individual with a coincidental patronym? I haven't cared enough to seek out a copy), and features the likes of Joe Estevez and Conrad Brooks in supporting roles. In other words, it looks like the path of intentional camp that *Return to Frogtown* started down is followed to its nadir.

Some Notable Totables:
- body count: 17
- breasts: 2
- explosions: 2
- ominous thunderstorms: 0
- actors who've appeared on *Star Trek*: 2
    - Charles Napier (Captain Delano) played "Adam" (the space hippie) in the classic episode "The Way to Eden," and "Denning" in the *DS9* episode "Little Green Men"
    - Douglas Denning ("Frog Soldier") was an uncredited Klingon in *Star Trek 4*

ZOMBIE BLOODBATH (1993)

UNEARTHED! UNSTOPPABLE! UNDEAD!

- Produced and directed by Todd Sheets
- Written by Todd Sheets and Jerry Angell
- Starring Chris Harris, Auggi Alvarez, Frank Dunlay, Jerry Angell and Jerry Angell's mullet

In the nascent days of the Internet in the mid-'90s, director Todd Sheets was a minor celebrity in the world of ultra-low-budget B-movies, second only to J.R. Bookwalter. (At least in that small community which cared about such things.) Partly it was timing; both had been active starting a decade before, and had a catalog of titles to their name by this time. But more importantly, the do-it-yourself ethic of the shot-on-video director meshed well with the democratizing ideals of the early World Wide Web; after all, both models proposed to break away from the old models of media sponsorship and distribution, and put the apparatus for the publication of creative works into the hands of the common man. Sheets, with his splattery shot-on-video "extreme" horror, stuck it to the watered-down mainstream horror features mandated by The Man in Hollywood.

Most of this praise and regard, mind you, was tossed around by people who admired Sheets in the abstract, never having seen his movies. This movie was my introduction to the output of Todd Sheets, and I can very passionately declaim that this is the movie for you if you want to see long, squishy scenes full of rubbery viscera being gnawed and fondled by hordes of cheap zombies.

In all other regards, i.e, by any of the parameters by which we presume to assess any example of the artform known as "cinema," it's utter crap.

The movie seems to start right off with a bang, the kind you don't want to hear: a meltdown in a nuclear facility (as represented by a board room, and a parking garage full of air conditioner fans). Things break down too quickly for an evacuation, and we get to see various employees melting like a hot creamsicle due to exposure. And those who don't get liquified, well—zombies! Groups and clumps of them, leaping out of doorways and dragging people away to masticate them.

Ten years later, the area that once housed the reactor is now a housing development. A trio of teens, brother and sister Joey and Beth (Chris Harris and Cheryl Metz) and their new neighbor Mike (Auggi Alvarez), wander out to explore a cave that looks more like a viaduct to me; in the dark, Beth and Mike fall down a hole to a lower level. Joey runs back home for help

And we need to stop right here for a moment, because co-writer Jerry Angell, playing Joey's dad Larry, has what I think might well be the ugliest mullet ever to profane the human skull. And I've seen my share of mullets. (Still see them, actually, most pathetically on the heads of some of my son's soccer teammates. Want to make kid look like he needs to be in Special Ed? Saddle the poor tyke with a bad mullet.) It's a distracting and fascinating abomination; when it's on screen, you can't drag your eyes from it. In fact, I declare the mullet to be the best performer in this film. Which isn't much of a stretch; the cast was assembled by the Friends 'n' Family method, and overall, the acting ability ranges between "adequate if you squint right" to "why are my gums bleeding?"

So. Joey's parents call Mike's dad Ralph (Frank Dunley), a hefty older ex-Special Forces guy who keeps a fifty foot length of climbing rope in his trunk, because he's just that prepared. They all go into the cave—which is strangely well-lit this time, in comparison to the darkness before—and easily haul the two trapped teens up.

Well! Crisis averted! Movie's over, right? No? Oh.

Later, Joey and Mike and Joey's little brother or somebody are watching a movie at Joey's house while the parents hang out with Ralph (the feature on TV, incidentally, is Sheets' earlier film *Zombie Rampage* (1989)) when—there are zombies at the door! And coming up the basement steps! And generally all over! For no stated reason! When dealing with our heroes, the zombies in this movie generally are pretty wimpy; pawing and grabbing but doing no damage. That's why, after the boys call their parents, Ralph and the other two can easily push their way through into the house. (Gem of dialogue from Ralph: "Sure is something weird going on around here, isn't it?")

In other scenes, a person we've never seen before (and is thus expendable) will be minding his/her own business when—suddenly there are zombies! The chase lasts about five seconds, and then we've got a circle of zombies around the victim, pulling and gnawing on bloody rubber entrails. In fact, if you simply assume that a scene like this occurs between every paragraph break, I can cut my recap in half.

One random person who encounters zombies and escapes to Joey's house is Daria (Kasey Rausch), otherwise known as Exposition Girl. She knows all about the nuclear plant implosion, which sank the complex into the ground and was simply covered over by the government. A literal cover-up! Also, the cave they were at earlier is the remaining entrance to the lower levels, which were never sealed up. Ralph decides that both families should go seal it up themselves, because Ralph's the kind of guy who keeps dynamite around for just such an occasion.

Somewhere around here, there is also what one might generously call a "subplot." There is a gang of girls in the city (about four of them) who are mad at another similar-sized girl gang for "invading their turf." Then there is apparently a "gang war" that take place off-screen. Then bodies get dumped in the hole in the tunnel. Then the surviving leaders of both gangs have to team up when they get attacked by—zombies! Then they die! I take it back; one couldn't call that a subplot, even generously.

Anyway. Our survivors go first to Ralph's

house for supplies and armaments, then through the woods to the tunnel entrance. Along the way, they lose Larry and his Fascinating Mullet—it's hard to tell with the crummy editing, but I think the zombies grab him and pull his guts out through his ass.

Then they go into the complex, which look like the corridors of a school or some other bureaucratic building, meeting groups of zombies that leap out ineffectually…

…And through the building some more, meeting more zombies…

…Eventually to a ~~bored room~~ excuse me, a boardroom, where Exposition Girl finds documentation sitting on a table to supplement her supply of exposition. The power plant was built over the site of an Indian burial ground! And when the government refused to relocate, the Indians (the live ones above ground, I mean) gave the place a five-year curse, which is why it melted down exactly five years later! As defined in the Jabootu glossary,* this would be an instance of "misdirected answering." Unless, unlike myself, most viewers would be saying, "Yes, the inability of the government to seal up the entrance themselves is plausible, and of course there's nothing unbelievable about the contaminated land being used immediately thereafter for a housing subdivision, and I naturally have no problem with scores of zombies choosing exactly this moment to start leaping out and fondling the internal organs of the living… but will somebody please address the question of what caused the initial meltdown? It inhibits the suspension of my disbelief!"

From there, they head back to the entrance, which is where Ralph wants to set the explosive charges. (Which means we went through the entire underground complex, hemorrhaging expedition members, exactly why?) The explosion is accomplished by rocking the camera along with some sound effects. And presto! Some old ex-military guy with a few sticks of outdated TNT has accomplished what the Army Corps of Engineers could not! Except that more zombies immediately leap out of the bushes and kill them. The end. Except for more chewing.

So, so many things wrong here. It's pretty clear that all Sheets really wanted to shoot was a string of scenes with a horde of zombies chewing on guts; the rest of it is just the obligatories to hold it together so sketchily that a medical professional could reasonably prescribe attention-deficit treatment based solely on the evidence presented in the movie. Whole chunks of what could have been plot are simply left out; for instance, I think we may possibly have been expected to infer that the zombie uprising was triggered by the initial two teens falling down the hole. But that just may be my order-loving mind, trying to construct a plot from the images on the screen in the same manner that I see bunny rabbits in cumulus clouds.

But even in a movie whose entire *raison d'etre* is zombie attacks, you'd expect there to be more effort put into the zombies themselves: a bunch of latex and greasepaint-smeared extras (with healthy arms and legs), adult and child, dressed in whatever casual street clothes they brought with them (as the initial crop of zombies is supposed to have sprung from the radioactive hole, I can only assume that they had a really, really lax dress code at this particular nuclear facility), stumbling around and grabbing at people. In almost every such scene, there's at least one zombie extra wearing a huge grin that says, "Boy, this is sure a fun way to spend my Saturday!" And absolutely priceless is the scene at the end of a horde of zombies shambling along a grassy knoll in this city which is supposedly "completely overrun" by the living dead—and right behind them, the commuters visible on the interstate are simply going about their business.

Now, you might want to forgive Mr. Todd Sheets because this was early in his career, such as it was, and every artist has creative skeletons in their closet. (Not everyone tries to market it to strangers, but whatever.) If he learned from this experience, built upon it, and grew as a filmmaker in subsequent productions, then *Zombie Bloodbath* might

---

* I don't have to tell you again that it's at Jabootu.net, do I?

be marginally forgivable, if you were yourself the spiritual lovechild of Mother Theresa and Gandhi. However, Sheets followed *Zombie Bloodbath* up with two sequels, one in 1995, the other in 2000. And they're not any better. In fact, the first *Zombie Bloodbath* may be the best of the bunch. This is a man coming out the gate at the pinnacle of his craft. And that's almost enough to make you despair for humanity as a whole.

Some Notable Totables:
- body count: 23
- breasts: 0
- explosions: 1 (implied)
- ominous thunderstorms: 1
- cars that won't start for no good reason: 1
- actors who've appeared on *Star Trek*: 0

ABRAXAS, GUARDIAN of the UNIVERSE (1994)

AN ADVENTURE ACROSS SPACE AND TIME.

- *Written and directed by Damian Lee*
- *Starring Jesse Ventura, Sven-Ole Thorsen, Damian Lee, Jerry Levitan and Marjorie Bransfield*
- *Produced by Damian Lee, David Mitchell, and Curtis Petersen*

It's a natural story idea for mindless entertainment: good space cop vs. bad space cop on Earth. It's not an ambitious premise, but, it shouldn't be a trial to squeeze ninety minutes of painless distraction from it, should it?

It shouldn't be. But in this case, it is.

We start with an explanatory voiceover, from the eponymous Abraxas (ex-wrestler, ex-Governor of Minnesota Jesse Ventura), explaining things we either don't need to know or would pick up on very soon, such as the fact that Abraxas is a "Finder," an interstellar cop with the mission to "protect all life," and that he's hard on the tail of Secundus (Sven-Ole Thorsen), his former partner who's turned renegade. Secundus is on his way to earth via "travel-warp" (a teleportation special effect that makes the transporter from the original *Star Trek* look really cool, and which saves on costly spaceship effects) in order to… uh…

Okay, here's what I was able to figure out. Secundus is trying to mate with an earth woman because his child could very well be the fulfillment of a prophecy—the Culmator. At least, that's what I want to think they're saying, because it would make at least half-sense as an idiot's version of "culminator," i.e., one who culminates or brings to pass—on the other hand, it sounds like everyone's saying "Comator," which makes absolutely no sense to me, unless they mean that he (and the movie as a whole) can cause comas, in which case I agree wholeheartedly. This Culmator would have the ability to calculate the Anti-Life Equation, which would open the door to the Anti-Life Universe, which Secundus thinks would give him ultimate power but which might actually destroy the universe. (If you're a comics geek, you might recognize that "Anti-Life" terminology as being cribbed from the legendary Jack Kirby's work for DC Comics in the '70s. I you didn't recognize it as such, the ghost of Jack Kirby thanks you.)

Abraxas follows him to earth, and they spend several minutes chasing each other through snowy woods at night, using guns that cause big explosions but don't actually hit the target. (Abraxas has been on the job for over 9,000 years and can't hit the broad side of a barn door? Um, is there any other interstellar police officer we could deal with?)

Unfortunately, Secundus stumbles across just what he needs, a couple parked in the woods for a little makeout. He tosses the guy

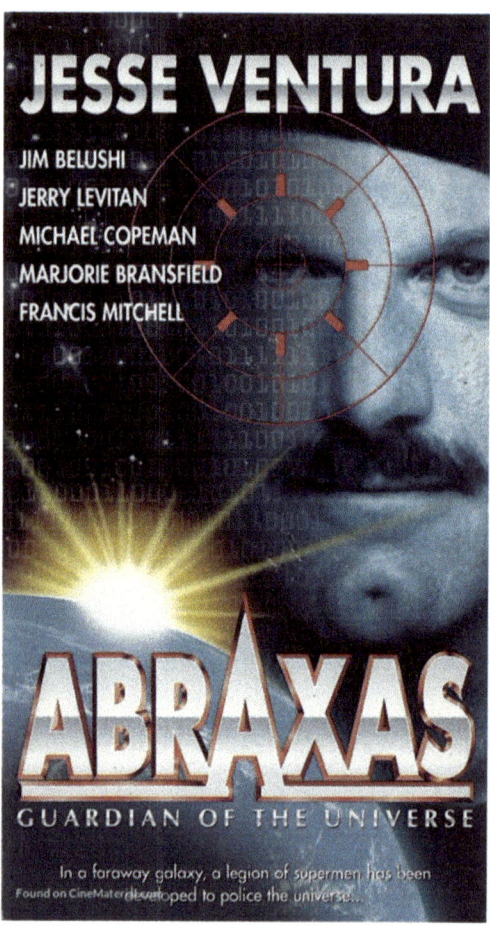

she's remarkably hale and hearty (I'd have thought that going through all of the changes of a nine-month pregnancy, plus delivery, in under five minutes would have some serious repercussions on the internal organs—silly me!). And five years later…

Now, let me pause and point out one of the sillier stylistic decisions here one among many, many silly decisions. I accept that Abraxas has the occasional voiceover, even though all of the stuff the first intrusive voiceover told us was repeated a few minutes later, almost verbatim, by the two jokers in the headquarters control room (one of whom is writer/director Damian Lee). But then Secundus gets his own couple of voiced-over scenes (and unfortunately, Thorsen has all of the enunciative skill of an inebriated André the Giant). And then, to make it even more comical, Sonia gets her own voiceover, explaining how in the last five years she's grown to love her baby, whom she named Tommy, but that he's peculiar in that he never ever speaks, didn't even cry as

on his keister, and thanks to an apparently instinctive understanding of the operation of terrestrial motor vehicles (it's a guy thing, I guess), he manages to get away from Abraxas's pursuit long enough to impregnate the young lady—or rather, to accomplish a "DNA infusion" by placing a glowing hand on her abdomen. Wow, that sure beats the old-fashioned way…

Abraxas catches up and sends Secundus back via travel-warp (since there's a law that any Finder, past or present, is immune from execution—maybe there's some other whole interstellar police force up there we could deal with?), and then finds the girl, Sonia (Marjorie Bransfield), in a state of advanced pregnancy. His "answer box," an annoying computer linkup with headquarters on his wrist (also cribbed from Jack Kirby), tells him he has to terminate the woman and baby to make sure it's not the Culmator, but he won't—instead, he just leaves her there in the snow with her newborn baby.

Not only is Sonia okay with the baby, but

a baby. (Yes. Also cribbed from Kirby.) Oh, and that she has the fear that someone or something is going to try to take him away from her. Foreshadowing, you know. (I'm just glad that Tommy is silent, otherwise he would probably deliver a voiceover, too.)

And as luck would have it, Secundus breaks out of the penal colony right about then and heads to Earth to try and get the Anti-Life Equation from his son's head, so Abraxas is sent back after him. And presto, we finally get down to what this film originally meant to be: a ripoff of *The Terminator* (1984), with Abraxas trying to protect young Tommy and Secundus trying to rip the Anti-Life Equation from his skull. But I don't think you need me to tell you that Jesse Ventura is no Michael Biehn, and Sven-Ole Thorsen is definitely no Ah-nuld.

But a simple summary doesn't show you all of the ways in which this movie bites. The dialogue is repetitive, yet not terribly informative (as evidenced by how many times they try to repeat that bit about the Anti-Life Equation, hoping that you'll get acclimatized to it); there's loads of backstory foisted on us that never makes one iota of difference; and the whole thing never bothers to pace itself, instead simply loading on events to fill out the running time (including, you guessed it, a visit to a stripper bar that exists for no other reason than for the movie to include a stripper).

Now, let me clue you in to what bothers me most about this. As you may have gleaned, I'm a story-focused movie viewer. I concentrate on plot and narrative and theme and such. So it simply appalls me when the most basic part of the movie, the story, is such a slipshod, unpolished, crude, lumpy affair, unfit for man or beast. Even if you're the director and co-producer, and really have no one higher to answer to as far as script quality goes, how can you not have that inner compulsion to get things as good as you can? How can you not hear the voice of the muse on your shoulder, pointing out the unreadiness of this draft?

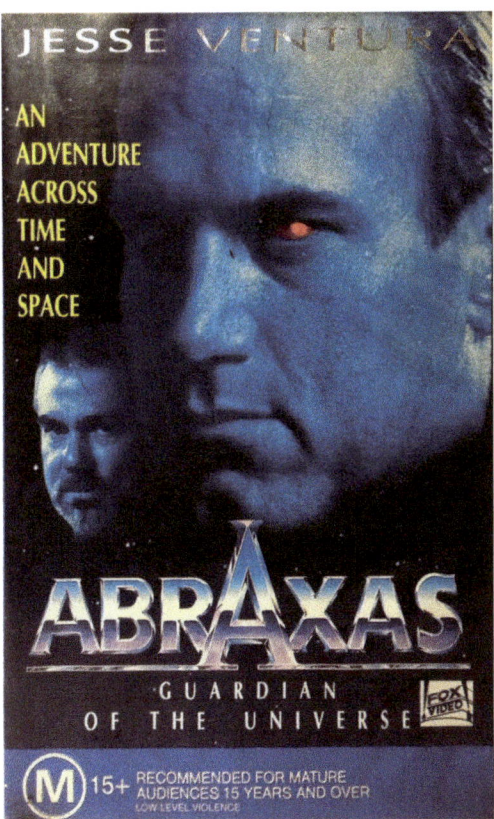

I know you can rarely be fair in criticizing a script from the finished project, since the producer and director can and do muck around with it to an appalling degree before it gets to the unwitting audience. But when the writer is also the director and the co-producer—really, who else is there to blame?

I can't tell you to absolutely avoid this one, but I will say that there are a lot of other movies to cross off your "to see" list before it would become worthwhile. You'll have more fun sitting in the dark for ninety minutes, imagining how fun a good space cop/bad space cop movie really should be.

Some Notable Totables:
- body count: 3
- breasts: 0
- explosions: 25
- ominous thunderstorms: 0
- actors who've appeared on *Star Trek*: 0

IMMORTAL COMBAT (1994)

INDESTRUCTIBLE WARRIORS PROGRAMMED TO KILL. THIS IS NO GAME.

aka *Resort to Kill*

- Produced and directed by Daniel Neira
- Written by Robert Crabtree and Daniel Neira
- Starring Roddy Piper, Sonny Chiba, Meg Foster, Kim Morgan Greene and Deron McBee

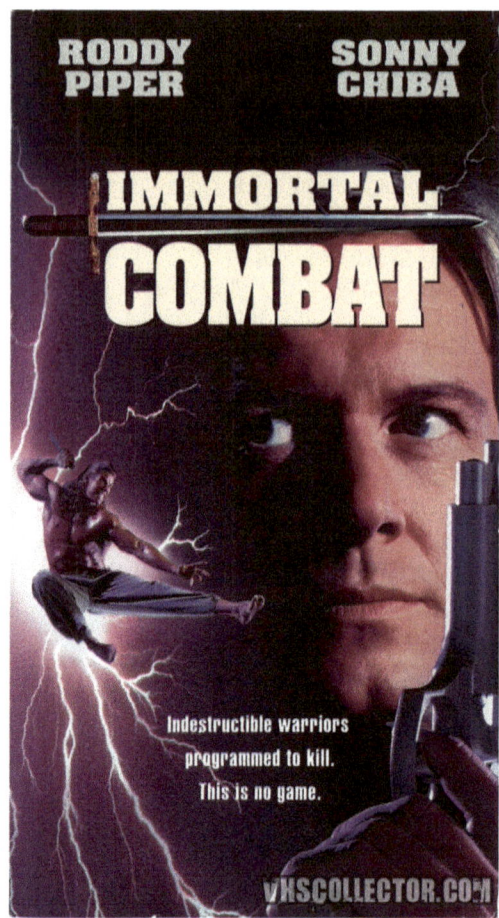

I have elsewhere alluded to my man-crush on late wrestler-turned-actor Rowdy Roddy Piper, paragon of all that is manly. That starry-eyed appreciation, though, doesn't keep me from noticing when the movies in which The Rowdy One stars aren't up to snuff. *Immortal Combat* is probably one of the worst movies on Roddy's resume, and thanks to the credits above, we can pin the blame squarely on one person, producer/co-writer/director Daniel Neira. This is another one of those all-too-common cases in which someone has an idea that they're just certain is great—and then manages to make sure no one around them is in a position to tell them otherwise. I will note, with approbation, that Mr. Neira did not direct or produce another feature film for eight years and has never again been given any kind of writing credit, proving that in some rare cases the wrong does fail, the right prevail.

What I've got to tell you makes very little sense when reduced to a synopsis, but let's see what I can muddle out.

First up, we get the inestimable pleasure (cough, cough) of seeing actress Meg Foster, she of the icy eyes, in bed with an incredibly burly Japanese guy named Osato (played by an incredibly burly Japanese guy named Woon). Meg then dismisses him with some cockamamie story about her dangerous husband coming home, and Osato sprints off into the night, only to be chased by armed guards and a killer Chippendale dancer. (Oh please, heavens preserve me as I try to get through this.) It's a setup, see, and the permed prettyboy Chippendale dancer (whose idea of being tough is to beat on his own well-waxed torso and then spread his arms, bear his teeth like he thought he was wearing plastic vampire fangs, and make high-pitched "Yii! Yii!" sounds) and Osato fight it out before Chippendale (his character's name is Muller, and the so-called actor's name is Deron McBee, and he used to be one of the American Gladiators, but he's going to be "Chippie" from here on out) kills Osato.

Next. Cop John Keller (Piper) is in his captain's office, explaining how his partner J.J. (Sonny Chiba) got shot. For this, we get a massive flashback to Keller, J.J., and their female third wheel Jill (don't get attached) doing some sort of stakeout at a glitzy party looking for someone named Delany. In the course of things, Keller manages to beat up a whole bunch of thugs for no reason I could see, and then be invited to participate in their own little kumite by none other than

Meg Foster. Her character's name is Quinn, and her performance here is the same display of somnambulism we've come to expect from the rest of her body of work. "Hey, I've got these spooky-ass eyes to do the heavy lifting—why should I exert myself acting?" Keller beats up a whole bunch more people in a row, and then he and J.J. try to arrest all hundred-or-so people, starting a stampede. Then they start shooting the hired thugs, and getting shot back at by them, which is how J.J. got shot.

But wait—Jill also gets herself killed, by Chippie! (It's in this scene that he really earns that nickname, as he shows up in black slacks, sneakers, and a sleeveless tuxedo shirt. That, and his luxurious Michael Bolton hair…) He carves her up with a knife, for no discernible reason.

Oh, and there's also a Japanese cop on the premises working separately, trying to find Osato, who's some Yakuza muckamuck last seen at one of these parties. He also gets to kick some ass, and shoots a familiar figure in a sleeveless tuxedo shirt who promptly, after getting shot, stands up unharmed. (The Japanese cop, meanwhile, promptly becomes a non-part of the story. Smart man.)

Got all that? Okay, here's more. Keller noticed that the invitation to the party has the same little "HCo" logo on it as a travel brochure for a Caribbean island, so he wants to investigate! And when the captain tells him that that's just a wee bit out of his jurisdiction, Keller declares that he's taking his saved-up vacation to do it on his own time.

I hope you've noticed by now that we're in a parallel universe. We've got two cops who just go in and start beating people up and shooting them—and Keller doesn't even have to stick around for any kind of internal affairs investigation. Nope, the captain's gonna curse at him a little, and then Keller's going to do what he wants. Thanks, but I think the last thing we need are more L.A.P.D. cops with that whole Judge Dredd "I am the law" attitude.

On to the Caribbean. The only noteworthy event on the trip down is that Keller beats up a slimeball who's bothering a single lady on the boat—gee, I guess she's going to become the love interest here. That whole process is helped along by the resort's mixup; see, his name is Keller, and her name is Karen Keeler (Kim Morgan Greene)—so they're accidentally given the same room! Oh, the hilarity of seeing her come out of the shower to find him eating from her room service cart! And to push it a little further, he manages to appropriate the jeep she's reserved for the next day, by exploiting that whole similar-name thing. (And then, when he shows back up again, she thinks the whole bit was jes' cute! Wouldn't you?)

You know that a movie's not really doing it for you when you find yourself unconsciously embarking on errands just so you have an excuse to put the video on pause and get away from it for a minute. During my screening of *Immortal Combat*, I checked the mail a couple of times, went to the bathroom thrice—and then, because that about dehydrated me, I went and got a big glass of Mountain Dew. And since poking around for snacks is always a good distraction, I also went through a half pound of Jelly Bellies and an entire roast suckling pig.

And why am I telling you this now? Same philosophy: you probably needed a break, too. Okay, we're back.

What, you may ask, has J.J. been doing all this time? You surely don't hire Sonny Chiba as L.A.'s least articulate cop just to have him shot down in the first ten minutes. No, we keep cutting back to him at home, being cared for by his Caucasian daughter (don't worry, we'll find out all about that), engaging in macho healing—kneeling for hours in his dojo, fighting candles and stuff, until his shoulder is all better inside of a week.

And when he's finally ready to join Keller in the Caribbean, we get his entire background dropped in our laps in a single scene. Why doesn't J.J. use a gun (which was mentioned in passing way back when)? Why does he have a white daughter named Andy? When he was a young cop in Japan, he pursued a perp through a park, shot at him, and accidentally killed Andy's mother. So out of guilt, he adopted her and stopped using guns. (And, presumably, left Japan for L.A., where I'm sure that the police department was overjoyed to hire a foreign national who still only barely speaks English and refuses to use firearms. Must have been those ninja skills that won them over.) Nothing revealed here has any relevance to the rest of the movie, but don't we all feel like we know J.J. better?

Meanwhile, back on the island, Keller's been mostly annoying the crap out of me. He's snuck into the HybriCo compound (that's what that "HCo" logo stands for), where Quinn is present for yet another bare-knuckles match—this time featuring the supposedly-deceased Osato. (You can't keep a good Woon down.) And as it must necessarily turn out, Karen is also a reporter investigating HybriCo. Keller gets many opportunities to beat up goons; then Karen gets kidnapped, and J.J. arrives with a shitload of ninja gear, and they go to town.

Want to know what the big secret is at HybriCo? They've found this ancient Mayan formula (the island was once inhabited by Mayans, you know, as indicated by some styrofoam sets and stock footage of Chichen Itza) that turns men into invincible warriors —but they have to die first, preferably by being run to ground. That matters. Really. Quinn is working on selling the formula to Third World countries (who are notorious for having a whole bunch of money to spend on military innovations, I guess); in the meantime, she keeps Chippie around, he being the Signature Killer, an L.A.-area serial killer that she revived and keeps under her thumb for no reason under the sun. (Maybe it's the collector mentality: she just wanted to be in possession of the world's least likely serial killer.) And it turns out that the only way to kill these immortal warriors is either by fire or... Wait, can you guess? Can you? Yup, decapitation. At this point, it would actually have been a plus to hear Sonny Chiba intone, "There can be only one." But it was not to be.

A bunch of Chiba ninja stuff happens (since Quinn naturally has her own ninja army, in addition to killer Chippendales— and I have to say, for being fifty-five Chiba's a dang spry and fast fighter, though he looks his age), Roddy gets to do that whole "I can't swim" thing that seems to come up frequently in his movies, and eventually the good guys win.

Where do I begin? A secret installation that still advertises itself on brochures and lighters? Immortal Chippendale serial killers? Yet another annoying reporter girl? Sonny Chiba as a cop in L.A.? Meg Foster with a big placard around her neck that reads EVIL JUST CUZ?

The only things saving this movie from a complete thumbs down are Chiba's ninja stunts and Piper's native charm (and even that—*even that*—wears thin long before the closing credits). Nothing else here comes close to winning friends and influencing people. The only reason I kept watching to the end, sidetrips and all, was the overwhelming need to see someone kick that damned Chippendale dancer's ass.

Some Notable Totables:
- body count: 19
- breasts: 2
- explosions: 4
- ominous thunderstorms: 0
- actors who've appeared on *Star Trek*: 1
  - Meg Foster (Quinn) played "Onaya" on the *DS9* episode "The Muse"

NECRONOMICON: BOOK of the DEAD (1994)

From the master of terror, comes a chilling tale of unspeakable evil.

- *Directed by Brian Yuzna, Christophe Gans, and Shusuke Kaneko*
- *Written by Brent V. Friedman, Brian Yuzna, Christophe Gans and Kazunori Ito, based on stories by H.P. Lovecraft*
- *Starring Jeffrey Combs, Bruce Payne, Richard Lynch, Maria Ford and David Warner*
- *Produced by Brian Yuzna and Samuel Hadida*

I can blame Stephen King for his own bad movie adaptations. He's had his hand in half of them, and he has the clout to step in on the rest if he so chooses. So I feel no pity for him. But poor H.P. Lovecraft was dead decades before anyone thought of trying to adapt his stories to the screen; he is wholly a victim of Hollywood, defenseless and spinning in his grave more often than not.

So it's a real pleasure to see a Lovecraft-based movie in which the filmmakers had at least read Lovecraft's work before they try to film it.

One problem with the adaptation of Lovecraft's works to screen is that he worked almost exclusively in shorter fiction (only *At the Mountains of Madness* could even be called a short novel), and thanks to his idiosyncratic style, much of the wordcount was devoted to description, which motion pictures can deal with in a split second. Most Lovecraftian movies have therefore ended up filling the running time with added material —some fairly good (*Re-Animator* (1985)), some not so good (just about all of the others), but almost all of it out of character of a Lovecraftian tale. Brian Yuzna, whose experience producing Lovecraft-inspired movies dates back to the aforementioned *Re-Animator* and *From Beyond* (1986), spearheaded this anthology feature in which he and two other directors provide short film versions of various Lovecraft tales. While the results are uneven, the format at least doesn't actively work against successful adaptation.

The framing story, directed by Yuzna, takes place in 1932 in, one assumes, Boston, where a mysterious monastery is being visited by none other than Howard Philip Lovecraft himself—and Lovecraft is being played by none other than Jeffrey Combs (star of *Re-Animator* and *From Beyond*), looking very much like H.P. in a prosthetic nose and chin. Lovecraft has discovered that a copy of the fabled *Necronomicon*, the "book of the dead" whose secrets can drive men mad, is to be had somewhere in the library holdings of the sinister monks. Having visited before, he is welcomed in to browse an alchemical encyclopedia, but quickly sneaks off with a pilfered key to a reading room with a wall safe, in which is the brass-bound volume. What Lovecraft doesn't notice as he takes it out and begins to read is that the back of the safe is also a door, and it slowly opens…

The structure of the rest of the movie is

that the stories presented are what Lovecraft reads in the *Necronomicon*. The first story, "The Drowned" (directed by Christophe Gans, later the director of *Brotherhood of the Wolf* (2001) and *Silent Hill* (2006)), is set roughly in the '50s, give or take a decade. The executors of the will of Jethro De La Poer have finally found an heir sixty years after his death, nephew Edward (Bruce Payne) who'd been living in Sweden, to take possession of the old family home on the edge of a New England cliff. After touring the sepulchral manse with the daughter of the executor, Edward settles in with a letter from Jethro included with the will, written before Jethro threw himself from the balcony onto the rocks.

In flashback we see that Jethro (Richard Lynch) denounced God and burned the Bible when his wife and son were taken from him in a shipwreck. But nature abhors a vacuum; that night, he is visited by a seaweed-bedecked fishman (in Puritan garb, no less) who delivers—a copy of the *Necronomicon*! (Gotta get your money's worth from those props.) In it, Jethro finds a spell for bringing back the dead, which apparently consists in its entirety of Lovecraft's famous couplet, "That is not dead which can eternal lie, / And with strange aeons, even death may die," accompanied by "In his lair, Cthulhu waits dreaming."

Jethro's letter warns the reader of the monstrous consequences of using the spell, but Edward has a tragic car accident in his own past which ended up with his beloved Clara drowning, so he finds the book where Jethro had hidden it…

Of all the stories, this is the most overtly Lovecraftian in detail and trope, despite the fact that it can't be identified as an adaptation of a specific story. (Some have tried to link it to "The Rats in the Walls," with which it shares the familial name and an ancestral house, but the story itself bears no resemblance to Lovecraft's.) It is, however, overflowing with other favorite Lovecraftian details: ancestral guilt and ancestral secrets, Innsmouth-type fishmen, and several tentacled thingies, including a huge one that

lives in the caverns beneath the house. (The best image is that of old Jethro's revived son, suddenly revealing a mouth like an octopus's, surrounded by tentacles.) Rather than an adaptation, it's more of a pastiche, with so many homages held together by a culminating action scene.

The second story, "The Cold" (directed by Shusuke Kaneko, who went on to direct the three '90s *Gamera* revival movies), is based on Lovecraft's "Cold Air," but I'm disappointed that a non-Hollywood director felt the need to make so many Hollywood changes to the story. (Not that it was one of Lovecraft's better stories to begin with.) Told from the present in flashback to a reporter looking for an explanation for forty years of murders, the protagonist is young Emily (Bess Meyer[*]), coming to Boston in the early '70s to escape an abusive stepfather (Gary Graham of *Alien Nation* fame). She rooms in the house of the reclusive Dr. Madden (David Warner), who keeps himself confined to his frigid third-floor suite, leaving the rest of the house to be run by his housekeeper Lena (Millie Perkins, who played Anne Frank in the movie). But through chance contact, a romance develops between Emily and Dr. Madden despite a generation gap beyond anything Emily can imagine.

I hope you already see all of the problems. Adding abuse and romance to Lovecraft is just plain silly; "human drama," after all, was about the furthest thing from Lovecraft's mind. This segment adds a lot of material to expand a slight story out to half an hour, and much of it is stock Hollywood cliché. In addition to needing cold, Dr. Madden in this version also needs spinal fluid, thus accounting for the murders.

The original story "Cold Air" is something of a one-trick pony, leading up to a "gotcha" ending that can be seen from miles away, as with many of Lovecraft's weaker tales. This adaptation emphasizes the flaws of the original and adds some of its own. While there's a nifty little twist at the

---

[*] And what do I recognize her from? Her single line in *Heathers* (1988), that's what.

end, it's far too little, far too late to justify the story. And it mystifies me why a foreign-language director would choose to do an adaptation that relies so much on dialogue and exposition.

The third story, "Whispers" (directed also by Yuzna), is probably the least Lovecraftian of the bunch in terms of overt detail; it's supposed to be an adaptation of "The Whisperer in Darkness," to which it bears not even a passing resemblance. Two cops, Paul (Obba Babatunde) and Sarah (Signy Coleman), are chasing a murderer, known as the Butcher, through the streets of Philadelphia; unfortunately, because they're also arguing about whether they should have slept together and what they should do now that Sarah's pregnant, they crash their police car. Paul's unconscious body is dragged off by parties unknown; Sarah tries to track him and enters a warehouse which apparently descends straight into Hell.

I said this is the least Lovecraftian of the lot in terms of outward props, but perhaps it's the most Lovecraftian in terms of pure, incomprehensible horror. Sarah's descent is

framed in a fluid reality where nothing is as it seems; there's an immense horror waiting around the periphery of this story, seen dimly in the intensely horrific imagery shown us, but far too big to be contained on the screen. It's a nightmare world which exploits Sarah's twin fears of motherhood and of losing the baby, of losing her partner, of being helpless and exploited by something she can't even imagine.

Yes, I know that's a terribly vague description, and purposely so. What Yuzna shows us here is a string of terrifying images, profoundly disturbing in their alienness and irrationality. This is, I think, a true successor attempt to Lovecraft, who in his later years tried to indicate on the page a cosmic horror that could never be defined and described in words. The true horror is the one which can never be tamed by comprehension; it always lies beyond those limits. While he probably would have run for a throw-up bucket, I think Lovecraft would have approved of this adaptation.

The three stories have individual faults and strengths. The framing device is also clever but, as you may have noticed, all three of the tales are set in eras after that in which Lovecraft is supposedly reading them. An early line of dialogue about the

Necronomicon revealing both the past and the future was probably supposed to band-aid this problem, but it doesn't work. All three stories contain the *Necronomicon* itself (even though it's only a briefly-seen bit of set dressing in the third), but none of them actually reveal the horror said to be within its pages. It's a clever framing device , but it sets up promises for the stories it introduces that they don't plan to fulfill.

Nevertheless, compared to all the in-name-only Lovecraft adaptations which have somehow gotten themselves made, this is a competent and sometimes beautiful little movie. Watching it awakened my desire to re-read Lovecraft, which is something which no other Lovecraft movie adaptation has ever done; that's got to say something.

Some Notable Totables:
- body count: 10
- breasts: 2
- explosions: 0
- dream sequences: 1
- ominous thunderstorms: 2
- actors who've appeared on *Star Trek*: 5
    - Jeffrey Combs is obviously a regular in the *ST* universe, with two recurring roles (Weyoun and Brunt the Ferengi, including one episode in which he was both) plus two other guest shots on *DS9*, a guest role on *Voyager,* and another recurring role on *Enterprise*
    - Richard Lynch (Jethro De La Poer) played Baran in the *TNG* two-parter "Gambit"
    - David Warner (Dr. Madden) was Ambassador St. John Talbot in *Star Trek 5*, Klingon Chancellor Gorkon in *Star Trek 6*, and Gul Madred (the one who tortured Picard) in the *TNG* two-parter "Chain of Command"
    - Dennis Christopher (Dale Porkel, the nosy reporter in "The Cold") showed up on a third-season *DS9*
    - Gary Graham (Sam, the abusive stepfather in "The Cold") guest starred on a second-season *Voyager* episode, then had a recurring role on *Enterprise* (he's also appeared in the fan franchise *Star Trek: Renegades*, but we can't count that, can we?)

ROCKWELL: A LEGEND of the WILD WEST (1994)

He brought black powder justice to a lawless land.

- Written and directed by Richard Lloyd Dewey
- Starring Randy Gleave, Karl Malone, Scott Claflin, Michael Ruud and Shantal Hiatt

Orrin Porter Rockwell is one of the most colorful figures in Western history: the rootin'est, tootin'est Mormon gunfighter ever. When he served as a bodyguard to Latter-day Saint prophet Joseph Smith, he was promised by Joseph that no bullet would ever fell him if he kept his hair long like Samson. Over the course of several decades, as he also provided personal security to Joseph's successor Brigham Young, he had plenty of encounters that should have proved Joseph wrong, but didn't. Legend has it that he would walk away from gun battles with several armed opponents, having taken them all down, shaking their bullets out of his coat. He's about the closest thing we have to a Mormon folk hero.

And he deserves a much better biopic than this.

The modern "Mormon cinema" subgenre —movies with both Latter-day Saint content and viewpoints, meant largely for a Mormon audience—began with Richard Dutcher's 2000 missionary story *God's Army*. Rockwell was an earlier attempt at moviemaking about and for that particular demographic, but it failed to find an audience or inspire imitators. For one thing, with a deserved R-rating, it was too violent for family-oriented Mormon fare. For another, it simply didn't tell its story well, or even know what its real story was.

We begin with our occasional narrator, Willie (Scott Claflin), the lone survivor of an attack on his father's homestead outside Nauvoo, Illinois by an anti-Mormon mob in 1844. It's a scene that works pretty manipulatively to establish black-and-white good guys and bad guys, since the mob rides in, shoots a woman and a little girl and a man in cold blood (and with gory exit wounds—remember what I said about the deserved R-rating?), and rides on. It's a situation devoid of the background that would make it comprehensible to someone unfamiliar with the history, and very little of that history is explained as the movie unrolls—none of the historic political tensions between Mormons and their neighbors, none of the clerical agitation over Mormon differences in belief and practice… These are bad guys. Just accept it and know who to root against.

A Mormon audience would know the context in which to place this scene, but it still reeks of emotional manipulation right out the gate. And would an audience familiar with the history sit still for inaccuracies like a Joseph Smith (Scott McMillan) in the next scene with salt-and-pepper hair?

Anyway. The attack on Willie's family is symptomatic of the widespread mob violence that the Mormons are attracting, and it's not long before Joseph Smith is arrested on politically motivated charges and dragged off to the jail in Carthage. In what is at best a distortion of history, the main instigator of this is one Chauncy Higbee (Michael Flynn), former confidant of Joseph who had been expelled from the church; he's now a capitalist slimeball who enjoys the taste of rattlesnake and lacks only an unctuous mustache to twirl. Joseph dies at the hand of a mob while supposedly in protective custody.

Anti-Mormon violence continues, in a cartoonish display of random acts of murderous cruelty and nefariousness, and Porter finds himself the individual target of Higbee's wrath. The only person he can count on to be as good a shot as he is Elijah Abel (novelty casting coup Karl Malone, who was near the beginning of his decade-long tenure with the Utah Jazz basketball team). One's a pudgy white mountain man; the other's a black basketball star. Together, they fight crime!

After being chased through the woods in his red long underwear (and having a twelve-year-old girl make eyes at him), Rockwell ends up in jail for four months, awaiting trial for the murder of one of Higbee's goons who was gunning for him. Eventually acquitted (making the whole episode nigh pointless), he joins the rest of the Mormons, who by this time have gone west to Utah. (He also gently rebuffs another twelve-year-old girl with starry eyes—this time, his jailer's daughter. I don't like this trend...)

Fast-forward to 1853, when Higbee has become the head honcho in a mining company, and plans to use a pet federal judge to allow him to run roughshod over Mormon mining claims in Utah. That's when Brigham Young (Michael Ruud) comes to Porter and offers him a marshalship to keep the territory safe. Porter also meets up again with Mary Anne Neff (Shantal Hiatt), once the first twelve-year-old who made eyes at him, now an educated young adult who's still got her eye on him.

Up until now, the plot has been meandering and disjointed. That was the good part; from here on out, it's merely a series of gunfighting episodes as various of Higbee's hirelings run afoul of Porter and receive a fatal case of lead poisoning for their troubles. There are also plenty of heavy-handed scenes of Porter and Mary Anne falling in love, though he has to push her off because, you know, the dangers inherent in the job and all. And just to make sure I'm thoroughly creeped out, he also rescues another twelve-year-old girl from claim-jumpers, and she's no sooner untied than she offers to braid his air and pronounces her readiness to be Mrs. Rockwell. Somebody, make it stop...

Many factors combine to keep this movie from generating any kind of spark. When a professional basketball player in your cast doesn't stand out as a worse actor than the rest, you know you're in trouble. Randy Gleave's version of Porter Rockwell mostly stares straight ahead, speaks in short sentences, and lets his hair do the acting. The script lurches between clumsily pointless and clumsily obvious. (Why, pray tell, do we have a sudden subplot about Porter Rockwell appearing as a conquistador in a community play two-thirds of the way through the movie?) Costumes too often show a decidedly non-historic flavor, and far too much of the movie (those parts not shot in the woodlands of Illinois or the mountains of Utah) was obviously staged in recreated historical village sites around Salt Lake City.

But most disappointing is that the whole production resolutely stays away from any of the features that make the Porter Rockwell of history and fable such an intriguing character. How does a man of violence reconcile himself to a religion of peace (or, at very least, of defense)? How does a rough and unsophisticated man relate to men who were revered as prophets of God? How much of the Samson-like blessing did people witness, and how much were legends that grew up around him while he was alive? A movie about Porter Rockwell should be a meaty, satisfying exploration, not an anemic, meandering gunfighter flick that only ends when the hero runs out of people to shoot.

Writer/director Richard Lloyd Dewey is also the author of *Rockwell: A Novel*, *Porter Rockwell: A Biography*, and *The Porter Rockwell Chronicles* (another novel, first in an announced series). With so much Rockwell on the brain, you'd dearly like to believe that he could generate a better, more engaging portrait of the man than the distant and lackluster version presented here.

Some Notable Totables:
- body count: 33
- breasts: 0
- explosions: 0
- ominous thunderstorms: 0
- springloaded scarecrows: 1
- actors who've appeared on *Star Trek*: 0

ADDICTED to MURDER (1995)

TIME TO FEED THE FEAR.

- *Produced and directed by Kevin J. Lindenmuth*
- *Written by Kevin J. Lindenmuth and Tom Piccirilli*
- *Starring Mick McCleery, Laura McLauchlin, Sasha Graham, Bernadette Pauley and Candace Mead*

Intellectually, I admire Kevin Lindenmuth's work. Another one of the godfathers of the shot-on-video independent microbudget cinema movement, he consistently manages to work with pizza-delivery-tip budgets and turn out something feature-length. And not content to do exploitative ripoffs, he writes scripts that are ambitious, complex, and intelligent, and attempts challenging storytelling techniques.

But I've never seen one of his movies that I really, you know, *liked*.

In the present offering, we have the tale of Joel Winter (Mick McCleery), a man with whom many readers may identify: he was a high-school geek, a beset-upon fellow with a premature paunch, bad hair and not much personality. He did have one friend at the time, though; a vampire, Rachel (Laura McLauchlin). He was a young child when he met her, and she was his "imaginary friend" as he grew up.

His relationship with her took on bizarre overtones, as she loved to be "killed" repeatedly and trained Joel to do it (in a sequence that unintentionally calls *Groundhog Day* (1993) to mind), making an unwilling killer out of him. Then she finally disappeared; now, he's a thirtyish handyman living a lonely life in New York, searching for Rachel or someone like her while trying to come to terms with his incredibly messed-up psyche.

What I've told you so far, by the way, is spread out all over the video, as we're not dealing with linear storytelling here. We leap from Joel's pointless job and sterile apartment, to flashbacks of his teen years (hey, same haircut!), to flashbacks of his short-lived marriage. Interspersed with all of this are film clips from television interviews after the events of the movie, psychologists and commentators and his ex-wife weighing in on what made Joel Winter such a proficient serial killer. The irony, I suppose, is that not a one of them knows what it was that warped him: his juvenile companionship with an emotionally needy vampire, who killed her rival for his affections: his mother.

As our present-day plot goes, Joel is divided and conflicted. On the one hand, he wants to break out of his shell and feel again, and to that end he starts a casual relationship with Kathy (Bernadette Pauley), a tenant in his building who relies on his mechanical abilities. On another hand, he seems to focus his left-over-from-high-school rage on Sabrina (Candice Meade), the haughty receptionist at his work. And on a third hand, he starts getting mysterious fliers in the mail which invite him by name to a new club called "The Hungry," where he meets Angie (Sasha Graham), a playfully seductive thing who reminds him of Rachel in more ways than one.

All of this is very interesting, but I'll be honest: for at least the last half hour, I didn't care. Not a bit. Reasons for such apathy are numerous, and I'll delineate them as is my habit.

First of all, our "protagonist" is a wishy-washy, reactive lump without a backbone. I understand the idea of a beset-upon high school nerd with oodles of rage beneath his socially inept exterior, but it just doesn't work here. McCleery's performance captures perfectly the somnambulistic resignation of the self-aware loser, but nowhere does he manage to convince us of the fires that ostensibly rage within.

Compounding the problem is the herky-jerky storytelling. While I do appreciate nonlinear storytelling in certain instances, it causes far more problems than it solves in this case. We spend so much time changing

time frames that the narrative thread of any one of them is easily lost, and by the end what happened when has blurred together and we can't tell when the events in front of us are supposed to have taken place. Causality, the essence of story, is completely destroyed. The fact that "helpful" captions are shown only sporadically doesn't help things; at best they seem an after-the-fact admission that the movie really doesn't flow as edited.

Which is really a shame, because buried in here is at least one really neat idea: the exploration of the psychological dissociation in a youth who has killed repeatedly to no ill effect on the victim. It's a sensation that Joel keeps trying to reclaim by killing women and imagining they're Rachel, and it could have really been a dominant theme, but because of the problems above it never gets any impetus.

There's such a thing as being too clever, and I think that's what we're seeing here, the cinematic analogue to the Chinese acrobat who spins those plates on the tops of pool cues. There are only so many plates that he can keep spinning; after a certain threshold, it's no longer entertainment—it's just one frantic guy running back and forth in the middle of a growing pile of smashed crockery.

Some Notable Totables:
- body count: 11
- breasts: 0
- explosions: 0
- dream sequences: 2
- ominous thunderstorms: 0
- actors who've appeared on *Star Trek*: 0

ARMAGEDDON: The FINAL CHALLENGE (1995)

THE FORCES OF GOOD BATTLE THE FORCES OF EVIL TO RECLAIM EARTH!

- *Written and directed by Michael Garcia*
- *Starring Todd Jensen, Graham Clarke, Joanna Rowlands and Toni Caprari*
- *Executive produced by Mark Bruno*

It's not often that I, with the callus built up on my soul by years of watching underwhelming cinema, find a movie that's so blasted annoying that I have to turn it off and wait until the next evening to finish it. Apparently there's always a movie that's worse than your resistance. It's not just how dreadful each scene of this movie is (it's all bad, but not horrendous). No, it's the fact that nothing makes sense when strung together. Nothing. Not a damned bit. Whatever story Michael Garcia thought he was writing and directing, someone should have told him that it thoroughly escaped being captured on the film he shot and edited.

And that's despite the massive amounts of gibberish-laden exposition we're served. We start, for instance, with a screencrawl explaining that in the post-holocaust future, the New World Order Bank (that's subtle) runs things, and they've created a line of "Fear-Permutator" clones who keep order and kill anyone who annoys the Powers That Be via a game called "multiple murdering." I'm pretty sure I've got these details correct, because the back of the box reproduces the crawl practically verbatim. Apparently the poor copywriter for the distributor couldn't make heads or tails of the movie either.

Once that's over, we get even more exposition, this time voiced over footage of spaceship and space station models hanging lazily from very obvious strings. And this exposition is completely unrelated, weaving a confusing tale of how there are loads of space platforms around the solar system, inhabited by refugees from earth who now can't afford to get back. Or something.

This background supposedly helps us understand what comes later, har-de-har. Next we see an earth city, represented by a cheap model of a *Blade Runner*-esque city constructed of shoeboxes and tinkertoys. A flying car model lands, and we meet our protagonist, thirty-year-old courier Michael (Todd Jensen), who is at first referred to as Michael Edelander, before his name inexplicably changes later to Michael Throne. It's his voice doing all of the voiceovers, by the way, and his amateurish delivery is not only irritating, but ironic considering events unfolded later.

He sees a commercial for a new sex droid and decides to trade in one of his older models for credit, but when he tele-calls the company, he finds out that he's somehow got a negative credit rating. He then spends ten minutes of our lives calling various banks, finding out that accounts he never had are overdrawn and judgments are being held against him. Eventually he ends up with a psycho bearded bank rep (Toni Caprari) who makes some menacing statements that I couldn't understand. Whee, we're watching a movie about the dangers of futuristic bank errors—almost as exciting as George Lucas's exploration of futuristic trade embargoes.

Later that night, he hears something and ventures outside (which reveals that, despite the city model we saw earlier, the back of his house just looks like a suburban brick home with a white wooden deck and very healthy trees) and finds a girl in the trash. So he brings her in. And then he has a dream about the bank psycho (whose name we were supposed to pick up on at some point, I suppose—it's Geiring) swordfighting him in his apartment and killing him.

After waking he finds that the girl he rescued is named Voyou (Joanna Rowlands), and she's kind of cute in a sad-eyed-waif sort of way. She's also not quite all there; she only knows that she was "looking for Daddy," who came "from the sky." Naturally, Michael falls head-over-heels for her, even though all she does is drifts aimlessly around his apartment, watching the rain, kissing mirrors, and fondling his android collection. I guess he just digs that "ethereal halfwit" thing.

Then there's another psycho bank guy dream, as he rips out Michael's heart—but this time it's Voyou's dream.

Then Michael runs into old bearded Plato (Graham Clarke), who is Voyou's father. He lives in the old prison complex, which is also the center of the Rebellion. Rebellion? Has anyone mentioned a Rebellion previous to this? And do we ever see any putative members of said Rebellion, aside from Plato himself? Plato is also a psychic painter, turning out canvases of the "Holocaust," the "great Chemical Disaster," etc., before they happen, earning him the nickname of Plato the Prophet. And his latest canvas shows a giant spaceship hovering over the city.

Well, Michael's awful confused about this (aren't we all?), so he does what any reasonable person would do: he enters the Dream Pod. It's a Brundlyfly-ish contraption which, I guess, sends him into a deeper consciousness. First he dreams about the day of the "Holocaust," which apparently wasn't that long ago, because he was married with a kid and working as a deejay at the time (spinning LPs, no less), and because he knew the bombs were dropping and his family was going to get obliterated, he uses the airwaves to send one last "I love you" out to them. He also dreams he's playing a VR game of chess against the bank psycho while dressed in white robes, superimposed on a star field.

Yeah, that's a deeper consciousness, all right. Sure hope he got more out of it than I got.

Since that wasn't much help, he spends time with Voyou in the apartment, until he goes to investigate a noise and ends up battling the psycho bank guy in an industrial catwalk place full of hanging chains. Amazingly, crazy Geiring acts just like he does in Michael's dreams (remember, this is the first time they've even met face to face), i.e., like a low-rent Joker. He even wears facepaint, though more along the lines of KISS. And Geiring proceeds to beat the snot out of Michael and leaves him. And when

Michael comes down out of Catwalk Land, he finds Voyou dead.

But wait, says Plato when next they meet. That wasn't the real Voyou; it was an android, and Plato arranged for Michael to meet her to bring him into the Rebellion (I guess Plato was getting lonely being a one-man resistance front). Why? Because Michael's voice has such an irresistibly persuasive quality, as evidenced by his last broadcast before the Holocaust, that he's needed to help convince the Masses to rise up against the State, and yes, you can hear the capital letters in his voice. Michael's ultra-voice qualifies as an Informed Attribute[*], as I've gotten nothing but numbness from listening to it this long.

Here's the plan. There is a real Voyou, who's a computer programmer on Venus. She can access the main interplanetary broadcast satellite which controls all media programming for all of the solar system as its defenses are lowered once every ninety days for maintenance. So she can get in and let Plato and Michael make a broadcast to everyone everywhere. Which they do, relaying to all the world the surprising truth of Plato's last vision: that Jesus Christ is coming back within the next 24 hours! They reveal this ("No, really!") and spout some anti-state pseudo-Christian propaganda and act all satisfied with themselves. (They expect anyone to believe this? "Gosh, honey, if you can't trust an anonymous pirate signal bursting into primetime, who can you trust?" I guess they don't have street-corner kooks spouting immanent apocalyptic predictions in the future.)

And things start coming true, because some of the space platforms burst into flame in such a way as to present evidence for the existence of an oxygen atmosphere in deep space.

Michael wears his *film noir* fedora to meet Voyou, who's coming in from Venus to meet him at a diner, but instead Geiring finds him and chases him down the rainy street, firing his laser gun into him several times. Apparently this does but minor damage, as Michael still manages to fight Geiring to a standstill, blast him several times, and then stop with his gun in Geiring's face and—you guessed it—refuse to shoot him because, really, that would only extend the insanity, you know? (You see this way too often in the movies. In the real world, we have a word for people who behave like that: corpses.) Geiring naturally grabs the gun and holds it to Michael's face—and then he laughs insanely, says that Michael was right, it really is pointless, and dances off into the rain, singing "It's Raining, It's Pouring."

Voyou shows up, and off they go in her car, and in the morning a big-ass golden spaceship shows up over the city, which Michael's voiceover proclaims to be "Christ's

---

[*] As defined at Jabootu.net: "When a character displays a mediocre or even inept level of skill in some discipline (anything from dancing to writing to fighting), yet we are shown other characters lauding their talents. This is to signal the audience that, at least in the universe presented in the film, these people are to be considered as highly proficient at their craft, however much this belies the evidence of our eyes and/or ears."

vehicle, the flying New Jerusalem"—and yes, there is some resistance to this Messianic reign, "but that is another story."

The credits roll, while I sit in stunned incomprehension, staring at the screen, wondering, *What the hell did I just watch?* This review may seem nonsensical, it may seem full of non sequiturs and fragmented scenes—but it's far more coherent than the feature it describes. My synopsis doesn't convey the often visible stage lighting used, nor the Roman Candle "laser guns," nor the completely godawful score—a New Agey synthesized piano abomination that sounds like what you'd hear on your local "cool jazz" FM station when the batteries in your radio are dying. Which, I suppose, is appropriate. You'd hate to find a competent score attached to a movie that should be floated out to see on a barge and sunk.

I take back my former words; every scene is inept. Practically every line of dialogue and every camera setup holds some element worthy of ridicule. It has the character of an overlong fever dream, and without the evidence of owning the videocassette, I would be inclined to regard it as such.

Some Notable Totables:
- body count: 1 (if you count the android Voyou)
- breasts: 0
- explosions: 6
- dream sequences: 3
- ominous thunderstorms: 2
- actors who've appeared on *Star Trek*: 0

CREEP (1995)

- Written and directed by Tim Ritter
- Starring Kathy Willets, Joel D. Wynkoop, Tom Karr, Patricia Paul and Dika Newlin
- Produced by Michael Ornelas
- Executive produced by Tony Granims and Joel D. Wynkoop

Florida-based moviemaker Tim Ritter is another of the forces behind the microbudget, shot-on-video feature film "revolution" of the '80s and '90s, and like the most successful of those other microbudgeters, he realized at the outset that he needed to compensate for the obvious deficiencies of self-financed video over studio-financed film. Much has been said about the "democratization" of film as a means of creative expression via the introduction of consumer-grade and consumer-affordable videocameras; recording audio and video no longer required massive outlays and forgiving investors. The means of committing an audiovisual narrative to permanent form, however crude, lay within the grasp of the committed hobbyist. That said, the independent moviemaker still had to put something in front of the camera, and an individual with a camcorder, no matter how high-end, still couldn't compete with the resources available to the professional industry production company.

The way to make video-based production feasible (i.e., appealing to a reasonable number of potential audience members and thus economically sustainable) wasn't to attempt to recreate what Hollywood production companies were doing with several more zeroes in their budgets; it was to provide a product that those corporate filmmaking bodies weren't producing. Yes, I could be speaking of porn; the first people to profit from both the home video explosion and the advances of video production were skin flick producers, who realized that lavish production values and artistic visuals were irrelevant to viewers simply hankering to look at nekkid people. I could also be speaking of "individual vision," which is cited in discussions of cinema to a "Methinks the lady doth protest too much" degree; despite the pretensions of the auteur theory, moviemaking is a heavily collaborative craft, and the idea that a film bears the fingerprints of its director to the same degree that a novel bears the marks of its author is simply ludicrous. At best, a movie could be said to retain some diffuse influence of its director which can be felt at varying strengths through each of the disciplines to whose practitioners the director is forced to delegate. Even a microbudget movie is a collaborative enterprise, and anyway, "individual vision" is responsible for those scores of art-indie film-school projects which no one but the director and his mom ever want to watch.

Ritter saw that his output would have to fill a niche that the majors and mini-majors weren't filling, and he decided to be "transgressive," as the kids say today. His 1995 "cult classic" *Creep* promises sex and violence (not just action) from the get-go. That it delivers on those elements is not open to dispute; how well they mesh into a good (if cheap) movie requires further discussion.

Just to get us off on the right foot, our prologue features a drugged mother and her strung-out manfriend pushing her son Angus into "bad touching" his sister in front of an 8mm camera. Don't worry, we see no actual children in this scene, just the camera in Mom's hands staring at us. But it's still plenty disturbing to hear the adults ranting "Touch your sister!" and "Be a good sissy!" for several minutes. And the severed head they toss around doesn't relax the ambiance.

In other words, it's absolutely no surprise that Angus grows up to be deeply, royally, completely screwed up.

When next we meet Angus Lynch, he's an adult (Joel D. Wynkoop, who has parlayed his role in this movie into a bizarre celebrity status among microbudget filmmakers and fans) in a bright orange jumpsuit, being transported between Florida prison facilities. A car crash on a lonely road gives Angus a chance to escape his police escort, and after killing the one live cop who tries to tail him, he's officially free from prison, with some grudges to settle and some psychoses to indulge.

Meanwhile, young lady cop Jackie Ketchum (Patricia Paul) suits up for another day of busting perps and the like. It seems that Jackie's main law enforcement training has been a steady diet of *Dirty Harry* movies; when she finds a sociopathic woman (Dika Newlin) mixing poison into baby food bottles on a grocery store shelf, she gets all steely-eyed and makes the suspect eat her own handiwork. Kind of unusual in uniformed patrol officers; you usually have to make detective and start wearing your own clothes to work before you can let your attitude handle your firearm, then walk away without doing any paperwork.

Jackie's got her own inner turmoil; she's haunted by the memories of her mother being stabbed by a mugger when she was little, and even the protective presence of her father, the world's most laid back police captain (Tom Karr), does little to ease her flashbacks.

I'll tell you right now: Angus' story and Jackie's story aren't going to intersect for a long, long time. So get used to switching back and forth.

Angus wastes no time in getting back to form. He finds a secluded church for shelter, and murders a homeless wino for his clothes and collection of bladed weapons. Then, with that unerring Serial Killer Radar, he finds a young couple screwing in their car in the woods and kills them both for their wheels.

How better to follow that than with a trip to see one's stripper-sister? So Angus stops by to watch his sister Kascha (Kathy Willets) show everyone the godawful things that some quack plastic surgeon attached to her chest. I've never made a secret of the fact that I don't much like breast implants that look like implants instead of breasts, but these cantaloupe-sized subdermal contraptions turn my dislike into utter revulsion. They look more like Googie-era hood ornaments than mammary glands. And combined with an over-aerobicized figure and skin made leathery by decades of cigarettes and other hard-livin', Willets is one stripper that I would pay to stay clothed.

After a few moments of catching up, Angus discovers that Kascha's current husband Donny is a little too abusive for his tastes, so Angus hitches a ride to Kascha's home to meet him. Donny (Lenny Blythe Jr.) looks like Dom Deluise's less-polished brother, and acts so repulsive that Angus almost comes across as a hero for gutting him with a hunting knife.

Jackie's day, meanwhile, hasn't been nearly as productive. She has to turn in her badge and gun today while on mandatory suspension for her convenience-store trick. Then she drops in on her boyfriend Graham's apartment, just barely missing the extended striptease his new girlfriend-on-the-side performed for him before they both ended up in the hottub. Oh yay, two stripteases not ten minutes apart; at least the teaser in this case is fifteen years younger than Kathy Willet, and her skin still looks like skin instead of naugahyde. But still. I don't know from experience, but I suspect that maybe a striptease is something you really have to see in person to appreciate, since I've never seen one in a low-budget movie that aroused more than my thumb on the fast-forward button.

So. Angus and Kascha decide that a life of perverse crime would be hunky-dory, so they terrorize another couple in the woods (this time with Angus decked out in drag), then dig up their mother's corpse from the cemetery just so Angus can hurl abuse at her. Then brother and sister decide that an open grave would be a terrific location to play some of those "games" that Mom forced upon them as kids... but in the middle, Angus slices open Kascha's throat instead, just cuz.

Back in our other storyline, Jackie's a wee bit paranoid, since her dad is the one who originally put Angus away, and serial killers are notorious for coming back for revenge. She runs into a small-time rapist she once helped convict (Dan "Rattlehead" Cleveland), and she's more than a match for him, but still, her suspension plus her breakup plus those incessant flashbacks to her mother's murder are taking their toll upon her, so Dad suggests she go up to "the retreat" (I'm not sure if this is their family cabin, or a police-owned facility) and he'll join her once he's put the department to bed.

Unfortunately, Captain Ketchum has other things in mind when he gets there; he bashes Jackie over the head with a vase and ties her to the bed. Why? Mostly because he's worried that her amnesia is fading, and she's about to remember that it was he who killed Mommy, because she was about to report him to his superiors for being abusive. (As luck or plot mechanics would have it, Jackie only flashes back to a complete recall of that day, including her father's face under the ski mask, while she's knocked out cold from Dad's blow. Oh, the irony!)

And finally, our two storylines intersect as Angus shows up—at Dad's invitation. See, Dad arranged for the prisoner transfer and the crash that gave Angus his freedom, on the condition that he show up to kill his troubling daughter and thus provide Dad an alibi. Of course, serial killers are notoriously unreliable employees, and Angus decides to kill Dad instead, then leaves Jackie alive when he's struck by the parallels in their lives—both screwed over by parents who done them wrong.

But that's scarcely a satisfactory conclusion, so instead we get another one that's... not much better, really. Jackie cuts her hair to be unrecognizable, tracks Angus for four months, then shows up in his apartment with a mountain of plastic explosives and brings the building down on top of them. The end.

I hope I don't need to point out to you that, even ignoring the primitive technical aspects of a movie with this limited a budget, we're not talking about a good movie here. The formless succession of events presented to us can scarcely be called a plot, and our nominal protagonist Jackie really doesn't do anything, or even participate noticeably in the story until the last ten minutes. And those last ten minutes are themselves especially problematic; the footage of the building crashing down obviously resulted from a demolition that Ritter captured on video and found a way to use, but couldn't it have been worked into the story (or a story) a little more organically? As it is, having Jackie blow up an entire apartment building just to kill Angus and herself means that, when our pseudo-protagonist finally actually does something, it's a self-centered and irrational act that takes the lives of probably dozens of innocent co-tenants.

That having been said, the movie does fulfill its promise of being transgressive. Wynkoop's performance as Angus is always fun to watch; I can't very well gauge his abilities as an actor because playing such an over-the-top, irrational character can hardly be called "acting," but it still means that the scenes involving our messed-up serial killer are more interesting than those involving our milque-toast, wanna-be-tough protagonist.

I would call Kathy Willets' boob job "transgressive" in and of itself, but apparently there's a market for that kind of thing. What a world.

Some Notable Totables:
- body count: 16 (plus however many people were in the apartment building)
- breasts: 10
- explosions: 2
- dream sequences: 3
- ominous thunderstorms: 0
- actors who've appeared on *Star Trek*: 0

CYBERZONE (1995)

You've entered Cyberzone. Let the chase begin.

aka *Droid Gunner*

- Produced and directed by Fred Olen Ray
- Written by William C. Martell
- Starring Marc Singer, Matthias Hues, Rochelle Swanson, Robin Clarke and Kin Shriner
- Executive produced by Andrew Stevens and Roger Corman

> "I'm cybertrained in judo and karate. I've got over a hundred hours on the simulator!"
> "Well, that's great. We run into any simulated killers, you can take over."

So one day, B-movie producer Andrew Stevens, who has a business relationship with the legendary Roger Corman, gets a brainstorm. The American Film Market trade show is coming up really soon, and he realizes he has access to some shooting locations near the AFM locale. What if he had a movie shooting then, so he could take people from the trade show out for tours of the set? It would be great advertising, not only for the movie being shot, but for everything that his company is coming out with.

Problem is, there are only a few weeks until the trade show. So he calls in Bill Martell, a low-budget screenwriter who's made a name for himself writing scripts to specific budgets. Stevens says, "Here's the stock footage we'll be using, here are the locations, here's the basic idea for the movie. You've got nine days to deliver a script."

Not a first draft. The final shooting script.

Bill goes home, and over the next nine days he consumes Juan Valdez's annual output and finishes the script. He walks into Stevens's office, hands it to him, and walks out the door. In the other door comes director Fred Olen Ray; Stevens hands him the script.

"Here," he says. "You've got a week for pre-production, and $225,000. Make it."

On movies like this, not only does the production story enhance one's enjoyment of the final product, it sometimes even proves more interesting.

The story itself is more than a little *Blade Runner*-esque. Marc Singer stars as Jack Ford, a "droid gunner" in a dystopian future Phoenix, AZ, where society is divided into "lower" and "higher," and Ford is definitely among the lower of the low; even in the dive bars he frequents, he and his entire gunner profession are looked down on. (Several references are made to the smell of "'bot oil," which makes me wonder why 'bot oil would smell so terribly different than any other mechanical oil.) Droids are illegal on Earth, just as in *Blade Runner*, but darned if they don't keep showing up; Ford is a bounty hunter specializing in 'bots.

His newest case is a little different, though. Professional thief Hawks (Matthias Hues) has stolen four pleasurebots from the Jupiter colony, with the help of some footage from *Battle Beyond the Stars* (1980), probably the most amortized movie ever made. Pleasurebots, in case you couldn't guess, are mechanical prostitutes, and afford a reason to show some gratuitous female flesh (how good-looking are they? Well, one of 'em's the late *Playboy* centerfold Lorissa McComas, hubba hubba). The rightful owner, Mr. Reginald (Cal Bartlett), has reason to believe that they've been smuggled into Phoenix, which is the new West Coast megalopolis now that L.A. has slipped into the Pacific, and he wants Ford to find them and get them back unharmed.

But since Ford's used to bringing in severed robot heads for the bounty, Reginald hooks him up with a technician who can disable the pleasurebots without damaging them—Beth (Rochelle Swanson), a hoity uptowner who looks down on Ford with disdain.

Together, then, the Odd Couple sets out to find the pleasurebots, exploring whorehouses and dive bars and all the settings you'd usually find in a Roger Corman film. Ford's main lead is a crimelord named Chew'Bah, played with a certain Jabba-the-Huttishness (including a chained dancing girl) by Robert Quarry; but since Chew'Bah is the one who set up the smuggling deal in the first place, he sends out goons after Ford and Beth. Fights, escapes, more stock footage…

After much this'n'thatting, they track the pleasurebots to the new Born-Again underwater city New Angeles (represented

by footage from *Lords of the Deep* (1989) and a conduit-lined corridor in a water treatment plant that shows up in just about every Corman sci-fi flick), where hypocritical religious leader Humberstone (Robin Clarke) has intentionally imported the pleasurebots as contraband to his sinless paradise—without some sin, see, his followers have no need for salvation. (Methinks Bill has some issues with organized religion.) But since Humberworth has tried to pull a fast one on Hawks without paying him, Ford and Hawks and Beth all team up to smuggle the pleasurebots back out again.

The first time I watched this, back right after its release in '95, my friend Chris and I got bored; it was out of desperation that we started counting breasts, thus beginning an august tradition. Now, however, knowing the story of the production and especially the creation of the script, it's much more entertaining. (That, and I think my standards have fallen in the meantime.)

I mean, if you've got to turn in a final, carved-in-stone script in exactly nine days, you don't have time for such niceties as ambition and originality. You've simply got to get a semi-coherent story down on paper, set in the locations available. And how do you do that?

Simple. You steal.

Similarities to *Blade Runner* have already been noted. Plus you've got that "man and woman who hate each other until they fall in love" thing that's best exemplified by (though by no means original to) *Romancing the Stone* (1984). Ford also has a musical pocketwatch right out of *For a Few Dollars*

More (1965), a borrowing emphasized by the fact that Ford ends up having a quickdraw competition over the watch with Humberworth's lieutenant Walsh (Kin Shriner). Naturally, the watch is emblematic of a hurt in Ford's past (apparently that subplot ended up on the cutting-room floor), which is one of Bill Martell's favorite tricks: assigning an object as a symbol of the protagonist's inner turmoil. (I know, it's not original to Bill—poet John Keats labeled it an "objective correlative" over a century ago—but Bill uses it with great frequency, to good effect.)

Despite all of this, Bill did let himself get creative in the patching together of these "homaged" parts, not to mention a bit playful. The pleasurebots are a pain to smuggle, as they won't keep from stroking their thief. (At one point Hawks tries to disguise them as nuns.) When Chew'Bah orders Ford's death, he also takes the occasion to set a budget for the flowers they should send to Ford's funeral. And when Humberworth sends an assassin droid to take Ford out, it's a big bruiser with an Austrian accent.

And then, of course, you've got Fred Olen Ray up to his old tricks, which is basically using the stock footage Corman gave him (*Battle Beyond the Stars*, *Lords of the Deep*, and a tiny snippet of *Star Hunter* (1995), which Ray also directed), and calling all his frequently used actors and offering them parts (Marc Singer, Rochelle Swanson, Robert Quarry, Ross Hagen as a one-eyed pirate bartender, Brinke Stevens as a mutant cat stripper, Bob Bragg and Sam Hiona as Chew'Bah's thugs, Peter Spellos as the employment "interviewer" for a whorehouse, Hoke Howell and Jeff Murray as street bums, Richard Gabai as a New Angeles plant worker, Steve Barkett as a space fighter pilot, etc., etc.). Say what you will about the final product, but it sure looks like the production was fun.

Which is probably why, despite its flaws, *Cyberzone* ends up being more entertaining than $225,000 should pay for on such short notice. Bill's a professional, Fred's a professional, and professionals know that you have to have fun under pressure or you'll crack. Don't take it seriously, and you can enjoy it for the throwaway low-budget trash it is.

Some Notable Totables:
- body count: 25
- breasts: 14 (same as that first viewing, six years ago)
- explosions: 4
- dream sequences: 1
- ominous thunderstorms: 0
- actors who've appeared on *Star Trek*: 1
    - Matthias Hues (Hawks) played the second Klingon general in *Star Trek 6*

CYBERZONE: Screenwriter William C. Martell's Comments

I had a treatment called *Steel Chameleons* about a female cop investigating a murder who uncovers an underground railroad for androids who want to pass as human. Her investigation takes her to a brothel with "pleasure droids"—designed for safe and sanitary sex. One of the PDs becomes her informant, she develops a relationship with him, and later decides to protect him from prosecution. She's with the PD (police department) and he's a PD.

Andrew Stevens wanted to start his own company and asked me to write three scripts that could be made cheap—I agreed to write two. The first was going to be *Steel Chameleons*. Andrew's scheme was to use other people's money to make the films—he would keep foreign rights and the partner would have domestic. So my treatment was sent over to Corman's company for approval.

Roger had these two guys running Concorde—Mike Elliott and Rob Kerchner. That's who I had my meetings with. They were making 30 films a year at the time, so Roger was only involved in the really important stuff... and you know how important the script is. I went into the meeting expecting notes on my treatment... instead they wanted to start from scratch. They liked the idea of pleasure droids. Could I write a script about robot hookers from outer space? I asked if they had to be from outer space... yes. Did they have to be hookers... yes. Did they have to be robots... yes. "Okay, I can write that."

Andrew was supposed to put up half of the budget, and in keeping with his "other people's money" plan, he needed to sell foreign rights at AFM. The money from foreign rights would make up his half of the budget. But he was a start-up company, so he needed to be able to show the foreign guys what they were getting. That meant the film had to be in production during AFM so that he could have these foreign guys on set. So now I had an insane deadline—I had to start from scratch with a new story and get the script finished in time to get it cast and in front of the cameras by AFM. When we counted back the time for pre-production we realized I had about two weeks.

Andrew's deal included five minutes of Corman stock footage. I decided to go from outer space to under water—lots of production value. There was also a cool futuristic car chase in one of the films, so I added that (it got cut out) and a foot chase scene through a rotating burning tube (also cut out).

I also couldn't really start writing until Andrew and Roger had signed the cast. That sounds weird, but we needed names that were available at a specific time (AFM). What if I wrote a tough guy sidekick and we ended up with Ruth Buzzi in the role? So the major roles were cast before I started writing. Matthias having a casual conversation with Marc while he had him in an arm lock would be funny—the same scene with Russ Tamblyn wouldn't work.

Andrew and Roger agreed on Fred as a director. I had a meeting with him before I started on the script. I had met Fred years earlier at AFM at a screening of some sci-fi film he directed that was produced by the guy who produced *The Blob* and *Dark Star*. I think the movie was called *Star Slammer* and was a women's prison movie in outer space. Anyway, Fred has a great sense of humor. I pitched him the story idea I had come up with, he thought it sounded okay and had some great story and stock footage ideas... Now I had nine days to write it.

(Fred's contributions included Brinke Stevens as a mutant... but she was supposed to be a hologram. When we couldn't afford the FX, she became "live" in the bar.)

I wrote the script. Not much sleep. Ten pages a day. The first couple of days at ten a day are okay, it's the last couple that are impossible. Your brain is just used up and needs a vacation. One thing I'd never mentioned to anyone—I couldn't take the robot hookers from outer space thing seriously, so I wrote a comedy. I thought it would be funny if these girls were the ultimate in boob jobs—they're 100% fake! All bod and no brains. In your review you wonder if I have organized religion issues—maybe I do, but the villain was based on the Christian Coalition guy (Reed?) who was headline news at the time. I think I even took some of his dialogue from the CC guy's speeches (he was making a speech every day at the time, and it looked like the country was going to adopt Christianity as its official religion). Fred even cast a guy who looked like the CC guy. What was social commentary at the time looks odd now.

Also in the review you mention some places I stole ideas from... but missed the main place: *The Empire Strikes Back*. I knew that Jabba had been played by a human in a *Star Wars* scene that was cut, so I used that as an in joke with Bob Quarry's character Chew'bah. The waterfront bar is the cantina from *Star Wars*, Matthias's space ship is some variation on Millennium Falcon, etc. My goal with the script was to make fun of *Empire* and every other sci-fi film I loved.

You also mentioned the pocket watch "twitch"—which was from a *Chinatown*-like plot thread that got cut. The villain trying to corner the robot hooker market was like Noah Cross cornering the water market... except silly. So I gave Marc's character a tragic past—a woman he loved who died. She gave him the watch. There's parts of this still in the film, but the big scene is gone. There was even a "Don't worry, Jack, it's New Angeles" line.

I also think I snuck in a James Bond theme song title, probably a Sam Fuller film title, and other stuff into the dialogue. And the names are all action film directors from the '30s.

Part of the fun: Marc's character is a guy who wants to get laid but can't, Matthias' character is a guy who has women throwing themselves at him but is more interested in making a buck. Every time Marc is about to get some luvin' bad guys attack.

By the way—the script was based around locations. That's why there are three scenes at the strip bar (a total of eight minutes), three scenes at Chew'bah's lair (eight minutes), three scenes in the office (eight minutes), etc. We struck it rich at this crappy warehouse converted into a studio because they had flats we could build into offices and were located in a bad part of town with lots of alleys. If you look closely at the villain's office—you can see the paint drying on the wall! That's how quickly this thing was shot. You might also notice that Matthias' space ship set is the same as his mini-sub set (eight minutes total)—but the section of the set with the ladder was put in a different spot.

So I turned in the script and had a meeting with Fred. He asked if the script was supposed to be funny and was relieved when I said yes—we were on the same page. Here was the problem: Andrew and Roger (or at least Mike and Rob) wanted a serious film about robot hookers from outer space. So everything was played straight—except the bimbo pleasure droids kept walking into walls and had one track minds, and the winos shared recipes for Mutant Cat Au Vin [a scene kept in the overseas release but cut from the domestic version—Nathan], and everything was silly—but done with a straight face.

While the film was shooting my friend Paul Kyriazi was in town from Japan for AFM. Paul gave me my first paid screenwriting job (*Ninja Busters*—also a comedy because I couldn't take the concept seriously). So Paul and I can be seen in the bar scenes. I'm sitting at a table with an eye patch, Paul is at the bar. We spent the day watching Brinke Stevens strip over and over again.

I'm at AFM sitting in the office watching buyers come in. Andrew has a bunch of posters on the wall for films that are just ideas at this point in time. There's a poster for *Invisible Mom* with my name on it. Andrew needs to presell these movies—to get foreign buyers to pay up front before the films are made. Why? Because that's where the money to make the films is coming from! That means the buyers have to have faith in the company based on their set visit to *Droid Gunner*. Will the company be able to turn those posters into movies... or go bust?

At the end of AFM they tally up the presales on *Droid Gunner*, and I'm sitting right there. The movies makes about four times its cost in profits! The other films sell well, too—Andrew's company is a success.

The film is screened for cast and crew, and afterwards we go to Dimples Karaoke Bar across from NBC—Fred buys us drinks on his credit card. (Fred is the nicest director I've ever worked with—I'd work with him again in a heart beat even though the budgets are so low the pay sucks). Everyone thinks this may be Fred's best film—they laughed throughout the screening and even liked the emotional scenes in the film (Marc giving the girl a coin, etc). Lucas was talking about doing more *Star Wars* movies, and I thought that might turn it into a big cult movie.

When Roger releases the film on video, the title is *Cyberzone*. I want to know what the cyber part is, and where's the zone? Plus, the video box is serious and the text on the back is about Marc Singer tracking down dangerous androids... Um, how dangerous are those bimbo-bots? Fred and I realize that nobody got the joke. I worry that people who rent it thinking it's going to be an action movie will be disappointed because it's silly. But I get email from Joe Bob Briggs—he liked it. *Entertainment Weekly* does a whole article on "pleasure droids" as a sidebar to their review. A couple of websites thought it was a great six-pack movie.

It's okay with me if people see *Cyberzone* and think it's crap, but I like the movie for personal reasons—I had a great time. The film is what it is... best viewed while drunk. I think Rochelle Swanson is great—she did the perfect "girl with glasses who is a babe when she takes them off"—taken to an extreme because every time she takes off her glasses it's to go undercover as a hooker. Hoke Howell cracks me up—he was perfect. Ross Hagen can make the worst lines I wrote sound good. The girls are all fantastic—they were playing parodies of themselves and were good sports about it. And Matthias delivered my favorite line in the script: "They're like leeches!"

DEATH MACHINE (1995)

IT FEEDS ON YOUR FEAR.

- *Written and directed by Stephen Norrington*
- *Starring Brad Dourif, Eli Pouget, William Hootkins, John Sharian and Martin McDougal*
- *Produced by Dominic Anciano*
- *Executive produced by Jim Beach*

This very easily could have been a forgettable movie. In many respects, in fact, it was; between the time I first saw it with my friend Chris in the mid-'90s and the present day, huge chunks of the story vanished from my memory. This was career FX guy Stephen Norrington's freshman effort both writing and directing, three years before he was tapped to helm *Blade* (1998), and it's a B-movie solidly in the *Alien* mold: a confined near-future setting, an *ee*-vil corporation, and an unstoppable killing machine with a head that's all teeth. But amidst the direct-to-video mediocrity, there are a couple of facets that rise above the level of required adequacy, and one which seared itself upon our hearts forevermore. I'll tell you when we get there.

In the meantime: the Chaank Armaments Corp. is in the middle of a public relations crisis. Their covert "Hardman" Project, involving cyborg soldiers, has become public knowledge thanks to one of the experimentees going AWOL and killing a half-dozen civilians. To top it off, the company's former CEO just recently died under mysterious circumstances, leaving the corporation in the hands of new chief executive Hayden Cale (Ely Pouget). The tough, androgynous name is supposed to make us think that she's tough enough to survive in a "man's world" and all, which is good because her actions when we meet her characterize her as the world's most naive Girl Scout thrust into the role of running an arms company. She is shocked—*shocked!*—to discover that there is illegal weapons research going on, and pledges to get to the bottom of it, over the objections of fellow executives Scott Ridley (Richard Blake) and John Carpenter (William Hootkins). Yeah. It's one of those movies, in which naming the characters after genre-beloved directors is considered "clever." Trust me, it's not. It never is. Especially because it always seems to be the same half-dozen directors who are so "honored." Even in *Night of the Creeps* (reviewed on page 47), one of the movies I love beyond all rational bounds, that particular contrivance is a sucking wound. And *Death Machine* is no *Night of the Creeps*.

That distraction aside, Cale vows to shut down this and any other illegal project being developed in the bowels of Chaank, and to fire the creepy weapons designer who lives in the vaults, Jack Dante (Brad Dourif). The name may be yet another directorial nod, but in this case it also fits the character, this diabolical mastermind who has infiltrated the entire Chaank network and security system, and of whom even Cale's fellow executives are deathly afraid. But not only is he the nigh-omnipotent computer antagonist, he's a fairly well-drawn character. He's underbelly-white, with lank hair and a bad wardrobe; his basement lair is festooned with action figures and taped-up centerfolds, which are as much an expression of his suspended adolescence as his fascination with neat 'n' cool weapons systems is; and his behavior betrays him to be not only antisocial, but socially maladaptive, relating poorly to others and misinterpreting social cues. He wants to be seen as an extremely dangerous individual, when what he really is is a petulant child-man with a certain dangerous skill. The only false note is that Dourif is skinny, whereas the real thing would be pudgy from a diet of Twinkies and Mountain Dew Code Red.

Oh, and he's got a tremendous crush on Cale. Just what every girl wants.

You may think that Dourif is thus the exceptional facet of this movie to which I referred. He is not. That is yet to come. Be patient.

Because in addition to Cale and Dante and the rest of the squabbling execs, we have three more characters, leftist terrorists-lite who want to wipe out Chaank's crimes against humanity. As we meet them, they're all puffing on massive joints; endearing, no? The leader is—sigh—Sam Raimi (John Sharian), who looks like a career surfer ten years past his prime. And the other two are Weyland (Andreas Wisniewski), the blond geek whose name is half of a reference to the *ee*-vil corporation in the *Alien* movies; and the other half of the reference: Yutani (Martin McDougal).

Or, as we dubbed him when his name wasn't quickly mentioned, Rising Sun Dude.

And yes, Rising Sun Dude is the shining centerpiece of this movie, a pseudo-Asian with the Japanese war flag painted on his face and shaved into his buzzcut. He speaks in clipped declarations and puts forward a face so stoic he makes your average samurai look like Paris Hilton's latest disposable pet. He embodies a coolness so overflowing, it leaks in excess from his person and leaves a glowing trail of coolth behind him. RISING SUN DUDE, I KISS YOU!!!

Right. So. Anyway. Everything comes to a head this particular night, as Cale tries to find a way to lock Dante out of the corporation without the approval of the other execs. The Three Revolutionaries stage a covert break-in to blow up the Chaank computer core. And Dante, pissed at Scott Ridley for trying to oust Dante's new "girlfriend" Cale, unleashes his latest toy on the exec: the Warbeast. Or, as we dubbed it when its name wasn't quickly given, the Killer Mechanical Squirrel.

You can probably already guess the design: an eight-foot-tall mass of hydraulics and carbon steel, with wicked-looking choppers occupying half of its head, and front limbs culminating in huge razor-sharp talons. It's a prototype meant as a "battlefield morale destroyer," and to that end it's been designed to sense fear and hunt the fearful via pheromone trackers. It's a stupid idea, naturally, and it would never make it out of prototype into production, but on the other hand it's the natural weapon for someone like Dante to design, since it'd be so ass-kicking cool to fight one on your XBox.

And that's it. Three execs (whoops—

make that two), three rebel good guys, one vicious computer nerd, and one Killer Mechanical Squirrel, trapped in the company highrise overnight. There are double-crosses among the execs, inflated idealism among the revolutionaries (they didn't even load any live ammo into their big-ass guns), and many attempts to trap or at least evade the Warbeast. Injuries and explosions abound, and Rising Sun Dude just keeps on being cool. How cool is he? You want to know? At one point he needs fabric for a tourniquet on his leg, so he reaches inside his belt, grunts, twitches, and *rips his boxers right out of his pants*.

This is the point at which Chris and I became totally gay for Rising Sun Dude. Pity he doesn't live to the closing credits (yikes, did I give too much away?); he should have been the focus of a whole franchise of über-cool action flicks.

By the end, Cale has become converted to the revolutionary cause, since being an exec at an arms contractor doesn't turn out to be nearly the dream job she thought it would be (yeah, it looks like they went cheap on your background check too, sweetie), and she and Raimi manage to bring ironic justice down both on the corporation and on Dante.

There's not much here that would indicate that Norrington had anything like *Blade* in him; there's certainly none of that hyper-caffeinated energy to be had. Granted, the budget for *Death Machine* was only a fraction of what he had to play with on *Blade*. I also don't know how much to credit his script for the interesting points of Dante's personality, since Dourif is a tremendously underrated actor and could easily be responsible for his own character quirks. But Rising Sun Dude? I can only imagine that the idea came along one day while Norrington was smoking what the revolutionaries smoke, and he decided to keep it in. For that alone, I thank him.

And Rising Sun Dude, you will live forever in our hearts!

Some Notable Totables:
- body count: 12
- breasts: 2 on Dante's porno video, plus about 20 on the pinups around his lair
- explosions: 15
- ominous thunderstorms: 1
- actors who've appeared on *Star Trek*: 1
    - Brad Dourif (Dante) played "Ensign Suder" in three episodes of *Voyager*

DRAGON FURY (1995)

THE FUTURE HAS JUST UNLEASHED THE ULTIMATE WARRIOR.

- Produced, written, and directed by David Heavener
- Starring Richard Lynch, Robert Chapin, T.J. Storm, Chona M. Jason and Deborah Sharon Stambler

You will recall David Heavener's name from the review of *Deadly Reactor* on page 115. It was an acutely painful experience, not unlike serious radiation exposure, and I was afflicted for days afterward with nosebleeds and eye-popping headaches. I'm happy to say that the current feature does not star David Heavener. True, he wrote it, directed it, produced it, and gives a "special guest appearance" (can any appearance by David Heavener really be considered special?), but he does not occupy the camera for the majority of the running time. It's still a stinky-bad movie, but my only side effect was a moderate case of diarrhea.

The future, as usual, is a gritty and cheap place, one in which bare-chested, ninja-masked goons with swords chase unarmed people around. (One man resists, which gives us a chance to see what looks like the fight choreography practice session filmed by mistake.) All appears hopeless for a mother and daughter, until a lone fighter appears—dressed identically to the goons. (Yup, that makes the fight easy to follow.) He easily dispatches a half-dozen opponents, mainly because they use the "wait your turn to attack a solitary combatant" style of swordplay. He then rescues the helpless twosome on his motorcycle and... Wait a second. No electricity (as evidenced by the artfully placed torches lighting up the night), no weapons more advanced than swords, but we've got a shiny bike and refined fuels? Sure. Whatever.

The lone warrior is Mason (Robert Chapin), who pulls off his ninja mask to reveal his shining golden mullet, and opens his mouth to reveal the reason that Heavener felt comfortable casting Chapin as the lead: he has exactly the same level of charisma and thespian prowess as Heavener himself. To wit, none.

He takes them back to the hideout of his compatriots: Milton (Chuck Loch), your standard inept smart guy (with glasses and all!), and Regina (Chona M. Jason), Mason's short, hot and feisty love interest. (By the way, I didn't find out her name until the closing credits. And I was listening hard.) The deal is—and no, this makes no more sense to me than it will to you—that people in the future like this mother and daughter are afflicted by the deadly Peeling Latex Plague, the treatment for which is only available through the AAMA, a medical organization which is now the only law in the land. Those who have the plague have to pay the AAMA for treatment, or the AAMA will hunt them down and kill them. (Look, I just told you it makes no sense.) Mason, Milton, and Regina are freedom fighters who help get sufferers to the "underground hospitals" before their makeup crumbles off all the way. Their opponent is the local Chief Medical Dictator Vestor (Richard Lynch with a caduceus tattoo on his cheek—and again, I didn't know the character's name until the credits rolled), whose "Dragon" goons we've already seen, and his right hand bad-ass, Fullock (T.J. Storm). With the state of Lynch's career through the '90s, it's not often that you can say he was "slumming," but I think this qualifies.

Milton, though, being a general purpose smart guy, has figured out through old newspaper clippings that, waaay back in 1999, Dr. E.L. White had come up with an inoculation for the just-beginning plague, but was murdered by the AAMA (and an 8.7 earthquake the next day effectively stymied investigation and threw all of the U.S. of A. back to the Stone Age because if Los Angeles goes, the entire world is soon to follow, right?). Boy, if only they had a time machine to go back and get the serum before the quake and... hey, what's this in the basement? By golly, if it isn't a time machine!

Since Vestor and his Dragons are breathing down their necks, Mason volunteers to go back for the serum. He's got a set of arbitrary rules: the time door will open again in 36 hours for only 20 seconds, and if he doesn't make it back, they can never try again to retrieve him. (Do not ask why. There is no reason, which usually means that someone will beat you up for asking.) He makes the jump, courtesy of some flashing lights. Then Regina runs down and makes the jump after him. Then Vestor arrives, and he sends Fullock and another Dragon through.

Mason gets the short end of the stick. He contracts all of the possible symptoms of a time jump—splitting headache, unconsciousness, amnesia—and ends up in the hospital as a John Doe. Regina's fate is even worse; she arrives without any symptoms at all, but does so in the middle of a "komedy" bit with David Heavener (what a special guest appearance!) as a groom in the honeymoon motel room; his bride takes violent exception to this beautiful girl that just appears on their mattress. (It doesn't help that Regina decides to go through the time machine topless for absolutely no reason.)

And Fullock and the other Dragon end up in back alleys where, after a moment of disorientation, they're well enough to kick the asses of some doped-up ne'er-do-wells who get in their faces in a fight with all of the heart-pumping immediacy of synchronized swimming. (Everybody arrives none the worse for wear, except our ostensible hero. Know what that makes him? A wimp.) And then Fullock pulls out his amazing Extend-O-Blade (everyone in the future has one—it snaps out from flashlight size to full katana with just a flick of the wrist and a splice of the film), which has a flashing detector in the pommel which homes in on Mason for them. What exactly is it detecting? I dunno, but Regina's does the same thing. My only guess is that it's a Mighty Mullet Detector.

So. Time travelers back to present-day Los Angeles, armed with swords. It's like the gruesome bastard child of the *Highlander* and *Terminator* franchises. As written and directed by David Heavener.

The nice Dr. Ruth (Deborah Sharon Stambler) little by little works on Mason's amnesia, but it doesn't really all come back until the Dragons and Regina all show up at the same time at the hospital for some more fighting. Dragon #2 gets offed, and Regina and Mason escape with Dr. Ruth's help. (Part of the escape chase features Fullock running after the car and leaping onto the back. Were they consciously trying to remind us how much this movie depends on the *Terminator* flicks?)

And then, of course, Regina gives Mason the best possible treatment for amnesia, i.e., sex. (Took me the longest time to figure out why she was even in this movie. Silly me.) Mason has dreams that explain his own backstory to him (how Fullock killed his wife and child, how Vestor thought that he could break Mason's will and make him a Dragon), and when he awakens, he remembers why they came back in time and what they're supposed to do. Good for you, Mason. It's now almost an hour into the movie, so could we get on with it, please?

Now that Regina has served her purpose in the movie, Fullock appears (the Mighty Mullet Detector runs on Duracells, you know) and slashes her across the stomach as soon as they walk out of their motel room. With her dying breath, she pleads with Mason to leave his grudge with Fullock for now and instead concentrate on getting the serum before the deadline. He runs off without a backwards glance, and we never do get anything resembling grief or mourning—but I guess that given the acting ability exhibited so far, we're lucky to be spared the display.

Since Mason needs to find a medical clinic (and better, get into it), he goes to Dr. Ruth, the only doctor he knows, at her house. (Wait a minute—how could he know where she lives? I swear, if you keep asking questions, I'll turn this car around!) Since there are only about seven doctors in the L.A. area, she of course knows one who works at the right place, and since we're two-thirds of the way through the movie, she swallows his cockamamie time-travel/conspiracy/earthquake story with no qualms. She even helps convince her associate, Dr. Stenton, who gives them all the security codes and combinations to get into the vault for the serum—but who should appear and cut Stenton down? (Hint: he's got a Mighty Mullet Detector.) Once again, running away is the strategy of choice, so off they go with only an hour to spare before the deadline, with Fullock tailing them in a stolen ice cream truck (komedy!).

Apparently Stenton worked at a place where no one even knew him, because Mason manages to bluff his way through using his name. While Mason and Dr. Ruth try to find the "secret passage" into the vault, Fullock just comes blazing through, mowing down security guards right and left, until we finally get the climactic battle.

But wait! When the time door opens (i.e., somebody turns on a blue light), Vestor jumps through from the future for his last battle, and chops Mason across the gut before expiring himself. So that means that Dr. Ruth has to take the serum through and save the future. What a happy ending. I mean, aside from the fact that the hard part is yet to come: synthesizing enough of the serum for mass inoculations in a wood-burning future, while avoiding the fascist AAMA and their omnipresent goons. But how hard can that be?

As usual with movies this stupid, I've had to gloss over the petty inanities that fill every scene in between the big notable whoppers, but trust me, they're there. Character stupidity, gut-wrenching dialogue, lackluster fight choreography, synth-in-a-box soundtrack, and all of those ill-conceived creative choices that characterize David Heavener's presence on either side of the camera. I'd like to say that, having seen it and written about it, I'm free of the *Dragon Fury* tale forever... but then I found out about *Dragon Fury 2,* and my curiosity got the better of me. But that's a review for another time.

Some Notable Totables:
- body count: 44
- breasts: 4
- explosions: 0
- dream sequences: 2
- ominous thunderstorms: 0
- actors who've appeared on *Star Trek*: 1
    - Richard Lynch (Vestor) played "Baran" in the *TNG* two-parter "Gambit"

GUNFIGHTER'S MOON (1995)

A LEGEND HAS MET HIS MATCH—HIMSELF.

- *Written and directed by Larry Ferguson*
- *Starring Lance Henriksen, Kay Lenz, David McIlwraith, Nikki Deloach and Ivan Sergei*
- *Produced by Douglas Curtis*
- *Executive produced by Larry Ferguson, Robert Kenneally, John Langley and Peter Rosten*

In first American and then world cinema, the Western has become a genre largely divorced from its historical setting, growing instead into an idiom for the expression of universal, larger-than-life archetypes. Unfortunately, given the whole topsy-turvy nature of this world of ours, positives are not always positives. Archetypes are good when handled properly; when fumbled, we call them "clichés," and they become a sign of lazy, unambitious thinking rather than an insight into the human psyche.

Part of the problem is, naturally, one of the Western's strengths. (Do statements like that make me a Postmodernist?) It's a tightly strictured genre, perhaps more limited in its elements than any other (at least, any other recognized as a full cinematic genre and given its own shelf at the video store). The historic and geographic setting are both rigidly confined, and moreover, they're stylized almost to the point of being unrecognizable for their real-world counterparts. (A lot of people, on visiting Texas, are surprised that it doesn't look like the Texas that John Wayne rode through—mainly because "Texas," as well as Arizona, New Mexico, Nebraska, and Dodge City, Kansas were usually either southern California or southern Utah.) The character templates are similarly limited, with the focus usually being on frontiersmen and gunfighters, forced to make their own law for good or evil in a land without adequate law enforcement; the supporting characters are those who would normally interact with such characters—namely, bartenders, downtrodden ranchers, and cheap women. In fact, sometimes it seems like the entire typical Western town is composed of the saloon, the cathouse, and the barber shop (where the barber doubles as the part-time judge or mayor).

What's the problem here? Well, aside from the fact that there are only so many stories to be told with these people in these locales without becoming hopelessly repetitive, the setting and situations are getting further and further removed from primary sources with each passing generation of filmmakers. Modern dramas and action-adventures can be informed by real-world events; science fiction, at least in theory, thrives on innovation. But the Western is locked into a finite set of stock elements, about which the current generation of directors and writers learns solely through the extant cinematic library. It is, in a word, incestuous.

That's not to say that good movies can no longer be made with these worked-over elements, but each of the recent successes only proves the point: a Western still has to fully reference the established tropes—touch all the bases, as it were—and knowingly play off the "canon." And the audience is expected to be fully aware of the standard elements being referenced. Imagine some poor foreign chap trying to enjoy, say, Sam Raimi's *The Quick and the Dead* (1995) without realizing the importance of the shootout in the climactic scene of 90% of Westerns, or wondering what all the hoopla was about Clint Eastwood's *Unforgiven* (1992) because he didn't know how familiar the story of "the legendary gunfighter who can't retire" is (and how associated Clint Eastwood had been with Westerns throughout his career).

Sooner or later, I have to start discussing *Gunfighter's Moon*, which is fully as referential to the standard tropes as either of the examples used above, but not nearly as successful. Gunfighter's Moon also uses "the legendary gunfighter who can't retire" as its mainspring, and it's a no-brainer that this one got the greenlight thanks to the success of *Unforgiven*. But that's not the only famous Western that gets "homaged" here. It seems as if writer/director Larry Ferguson, when given the opportunity to make a Western, decided to make all of them.

Lance Henriksen is perfect as Frank Morgan, legendary quickdraw—now old, skinny, tired, and still tough enough to chew through your arm. Tough enough that, when two young turks from Kansas track him down to a small town in Colorado just to challenge him, he has no qualms about blowing one away and shooting the other in the leg when his attempts at dissuading them fail. (Regarding that omnipresent urge to find and fight the top gunslinger in these movies: I'm gratified that stupid macho obsessions are not merely a product of a more modern era, and a little disappointed that the terminally stupid and belligerent have no analogous method of removing themselves from the gene pool these days.) Such is life at the top.

That life, such as it is, is interrupted by a telegram that Morgan's woman Rosa (Yareli Arizmendi) tries to keep concealed from him; but he's far too canny for that. His past has come calling, and he leaves that morning on his horse, with the dog that isn't his but follows him everywhere anyway tagging along. (Don't all gunfighters have one of those?)

Now, this next complaint may seem over-finicky, but it's more important than it looks at first blush. Or rather, than it sounds at first blush, because the nit I'm picking at here is the music. Our opening theme was done entirely with keyboards—passable, until we got to the "muted guitar," which had "CASIO" stamped all over it. But here, as Morgan takes a five-day montage to Red Pine, Wyoming, we're treated to overly-valiant, fanfarish bombast, more appropriate for the Cartwrights on the ride than for our over-the-hill outlaw. Had I known that this was going to be a three-minute montage, I would've turned down the sound on the TV and thrown a Ry Cooder soundtrack CD on the stereo.

Eventually he arrives at what's supposed to be Wyoming, although it looks suspiciously like the environs of Vancouver. (Hmm. The Colorado village is shown as a dusty, arid place, whereas Wyoming is moist and verdant. I wonder if Ferguson had ever visited either locale.) He's immediately recognized by one of the town's old-timers (must've had the trading card) and reported to the sheriff. Unfortunately, the sheriff isn't really the sheriff, as the real sheriff was killed in a botched bank robbery the week before; the temporary sheriff is storekeeper Jordan Yarnell (David McIlwraith), in charge of keeping Morris (Dave Ward), their single prisoner from the robbery, in jail until his hanging next week. Yarnell's not happy to have the wildcard Morgan in town, especially because he has no idea why Morgan's there, unless it's to spring Morris.

It doesn't take us nearly so long to figure things out, though, since Morgan's very obviously got some history with Yarnell's wife Linda (Kay Lenz), and takes a keen interest in the Yarnells' seventeen-year-old daughter Kristen (Nikki Deloach). So it doesn't come as a surprise to us when Linda visits Morgan privately and reveals that yes,

Kristen is actually his daughter, and no, neither Jordan nor Kristen know; Linda has told them that her husband died a decorated hero in the Civil War, rather than raise Kristen knowing her father was a notorious outlaw. It's Linda who called Morgan here, because Morris' cousin Walt Shannon (Brent Stait) is on his way to town to free his kin, and there's no way that a storekeeper with a badge can take on a professional goon like Shannon. How she expected to get Morgan's help while keeping her dark little secret from Jordan and Kristen remains a mystery.

There are admittedly many nifty ideas in here, but they're spaced out from each other so neatly that it seems like several different versions of the movie. For ten minutes, after Morgan takes compassion on a downtrodden Mexican servant in the saloon (James Victor), there's much discussion of the idea that "a man on his knees is only half a man." I kept expecting them to grow what they planted there, and have Morgan either end up in contrition in a church or shot to his knees by an opponent; but apparently Ferguson got bored with that particular subtext after hammering on it for ten minutes, as it's never referenced again. Even more maddening, the story we're promised in the opening scene—that of a gunfighter trying to run from his own reputation and get out of the "business"—isn't the story we're told; once Morgan gets that telegram, he's gunfighter through and through for the rest of the movie. He may regret not having lived with Linda and Kristen as husband and father, but that's not the same as trying to step out from beneath the shadow of a reputation that's outgrown him.

As you've no doubt gathered, one doesn't watch a Western in this day and age and expect originality. But unlike one of the good modern Westerns, which is derivative but manages to blend its borrowings smoothly, *Gunfighter's Moon* is lumpy in its assemblage. I imagine that Ferguson watched a different classic Western each night while writing the script, and woke up the next day determined to immortalize the previous night's viewings in his own movie. I'll not list for you all of the many echoes of previous movies; I don't have the expertise to label them all anyway. Suffice it to say that, while the first half leans heavily on themes from *Unforgiven*, the second takes its cues directly from *High Noon*, as Yarnell finds that the town is willing to release the bankrobber rather than have Shannon and his posse shoot up the town, and only Yarnell's willing to stand firm. Of course, Morgan's in town to help him, but Yarnell doesn't know that—and anyway, once Morgan gets shot in the back by the brother of the Kansas kid he waxed right after the opening credits, it's doubtful whether he'll be able to help anybody.

The worst part of the story's lumpy consistency is the way in which it continually reminds you very clearly of the movies from which it's taking its inspiration, all of which were definitely superior to this one. Maybe the best audience for this one is the unschooled audience, after all—viewers who won't see it as a patchwork of favorite scenes from a dozen other movies, and maybe find a way to appreciate it as a discrete work.

Some Notable Totables:
- body count: 5
- breasts: 0
- explosions: 0
- ominous thunderstorms: 1
- actors who've appeared on *Star Trek*: 0
- actors who've appeared on *The X-Files*: 9 (hey, Vancouver's a small acting community)

INVISIBLE MOM (1995)

NOT SEEING IS BELIEVING.

- *Directed by Fred Olen Ray*
- *Written by William C. Martell*
- *Starring Dee Wallace Stone, Barry Livingston, Trenton Knight, Russ Tamblyn and Stella Stevens*
- *Produced by Fred Olen Ray and Andrew Stevens*

Hollywood is a sausage grinder; low-budget Hollywood, doubly so. It's got all of the drawbacks of any major manufacturing industry—rigid production schedules, redundant layers of management, ultimate decisions made by beancounter committees —and one besides: unlike sausages, each of its products is supposed to be different enough to attract by its novelty while maintaining a predictable level of quality. Given those conditions, it's not surprising that even experienced professionals such as producer/director Fred Olen Ray and screenwriter William Martell can collaborate on a supposedly simple project—in this case, a kid's movie in the vein of the *Honey, I Shrunk the Kids* franchise—and still have underwhelming sausage come out the other end of the grinder.

Josh Griffin (Trenton Knight) is at that awkward junior-high age, which in movie terms means he's got a girl he likes and a bully who's giving him grief. He's also got a dad (Barry Livingston) who's an inventor for Applied Technologies, and a mom who's Dee Wallace Stone. (Well, what else can I say about her? I mean, it's not like we see her going to work, but keeping house after one child is kind of light work for a homemaker...) Mom is a rare breed in cinema: a parent who tells her child, "If you're in the wrong, back down—but if you're right, stand up for yourself." None of this namby "Ooh, violence doesn't solve anything" crap that I hear spouted by people who apparently sprang full-grown from the head of Zeus and never went to grade school. (Me, I teach my kids, "There are problems that violence doesn't solve, and problems that violence does solve—make sure you're using the right tool for the right job. And while I don't want you starting fights, you have my permission and blessing to finish them.")

Where was I? Oh, yeah. Apparently Dad Griffin needed a mom like his wife, because he's a non-confrontational type, which means that his boss Dr. Woorter (Russ Tamblyn) both insults him for being a slacker, and then steals his inventions and presents them to the military as his own, making manymany bucks. Dad's not going to stand up to his boss, though (he even tries to give Josh the "Fighting never solves anything" crap before Mom gently contradicts him). Mom gives him a non-confrontational solution, then; why not invent something here at home, so Woorter will have no claim on it?

It's a great idea, so Dad starts working in

his basement lab, mixing beakers of Kool-Aid and dry ice—I mean, really important chemicals and stuff. And after a couple of false starts, he comes up with his great invention: an invisibility potion! He tests it on the dog, and yup, the dog disappears.

He keeps this a secret even from his family for a couple of days as he tests it out, which gives the invisible dog time to get Josh in trouble (making messes, unmaking beds, etc.) to the point that Mom grounds him. And somehow she forgets to lift the grounding when Dad finally reveals that the dog's right here, folks! Look at that dog collar walking around by itself!

And since he's still grounded, he won't be able to ask that special girl out to the sci-fi double feature on Saturday, and when the bully teases that he's going to ask her out instead, well, that's the last straw. Josh and his friend Skeeter (Phillip Van Dyke) get into the invisibility potion in the basement, testing it first with an eyedropper on Skeeter's iguana (yeah, just what we need—invisible lizards running around under foot). But then Mom interrupts, and in desperation Josh squirts the remainder of the eyedropper into his RC Cola. She gently kicks Skeeter out ('cause Josh is still grounded, you know), and confiscates the RC Cola. And before Josh can sneak it back, Mom gets thirsty, and well…

There she goes.

I'm pretty okay with things up to this point. Sure, there was some distressingly bad technobabble in the Applied Technologies lab, and the "invisible dog" effects were noticeably primitive, but those are pretty much par for the course. But from here on out, we start piling up annoyances. One annoyance is ignorable; a couple can be ignored with some effort; but after a while, the sheer weight of the combined annoyances really detracts and distracts.

See, Dad hadn't come up with an antidote yet, so he takes a sample of the formula to work to take advantage of the computers and greater supply of chemicals. But then Woorter gets wind of the project, so Dad has to break his test tube to keep Woorter from getting his hands on it. Woorter then cans him and calls security to drag Dad away.

But then Josh gives Dad the "stand up for yourself" speech—which is okay, except by the end it becomes "You have the right to break into the laboratory!" Okay, time out. Did I mention that this is a kid's movie? I'm all for putting strong moral messages in kid vids, and I like the "stand up for yourself" idea, but we've just crossed the line into a highly questionable moral.

So the next day, Saturday, Dad and Josh go back to the lab to "clean out his desk," made easy by the fact that Dad still has his keys. He was fired from a (supposed) defense contractor lab and declared "banned for life," and nobody took his keys? And security will just allow a terminated and quite possibly disgruntled employee back in to "clean out his desk" without even having someone hovering over his shoulder?

In security's defense, they do call Woorter at home, so Josh and Dad are on a time budget to find an antidote—and just as they think they've got it (testing it on the iguana to be sure), Woorter and the security guy burst in. And then, when Dad pleads to Woorter, "My wife is invisible! You've got to let me work on the antidote!" Woorter uses that as evidence that Dad is unstable and has the State Mental folks come and pick him up, and drag Josh off to an orphanage. Whuh? The state will lock up nonviolent private citizens on the say-so of their ex-bosses? They'll trundle a child off to an orphanage without even checking to see if there's a second parent to take care of him? Hell, the first and only notice Mom gets that anything's amiss is when the orphanage allows Josh a single phone call.

So Mom grabs a cab to the lab to try and find the antidote herself, but that's exactly what Woorter was planning on, because he needs a living specimen of the effects of the formula to show the boys at the Pentagon. He catches her, and his offer to her is that, if she cooperates and allows herself to be transported to Washington in a crate, he'll have her husband and son released. Whuh? Let's see how many implausibilities we have here: A) that the Pentagon will take kindly to one of its civilian contractors kidnapping a private citizen and shipping her like livestock; B) that Woorter's got the kind of far-reaching civic powers that he can, with a word, have people released from state institutions at will.

The annoyances are really stacking up by this point.

I've got to leave some surprises for you in case you ever watch this, but the ending revolves around a competency hearing like they have in some completely dissimilar parallel universe. Order (and visibility) is eventually restored, good is rewarded, evil is punished, and all is right with the world.

Oh, did you miss the girl-and-bully subplot in there? It ends about halfway through, when the bully (who's also the Griffins' paperboy—have you ever met a bully paperboy?) gets slapped by the invisible Mom. (There's some slight implication at that point that Mom is therefore cruising around the house with nothing on, but thankfully they don't go too far down that particular road.) And that's it. Neither bully nor girl are ever brought up again.

But it's not surprising that minor characters get lost in the shuffle, as the major ones do too. I never was able to figure out who the actual protagonist was; Mom was obviously the title character, but she was involved very little in either the onset of her problem or its solution, and spent too much of the time in between being passive. Josh was the instigator of the action, but he wasn't really as involved in the solution, and as for any "character arc" he might have had, well, that was short-circuited about halfway through when Mom took care of his bully problem for him. Dad does most of the running around, but the resolution of his problem at the competency hearing is mostly taken care of by Mom and her invisible hijinks. I suppose I'd put the protagonist hat on Dad, but the fact that I have to dissect it this much is yet another annoyance for the pile.

And how did I forget to mention Mrs. Pringle (Stella Stevens), the neighborhood's Mrs. Kravitz-wannabe who watches the Griffin household with her binoculars while her husband reads the paper? Did we not have enough clichés here without this one tacked on?

If we can condense all the transgressions into one venial sin of children's movies, it is this: making them "just for kids," and forgetting that parents are going to be watching these things too. Take a good children's movie like *The Iron Giant* (1999); it's certainly aimed at the juvenile set, but there's nothing precluding it from being enjoyed by the parents too, or even childless adults. It's just plain good cinema, regardless of age group. *Invisible Mom*, by contrast, cuts all sorts of plot and production corners with the apparent attitude that, hey, we don't have to make it good; it's just for kids, after all.

Well, it's true. My kids enjoyed it. But I'm the one that rents tapes, and I'm the one that buys them, and I'm probably not going to do either for this one.

Some Notable Totables:
- body count: 0
- breasts: 0 (I mean, technically, they're supposed to be present, since Mom's running around naked and all, but…)
- explosions: 0
- ominous thunderstorms: 2
- actors who've appeared on *Star Trek*: 0

INVISIBLE MOM: Screenwriter William C. Martell's Comments

The original script was about a working mom who was invisible to her husband and kid—they took her for granted. After the line producer has scheduled the whole shoot, Andrew finally got around to reading the script (or maybe just the coverage) and came up with a list of changes. First—she doesn't work. He wanted mom to be more of a June Cleaver type and less of a realistic mom. Next, he wanted the kid and dad not to take her for granted (there goes the character arcs for both of them). Also—originally the script was written for three days of Dee Wallace Stone on camera (the rest is voiceover when she's invisible) but Dee really liked the script, and said she'd work more days. Andrew said, "Show Mom more." ("But she's invisible!" "Then make her visible!") That's why she saves the day instead of the son and dad saving the day (and coming to appreciate her). Whole rewrite had to be done in less than a week, then it was immediately shot. I was doing rewrites on *Night Hunter* for Ashok Amritraj at the same time, got no sleep, and had walking pneumonia when we shot the Teamster #2 scenes [in which Bill does a cameo—Nathan]. Other things that went wrong on that film—we shot at the Van Nuys Sewage Treatment plant which has a huge high tech lab... but the location person rented the wrong lab (this little one) and we didn't discover it until we showed up to film. We also didn't get access to their computer room with this huge computer from 1970s movies (so our "super computer" was a lap top)....

The film was shot in two weeks (including FX days shot in a studio). I don't think you can shoot a movie that fast and have it turn out good. Too many things went wrong (etc). But my nieces loved it.

Fred is a great guy. He always tries to make the best movie with whatever he's given. He likes movies. The only "negative" thing I can say about him is that he and I have totally different visual styles (he likes to set up the camera and have the actors move, I like to move the camera), but that's an artistic difference. On the last day of shooting Fred buys a bottle of champagne for everyone on the crew out of his pay check. He's also funny... I like Fred more than any other director I've worked with (to date). He actually fought for my script on *Mom* when Andrew finally gave us his notes.

TERMINAL RUSH (1995)

A NATIONAL MONUMENT HELD HOSTAGE. A FORGOTTEN HERO RISES WITH A VENGEANCE.

- Directed by Damian Lee
- Written by Mark Sevi
- Starring Don "The Dragon" Wilson, Roddy Piper, Michael Anderson Jr., Brian Warren and Kate Greenhouse
- Executive produced by Don "The Dragon" Wilson

Remember that *Far Side* cartoon that shows the "People Who Didn't Like *Dances With Wolves*" convention? There are three people standing around the punchbowl in a big empty meeting room, complaining bitterly.

Die Hard is even more like that than *Dances With Wolves*. It's the action movie that just about everyone in the world loves, and with good reason: it's got a zesty premise, good suspense all the way through, and engaging characters, both good and bad. Nevertheless, if I had a time machine and was changing the past to engineer the present, I'd be sore tempted to delete *Die Hard* from reality. Sure, we'd lose one of the greatest action movies of all time, but on the other hand we'd be spared the growing hordes of lame-ass *Die Hard* ripoffs.

The saying in Hollywood is, "Everyone wants to be first to be second," meaning that everyone wants to jump on the bandwagon just as soon as someone else has shown that that bandwagon is profitable. And movies are often made solely on the writer/director/whoever's ability to describe it in one sentence, especially if that one sentence compares this project to a previous successful movie. What could be easier than saying, "It's *Die Hard* with a slight variation"? Thus, we have been inundated with "*Die Hard* on a ship" (and its sequel, "Die Hard on a train"), "*Die Hard* on the President's plane," "*Die Hard* with supermodels," etc. (There's another Hollywood joke about the starlet so stupid she agreed to appear in "*Die Hard* in a skyscraper." That was before Anna Nicole Smith starred in *Skyscraper* (1996).)

Terminal Rush, in case you were wondering, is "*Die Hard* on a dam." It's got to be one of the most meticulous imitators of the original *Die Hard*, and yet somehow manages to also be one of the lamest.

First, an ominously unexplained scene in which the governor, an Air Force general, and an executive discuss a "test flight" surrounded in secrecy. There's talk of a media blackout, talk of a special microchip making everything work... Trust me, you're not supposed to understand this until later.

Our hero is Jacob Harper, a deputy sheriff in this unnamed desert town, played by Don "The Dragon" Wilson, former World Kickboxing champ turned actor who is unwilling to give up that nickname that makes him distinct from all the other Don Wilsons in the world. Because Wilson's half-Asian features put him in the "vaguely ethnic" category of actors, Harper here is part Indian, thus evincing the normal racial epithets like "Tonto." We're introduced to him at a redneck bar, where a generically inconsiderate redneck is making life hard for a teenager working there (throwing darts at his head and such). Harper wipes the floor with the redneck and his associates, because good guys don't let pointless cruelty go unanswered. On the other hand, this scene doesn't bode well for the rest of the movie, because the fight is notably ill-choreographed. In fact, it looks *un*-choreographed, as if director Damien Lee had simply said, "Okay, Don, go out there and, you know, kick some ass around. Rolling!"

Meanwhile, a phalanx of black SUVs drive up to the dam (I will admit to not knowing which dam this is on sight, but given its stated proximity to Nellis AFB, plus the stock footage used throughout, I can only assume it to be Hoover Dam). Out hop about a bazillion goons in paramilitary black with semi-automatic weapons, led by Dekker (Michael Anderson Jr.) and right-hand man Bartel, accent on the first syllable (paragon of manhood Roddy Piper, unrecognizable with finger-gelled hair and raccoon makeup around his eyes). They promptly pepper the guards with bullets and make their way into the bowels of the dam.

But lest we're too excited by all this action, we then cut to, you know, personal stuff. Harper is estranged from his wife Katherine (Kate Greenhouse), largely stemming from the fact that she wants desperately to get out of this desert boondock, while he feels bound there by his mother's Indian heritage. Hmm, marital discord regarding location of residence—gee, wow, just like *Die Hard*! Even Harper's father tells him he ought to leave town to be with his wife. Dad, by the way, is a security guard at the dam, and right after he imparts his intergenerational wisdom to Harper, he reports to work late and is promptly nabbed as one of the dozen hostages that Dekker has refrained from shooting. A family member as a hostage—gee, wow, just like *Die Hard*!

Dekker has delivered an ultimatum to FBI Special Collins (Dave Nichols) that he wants $25 million or he'll start executing hostages in four hours. Collins hems, haws, and promptly takes over the sheriff's department as his base of operations, to the consternation of Sheriff "Snookie" (Brian Warren—unexpectedly for a rural community, a younger black man). As is standard in these movies, the FBI is high-and-haughty with the local gendarmerie, and as a result they don't find out that Harper's dad is one of the hostages —or that Harper knows a secret "construction tunnel" into the dam that isn't on any of the blueprints.

From here, it's mostly standardized *Die Hard* stuff. Harper goes inside alone, kills a couple of patrolling goons, and gets his hands on a headset with which he can listen in on the baddies' plans; Dekker orders a couple of hostages killed, which Bartel carries out with relish; and the FBI wanders around with their thumbs up their butts, trying to figure out what Dekker, a career arms dealer, and Bartel, a mercenary, are doing playing the terrorist game.

Remember that part about the Air Force microchip?

It all comes clear when Snookie informs Collins that the highway patrol has a deal with Nellis AFB to call out their soldiers as needed for emergencies, such as the crowd control needed now (we don't see any need, but we're told that there are riots and general unrest due to the televised threat to blow the dam—although, given that this is rural Nevada, a state with a population density of 16.5 per square mile, I can't see how it would really be an issue). Let's see, depleting the forces at Nellis—could this work into Dekker's plans? Supposed terrorists with a hidden ulterior motive—gee, wow, just like *Die Hard*!

The high point, such as it is, is the fight between Harper and Bartel. Given the lackluster quality of the initial action we see, I had feared that the showdown between two of my "guilty pleasure" action stars would end up being a shootout between two catwalks (of which there are plenty), but no, they do go at it hand-to-hand—and because both Wilson and Piper are consummate professionals, they still manage to make the fight look good despite any technical shortcomings.

Much of the rest of the movie is predictable blah-blah, but I have to tell you something from the climax. Harper goes single-handedly to stop the acquisition of the chip that is the terrorists' real goal and holds a gun on Dekker and Bartel, but gets shot in the leg by a hiding third man. Bartel instructs Harper to put his hands behind his head, which he does—having conveniently hidden two throwing knives right there. Weapons hidden at the back of the neck, right at the climax of the movie. All together now: Gee, wow, just like *Die Hard*!

Despite how diligently *Terminal Rush* photocopies all of *Die Hard*'s plot points, *Terminal Rush* still misses out on *Die Hard*'s success. The peril of the hostages never gets ratcheted up a notch; Wilson's Harper isn't nearly the charismatic everyman that Willis's McClane is (owing, largely, to Wilson's lack of charisma himself—he's got a modicum of boyish charm, but it largely vanishes whenever he opens his mouth). Piper, on the other hand, has loads of native charm, but his humorless role here lets absolutely none of it come out. And that raccoon makeup is just damned funny-looking.

The final product looks like the initial feature project of a a film school graduate whose enthusiasm overreached his skills, but it isn't so. Producer/director Damien Lee has been making movies since the early '80s, with such genre credits to his name as *Food of the Gods 2* (1989) and *Abraxas* (reviewed back on page 209)—not high art, granted, but certainly he's no neophyte. Writer Mark Sevi also has string of credits, including *Sci-Fighters* (reviewed on page 265) and *Arachnid* (2001) with a predilection for sequels—*Relentless 4* (1994), *Ghoulies 4* (1994), *Dream a Little Dream 2* (1995), *Class of 1999 2* (1994), and the marvelously titled *Excessive Force 2: Force on Force* (1995)). Again, no award-winners here, but both Lee and Sevi are definitely in the ranks of People Who Should Know Better.

If you ever get the urge to watch this one, fast-forward about an hour into it and watch the fight between Don "the Dragon" Wilson and "Rowdy" Roddy Piper. Then go watch *Die Hard*. It'll be just like watching *Terminal Rush* in its entirety, but better.

Some Notable Totables:
- body count: 29
- breasts: 0
- explosions: 9
- ominous thunderstorms: 0
- actors who've appeared on *Star Trek*: 0

The MANGLER (1995)

From the three masters of horror, the ultimate tale of terror is about to begin.

- *Directed by Tobe Hooper*
- *Written by Stephen Brooks, Tobe Hooper and "Peter Welbeck" (Harry Alan Towers), based on the short story by Stephen King*
- *Starring Robert Englund, Ted Levine, Daniel Matmor, Jeremy Crutchley and Vanessa Pike*
- *Produced by Anant Singh*
- *Executive produced by Sudhir Praglee, Sanjeev Singh, Helena Spring and "Peter Welbeck"*

Somebody once said (and if no one can remember who originally said it, I'll just go ahead and take credit for it) that there have been more cinematic atrocities committed in Stephen King's name than in any other. I suppose it's the price you pay for fame—Stevie has sold over 350 million books, so everyone is lined up to buy the film rights to all his short stories (since the novels are already spoken for by the big studios) and turn them into a movie that they can proudly slap his name on, while King cringes and doesn't dare go near a multiplex in his hometown.

This movie shows all the earmarks of being conceived entirely by the marketing department. "Just think of the voiceover for the coming attraction, Leo! 'From master of horror Stephen King and director Tobe Hooper of *The Texas Chainsaw Massacre*, starring Robert Englund of the *Nightmare on Elm Street* series and Ted Levine of *The Silence of the Lambs* —a new kind of horror!' Now all we need is a script, and we're in business!"

So they came up with a script, and that's where the carefully constructed house of cards came crashing down.

If you've read the original short story, from Stephen King's *Night Shift* collection, then you already know it's about a demon-possessed industrial laundry iron. (Why? Because King did a stint in an industrial laundry back in his starving writer days, and a lot of his work is based on his personal experiences. That explains why so many of his later novels have full-time novelists as their protagonists.) Those things are big, scary-ass machines, so it's no wonder that he wrote a horror story about it. But short stories are, well, short. There's just enough space in there to put forth a concept and sketch in a scary situation. To make a feature film out of a short story, you either have to flesh out ancillary situations and concerns that are only indicated in passing in the story (the classic King example being *Children of the Corn* (1984)), or you have to add entirely new characters and situations to fill up a two-hour running time (as happened in *The Lawnmower Man* (1992), which has exactly two points of similarity to the Stephen King story: the title, and a single line of dialogue).

The Mangler tries to do both of these simultaneously. Comparisons to walking and chewing bubblegum are apt.

The most effective moments in the movie come at the very beginning, as we're introduced to the harried and sweaty women working in the Blue Ribbon Laundry, and the huge steam iron nicknamed "the Mangler." It's an imposing piece of machinery, with huge rollers and exposed bicycle-style chains with links the size of a loaf of bread, hungrily pulling sheets into its cast iron maw as fast as the workers can carefully lay them in the opening. All of this is overseen by evil old man Bill Gartley (Robert Englund under layers of latex), a sneering capitalist in leg braces.

Things start to go wrong when Gartley's teenage niece Sherry (Vanessa Pike), also a peon employee, cuts her hand on a handle of the Mangler just as two doofuses (doofi?) bump into the machine while carrying an old-style icebox. Sparks fly and such. Then a little later, elderly Mrs. Frawley (Vera Blacker) accidentally spills her antacids into the machine, and while trying to pick them off the conveyor belt, she gets pulled in and Mangled. (The machine's also got the auto-folding attachment, which doesn't help any.)

The cop called in is world-weary burnout John Hunton (Ted Levine). Naturally, he's tortured by the death of his wife in an auto accident, because all police detectives have to be battered and traumatized by life, right? But before he can do more than puke at the sight of the hospital-cornered Mrs. Frawley, the sheriff and coroner show up, immediately rule it an accidental death, confirm that the safety cutoff bar on the Mangler is in fact working as it should be, and everything's back to business as normal.

Hunton goes home and uses his next door neighbor as his shrink. Fortuitously, said neighbor Mark (Daniel Matmor) also happens to be the brother of Hunton's deceased wife, as well as a PhD parapsychologist. Boy, I bet those are in demand in semi-rural Riker's Valley, Maine.

Good thing that he's there, though—because as other accidents start happening around the laundry (a steam hose breaks loose and scalds three women), who else would put together the pieces and start to suspect that the machine is actually possessed through a freak set of circumstances which randomly turns out to be a summoning spell?

All of which is an expansion of King's original story—all except that part about the sheriff and the coroner covering things up as fast as they can. It seems that Gartley's got some strange power over the high and mighty in town, linked somehow to the Mangler which has been a fixture in the laundry for generations. According to this storyline, the Mangler's always been possessed, and there's a string of missing sixteen-year-old girls stretching back for years, girls all coming from the town's wealthy families; apparently they were sacrifices to the machine, in return for... um... Boy, that part really never comes together, since it's never made clear exactly what a possessed steam iron can grant to its supplicants. April freshness, maybe? And there's also some falderall about how those who lose body parts to the Mangler become in some way connected to it, and thus infused with its pernicious *ee*-vil.

And frankly, not only does this subplot not gel with the main one derived from King's story, it flat-out contradicts it. Why are we worrying about the Mangler just now being possessed, when it's already supposed to be long-possessed?

Most of this information is revealed by the "Pictureman" (Jeremy Crutchley), the ancient police photographer who has intimate knowledge of the darker goings-on in town. Unlike most of the other characters, who manage to be one-dimensionally annoying, the Pictureman's got two entirely separate annoying sides to him. First up, the actor's a young guy—probably in his twenties—done up with some incredibly unconvincing age appliances. One wonders if they did it that way solely for the purpose of making Englund's makeup job look credible by comparison. Secondly, he's a walking anachronism, with his pork-pie hat and antiquated single-flash camera. In fact, the whole production seems plagued with a half-hearted attempt to go for a stylized, period look, but never accomplishes more than making you wonder why. (I guess it's hard to keep the production design consistent when the production's split between Hollywood, London, and South Africa.)

The movie works hard to distract us from looking askance at the plot, if only by providing intensely silly distractions. For instance, there's the possessed icebox! That's right, the coil-topped icebox that the two yayhoos were carrying in the laundry gets delivered to a suburban house—conveniently, in Hunton's own neighborhood. No clue is given as to why an obsolete icebox is delivered to a house at random and left sitting in the front yard, but no matter; the point is that the icebox is also *ee*-vil from its contact with the Mangler, and thus it lures in and suffocates a little boy, as well as a handful of birds—and it almost eats Mark's arm! Enraged, Hunton takes a sledgehammer to it, and when he knocks the coil off the top, a spray of post-production blue energy shoots out the top. This convinces Mark that the Mangler is indeed *ee*-vil, and they have to be careful in trying to exorcise it so that they don't accidentally release the *ee*-vil. (Which only raises the question, What exactly are they going to do about all that *ee*-vil blue light that just sprayed out of the top of Lucifer's beer-cooler?)

If you've read the story, then you know exactly how the "surprise" ending works— and even if you didn't, you can probably figure it out with all of the meaningful shots of Mrs. Frawley's antacids (which Hunton swipes on the sly—tortured detectives all have ulcers). Or at least, you know one of the endings; given the many disparate plot threads here, it's only natural that the movie take ten minutes to end all of them—and as long as we've got two mutually exclusive plot threads running in tandem, we might as well throw credibility to the wind and end up with the offhand revelation that the laundry building has a basement foundation which is actually a miles-deep pit, complete with a stone-arched spiral staircase running around the edge like an ancient catacomb.

As I mentioned, the movie's at its best in the opening scenes; the impersonal, grinding power of the Mangler when it's working as it's supposed to is the most memorable image to be found here. After that, it's just a steady decline into storytelling ineptitude, until the only meaningful conflict to be found at the climax is the one between boredom and ridicule.

Some Notable Totables:
- body count: 7 (plus 4 birds)
- breasts: 0
- explosions: 1
- ominous thunderstorms: 1
- actors who've appeared on *Star Trek*: 0

CROSSWORLDS (1996)

IMAGINE A PLACE WHERE ALL DIMENSIONS OF THE UNIVERSE COLLIDE...

- Directed by Krishna Rao
- Written by Krishna Rao and Raman Rao
- Starring Rutger Hauer, Josh Charles, Stuart Wilson, Andrea Roth and Perry Anzilotti
- Produced by Rupert Harvey and Lloyd Segan
- Executive produced by Mark Amin and Stephen Hopkins

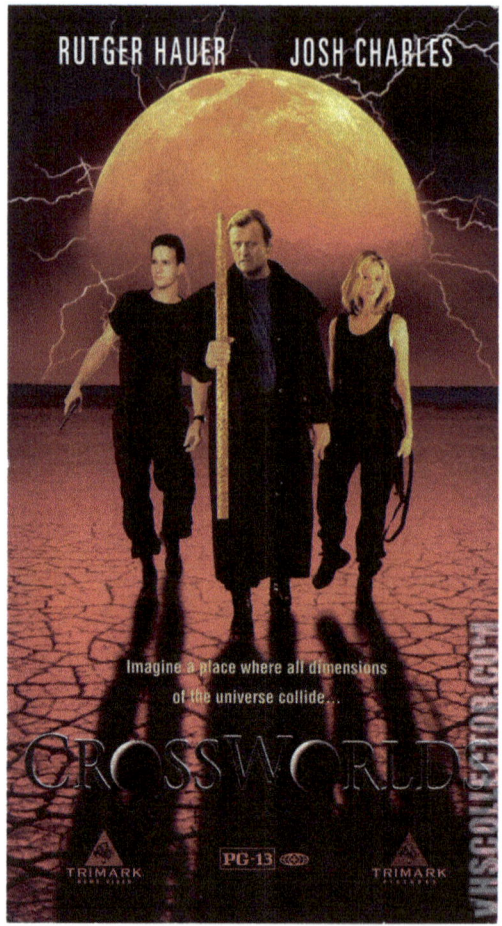

A movie like this one doesn't qualify for hyperbole from either end of the spectrum. It's not superlative; it's not horrendous. It certainly doesn't hurt going down, despite being a fairly unambitious production. If there's a particular complaint to pin on this one, it's that the "hook" concept—inter-dimensional guerrilla warfare, and the convoluted goings-on associated with it—is simply too rich and meaty, too fertile with nifty ideas, to be dealt with without more production oomph to back it up.

Well, that and the occasional slips into numbing stupidity, like the one on display in the opening scene. Twenty years ago, a mysterious archaeologist explores a mysterious tomb in mysterious Albania (can you stand the tension of a full two minutes of a flashlight beam lancing through dusty air?) and opens a crypt to pull a carved scepter from a corpse's hands. Just as he does so, though, other mysterious guys in two-piece suits (aha! evil!) show up, take the scepter from him, and demand to know where the other part of it is. "Somewhere you'll never find it," the archaeologist bravely says.

Well, yeah, that's true—unless the bad guys ever think to check with his wife or son.

Twenty years later, the son in question, Joe (Josh Charles—even after all his other films, you still know him as "one of those *Dead Poets Society* kids"), is an L.A. college student with some serious social problems. One is that he hasn't been able to get back on his feet after his last girlfriend dumped him; the other is that one of his two best friends is a pre-stardom Jack Black, bellowing and grunting like an entire frat house rolled into one sweatshirt.

Joe thinks his luck may about to change when stunning and intense blonde Laura (Andrea Roth) starts checking him out from across the room at a party. Well, it is changing, but not the way he'd like, because Laura's really after one thing: the crystal Joe wears on a thong around his neck. As far as Joe's concerned, it's just a souvenir of his long-lost dad, but Laura's interest in it is a little more expansive: it's a key part of a device that may help her people free her enslaved home dimension.

To get the other half of the McGuffin, she drags Joe along through a hailstorm of enemy bullets to something he never thought he'd see: Rutger Hauer welding his balls. Hauer is A.T., a former agent in the inter-dimensional conflict who's now retired and lives in a TARDIS-like motel room (bigger on the inside than on the outside), where he creates huge metallic modern-art spheres. (And yes, I'm including that detail just to justify the "welding his balls" line.) A.T. wants nothing to do with Laura's mission until he finds out whose kid Joe is, at which point he grudgingly shrugs back into his bad black trenchcoat out of a sense of duty.

The other half of the device is, of course, the scepter from the prologue. Together, the crystal and scepter can transport people not only to any place in our world, but to the titular Crossworlds (will you please stop giggling every time I use the world "titular"? it's a perfectly good word!), sort of the antechamber leading to any of a dozen different dimensions. Individual mystics and such can cross the dimensional divide on their own, but the scepter is necessary if you're going to transport larger numbers of fighters and grunts, either to conquer a dimension or to fight back against the enslaving warlords.

That's right, there are bad guys here, led by Ferris (Stuart Wilson), who spends his days posing as the curator of the museum where the scepter is on display, just waiting for idealistic freedom fighters to come in after it. Pretty soon, battle is joined—a battle that rages all over the multiverse!

Or all over convenient parts of California, anyway. There are some cost-cutting measures that use their understated nature to good advantage: the simple CGI ripple effect that results whenever someone pops the crystal into the scepter, the equally simple camera tricks to show transitions of space and time. But it seems that while the scepter can bend the laws of spacetime, it can't breach the restraints of budget, and thus everything takes place either in California or an alien dimension that looks just like California. When A.T. uses the scepter to send them someplace random to escape from Ferris, they end up on a rocky seashore—which is promptly visited by surfers. When Ferris makes a deal with A.T. and sends Joe and Andrea someplace out of his hair, they land face-down in gritty sand... in a local playground. And in one of those twists of cosmic fate, Crossworlds itself looks exactly like a Mojave desert valley (with a red filter on the camera).

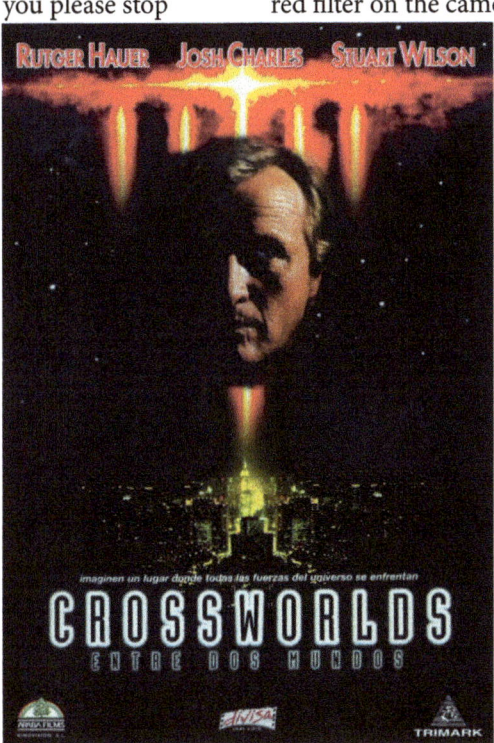

But if things fall apart on the macro level, the micro details are still perfectly adequate. Rutger Hauer is, of course, one of the coolest people on the planet, and he's here in a role which doesn't pretend he's still a young action hero; he's the crusty-but-tough soldier roped back out of retirement. Josh Charles plays Joe as a young man of uncertain confidence but a level head, and deftly keeps him from descending into annoying whininess as he tries to get A.T. and Laura to stop long enough to explain what the hell is going on. Andrea Roth is very easy on the eyes, and Stuart Wilson eschews malevolent scenery-chewing in favor of the easy-going attitude which accepts base evil as part of the cost of doing business. And I have to note Perry Anzilotti as Ferris' henchman Rebo, who also shows remarkable restraint in a role that begs to be played as an over-the-top Peter Lorre pastiche.

In fact, "restraint" is the saving grace of the production. With true universe-spanning spectacle out of the question, Krishna Rao wisely gives us a uniformly understated production so that the budgetary restrictions don't chafe as visibly, while he refrains from using easier, cheaper substitutes to retain our interest (you know, breasts 'n' explosives 'n' stuff).

Crossworlds never got a theatrical release, and that's for the best; the low-key approach would have seemed bloodless and anemic on the big screen. As it is, the best vibe *Crossworlds* gives off is that of a made-for-TV movie (back before the SyFy Channel made that an insult), a production that has pretty stringent limitations and works professionally within them.

Some Notable Totables:
- body count: 6
- breasts: 0
- explosions: 3
- dream sequences: 1
- ominous thunderstorms: 2
- actors who've appeared on *Star Trek*: 2
    - Ellen Geer (Joe's mom) played "Dr. Kila Marr" in the *TNG* episode "Silicon Avatar"
    - Michael Wiseman ("Cop #2") played "Beta Hirogen" in the *Voyager* two-parter "Flesh and Blood"

SCI-FIGHTERS (1996)

In the year 2009, they're your only hope.

- Directed by Peter Svatek
- Written by Mark Sevi
- Starring Roddy Piper, Jayne Heitmeyer, Billy Drago, Tyrone Benskin and Richard Raybourne
- Produced by Danny Rossner and Murray Shostak
- Executive produced by Mark Balsam

The biggest plus Rowdy Roddy Piper has going for him in his action-adventure flicks is his relaxed on-screen demeanor and a natural amiability around which most of his roles are built; he may not be Olivier, but he's got a rough-hewn charm that's just plain fun to watch. Billy Drago, on the other hand, was born a natural bad guy. His hooded eyes and languid acting add up to a positively reptilian persona; watching him perform holds the same sick fascination as watching a snake swallow a gerbil whole.

So when a movie starring both of them ends up lukewarm, you know it must have a lot working against it.

We begin on Lunar Base 4 Correctional Facility in the far-flung future of 2009, where, under uncannily normal gravity, Adrian Dunn (Drago) gets into an altercation with another prisoner over a cigarette. Using available power tools, Dunn cuts open his sick-looking opponent, causing green bile to spurt from his abdomen. As Dunn bends over the body, a little critter that looks like one of those gum-machine gummy octopuses bursts from the corpse's face, landing in a wound in Dunn's arm. Dunn is rushed to the infirmary, but dies soon thereafter.

Meanwhile, in Boston, Officer Cameron Grayson (Piper) gets himself into an altercation with some street hoods he's supposed to bring in. His captain tries to bust his balls over his failure, but Grayson's got a trump card: he's a "Black Shield" officer, which makes him part of an elite squad that gets to assign their own cases, ignore their commanding officers, etc. I really can't see the logic behind empowering such officers and then spreading them one-to-a-precinct; as one character says later, "Sounds like a cop's wet dream." It also makes all of the requisite "fighting with the captain" scenes pointless—we already know Grayson can do whatever he wants, so why's the captain even bothering?

Grayson's shield isn't the only thing that's black; the world is enshrouded in "Econight" because three months ago, some volcano went off and spewed enough dust into the atmosphere to cause blackness 24-7 and an effective nuclear winter. There are some lights set up in public areas to maintain circadian rhythm, but other than that it's just a lot of night shooting. How does this affect the plot? In no way that I could tell. (Perhaps it was to justify all the night shooting or order to disguise the fact that "Boston" is actually Montreal.)

So Dunn's body bag is shipped back to Boston for an autopsy, but en route Dunn revives, breaks out of the spaceport, and wanders the city, becoming steadily grosser as the organism takes over his body. He also takes to raping women at random, who then become infected as well. Oddly enough, his victims run the course of their infection much faster than he does; his first victim explodes with little octopus critters in about 24 hours, whereas Dunn keeps wandering around for the length of the movie.

When Grayson gets Dunn's description from the rape victim, he goes ballistic; not only is Dunn supposed to be dead, but Grayson's the one who put him in prison, and apparently it's a personal thing. (We get the backstory later.) And because a love interest is obligatory, Kirbie (Jayne Heitmeyer) the virologist working with the rape victim is young and pretty, and she goes through the whole "antagonism to attraction" process with Grayson. After all, who can resist his boyish charm, not to mention the heavy-handed musical cues?

So for most of the movie, Dunn wanders around the city, raping women and calling them "Katie," while Grayson and Kirbie try to figure out what the infection is and how to catch Dunn.

The explanation for the organism doesn't help things: apparently, it causes the infected to breathe out methane, and the brilliant scientists figure it was bioengineered by aliens to terraform our world into something habitable for them. No hypothesis is tendered for how the first prisoner on the moon was infected, or why the organism uses such a patently inefficient method of transmission (sexual contact), or why the breath of a few infected people is going to make more difference than herds and herds of methane-belching cattle that we've been keeping for hundreds of years. (Maybe the hypothetical aliens convinced us to like beef. Maybe they started the Hindu religion. Who knows?)

So Grayson uses the small-time hood from the first scene to put out feelers for Dunn in "Little Beirut" (you know, the bad part of town), and there are shootouts, and Dunn seems to be impervious to bullets, and even when he's killed he gets up again and wanders around Boston some more. And we finally get the backstory: Dunn used to be a cop and Grayson's best friend, and they were both in love with Katie,

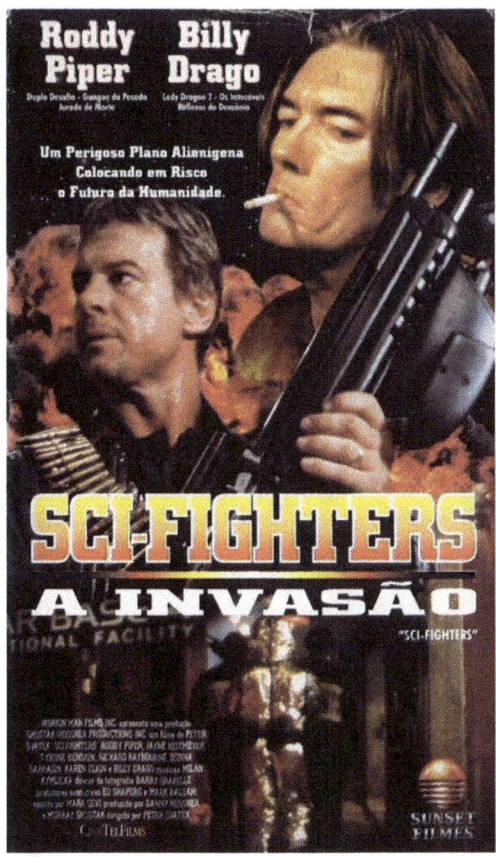

and when she married Grayson, Dunn raped and murdered her. Oh, and of course, Kirbie looks like Katie, enough so for A) Grayson to be attracted to her, and B) Dunn to get fixated on her, prompting the final confrontation.

All in all, it's a melange of elements that don't quite fit together, and the fact that Dunn starts talking with Cookie Monster grammar as the infection progresses just makes it sillier. (Apparently the aliens don't like articles or conjunctions.) And not even Piper's laid-back charm can hold it together.

But to end on a positive note, I'll tell you the two cool things in the entire movie:

1) To get a composite sketch from the first rape victim, the police use a computer which scans her face as she looks at flashing images on the screen; it reads her subliminal, unconscious reactions to the images and comes up with an accurate portrait.

2) There's a dildo-shaped knife… Okay, maybe there's only one cool thing.

Some Notable Totables:
- body count: 12
- breasts: 5
- explosions: 3
- dream sequences: 0
- ominous thunderstorms: 0
- actors who've appeared on *Star Trek*: 0

STREET CORNER JUSTICE (1996)

THE LAW OF THE LAND JUST CAME HOME TO STAY.

- Directed by Charles Bail
- Written by Stan Berkowitz, Gary Kent, and Chuck Bail
- Starring Marc Singer, Steve Railsback, Kim Lankford, Beverly Leech and Soon-Tek Oh
- Produced by Charles Bail and Jack Brown
- Executive produced by Benjamin R. Reder, Joe Restivo and Steve Restivo

*"There is no justice—just **us**."*

In this movie, Marc Singer wears his beard from *Cyberzone* (reviewed on page 238) and the cool haircut from *Beastmaster 3* (1996), but the front cover shows him wearing his Steelers cap pulled down low on his forehead, which makes him look like a homeless guy, and the screencaps on the back are so blurry I feared this flick might be shot on video. I'm glad to report that the movie inside the case is better than the case makes it look—which isn't much, but we take what we can get.

Not that the first thing we see during the opening credits is all that pretty either. Because in a dumpster on a Pittsburgh street, Clint Howard is graphically raping and mutilating a whimpering woman. I don't know how Clint Howard, character actor and younger/uglier brother to Hollywood success story Ron Howard, hasn't blown his brains out by now. There are a lot of actors who rely on sucky roles, and there are a lot of actors who usually play bad guys, but few people in Hollywood so consistently play such despicable dregs of humanity as Clint Howard. At best he gets roles that are solidly annoying; more often, well, did I mention that he's raping and mutilating here? That's the kind of role he normally has. It seems to me that immersing one's self in personalities like that for a living would just rot the soul completely. (The only other actor I can think of whose oeuvre should inspire such self-loathing is Billy Drago, and even then it's not a fair comparison.) Bottom line, I Would Hate To Be Clint Howard.

I would especially hate to be him when Marc Singer's plainclothes cop character, Mike Justus (ooh, I so appreciate subtlety) is the first to arrive on the scene. Justus chases the waste-of-sperm across rooftops, endures his goading about how the system has consistently put him back on the streets, saves the rapist scum's life from a fall and gets a kick in the balls for his efforts… You know the tables are going to turn, because hey, Clint Howard's only going to get so many lucky hits in on Marc Singer, and pretty soon Justus is beating the well-deserved shit out of the puke. Unfortunately, an apartment-dweller nearby catches only this last part on videotape, and without the inciting preamble, it looks like a case of police brutality. The upshot is that the rapist goes free, and Justus is "persuaded" into early retirement.

Sick of all of it anyway, he decides to take some time off in the North Hollywood neighborhood of Norwood, cleaning a house his aunt left to him that's just been vacated by renters. Unfortunately, the place looks like a hellhole compared to the circa-1957 photo he has, so he decides he'll take the next couple of weeks for some major maintenance before selling the house and moving on to who knows where.

But as you can imagine, this isn't some quiet little suburb. No, this is gang territory, and the merchants of the nearby strip mall are being terrorized by hoodlums who deal drugs in plain sight, accost little old ladies, and express disapproval by pissing on cupcakes. (Not their own cupcakes. That wouldn't make much sense.) When three of them break the windows of a Korean storeowner's (Soon-Tek Oh) donut shop, Justus leaps into action and dispenses some well-deserved whupass. He thus gets himself a reputation among the local hoods, as well as an introduction to the local police, in the person of Sgt. Freeborn (Steve Railback), who laments the inability of their budget to cover more adequate patrolling.

Although Freeborn is sympathetic, the city attorney is more of a buttwipe—in fact, at the town meeting they have to complain to the authorities, he actually puts the onus back on the storekeepers, threatening to shut their businesses down because of the "unhealthy environment" their presence encourages. Justus, not wanting to get involved, stands back and watches as the shopkeepers and other locals, led by Father Brophy (Bryan Cranston) and his indeterminate accent, organize a neighborhood watch around the slogan of "Take Norwood Back," abbreviated to "TNB" on the backs of the bright red jackets they wear on patrol.

Bright red jackets? Didn't any of these people ever watch the original *Star Trek* series? That's just asking for more trouble!

Of course, when I say that Justus stands back, that's all relative. He has a hard time standing back from Jeanette (Kim Lankford), the video store owner who's so desperate for a man it's almost embarrassing to watch. Despite her charms, Mike insists that he's not planning on staying around long enough to be a part of the community, and aside from advising them to patrol armed (advice that they ignore), he doesn't intend to contribute much.

All of that changes when the whole red-jacketed patrol gets ambushed in the school playground and gets the snot beat out of them, including Jeanette. There is, after all, a Breaking Point in all of these movies, and at this point Justus decides he's not selling the house; he's sticking around to whup these punks once and for all.

Which is all well and good, except that we're now a full hour into the movie, and the story's just now about to take off. Justus calls back his old partner and gets info on a few criminals now living in L.A. who owe Justus a favor. One, Willie (Beverly Leech), is a kung-fu hooker/scam artist. The other, Angel (Tiny Lister), is—as he describes himself—"big, bad, blind [in one eye], and Born Again." Together, they form a *posse comitatus* and start on their little crusade, including knocking over meth labs and stealing the gangsters' money to buy weapons to fight those very gangsters.

Now, I love a good wish-fulfillment ass-kicking movie as much as the next person. More, actually, as I have a highly developed sense of outrage (an uneasy bedfellow with my equally developed cynicism), and I often dearly wish that the ethically challenged of our species could be taught remedial morality by a vicious beating (and though I know it won't work, I'd still like to make sure by trying just one more time). And heaven knows, there's no shortage of movies willing to show me that Right Makes Might, and Might Conquers All.

The problem is that I know it isn't true, and if you want me to suspend my willing and eager disbelief, you have to keep from distracting me with the truth. Posit a single gang of hoodlums in an otherwise peaceful locale, preferably commanded by a charismatic scumbag, and I'm more than willing to trust that the conflict will be resolved when said scumbag has had his ass decisively handed to him. But when you paint a moderately accurate picture of actual gang culture, of the degree to which young people have co-opted those warped values to instill a sense of purpose and importance in their lives, I have a hard time swallowing the idea that a single ex-cop accompanied by two quirky accomplices and the strength of his Pure Heart can conclusively end a societal problem with roots that go far beyond a local gang of humanity-deficient punks. Even if that ex-cop is Marc Singer.

Other problems: the truncated and sketched-in romance (the main purpose of which is to give the bad guys a hostage to hold over Justus's head in the end); a similarly sketched-in hint of a love triangle between Justus, videostore Jeanette, and kung-fu hooker Willie; the disappearance of the spiritually distraught Angel from the plot after he loses control and beats a gangbanger to death; the upbeat *Highway to Heaven* tenor of the first half, leaving little time to get into true whupass mode; and a showdown which takes place in—you guessed it—an industrial setting in which young punks jump out at random like the targets in a video game, when it would have taken all of three brain cells to set up an effective ambush and wipe Justus out once and for all. Oh, and the tippy-top of the climax, in which Justus saves the main baddie from certain and deserved death, only to have the baddie pull a gun and justify his immediate dispatch with self-defense. (Here's a sense of my own morality: if the guy has hurt innumerable people without a thought, and will undoubtedly do the same thing once saved, you can probably just let him plummet to his death with a clear conscience.) The main baddie, by the way, is the "secret power" behind the gangbangers, and it's absolutely no secret who it is once they introduce the concept of his existence.

Was it too much cheese with my vitamins, or two much vitamin with my cheese? Whichever it was, the movie ended up hurt by being unable to decide its focus, either mindless action or hard-hitting drama. For all that, it's certainly not a painful movie, and, as indicated to begin with, certainly better than the cover design would indicate. (Note how that brings a nice sense of closure to this review.)

Some Notable Totables:
- body count: 12
- breasts: 3
- pasty male butts: 1
- explosions: 2
- ominous thunderstorms: 0
- cupcakes you really don't want to eat: two dozen
- actors who've appeared on *Star Trek*: 6
    - Tom "Tiny" Lister (Angel) played "Klaang" in the *Enterprise* pilot "Broken Bow"
    - Clint Howard (the rapist) played "Balok" in the original episode "The Corbomite Maneuver," and "Grady" in the second half of the *DS9* two-parter "Past Tense"
    - Juan Garcia ("Federico") played "John Torres" in two episodes of *Voyager*
    - Harvey Jason ("Lou") played "Felix Leech" in the *TNG* episode "The Big Goodbye"
    - Shelly Desai ("Rasool," the real-estate agent) played "V'Sal" in the *TNG* episode "Data's Day"
    - Ron Soble ("Chief McTighe") played "Wyatt Earp" (or a reasonable facsimile thereof) in the original episode "Spectre of the Gun"
    - (Beverly Leech (Willie) did the voice of Ensign Yraxys in the video game *Star Trek: Away Team,* but I don't think that counts)

VICTIM of DESIRE (1996)

SOME WOMEN ARE DESIRABLE... OTHERS DEADLY.

- *Directed by Jim Wynorski*
- *Written by William C. Martell*
- *Starring Marc Singer, Shannon Tweed, Johnny Williams, Julie Strain and Wings Hauser*
- *Produced by Andrew Stevens*
- *Executive produced by Ashok Amritraj*

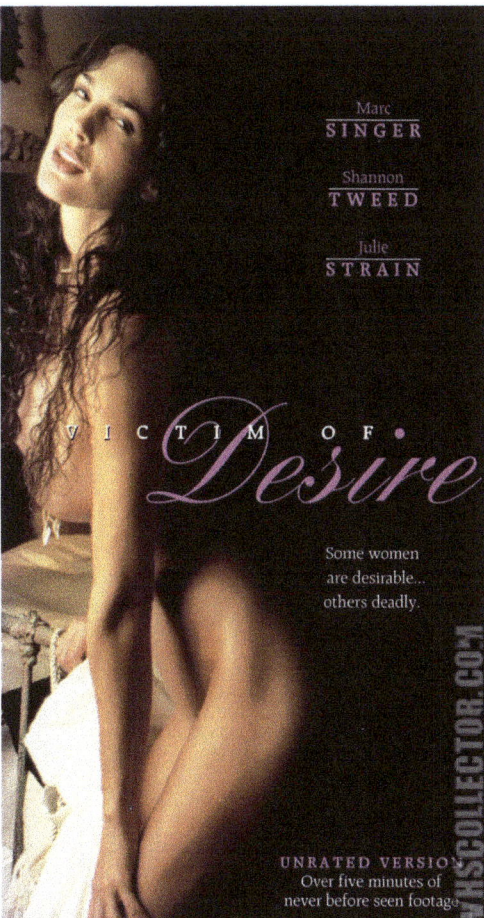

In the specific cinematic ghetto of the direct-to-video "erotic thriller," what you see above amounts to an all-star cast and crew. Unfortunately, there's no more guarantee that a group of household names (in my household, anyway) will automatically produce a good film on a low budget than there is with a summer blockbuster pricetag.

Peter Sharky (Marc Singer) is an investigator for the Securities & Exchange Commission, looking into the case of one Leland Duvall (Wings Hauser), a corporate CEO whose company is currently being hit with a wrongful death suit over a hundred-plus fires caused by the company's faulty electric blankets. (Honestly, I don't think I've ever heard this one before in a suspense flick.) But that's not why Sharky's nosing around; it seems there's also $70 million mysteriously "missing" from corporate coffers, and the smell of embezzlement is in the air.

So to kick off our story, Sharky shows up at Duvall's house, meets his stunning wife Carla (Shannon Tweed—and let me say right here that I find Tweed such an attractive woman that I cannot wholly begrudge any film that puts her in my field of vision for a goodly proportion of the running time), and overhears a bit of an argument between Duvall and his Vice-President Richard Jordan (Jay Richardson, working for a weekend). He also meets Jordan's girlfriend Linda (Julie Strain—and the fact that I find Strain much less appealing than Tweed probably lowers my fanboy credibility, doesn't it?).

And we then get about ten minutes of crammed in exposition and twists, to wit: Duvall did embezzle the $70 million, though he's willing to blame it on Jordan if Jordan doesn't back off; Jordan and Linda stage an argument in order to leave Linda behind at the house and give her an occasion to nose around and find out where Duvall stashed the money; and Duvall and Linda are also having an an affair—because why pay Julie Strain to be on the set if you're going to keep her clothed, right?

All of which we know but Sharky doesn't, because his idea of investigation seems to be to show up and let Duvall know he's under investigation, then wander around a bit. He wanders into the police station, and after talking about his investigation, gets himself temporarily partnered with homicide cop Marv Riker (Johnny Williams, bit-part fat man supreme). I couldn't figure out why a homicide cop is so hot to get to work on an embezzlement case, which is the only criminal charge involved here (wrongful death suits are civil cases, and even a criminal negligence charge still wouldn't concern homicide).

Homicide turns out to be the proper department, though, because that night shots ring out at the Duvall house, and we see a shadowy tableau of two ski-masked figures dumping a body into a car and the car over a cliff, ka-boom.

The car is identified as Duvall's. Since Sharky's investigation is ongoing, he's around when Carla comes in to identify the badly charred body. He's also the one who takes her home afterward, and tries gently to continue his investigation (assuming, quite reasonably, that the person who offed Duvall would be the same one who took the money). Of course, Carla is also prime subject number one as soon as the autopsy confirms that Duvall was shot dead before the car exploded.

From here, Sharky and Riker switch off twelve-hour shifts surveilling Carla, hoping to find a clue one way or another. They don't have enough for a search warrant, but they get permission to bug the house, which gives them long shifts of sitting in their cars on the curb, listening to headphones, and watching as the mourning widow keeps changing her clothes in front of the open upstairs balcony window.

Let's see—attractive widow who may be the murderer… What are the odds that she and Sharky start getting it on? (A hell of a lot better chance than fat Riker has, right?)

Naturally, because she's under investigation, Sharky has to keep his "involvement" under wraps, which is especially hard with bugs all over the house (good thing Carla takes him for the "strong silent" type, especially the "silent" part). But as he uncovers evidence for or against Carla's guilt, he naturally muddies the waters, since he's finding it at times and in ways in which he's not supposed to have access to the premises. And anyway—does he want her to be the guilty party?

Which is, of course, the general premise of half of the "erotic thriller" videos on the Drama section of the video store (the other half all involving strippers, or policewomen undercover as strippers). That's not an indictment in and of itself—it's a solid dramatic premise after all, involving desire and trust as opposing impulses.

But for it to work, it's got to be presented competently. Which this one isn't.

I was smart enough to get comments from screenwriter Bill Martell before I wrote this review so that we wouldn't overlap overmuch, and I'll let his comments stand as a unit afterward. But here are the things that stuck out for me, independent of Bill's info:

- Marc Singer was either hideously miscast or instructed to perform as if he were hideously miscast. I can buy Singer in a natty suit—as a neat-as-a-pin bad-ass hitman, maybe. But as a squeaky-clean white-collar securities investigator? He doesn't seem comfortable in his own skin, much less his conservative two-piece.
- The plot, as it appears in the final product, is lumpy. There's that whole section of twists in the first ten minutes, a similar set of twists in the last ten

minutes, and in between the investigation just sorta lopes along, punctuated by sex scenes.

The good news (at least to me) is that none of the stuff I didn't like was Bill's fault. Remember, the screenwriter is the person least responsible for how bad a movie is, what with all the other people who muck with it before it hits your eyeballs. (Funny—if every director thinks he can do better than the writer, why doesn't he just write it himself instead of hiring a writer to give him a script that he can "improve upon"?)

Some Notable Totables:
(all taken from the R-rated version, though I doubt the count changes in the unrated version)
- body count: 4
- breasts: 4
- explosions: 1
- ominous thunderstorms: 1
- jocular coroners who eat around cadavers: 1
- actors who've appeared on *Star Trek*: 1
    - Brad Blaisdell ("technician") played "Yint" in the *DS9* episode "Honor Among Thieves"

VICTIM of DESIRE: Screenwriter William C. Martell's Comments

Victim of Desire began as a script called *The Victim's Wife* which was supposed to be a theatrical. You see, *Treacherous* [one of Bill's earlier scripts—Nathan] was set up at Hemdale with Mickey Rourke (before he took a nose dive) and Brian Dennehy and a budget of $8 million. Everybody liked that script because it took place at a central location—it could be shot inexpensively with most of the budget going to cast. So I decided to write another one with a central location.

There's this great '40s movie written by Dan Mainwaring called *Roadblock* about a cop who falls for a sexy crime suspect... and ends up covering up clues that lead to her in order to prolong his relationship. I really liked that idea—you love a woman so much you'll let her get away with murder. So I added a touch of *Stakeout* and a portion of *Sea of Love* and came up with *The Victim's Wife*. As I was finishing the first draft, Hemdale went bankrupt... *Treacherous* was a dead project and I had no one to sell *The Victim's Wife* to.

Two years later, *Treacherous* is made with C. Thomas Howell and Adam Baldwin for $1.2 million. So I start looking at producers who make films at that budget range... I try to sell it at American Film Market.

At AFM I stumble onto a familiar name—Ashok Amritraj. He producer some Jean-Claude Van Damme movies, and was now making erotic thrillers. But Ashok wasn't listed in Hollywood Creative Directory, so I had no idea how to get a script to him. I decided to go down to the library and look through the phone books—found him listed in the white pages, called, pitched the script, and he asked to read it.

What I didn't know is that another producer I had sent the script to had already given a copy to Ashok because he liked it. They'd read it, liked it, but didn't want to work with the producer. So my script was kind of "pre-approved."

As soon as I signed my contract, things went wrong. Something happened behind the scenes and the budget for *Victim* went from about $1.2 million down to $350,000. I had to do a massive rewrite to take out locations, action scenes, and characters. The script would have been okay, but then they hired the director.

I did not get along with the director at all. The director has a temper. The director makes sex comedies and doesn't seem to understand suspense or plot twists. I remember a conversation with the director about the scene in the script where our hero realizes that the woman he loves is the killer—this was the pivotal scene in the script... the director cut it. I may have lost my temper at that point.

I can't blame everything on the director. Casting made changes in the script. When Julie Strain was cast as the lead suspect's girlfriend, they wanted more scenes with her. Naked scenes. The problem is—the character is supposed to be out of the country after page 15... so now the plot doesn't work. I tried explaining this, but was told that nobody cares about plot holes, they care about cast.

When they cast Burt Gilliam (Flying Elvis) as the crime lab guy, I had to write 10 pages of material for him. They wanted to get their money's worth. I wrote some great stuff—how he got his dog from the DEA: a retired drug sniffing dog. Turns out the dog is a drug addict. I managed to milk the story—keep it going—through every scene Burt was in. When they shot it, the crew had trouble not laughing. Well, it didn't make it into the film. I wrote tons of pages for every seminame they cast, none made it into the final cut. There are a bunch of Pete Spellos scenes that aren't in the film (one featuring me as the dead guy he's autopsying). The script was turning to crap! All of these pointless scenes!

And one scene got added by the director: here I am cutting cast down to the nubs—removing secondary suspects so that it's obvious who done it—and the director adds a speaking part. Some bimbo walking down the street who drops a steaming pile of exposition into the laps of the cops. Why did the director create this role? I think you can figure it out.

Then they film this piece of crap. The director—for reasons that nobody knows—has Marc act like Jerry Lewis. When I wrote the script, I'm thinking Robert Mitchum. The director seems to think it's a comedy! He doesn't think it's important to shoot clues, or suspense scenes, and he telegraphs all of the twists. At the screening I cringe throughout—this film sucks! But at AFM they sell it like crazy—all they care about is the cast!

One of the days I'm on set, someone breaks something and the director screams for someone to sweep it up right now! Everybody scrambles. One guy comes back with a broom, sweeps up the broken glass and makes sure there aren't any hidden pieces people might cut themselves on... the guy with the broom was Marc Singer. The director said, "I didn't mean you, Marc." Marc shrugged and said he was the first one to get to the broom. That's Marc Singer in a nutshell—he was the star of the movie, but he was happy to help out on the set.

I call the movie *Victim of Director*. The original script was like *Sea of Love*, the finished film is like Jerry Lewis starring in a *Night Eyes* knock-off. No matter how good the script is, it's gonna get cheesed on the way to the screen.

People see terrible movies and think that they could easily write something like that, but what they don't realize is that no producer would ever buy a script that bad. They need to buy a great script, so that once it goes through the big sausage machine, what comes out the other end is something people can watch without their brains exploding. The screenwriter joke at American Film Market is that they made an awful B-movie from the same screenplay they got you meetings at Warner Bros. and Paramount and Universal. So why the heck would you sell the script to a company that's going to ruin it? Hey, the studios ruin stuff every day! Track down the story of how the brilliant screenplay *Dead Drop* about the Q-like gadget guy for the C.I.A. who goes on the run when he realizes his gadgets are being used to topple third-world democracies... is turned into *Chain Reaction* with Keanu Reeves playing a welder who outruns a nuclear explosion on a motorcycle. It's a wonder any movie turns out watchable. A big studio only makes 10% of the screenplays they buy—I have scripts collecting dust forever at all of the major studios—but when they buy a script for a B-movie, they can't afford not to make it. So I would rather have the script get made than shelved—even if what ends up on screen isn't exactly what I wrote.

Victim of Desire was my second "Hollywood" film that made it all the way to the screen (*Treacherous* was first), and despite my not being able to watch it without trying to gouge out my eyes with a #2 pencil, it's like one of my children. I love it, even though it grew up to be a fat biker babe with face tattoos and a million piercings and a prison record. She was a cute baby, wanna see the pictures?

Maybe the next one will turn out better...

BLEAK FUTURE (1997)

MUTANTS. DAMN.

- Directed by Brian O'Malley
- Written by Brian O'Malley and Steven Darancette
- Starring Frank Kowal, Brad Rockhold, Wendie Newcomb, Rob Cunningham and Steven Kowal
- Produced by Steven Darancette

This movie, shot on Super-8, is further support for the thesis that the premise for any movie can be turned into a comedy by putting the words "Wackiness ensues when…" at the start. Despite that, post-apocalyptic comedies are few and far between; in fact, the only other ones I can think of offhand are *Hell Comes to Frogtown*, reviewed on page 72 (more of a tongue-in-cheek action/adventure than a pure comedy) and *Six-String Samurai* (1998), which we'll get to in a few pages. I'm speaking, obviously, of intentionally humorous movies, not movies so pathetic and piss-poor that they can inspire nothing but derisive laughter. There's no shortage of the latter.

I think the main reason for this is that comedy is what happens to other people. Everything from a banana peel-induced pratfall to a first visit with a fiancee's parents is funny only if you aren't currently sharing that situation. End up in traction, or schedule a trip to the intended's home for the coming weekend, and suddenly the comedy loses its yuks. Comedy isn't funny when it's us.

And during the main boom of post-apocalyptic adventure movies in mid-'80s, it *was* us. The threat of Mutually Assured Destruction was keeping many an American awake at night. No one would have been able to see the funny side of it, because during the days of nuclear brinkmanship, there *was* no funny side to it. (Come for the movie reviews; stay for the psychoanalysis of Western culture!)

And by the time the Soviet Union crumbled and foreign relations weren't based on a philosophy of perfectly balanced antagonism, the trend had passed. The glut of bottom-scraping post-apoc adventures at the local video store had buried any innovation in the subgenre, as well as all viewer enthusiasm. The field was too played out to sustain a parodied or satirical version. People by and large just weren't interested anymore.

But fans eagerly go where the general populace fears to tread (or simply doesn't want to), which means that eventually there would be at least a couple of comedic takes on the tropes and clichés of the genre.

The protagonist of *Bleak Future* goes by the name of Slangman (Frank Kowal), a bearded and bespectacled wanderer in a world that greatly resembles Death Valley. Actually, rather than a wanderer, he's more of a traveling salesman—but what he's selling is information! He has, to the best of his (and anyone else's) knowledge, the last book in existence: a dictionary. And for a price, usually measured in batteries or some other commodity, he'll tell you what a word means. Granted, it's usually a word he's just barely used expressly to fish for customers, but hey, you gotta create a market, right? He supplements that with other found objects for sale: egg beaters, Pepsi cans, etc.

When one local mutant lord makes the obvious leap—that he ought to just get his hands on the book, instead of dealing with the middle man—Slangman find himself on the receiving end of a mutant ass-whupping, and the only thing that saves him is...

...a mute Scotsman (Brad Rockhold). How could you dislike any movie with a mute Scotsman sidekick?

Said Scotsman, after whupping the whuppers, gives Slangman a valuable artifact: a beat-up golden CD-R. Slangman instantly recognizes it as coming from The Source, the fabled library and repository of all pre-apocalypse knowledge. And being something of a knowledge-worshiper (all right, he's a trivia geek), he immediately sets out northward to find the source of the CD-R, with the grunting Scotsman in tow. (He dubs the Scotsman "Atlatl," after his proficiency with spears. Never let a pseudo-intellectual name a Scot.)

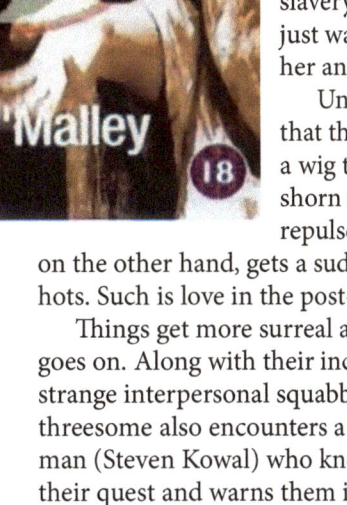

Their journey takes them through the territories of hostile tribes, as tradition dictates. Well, "hostile" may not be the word for it. The only people they encounter are "nomads" that don't appear to travel anywhere; they just stand around wearing cloth-paper cleansuits, speaking in fake Cockney accents and acting grotesquely stupid. But that's okay, because Slangman and Atlatl's true danger is behind them: a black-clad mutant, Atlatl's former master, who wants the golden CD-R. (Wouldn't they all be surprised if it just turned out to be a home-burned collection of alt-rock MP3s or a warez copy of PhotoShop?)

Also following in tradition's footsteps, they find themselves at the only commercial establishment to survive in the wasteland. That's right, a bar. And there, Slangman beholds a vision of loveliness—a blonde airhead named Femme (Wendie Newcomb) performing on stage in a little two-woman dramatic scene that lacks the thespian merits of a preschool graduation. (I've been to a preschool graduation recently. I know.) But blind to her inadequacies, he purchases her from her partner for a Twinkie.* She's like "whatever" about the arrangement, which really isn't bad as slavery goes; he really just wants to admire her and stuff.

Until he discovers that the blonde hair is a wig to cover her shorn scalp. Then he's repulsed by her. Atlatl, on the other hand, gets a sudden case of the hots. Such is love in the post-atomic world.

Things get more surreal as the movie goes on. Along with their increasingly strange interpersonal squabbles, the threesome also encounters a beatnik holy man (Steven Kowal) who knows all about their quest and warns them in the strongest possible stoner terms against seeking The

---

* I'm not saying that *Zombieland* stole that idea from *Bleak Future*; I'm just saying that *Bleak Future* used it first.

Source. Also on the trail of The Source is Dr. Obvious (Rob Cunningham), a zoot-suited mastermind with an interesting haircut. Don't forget that mutant on their tail, either. Eventually, it all comes down to a whole lotta violence, and Slangman in latex lingerie.

I'm very much reminded of Peter Jackson's *Bad Taste* (page 60) not just because of the low budget, but because of the energy and enthusiasm on the part of both cast and crew that shines through the technical limitations. *Bleak Future* isn't as memorably extreme as *Bad Taste*, but I'd like to think that the people who fell in love with Peter Jackson before *Dead Alive* and later films brought him into the international spotlight would also see a lot to appreciate in *Bleak Future* despite the technical demerits.

Which leads me to one of those ambiguous, inconclusive conclusions. I enjoyed this movie. I understand, though, that a lot of people wouldn't. And I do have to admit that, in the inevitable comparison between *Bleak Future* and *Six-String Samurai*, the latter is clearly the superior movie, both in inspired premise and in technical execution. But if you A) have seen plenty of post-apocalyptic movies, B) have enjoyed those movies despite the flaws, and C) have enjoyed making fun of those movies, you'll probably be able to see and appreciate the merits of *Bleak Future*.

Some Notable Totables:
- body count: 19
- breasts: 0
- explosions: 2 (plus 6 in stock footage)
- dream sequences: 1
- ominous thunderstorms: 0
- actors who've appeared on *Star Trek*: 0

HOSTILE INTENT (1997)

His government is hunting him down.

aka *Lethal Games*

- Directed by Jonathan Heap
- Written by Manny Coto
- Starring Rob Lowe, Sofia Shinas, James Kidnie, John Savage and Saul Rubinek
- Produced by Julian Grant and Stephen Ujlaki
- Executive produced by Lewis B. Chesler, Deborah Del Prete, John Fremes, David Perlmutter and Gigi Pritzker

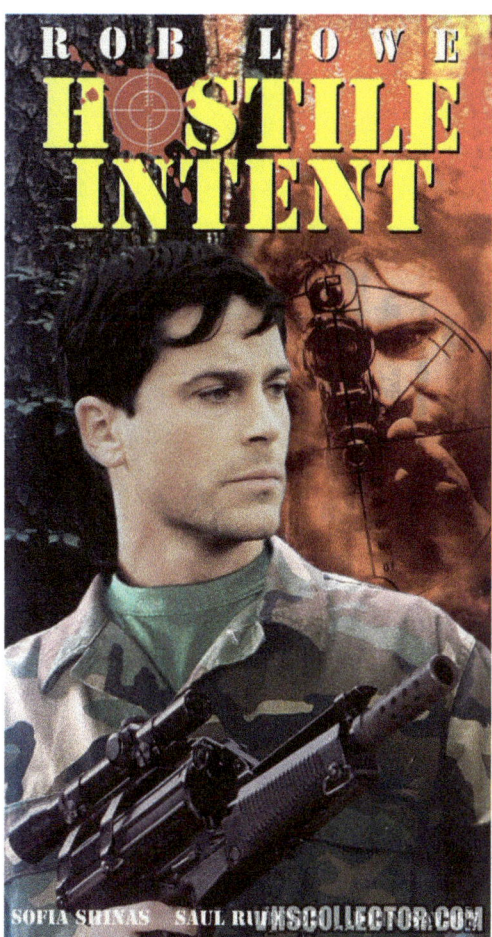

Evil government goons. They're a staple of action/suspense movies, and done right, they're intensely believable; many of us have seen the evidence of the depths to which a faction of the monolithic U.S. government can stoop in response to an ideological agenda. (I say this after having lived in Southern Utah, where the Downwinder movement has gained impetus due to a declassified memo to President Eisenhower labeling the residents a "low-use segment of the population," and therefore acceptable to coat with bomb test fallout.)

When done right, they're intensely believable. *Hostile Intent* doesn't do it right.

We open with a boogah-boogah title card stating that by the year 2000 there will be a full billion home computers. The next one states that in 1999, the government will pass legislation requiring that the Clipper Chip, a monitoring system the government can access, be inserted into all new computers.

With that glaring unlikelihood as a given premise, we open on four men in fatigues and greasepaint trudging through a nighttime thunderstorm in the woods. We soon discover that these are computer programmers, playing paintball against a rival company. We also find out that they pretty much suck, as the rival company takes them out easily from hidden positions.

"Our" guys work for Mike Cleary (Rob Lowe, in one of the troughs of his career), an obsessive ex-hacker now putting the finishing touches on Guardian, the ultimate "non-hackable" privacy shield. In celebration of the final working beta version, Cleary and his employees (you know the roll call—there has to be a bald fat guy, a punk kid, and an improbably attractive girl who apparently got into computers because she liked hanging out with the most socially inept guys in high school) head off to the Dotcom Café to unwind, and to plan their next paintball encounter with their rivals. Cleary used to work for the rival Gordon, and is still pissed that Gordon sold Cleary's under-contract work to the Feds, so Cleary uncharacteristically agrees to join in on the next paintball game to even some scores.

On the way to the playing field, three hours out of Chicago (with all the shooting locations actually being in Canada), their car breaks down on a secluded stretch. The first Good Samaritan along isn't exactly what they

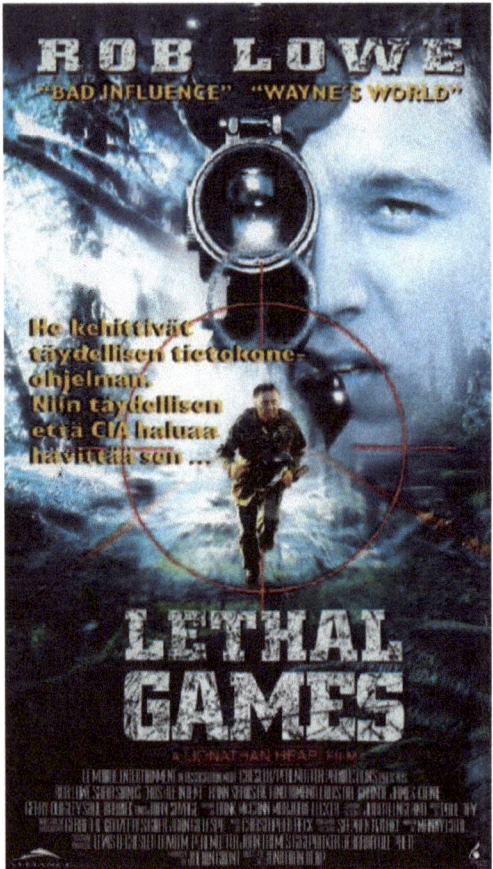

expected; it's survivalist John "Bear" Barrington (John Savage), who belligerently agrees to help them get a new fan belt. In fact, he takes one carload back to his secret base (an odd move, that), where he and a survivalist friend make fun of their fatigues, snoop suspiciously in their paintball equipment, and finally give them the fan belt.

Not too long after, they reach the playing area—three hundred acres ringed by a sheer cliff—and the game begins.

And then people start dying.

Unseen snipers start taking out players. Obviously, the front-and-center suspects are Bear and friend, who are also out in the woods with rifles for some hunting, but that suspicion dissolves when Bear's friend also falls prey to a sniper bullet.

Much of the rest of the movie is exactly what you'd expect: the survivors of both teams, plus Bear, band together to fight the evil government agents who are trying to get their hands on Guardian. There's guilt on Cleary's part as his employees are picked off, there's something of a reconciliation between Cleary and Gordon, and there are more improbabilities than a winning streak in Vegas.

Observe: at one point, another team of three or so goons, under the characteristically polite leadership of Saul Rubinek, show up at Guardian's urban office building, shoot up all the drywall along with the sole on-duty employee, and try to get the Guardian program out of their system. Unfortunately, that scene actually started my brain working, and once that starts no plot point is safe.

Because if these goons feel safe shooting up a downtown office, why didn't they just attack there instead of playing this protracted cat-and-mouse game in the hinterlands? Especially with an entire other officeload of people out there in the woods who are "collateral damage" unrelated to the Guardian program?

And then I wondered, why did the government send maybe six or eight agents,

equipped with $25,000 palmtop "tricorders," but couldn't manage any air support for the on-foot ground troops? (In fact, the only vehicle we see is a snazzy black penis car that the two surviving government baddies escape in—and you're not telling me that that's what the motor pool came up with instead of a troop carrier.)

And when the computer geeks start fighting back and scoring casualties of their own, why does the word "backup" seem absent from the goon commander's vocabulary?

The government agency in question is never explicitly identified (though the credits list a couple of people as ATF agents); in any case, one of the major saving tropes of the "evil agency" cliché has been ignored: that the agency is question is working alone, under its own warped agenda counter to that of the rest of the "good" government. In every instance here, both the goon commander and Saul Rubinek identify themselves as working for "the government" as a whole—as if gunning down civilians in a clandestine operation is quite obviously what your tax dollars are meant for, duh!

And just to make sure that we don't come up deficient with ridiculous plot devices, Cleary manages to reprogram one of the Infinity devices by poking at the circuit board itself. (Why do you think I call them tricorders?)

I suppose that director Jonathan Heap and writer Manny Coto (soon afterward the head writer on TV's *24*) thought they were being terribly topical in presenting a story of Evil Government vs. Privacy Rights Activists & Survivalist, but by the end it seems like the militia version of one of those fundamentalist features dramatizing the prophecies of the Book of Revelation—a screed in which plot coherence is sacrificed to make an ideological point.

All I can say is, it was probably a good idea to make this one in Canada.

Some Notable Totables:
- body count: 16
- breasts: 0
- explosions: 4
- ominous thunderstorms: 1
- obligatory Oz references: 1
- actors who've appeared on *Star Trek*: 2
  - John Savage (Bear) played "Captain Ransom" on the 6th-season *Voyager* two-parter "Equinox"
  - Saul Rubinek (the evil bureaucrat) was "Kivas Fajo" on the 3rd-season *TNG* episode "The Most Toys"
  - (also, Rino Romano (Press, one of the programmers) played "Alexander Munro" in the *Voyager* video game "Elite Force"—which is almost like appearing on the series, right?)

FREE ENTERPRISE (1997)

LIVE LONG AND PARTY.

- Directed by Robert Meyer Burnett
- Written by Robert A. Altman and Robert Meyer Burnett
- Starring William Shatner, Rafer Weigel, Eric McCormack, Audie England and Carl Bressler
- Produced by Mark A. Altman and Dan Bates

The basic premise of *Free Enterprise* is, "What if your life were like a big sci-fi convention?" I can't give a full plot outline here; I'd want to include all of the throwaway fanboy jokes, which would end up with this review being a transcription of the entire script. Here's what I can say in a linear fashion:

In 1980 we meet Mark, who's being turned away from the ticket office for the premiere of *Star Trek: The Motion Picture* in New York for being too young, and Robert, who's getting the tar beaten out of him in Washington state for wearing a *Star Trek* uniform to junior high. Both boys get the courage to stand up for themselves from visions of their common imaginary friend—William Shatner (who notes that he's one of the top ten imaginary friends).

Flash forward to the present: both guys are living the fanboy's wet dream in Los Angeles. Mark (Eric McCormack from TV's *Will & Grace*) is editor of "Geek Magazine," which caters to the whole episode-memorizing, toy-buying crowd, and Robert (Rafer Weigel) is a film editor at Full Eclipse (based on Full Moon Entertainment, the schlock genre production company). Of course, life isn't completely rosy: Robert's being dumped by his girlfriend, who can't understand his obsessions (and who, out of spite, takes back his birthday present, a mint-in-box *U.S.S. Enterprise* Christmas ornament). And Mark's only love life is an ex-girlfriend who annoys him, and an anonymous "moaning girl" who leaves orgasmic messages on his answering machine.

And then come the big changes in their lives. They run into William Shatner in a bookstore, and after frightening him with their fanboy geekiness, they discover he's working on a project: a six-hour musical version of *Julius Caesar*, with Bill himself as all of the male lead parts. ("And maybe I could get Heather Locklear—I know Heather, you know.")

But that's not all—after a string of one-night stands with starlet types, Robert finds the perfect woman in a comic book store: a beautiful girl named Claire (Audey England) who can list the comics she reads, and is attracted to his description home entertainment system and the fact that he has the Japanese-import laserdisc boxed set of *Planet of the Apes*. I correct myself: *This* is a fanboy's wet dream.

I can't convey in a short review how much fun this is to watch a movie composed almost entirely of in-jokes that you get, and that the movie expects you to get. Aside from all the obligatory *Star Trek* references, *Logan's Run* riffs also abound; Mark is almost thirty, and as he puts it, "My crystal's flashing." He even has a dream about being chased as a runner. And when he stumbles into his surprise birthday party, everyone chants, "Renew! Renew!" And what's that guitar solo in the background? It's "She Sells Sanctuary" by The Cult.

Now pile on gratuitous references to *Wonder Woman*, *The Lathe of Heaven*, *Speed Racer*, *Apocalypse Now*, the Justice Society of America, *The Mighty Isis*, *Tombs of the Blind Dead*, *Conan the Barbarian*, *Soylent Green*, *TJ Hooker*, *Belle de Jour*, *The Beastmaster*, *Terminator 2*, and just about everything else you can think of with a geeky pop-culture fanbase.

If I weren't married and settled, this is probably the lifestyle I'd have (minus at least some of the gratuitous sex, of course).

Some Notable Totables:
- body count: 0
- breasts: 2
- explosions: 0
- dream sequences: 3
- ominous thunderstorms: 0
- actors who've appeared on *Star Trek*: 5
  - William Shatner, obviously
  - Diana Cignoli (Illa) was a Dabo Girl on both the pilot and another episode of *DS9*
  - Thomas Hobson (young Richard) was "Young Jake" on the *DS9* pilot
  - Lori Lively (Leila) was in a 7th season *DS9* episode
  - Deborah Van Valkenburgh (Marlena) was "Det. Preston" in the *DS9* two-parter "Past Tense"

The LOST WORLD (1998)

THE ORIGINAL TALE OF PREHISTORIC TERROR.
MORE HORRIFYING THAN ITS IMITATORS.

aka *Sir Arthur Conan Doyle's The Lost World*

- *Directed by Bob Keen*
- *Written by Jean LaFleur and Leopold St-Pierre, based (hah!) on the novel by Arthur Conan Doyle*
- *Starring Patrick Bergin, Jayne Heitmeyer, David Nerman, Julian Casey and Michael Sinelnikoff*
- *Produced by Danny Rossner and Murray Shostak*

At various times in my life, I have sneered at all of the inadequate movie adaptations of Sir Arthur Conan Doyle's adventure novel *The Lost World*. I would like here to publicly apologize to all involved in those adaptations; I had not known how far this novel could be bastardized until I saw this 1998 version. What we have here is a perfect example of exactly how Hollywood (the mindset, not the location—in this case it's Canadian Hollywood-wannabes) can screw up a terrific story. You know that saying, "If it ain't broke, don't fix it"? People in the movie biz have never heard it; apparently, their motto is, "If it ain't broke, it can obviously take some more screwing."

I went back and reread the novel between watching and reviewing this movie, just to make sure that, yes, there was a great story at the base of a string of bad adaptations. I'm now starting to believe that, with the debatable exceptions of *Dracula* or *Frankenstein*, no good novel has been the subject of so many poor movies as *The Lost World*. I'm hoping that, as piss-poor as this one is, it will define the absolute nadir of these adaptations. Really, there's nowhere to go but up.

That sinking feeling can only barely wait until the credits are done before it settles in the gut, attached to the words we see on the screen: "Mongolia 1934." Mongolia? What in hell are we doing in Mongolia?! (I thought it was bad enough that a 1992 version transplanted the story from South America to Africa.) What possible rationale could there be for this? And furthermore, 1934? That's a pretty good trick, seeing how the original novel was published in 1912. This small message, "Mongolia 1934," should be read with the following subtext: "We, the producers, care not a whit about the legitimacy or integrity of this production, and shall feel free to change and delete features of the original for no reason but our own inscrutable whims. Abandon hope, all ye who enter here."

We start off with a short voiceover, as Malone, the expedition's reporter, tells us that he's going to recount the entire sordid tale. What's wrong with this? Well, he also lets us know that somehow he's still trapped alone in the Lost World. Hmm…

The story starts for real as explorer Maple White (Jack Langedijk) and his Mongolian sidekick Azbek (Russell Yuen) explore a cave in the Lost World plateau and discover a nest with a dinosaurian egg in it. Exulting that this is exactly the proof they need, White opens the bubbly and cranks up Beethoven's Fifth on his Victrola. (He's been backpacking through Mongolia with a record player on his back in case he found something to celebrate? Apparently.) Alas, those stirring chords manage to stir up about a gazillion mutant bats (rod puppets and mediocre CGI), and Azbek soon bites it, while White plummets from the cave down a cliff. He's gathered up and taken back to the Mongolian village where he's cared for by Azbek's brother and sister until Professor Challenger (Patrick Bergin) arrives.

Let me repeat that: Professor Challenger is played by Patrick Bergin. Now, as anyone who read *The Lost World* knows, Challenger is a short, powerfully built man, with the black beard of an Assyrian idol and the bombastic demeanor of a bull. In other words, he's John Rhys-Davies (the one thing the 1992 version got absolutely right). Patrick Bergin, on the other hand, is tall, of average build (though his face is getting a little doughy in these latter years) and cleanshaven except for the expected "explorer's stubble," and plays Challenger as this script presents him, with deferential firmness and no hint of an British accent (this despite the fact that Bergin was born in Ireland). Apparently this is not the famous Professor George E. Challenger of the novel, but perhaps his lesser-known cousin Lou Challenger. (This was during the period in which Bergin had somehow become the go-to lead for low-budget movies meant to capitalize on historical blockbusters; between 1991 and 2002, he also starred in off-brand versions of the stories of Robin Hood, Jack the Ripper, King Arthur, St. Patrick, *Frankenstein*, *Treasure Island*, *Dracula*, and something that bears a suspicious resemblance to *Gladiator* (2000).)

Challenger and White are seemingly old acquaintances, but Challenger gets little from White before the latter expires. He does, however, find White's sketchbook with pictures of several fantastic creatures, and the egg, which breaks open to reveal an embryonic pterodactyl.

Cut to London, one month later, as Challenger presents the sketchbook and pterodactyl-in-a-bottle to the assembled skeptical scientists. He manages to persuade his main detractor, Professor Summerlee (Michael Sinelnikoff), to accompany a new expedition. A Frenchman then stands up (and perhaps Bergin's lack of accent is the better choice, as the French accent here is atrocious) and offers to fund the expedition, and furthermore offers a $100,000 reward for the first person to bring back a live specimen. Unfortunately, his price for his assistance is the inclusion in the expedition of hunter John Roxton (David Nerman), a swaggering unintentional parody of the Indiana Jones-style American male: beaten fedora, black turtleneck under a leather jacket, a smooth week's stubble, and a cigar the size of a table leg. I'm sure we're not meant to like him, but I'm not so sure that we're supposed to start giggling as soon as his nefarious face is introduced.

Who else is in the party? Young Malone the reporter (Julian Casey), of course; he is the ostensible viewpoint character after all. Despite an earlier comment about Challenger's well-known distrust of the press, he and Challenger hit it off famously when Malone offers his services on the expedition and suggests a balloon to ascend to the Lost World plateau.

And who else do we need in our expedition? Why, the obligatory female that every producer feels the need to shoehorn into the all-male expedition of the original novel. In this case, it's Amanda White (Jayne Heitmeyer), daughter of Maple, coming along to preserve her father's memory and protect his interests.

So, off to Mongolia. Now, for comparison, let's take a look at Roy Chapman Andrews' famous real-world Mongolian paleontological expedition of 1922, in which he ventured into the desert with a dozen automobiles, plus an entire herd of camels carrying gasoline for the motorcars. In this movie, in contrast, we have a single halftrack that either makes use of a Mr. Fusion™, or stops in at the Amoco stations that dot the outer Mongolian landscape; somehow, without an external gas tank, they manage to drive for at least three weeks before they have to leave the halftrack behind. Tensions between Challenger and Roxton give ample opportunity to both to try and prove their Alpha Male status by being protective of Amanda; Challenger really pulls out the big guns when he accuses Roton of shooting animals "on the Endangered Species list," which is a meaningless and anachronistic charge in 1934, seeing how the Endangered Species List was first published in 1964—in 1934, people were still picking the last bits of roast dodo bird out of their teeth.

And it's right here that the last straw is uncolonially dumped on the back of my suspension of disbelief (already a much belabored animal by this time): there's a volcano. Just for the hell of it, apparently. Behind the halftrack, a volcano erupts with a gout of clean white smoke, and our expeditioners ooh and ahh unconcernedly at it as they drive away. It makes no further impact on the story; it's simply a volcano. Perhaps one of the producers' children said, "Daddy, howcome you never make a movie with a volcano?" So he did.

Onward they trek, stopping at the Mongolian village to pick up the late Azbek's brother Myar (also played by Russell Yuen) and sister Djena (Gregorlane Minot-Payeur), at whom Malone immediately starts making moon eyes. It's odd that this adaptation goes to great lengths to introduce a poorly developed interracial romance. Yes, boys, we know you're all really liberal and open-minded and all; you can stop trying so hard now.

And onward still they trek, through the snow, and into one of the strangest scenes to be had. This exchange comes from the novel, verbatim:

Summerlee: May I ask, sir, in what capacity do you take it upon yourself to issue these orders?
Challenger: I do it, Professor Summerlee, as leader of this exposition.
Summerlee: I am compelled to tell you, sir, that I do not recognize you in that capacity.
Challenger: Indeed! Perhaps you would define my exact position.
Summerlee: Yes sir. You are a man whose veracity is upon trial, and this committee is here to try it. You walk, sir, with your judges.
Challenger: Dear me! In that case you will, of course, go on your way, and I will follow at my leisure. If I am not the leader I cannot be expected to lead.

Now, this makes perfect sense in the novel; the expedition had been mounted under the leadership of Summerlee, but Challenger had shown up once it had begun and had become through sheer force of character its *de facto* leader. However, in this movie, there had never been any question that Challenger was the leader, with Summerlee along as an observer. And so I have to ask—of all the ignored facets of the novel, of all the really nifty things that were glossed over in order to make this steaming pile of dino poop, why in the world would they choose this little spot in which to be faithful to the text, despite the fact that the context which supports it has been completely removed?

And we're only marginally over a half hour into the movie.

They trek through the snow to the base of the plateau, where they start constructing their balloon. But then the females of the party are kidnapped by a tribe of Neanderthals with a dinosaur cult fetish, and it's only by blasting most of them away that Challenger and Roxton rescue them. Then it's a dizzying escape ride in the balloon, which drifts up and over the lip of the plateau, revealing the supposedly tropical interior. Then a bevy of pterodactyls attacks the balloon, and they crash-land.

Did you notice the word "supposedly" in the preceding paragraph? Here's why; after the crash, we see a number of establishing shots establishing the tropical nature of the surroundings—but as soon as we see the characters *in situ*, it's obvious that we're in a temperate coniferous forest (such as would be found in, say, British Columbia, where these scenes were shot), with a fog machine turned on low to add that "tropical steam" to the air. One of the advantages of watching most of the seven seasons of *Highlander: The Series* is that you get to know exactly what environments British Columbia is a good stand-in for, and tropical climes ain't one of them.

We're given our first dinosaur now, in the form of a brachiosaurus-style critter with stegosaurus-style spikes on the tail. Just to prove how stupid they are, both Challenger and Summerlee immediately identify it as a brontosaurus with peculiar modifications. (I'm sorry, but viewers these days are a little more sophisticated than they have been in the past—could you please go to the trouble of correctly identifying your dinosaurs?) The party also finds ruins of some ancient civilization, which the Neanderthals keep boobytrapped; eventually they find a place to bed down for the night.

The movie gets a little more exciting now that we've reached the Lost World, though no smarter. We do get some action as Roxton tries to pull a double-cross to get the balloon prepared and get back on his own with a live specimen, but gets eaten by a giant crocodile that lives in tunnels and has the brains to bait traps. And then Summerlee wanders off, to be attacked by a predator he identifies as a Tyrannosaurus Rex but which is very obviously something halfway between an allosaurus and one of the raptors (I'm kind a glad my six-year-old didn't watch this with me; he would have been disgusted by the misidentifications); said dinosaur punishes Summerlee for his stupidity by dismembering him and pointlessly not eating the parts.

Eventually, having survived Neanderthals, explosions, the mutant bats again, and vicious little eoraptor things, we end up with the two survivors, Challenger and Amanda, escaping by using the balloon material as a parachute. They get back to London, where Challenger declares that the Lost World is nothing but a fable.

Ah, but what about Malone? Mistakenly left for dead, he's now living and looking like a caveman as he finishes the account in his notebook and throws it from the plateau, for someone to maybe find someday. The end.

You may think that the above is uncharacteristically bilious on my part, but believe me, I haven't even managed to vent as much bile as I would like. Few things annoy me more than watching a cinematic screw-up on which professionals obviously worked hard and long to screw it up as bad as they did. It had to take several drafts to get the story line as far from the plot and spirit of the original novel as this ill-conceived monstrosity got. I can't attribute it to anything but a malicious intent to consciously make this as bad a version of *The Lost World* as is possible, and I can only reply with contempt. And to top it off—to cement someone's reserved parking in Hell—the producers had the audacity to pin "Sir Arthur Conan Doyle's" before the title, despite the fact that very little of what is inflicted on us in the ensuing ninety minutes can be laid at the feet of Doyle.

Add that to simple poor filmmaking—CGI work that would be barely adequate on an episode of contemporary television, the clearly visible arm of a stagehand throwing boulders during an explosion—and we have here a world-class stinker with all of the appeal of a post-burrito fart in an elevator.

Some Notable Totables:
- body count: 15
- breasts: 0
- explosions: 5
- ominous thunderstorms: 1
- actors who've appeared on *Star Trek*: 0

SIX-STRING SAMURAI (1998)

Vegas needs a new king.

- Directed by Lance Mungia
- Written by Jeffrey Falcon and Lance Mungia
- Starring Jeffrey Falcon, Justin McGuire, Stephane Gauger
- Produced by Leanna Creel
- Executive produced by Michael Burns

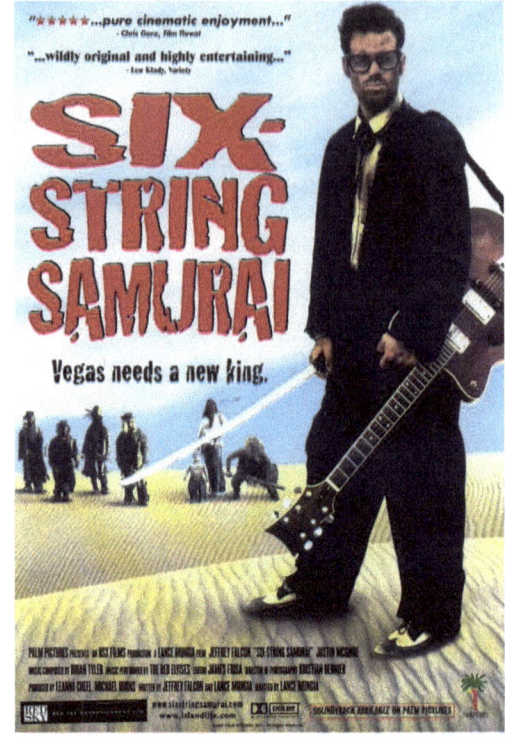

Six-String Samurai is a kung-fu rockabilly post-holocaust movie. It's not a deep movie, but it keeps its promises simply by mining the fun to be had in that simple premise. What results is the best kung-fu rockabilly post-holocaust movie ever.

As is promptly explained to us (against a background of now-familiar nuclear test footage), the bombs dropped in 1957, and the Russkies took over what was left of the U.S.—all except that last bastion of All-American freedom, Lost Vegas, as ruled by (who else?) the King himself, Elvis. Now it's forty years later, Elvis has died... and Vegas needs a new king.

That's is as good an excuse as any for us to watch our protagonist, "Buddy" (Jeffrey Falcon, who had previously made his living in a dozen Hong Kong movies as a *gwailo* martial artist), a wanna-be claimant to the throne, journey across the Nevada badlands in his beat-up zoot suit, his glasses held together by masking tape, his samurai sword duct-taped to his vintage guitar. All to the accompaniment of one of the best rockabilly soundtracks ever, mostly courtesy of the Red Elvises (an appropriately Russian surf quartet who make an on-screen appearance).

And because Buddy can't travel alone (that would be boring), he starts out the movie by rescuing a young kid (Justin McGuire, credited as "The Kid") whose mother had just been done in by some uncouth neo-savages. Naturally, the ragamuffin tags along with the gruff and consternated Buddy, and I will admit that I didn't mind the kid one bit. Usually I'm not in favor of cute juvenile characters, but here it seemed more an honest homage to both the samurai and western genres, from both of which this flick draws some inspiration.

A blow-by-blow plot synopsis is almost an exercise in futility (hey, if it weren't for exercises in futility, I'd get no exercise at all). The general gist is that Death himself, a big scary guy who looks like the fetish-totem version of Slash from Guns N' Roses, wants to be the next King of Lost Vegas, and is thus bumping off all the other wanna-be claimants on the road. So Buddy and the kid trek across Nevada, staying ahead of Death and running into all sorts of other interesting characters. Among them:

- Semi-mutant toughs reminiscent of the clan from *The Hills Have Eyes*, but with more style.
- A warped version of the "nuclear family" (Haw!) with whom Buddy tries to leave the kid. Unfortunately, they're cannibals; fortunately, their dinner is interrupted by...
- The Windmill People, who live among the power-generating windmills and wear spacesuitish outfits made of

fishbowls and water coolers and lots of duct tape.
- The leftover Soviet Army, trying to keep control of the wastelands outside Lost Vegas.

Over time, the kid grows on Buddy, and what started out as a reluctant semi-partnership ends with Buddy squaring off in a guitar duel against Death himself for the fate of the boy.

As I said, the plot ain't much to speak of—but then, it wasn't meant to be. The episodic scenes are strung together in a rough chronological order, but all the way through you can practically hear Mungia and Falcon saying to each other, "Hey, wouldn't it be cool to do a scene where…" Thus, we get scenes of well-choreographed kung fu (and guitar fu) that simply sing.

Now, I realize that there are deficiencies to this movie. In particular, because too much attention is paid to scene-by-scene perfection, the movie as a whole fails to build up as much steam toward the end as it should. And you have to wonder where those electric guitars are getting their power.

But hell, don't let those things stop you. The whole production is so stylized it's almost surreal; just accept the fictional universe created for your enjoyment, and, well, enjoy it. It's a beautifully shot and edited movie (and I'm not alone in thinking so—it took top honors in editing and cinematography at the 1998 Slamdance Festival); if other post-apocalyptic movies had taken half the effort to make themselves look good, the entire subgenre would be a respected category of cinema instead of the laughingstock of the video store.

It may not be the greatest movie ever made… but I watched it twice, two days in a row. I can't remember the last time I did that.

Hail to the King, baby.

Some Notable Totables:
- body count: 83
- breasts: 0
- explosions: 7
- ominous thunderstorms: 0
- actors who've appeared on *Star Trek*: 0

EPILOGUE

The End of an Era

1998 is as good a place to draw a line as any, I suppose. Once again, a new distribution model came along and changed the face of the motion picture industry in ways that even its proponents didn't predict.

On the surface, the introduction of DVDs seemed just like a slightly different delivery method for the same movies that audiences were viewing anyway. But along with greater picture resolution and instant access to any part of the feature (no more "Be Kind—Rewind"), DVDs allowed for modified viewing experiences: subtitles vs. dubbing for foreign films, fullscreen vs. widescreen, and even running audio commentaries by directors and others involved with the making of the movie (or, in the case of older features, film historians). Mostly, these were ways to get current videocassette owners—both rental outlets and consumers—to buy again a movie that they already owned.

However, the VHS market had already started to be more "buyer-friendly." At the start of the rental era, most videotapes were priced well upwards of $50 on release, with rental stores being their target markets; only after a period of months or years had elapsed would those same features be made available at "sell-thru" prices under twenty dollars for home viewers to add to their permanent collections. By the time DVD was introduced, the gap between rental pricing and sell-thru pricing had narrowed, both in cost and in delay.

With the introduction of DVD, the market slowly but inexorably became focused on consumers who bought, instead of those who rented. After all, there were so many features packed on the DVD releases of studio blockbusters that there was no way for a viewer to get through them all during the term of one multi-day rental. If it was going to cost three to four dollars to rent the movie, and fifteen to twenty dollars to buy it, it made sense to buy it if one was ever going to take the time to peruse the making-of featurettes, deleted scenes, commentaries, etc. that were packed on the disc.

The other upshot, however, was that consumers weren't as willing to risk fifteen or twenty dollars to buy a movie on a gamble as they had been to rent that same movie. And with the studios getting smart about marketing ancillary products to their theatrical releases in the form of direct-to-DVD sequels and spinoffs, the B-movie producers felt the squeeze of a collapsing market.

Now, well into the 21st century, the market for B-movies has transformed considerably—and ironically, one of the contributors is the microbudget film movement. Thanks to "prosumer" digital equipment (professional grade at consumer prices), there's plenty of watchable, distributable content out there for a tenth of what distributors used to pay for direct-to-video movies. 90% of the new feature films first on DVD and then on streaming services have still never been in wide theatrical release, but the days of the $5 million non-theatrical release are largely over, because distributors can better recoup their costs with an independent feature that cost $500,000 or less. Charles Band, once a mainstay of theatrically released B-movies and then the purveyor of $2-3 million direct-to-video features through his Full Moon label, now survives on bottom-scraping productions costing $100,000. Fred Olen Ray, the consummate B-movie professional, now makes his living throwing together softcore genre quickies that can be filmed on digital video in four days.

That's not to say that the B-movie is going the way of the buggy whip; there's too much naked capitalism motivating that cinematic niche to let itself go extinct. But the future will definitely be different from the past, and whatever we end up gaining, the necessary losses will be conspicuous.

INDEX

24 (TV) 281
1990: Bronx Warriors (1982) 66
A.P.E.X. (1994) 192
Abraham, Ken 104-106
***Abraxas, Guardian of the Universe* (1994) 209-211**
Ackerman, Forrest J. 135
Adams, Andrea 50-52
Adams, Grizzly 86
Adams, Nick 163
***Addicted to Murder* (1995) 224-226**
After Death (see *Zombie 4: After Death*)
Alahani, Sheeba 63
Alicia, Marta 143-145
Alien (1979) 101, 200, 242
Alien Nation (TV) 218
Allen, Ginger Lynn 104-106
Allen, Richard 46
Allen, Woody 173, 174
Altman, Robert A. 282-283
Alvarez, Auggi 205-208
***America's Deadliest Home Video* (1991) 159-161**
American Film Market 235, 238, 274
American Gladiators (TV) 212
American Ninja (1984) 22, 24
Amin, Mark 262-264
Amritraj, Ashok 253, 271-273, 274
Anciano, Dominic 241-243
Andelman, Juli 25-27
Anderson, Clyde (see Fragasso, Claudio)
Anderson, Michael, Jr. 254-257
André the Giant 210
Andreef, Starr 94-96
Andrews, Roy Chapman 285
Angel, Mikel 140-142
Angel Blade (2002) 115
Angell, Jerry 205-208
Angry Red Planet, The (1959) 86
Anthropophagus (1980) 14
Anzilotti, Perry 262-264
Apocalypse Now (1979) 283
Appignani, Lucciano 66-68
Arachnid (2001) 256
Argento, Dario 85

Arizmendi, Yareli 248
***Armageddon: The Final Challenge* (1995) 227-230**
Armstrong, Alun 193-197
Asimov, Isaac 94-96
At the Mountains of Madness (novel) 216
Atkins, Tom 47-49
Ator the Fighting Eagle (1980) 14
***Auntie Lee's Meat Pies* (1993) 140, 176-178**
Baer, Parley 39
Babatunde, Obba 219
Back to the Future (1985) 42
Bad Movie Report, The 69
***Bad Taste* (1987) 60-61**, 278
Baglivo, Maurizio 107
Bail, Charles ("Chuck") 268-270
Bain, Cynthia 100-103
Bakke, Brenda 153
Baldwin, Adam 274
Baldwin, Michael 97
Balsam, Mark 265-267
Balsam, Talia 53-55
Band, Charles 9, 40-43, 146, 290
Bangers (1997) 104
Bannister, Reggie 97-99
***Barbarians, The* (1987) 62-65**
Barkat, Moshe 38-39
Barkett, Steve 237
Barnett, Steve 143-145
Bartlett, Cal 236
Barton, David 150
Bass, Bobby 181
Bass, Linda 75-77
Bates, Dan 282-283
Batman (TV) 146
Batman (1989) 150
Batman Returns (1992) 188
Batman: The Dark Knight Returns (comic) 147
Battle Beyond the Stars (1980) 236
Beach, Jim 241-241
Beasor, Terrence 155
Beast With Five Fingers, The (1946) 86
Beastmaster, The (1982) 283

Beastmaster 3: The Eye of Braxus (1996) 268
Beautiful Creatures (1994) 61
Bechtel, Joan 130
Becker, Mary 143-145
Begg, Ken 89, 89
Behar, Wayne 78-81
Bellazecca, Pasquale & Luigi 62
Belle de Jour (1967) 283
Bellistri, Jim 84
Beltrane, Robert 19-21
Benskin, Tyrone 265-267
Benson, Steve (see D'Amato, Joe)
Benson, W.E. 82-84
Bentley, Gary F. 55
Benz, Donna Kei 38-39
Berger, Richard 163
Bergin, Patrick 284-287
Bergman, Sandahl 72-74
Berkowitz, Stan 268-270
Berryman, Michael 63, 65, 140-142, 154, 176-178
Bessho, Tetsuya 153
Bessi, Roberto 15-18
Beswick, Martine 140-142
Betzer, Just 56-59
Beyond Bedlam (1994) 200
Biehn, Michael 211
Bilson, Danny 40-43
Birney, David 94-96
Bishop, Edward 82-84, 85-87
Black, Jack 262
Black, Karen 140-142, 176-178
Black Caesar (1973) 66
***Black Cobra* (1987) 66-68**
Blacker, Vera 258
Blade (1998) 241
Blade Runner (1982) 227, 235
Blair, Bill F. 25-27, 50-52, 69-71
Blair Witch Project, The (1999) 138, 159
Blaisdell, Brad 273
Blake, Nill 100-103
Blake, Richard 241
Blalack, Stella 156-158
Blast From the Past (1999) 22
***Bleak Future* (1997) 276-278**
Bleeders (1997) 136
Blob, The (1958) 238

Blood Cult **(1985) 25-27**, 50, 82, 84
Blount, Lisa 22-24
Blythe, Lenny, Jr. 232
Boa (2001) 192
Boen, Earl 114
Bolkan, Edna 28-31
Bolt, Crispan 152-155
Bonaduce, Danny 159-161
Bonaduce, Gretchen 159-161
Bond, James 239
Bookwalter, J.R. 124-126, 127-128, 146-149, 150-151, 169-170, 205
Booth, James 38-39
Boss Nigger (1975) 66
Bowen, Michael 19
Boyle, Peter 152-155
Bragg, Bob 237
Brain That Wouldn't Die, The (1962) 175
Braindead (see *Dead Alive*)
Brainslasher (see *Mindwarp*)
Brancato, John D. 143-145
Bransfield, Marjorie 209-211
Bremer, Brian 101
Bressler, Carl 282-283
Briggs, Joe Bob 240
Brooks, Conrad 204
Brooks, Stephen 258-261
Brosnan, John 198-201
Brotherhood of the Wolf (2001) 217
Brown, Jack 268-270
Brown, W. Earl 180
Bruno, Mark 227-230
Bryant, Edward 135
Bryant, Todd 49
Bryant, Virginia 62-65
Buechler, John Carl 88-90, 133, 135, 200
Buenfil, Erika 28-31
Bunstein, Richard A. 78-81
Burke, Graham 182-184
Burlington-Smith, Anthony 82-84
Burnett, Robert Meyer 282-283
Burns, Michael 288-289
Burton, LeVar 53-55
Burton, Tim 40, 150
Buzzi, Ruth 238
Calfa, Don 111-114
Calhoun, Rory 72-74
Caligula 2 (1982) 14
Campbell, Bruce 121-123, 143-145

Campbell, David 69
Cannibal Holocaust (1980) 159
Capetillo, Eduardo 29
Caprari, Toni 227-230
Capricorn One (1978) 176
Captan, Talaat 189-192
Cardona, Rene III 29
Carducci, Mark Patrick 100-103
Carlen, Catherine 111-114
Carnosaur **(1993) 198-201**
Carnosaur 2 (1995) 200
Carol, Linda 32-37
Carpenter, John 25, 153, 202
Carr, Paul 155
Carrot Top 156
Cars That Ate Paris, The (1974) 67
Casey, Julian 284-287
Castle Freak (1992) 182
Castro, Jacqueline 29
Catcher in the Rye, The (novel) 47
Cattrall, Kim 193-197
Caulfield, Maxwell 53-55
Cavele, Kevin 193-197
Cemetery of Terror **(1985) 28-31**
Cementerio del Terror (see *Cemetery of Terror*)
Chain Reaction (1996) 275
Chapin, Robert 244-246
Charles, Josh 262-264
Charles in Charge (TV) 199
Chatfield, Karen 69
Chen, Moira (see Gemser, Laura)
Chesler, Lewis B. 279-281
Chiba, Sonny 212-215
Children of the Corn (1984) 258
Children Shouldn't Play With Dead Things (1972) 30
Chinatown (1974) 239
Chiodo Brothers 91-93
Chopper Chicks in Zombie Town **(1989) 111-114**
Christopher, Dennis 220
Cignoli, Diana 283
Cinema Home Video 146
Citizen Kane (1941) 27
Claflin, Scott 221-223
Clark, Lester 124
Clarke, Graham 227-230
Clarke, Robin 235-237
Class of 1999 2 (1994) 256

Class of Nuke 'Em High franchise 82
Cleveland, Dan 233
Cliver, Al 11-14
Cobra (1986) 66
Cohen, Michael 56-59
"Cold Air" (short story) 218
Coleman, Signy 219
Coleman, Thomas 19-21
Collins, Clifton, Jr. 182
Combs, Jeffrey 182-184, 216-220
Conan the Barbarian (1982) 72, 283
Conti, Perluigi (see Cliver, Al)
Cooder, Ry 248
Coogan, Rif (see Rifkin, Adam)
Coolidge, Calvin 175
Coote, Greg 182-184
COPS (TV) 161
Corbitt, Chance, Jr. 100
Corman, Julie 94-96
Corman, Roger 9, 37, 40, 198-201, 235-237, 238
Coscarelli, Dac 97-99
Coscarelli, Don 97-99
Costa Chica (2006) 115
Costello, Lou 113
Costo, Oscar L. 179-181
Coto, Manny 279-281
Coulj, Paul 189-192
Couture, Randy 86
Cover, Arthur Byron 135
Crabbe, Buster 26
Crabtree, Robert 212-215
Cramer, Grant 91-93
Cranston, Brian 269
Crawlspace (1986) 40
Crazies, The (1973) 200
Creel, Leanna 288-289
Creep **(1995) 231-234**
Creepozoids (1987) 146
Crichton, Michael 198
Chiodo Brothers 91-93
Crick, Ed 32-37
Crossworlds **(1996) 262-264**
Crowe, Russell 16
Crowford, Wayne 19-21
Cruise, Tom 27, 179
Crutchley, Jeremy 258-261
Cult, The 283
Cunningham, Dale 78-81
Cunningham, Rob 276-278
Curtis, Douglas 247-249
Cut and Run (1985) 140
Cyberzone **(1995) 235-237, 238-240**

Cyborg (1989) 22
D'Amato, Joe 11-14
D'Aquino, John 100-103
Daly, Candice 107-110
Dances With Wolves (1990) 152, 254
Daniels, Gary 185-188
Dano, Royal 91
Darancette, Steven 276-278
Dark Heritage: The Final Descendant (1990) 136-139
Dark Shadows (TV) 171
Dark Star (1974) 153, 238
David, Allyson 115-120
Davis, Jack 11-14
Davis, John 182-184
Davis, Ken 85
Dawn of the Dead (1978) 20, 85, 107, 124
Dawn of the Living Dead (2004) 115
Day of the Dead (1985) 126
De Benedetti, Alex 100-103
De Meo, Paul 40-43
Dead Alive (1992) 49, 61, 278
Dead Next Door, The (1989) 124-126, 127-128, 146, 150, 171
Dead Pit, The (1989) 129-132
Dead Poets Society (1989) 262
Deadly Reactor (1989) 115-120, 244
Deadrick, John 155
Deans, Darla 83
Death Force (2000) 115
Death Machine (1995) 241-243
DeCoteau, David 146-149
DeHaven, David 86
DeHaven, Gloria 86
DeHaven, Lisa 82-84
Dekker, Fred 47-49
Dekker, William-Livingston 82
Del Prete, Deborah 279-281
Deliverance (1972) 84
Deloach, Nikki 247-249
Deluise, Dom 232
Dennehy, Brian 274
Denning, Douglas 204
Deodato, Ruggero 62-65, 140, 159
Desai, Shell y 270
Detective Malone (1990) 68
Detroit Rock City (1999) 158
Dewey, Richard Lloyd 221-223

Di Cicco, Bobby 54
Diamant, Moshe 38-39
Die Hard (1988) 179, 254, 256
Die Hard 2: Die Harder (1990) 152
Dirty Harry (1971) 68, 232
Doctor Mordrid (1992) 40
Dominguez, H. Frank 22-24
Dominick, Henry (see Brancato, John D., and Ferris, Michael)
Douglas, Sarah 94-96
Dourif, Brad 241-243
Dowhen, Garrick 44-46
Doyle, Arthur Conan 284-287
Doyle, Shannon 169-170
Dr. Alien (1989) 146
Dr. Strangelove (1964) 200
Dracula (novel) 284
Drago, Billy 265-267, 268
Dragon Fury (1995) 244-246
Dragon Fury 2 (1996) 246
Dream a Little Dream 2 (1995) 256
Dream System (see *Mindwarp*)
Dreamaniac (1986) 146
Droid Gunner (see *Cyberzone*)
Drudi, Rossella 107-110
Dudikoff, Michael 22-24
Duff, Denise 202-204
Duncan, Neil 193-197
Dunlay, Frank 205-208
Dutcher, Richard 221
Duz, Akut 44-46
Dyke, Robert 121-123
East, Jeff 100-103
Eastman, George 11-14
Eastman, Marilyn 173-175
Eastwood, Clint 67, 248
Eaton, Premika 134
Eberhardt, Thom 19-21
Edlund, Richard 152-155
Edwards, James L. 147
Effner, Ryan 135
Elias, Louie 155
Elliott, Mike 198-201, 238
Ellis, Charles 25-27
Empire Pictures 42, 146
Empire Strikes Back, The (1980) 9, 146
Endgame (1983) 11-14
England, Audie 282-283
Englund, Robert 258-261
Entertainment Weekly 240
Epper, Eurlyne 155
Epper, Tony 181

Esparza, Moctezuma 22-24
Estevez, Joe 204
Evans, Roger 69-71
Everett, Gimel 129-132
Everett, Mara 130
Everybody Loves Raymond (TV) 153
Evil Dead, The (1981) 85
Evil Spirits (1990) 140-142
Ewing Jr., Floyd 124, 146-149
Excessive Force (1992) 179-181
Excessive Force 2: Force on Force (1995) 256
Eyes of the Stranger (1993) 115
Fabian, Ava 176
Faison, Matthew 39
Falcon, Jeffrey 288-289
Fangoria 133, 135
Fangoria Films 145
Fangoria Weekend of Horrors 203
Far Side, The 254
Fast Game Fast Money (1992) 86
Farrell, Sharon 19-19
Feinberg, Steven 182-184
Ferguson, Jessie Lawrence 55
Ferguson, Larry 247-249
Ferrigno, Lou 202-204
Ferris, Michael 143-145
Ferry, Pete 124-126
Fidello, Manuel 88-90
Field, Robert Scott 164
Fighter (2006) 86
Final Experiment (see *Prototype X29A*)
Finnegan, William 47-49
Flashdance (1983) 23, 50
Flock, John 182-184
Florio, Aldo 11-14
Flynn, Michael 222
Food of the Gods 2 (1989) 256
Footloose (1984) 23
For a Few Dollars More (1965) 237
For Your Height Only (1981) 32
Ford, Maria 216-220
Forever Evil (1987) 69-71
Fortress (1992) 182-184
Foster, Meg 212-215
Foster, Stephen Gregory 129-132
Fox, Terry Curtis 182-184
Fragasso, Claudio 107-110
Frakes, Randall 72-74
Frankenstein (novel) 284

Frazetta, Frank 64
Freddy vs. Jason (2003) 90
Frederick, Vicki 111-114
Free Enterprise (1997) **282-283**
Freeman, Morgan 182
Fremes, John 279-281
Friday the 13th: The Final Friday (1984) 88
Friday the 13th Part VI: Jason Lives (1986) 88
Friday the 13th Part VII: The New Blood (1988) 88-90
Friday the 13th Part VIII: Jason Takes Manhattan (1989) 90
Friedman, Brent V. 216-220
Frighteners, The (1996) 61
From Beyond (1986) 182, 216
Frost, Gregory 134
Fugitive X (1996) 115
Full Moon Entertainment 40, 42, 146, 282, 290
Fuller, Samuel 239
Future Cop (see *Trancers*)
Future Hunters (1985) 32-37
Gabai, Richard 237
Gaines, Jim 107-110
Gale, Ed 111
Galindo, Raul 28-31
Galindo, Rodolfo 28-31
Galindo, Ruben, Jr. 28-31
Gannon, Joe 152-155
Gamera 218
Gans, Christophe 216-220
Garcia, Andres Jr. 29
Garcia, Juan 270
Garcia, Michael 227-230
Garret, Frank 44-46
Gaudenzi, Franco 107-110
Gauger, Stephane 288-289
Geer, Ellen 264
Gemser, Laura 11-14
Gerani, Gary 100-103
Getz, Geha 129-132
Ghostbusters (1984) 199
Ghoulies 4 (1994) 256
Gilbert, Kent 164
Gilliam, Burt 274
Ginty, Robert 15-18
Gladiator (2000) 285
Glasse, Kayce 69
Gleave, Randy 221-223
Globus, Yoram 62-65
Gochnauer, Danny 129-132
God's Army (2000) 221
Godzilla 1985 (1985) 5

***Godzilla vs. King Ghidora* (1991) 162-168**
Golan, Menahem 62-65
Goldring, Danny 181
Good, the Bad, the Ugly, The (website) 104
Gordon, Charles 47-49
Gordon, Stuart 182-184
Gossamer 112
Graham, Gary 218
Graham, Reavis 121
Graham, Roger 125
Graham, Sasha 224-226
Granims, Tony 231-234
Grant, Julian 279-281
Graver, Gary 140-142
Grease 2 (1982) 54
Green, Kim Morgan 212-215
Greenhouse, Kate 254-257
Gregory, Laura 193-197
Griffith, Thomas Ian 179-181
Grimaldi, Eva 66-68
Grossi, Michael 124-126
Groundhog Day (1993) 224
Groves, Bill 50-52
Guerra, Danny 78-81
Guerrero, Franco 56-59
Guest, Nicholas 188
***Gunfighter's Moon* (1995) 247-249**
Guns N' Roses 288
Hackett, Martha 201
Hadida, Samuel 216-220
Hagen, Ross 237
Haggerty, Dan 76
Hall, Huntz 178
Halloween (1978) 28, 88
Hamil, Jayne 104-106
Hammer (1972) 66
Haney, Daryl 88-90
Hankin, Larry 96
Hanks, Tom 179
Hanley, Chris 193-197
Hardman, Karl 173-175
Hardt, Josef 25-27
Harewood, Dorian 153
Harpster, Michael 179-181
Harris, Chris 205-208
Harvey, Rupert 262-264
Hatcher, David 136
Hauer, Rutger 193-197, 262-264
Haunting Fear (1991) 140
Hauser, Wings 271-273
Hayes, Julie 80-139
Hayward, Charles 95

Heap, Jonathan 279-281
Heathers (1988) 218
Heavener, David 115-120, 244-246
Heitmeyer, Jayne 265-267, 284-287
Hell Up in Harlem (1974) 66
***Hell Comes to Frogtown* (1987) 72-74**, 202, 276
Hell Comes to Frogtown 3 (see *Toad Warrior*)
Henriksen, Lance 100-103, 179-181, 185-188, 247-249
Henry: Portrait of a Serial Killer (1986) 182
Hercules in New York (1970) 74
Herd, Richard 43
Heroes in Hell (1987) 66
Hess, Jon 179-181
Hessler, Gordon 38-39
Heston, Charles 152-155
Hiatt, Shantall 221-223
Highlander (1986) 245
Highlander: The Series (TV) 287
Hitchhiker, The (TV) 176
Hideous Sun Demon, The (1959) 173
Hideto, Furuoka 152-155
High Noon (1952) 249
Highway to Heaven (TV) 270
Hildebrand, Frank 15-18
Hills Have Eyes, The (1977) 140, 288
Hilton, Paris 242
Hiona, Sam 237
Hirschman, Ray 78-81
Hitchcock, Alfred 25
Hobson, Thomas 283
Hodges, Tom 179, 181
Hollow Man (2000) 157
Holmes, Paul 35
Home Alone (1990) 152
Honey, I Shrunk the Kids (1989) 250
Hooper, Tobe 258-261
Hootkins, William 241-243
Hopkins, Stephen 262-264
Hopkins, Telma 40-43
Hoskins, Dan 111-114
***Hostile Intent* (1997) 279-281**
House (1986) 49
Housely, James H. 82-84
Howard, Alex 100-103
Howard, Clint 198-201, 268
Howard, Ron 268

Howell, C. Thomas 274
Howell, Hoke 141, 237
Hues, Matthias 235-237
Huffman, Tracey 69-71
Humanoids From Atlantis (1991) 146
Hunt, Helen 40-43
Hurley, Matthew 100
Immortal Combat (1994) 212-215
Incredible Hulk, The (TV) 204
Independence Day (1996) 19
Inglorious Bastards (1978) 66
Interceptor Force (1999) 192
International Secret Police: Key of Keys (see *Kokusai Himitsu Keisatsu*)
Invisible Maniac (1990) 156-158
Invisible Mom (1995) 239, **250-252**, 253
Invisible Sex Maniac (see *Invisible Maniac*)
Iron Giant, The (1999) 252
Irvine, Paula 97-99
Isaac Asimov's Science Fiction Magazine 135
It Came From Outer Space (1952) 19
Ito, Kazunori 216-220
Ito, Robert 39
Jabootu.net 207, 229
Jackson, Donald G. 72-74, 202-204
Jackson, Peter 60-61, 278
Jackunas, Jolie 124-126
Jacobs, Norman 143-145
Jacobs, Steven 143-145
Jacobsen, Howard 69-71
James, Brion 202-204
James, Michael 56-59
Jason, Chona M. 244-246
Jason, Harvey 270
Jason Goes to Hell: The Final Friday (1993) 90
Jason X (2001) 90
Jaws (1975) 9
Jennings, Joe 137
Jensen, Todd 227-230
Jenson, Roy 155
Johnson, Arte 140-142
Johnson, Diane 69-71
Johnson, Kent T. 70
Jones, Duane 173-175
Jones, James Earl 179-181, 188
Joseph, Adrianne 109

Judas Priest 56
Judge Dredd 213
Jurassic Park (1993) 164, 198
Justice Society of America 283
KNB EFX 144
Kagen, Larry 133-135
Kaneko, Shusuke 216-220
Kanner, Alexis 94-96
Karis, Vassili 66-68
Karnowski, Tom 22-24, 185-188
Karr, Tom 231-231
Kawata, Takeshi 152-155
Keats, John 237
Keen, Bob 284-287
Keim, Krista 134
Kelly, Brett 170, 172
Kenneally, Robert 247-249
Kennedy, George 22-24
Kent, Elizabeth 143-145
Kent, Gary 268-270
Kerchner, Rob 238
Kerek, Barbara 115-120
Kidnie, James 279-281
Kill Crazy (1990) 115
Killer Klowns From Outer Space (1988) 91-93
Killough, Jon 125
Kilpatrick, Lincoln 182-184
Kimura, Ken 44-46
King, Rob 114
King, Stephen 5, 216, 258-261
King of the Rocket Men (1949) 202
Kingdom of the Vampire (1991) 146, **169-170**, 171-172
Kirby, Jack 209, 210
Kis, R.J. 72-74
Kiser, Terry 88-90
Knight, Harry Adam (see Brosnan, John)
Knight, Trenton 250-252
Knight Rider (TV) 16
Knights (1992) 185-188
Koenig, Walter 121-123
Kokai, Robert 124-126
Kokusai Himitsu Keisatsu (1964) 173
Koslo, Paul 153
Kosugi, Kane 38-39
Kosugi, Shane 38-39
Kosugi, Sho 38-39
Kotis, Peter 44-46
Kowal, Frank 276-278
Kowal, Steven 276-278
Kristofferson, Kris 185-188

Krueger, Freddy 76, 101
Kurcz, Robert 121-123
Kyriazi, Paul 239
La Fleur, Art 40-43
La Rue, Eva 62-65
LaCour, Mark 136-139
Ladd, Diane 198-201
Lady Dragon (1992) 15
Lady Dragon 2 (1992) 15
LaFleur, Jean 284-287
Lamb, Debra 141
Lambert, Christopher 182-184
Land of Doom (1986) 44-46
Landgren, Karl 66-68
Lane, Andrew 19-21
Lane, Jeffrey 69
Lange, David 147, 150
Langedijk, Jack 284
Langley, John 247-249
Lankford, Kim 268-270
Lantz, Frank 84
Last Starfighter, The (1984) 19
Lathe of Heaven, The (1980) 283
Laughing Dead, The (1989) 133-135
Law & Order (TV) 180
Lawless, Sebrina 75-77
Lawnmower Man, The (1992) 258
Lawson, Cheryl 129-132
Leavitt, Judy 123
Lee, Damian 209-211, 254-257
Leech, Beverly 268-270
LeFlore, Julius 74
Leger, Todd 137
LeGros, James 97-99
Leland, Beau 75-77
Lenhart, Lane 189-192
Leno, Jay 173, 174
Lenz, Kay 247-249
Leonard, Brett 129-132
Leone, Sergio 67
Leprechaun (1993) 7
Leslie, Bill 75-77
Lethal Games (see *Hostile Intent*)
Levin, Don 53-55
Levine, Ted 258-261
Levitan, Jerry 209-211
Lewin, Bruce 115-120
Lewis, Charlotte 180
Lewis, Christopher 25-27, 50-52
Lewis, Geoffrey 20
Jewis, Jerry 275

Lewis, Linda 25-27, 50-52
Lewnes, Pericles 82-84
Li, Bruce 32-37
Light, David 32
Lindenmuth, Kevin J. 224-226
Lister, Tiny 269
Little, Michele 23
Lively, Jason 47-49
Lively, Lori 49, 283
Livingston, Barry 250-252
Loch, Chuck 244
Locklear, Heather 282
Locklin, Loryn 182-184
Lofton, T.F. 75-77
Lofton, Terry 75-77
Logan's Run (1976) 282
Lombardi, Leigh 121-123
Long, Kathy 185-188
Looney Toons 60
LOOP (2007) 86
Lord of the Rings trilogy, The 60, 152
Lords of the Deep (1989) 236
Lorre, Peter 263
Lost World, The (1998) 284-287
Lowe, Rob 279-281
Lucas, George 228
Lunt, Susan 69
Lovecraft, H.P. 136-139, 216-220
"Lurking Fear, The" (short story) 136-139
Lurking Fear, The (1994) 136
Lynch, Richard 62-65, 216-220, 244-246
Maharaj, Anthony 32-37
Mainwaring, Dan 274
Malone, Karl 221-223
Maltese Falcon, The (1941) 32
Manard, Biff 43
Mancuso, Frank, Jr. 88-90
Mangler, The (1995) 258-261
Manoogian, Brian C. 121-123
Manzetti, Cervando 29
Maris, Peter 44-46
Markovic, Maria 146-149
Marks, Anthony 156-158
Maroney, Kelly 19-21
Marshall, Steve 47-49
Martell, William C. 235-237, 238-240, 250-252, 253, 271-273
Martin (1978) 171
Mason, Lowell 173-175
Mason, Paul 91-93

Massi, Danilo 66-68
Massi, Stelvio 66-68
Mastroianni, Armand 53-55
Matheson, Tim 152-155
Matmor, Daniel 258-261
Matrix, The (1999) 143
Matthews, Fritz 115-120
Mayersberg, Paul 94-96
Maylam, Tony 193-197
Mayo, Virginia 140-142
Max Hell Comes to Frogtown (see *Toad Warrior*)
Max Hell Frog Warrior (see *Toad Warrior*)
McBain, Ed 180
McBee, Deron 212-215
McBride, Alex (see Vanni, Massimo)
McCallum, Robert (see Graver, Gary)
McCleery, Mick 224-226
McComas, Lorissa 236
McCormack, Eric 282-283
McCormick, David 136-139
McDougal, Martin 241-243
McGowan, Bennie Lee 25-27
McGuire, Justin 288-289
McIlwraith, David 247-249
McKinstry, Jeff 86
McLauchlin, Laura 224-226
McMillan, Scott 221
McNamara, J. Patrick 99
Mead, Candace 224-226
Mead, Syd 152
Meet the Feebles (1989) 61
Menning, Sam 141
Meraz, Raul 29
Metalstorm: The Destruction of Jared-Syn (1983) 40
Metcalfe, Ken 56-59
Metz, Cheryl 205
Meyer, Bess 218
Meyer, Michelle 75-77
Miami Vice (TV) 180
Mighty Hercules, The (TV) 16
Mighty Isis, The (TV) 283
Miller, Dick 47, 49
Miller, Frank 147
Millian, Andra 94-96
Mindwarp (1990) 143-145
Minett, Mike 60-61
Minot-Payeur, Gregorlane 286
Mitchell, David 209-211
Mitchell, Gordon 12
Mitchell, Red 69-71
Mitchum, Robert 275

Molloy, Patrick 78-81
Moncure, Lisa 201
Monster Squad, The (1987) 49
Monty Python and the Holy Grail (1975) 60
Moody Blues, The 197
Moontrap (1989) 121-123
Moore, Deborah 56-59
Moore, Eddie 136-139
Moore, Melissa 156-158
Morishima, Morris 152-155
Morita, Pat 176-178
Morrison, Bill 147
Moss, Jim 110
Mötley Crüe 140
Mouse Hunt (1997) 158
Muller, Harrison 15-18
Mungia, Lance 276-289
Muppet Show, The 61
Murder Weapon (1989) 150
Murphey, Michael S. 53-55
Murray, Don 22-24
Murray, Jeff 237
Mutant Hunt (1987) 55
Mutant Kid, The (see *Plutonium Baby*)
Naff, Lycia 111-114
Nail Gun Massacre (1987) 75-77
Nakagama, Anna 162-168
Nakashima, Lex 133-135
Napier, Charles 202-204
Necronomicon, The 70
Necronomicon: Book of the Dead (1994) 216-220
Neeson, Liam 16
Neira, Daniel 212-215
Nelson, James 152-155
Nelson, John Allen 91-93
Nemec, Corin 152-155
Nerman, David 284-287
New Barbarians, The (1982) 66
Newcomb, Wendie 276-278
Newlin, Dika 231-234
Nichols, Dave 255
Nichols, Nichelle 53-55
Nicholson, Nick 110
Niekirk, Sidney 140-142
Nielsen, Brigitte 68
Night Eyes (1990) 275
Night Hunter (1996) 253
Night of the Comet (1984) 19-21
Night of the Creeps (1986) 47-49, 241

Night of the Day of the Dawn of the Son of the Bride of the Return of the Revenge of the Tterror of the Attack of the Evil Mutant Hellbound Flesh Eating Subhumanoid Living Dead, Part 2 (1991) 173-175
Night of the Day of the Dawn of the Son of the Bride of the Return of the Revenge of the Terror of the Attack of the Evil, Mutant, Hellbound, Flesh-Eating Subhumanoid Zombified Living Dead, Part 3 (2005) 175
Night of the Living Dead (1968) 126, 173, 200
Night of the Living Dead (1990) 182
Nightfall (1988) 94-96
Nightmare on Elm Street franchise 258
Nightmare Sisters (1987) 146
Ninja III: The Domination (1984) 64
Ninja Busters (1984) 239
Nishioka, Tokuma 163
Norcia, Jo 169-170
Norrington, Stephen 241-243
Norris, Chuck 179, 181
Norton, Richard 32-37
Nostradamus 155
O'Dea, Judith 173-175
O'Herne, Pete 60-61
O'Malley, Brian 276-278
Odaka, Megumi 162-168
Oh, Soon-Tek 268-270
Oliver, David 49
Oltre la Morte (see *Zombie 4: After Death*)
Omori, Kasuki 162-168
Operation Overkill (see *Warriors of the Apocalypse*)
Ornelas, Michael 231-234
Outer Limits, The (TV) 94
Outlaw Force (1987) 115
Outlaw Prophet (1999) 115
Outlaw Josey Wales, The (1976) 53
Ozone (1994) 151, 171
Pacino, Al 149
Page, Harrison 198-201
Palance, Jack 152-155
Paloian, Nancy 111-114
Parcero, Jose Gomez 28

Park-Lincoln, Lar 88-90
Parker Lewis Can't Lose (TV) 153
Parmalee, Joan 136-139
Parry, David 177
Paterson, Iain 88-90
Patrick, Robert 32-37
Patterson, Rocky 75-77
Paul, David & Peter 62-65
Paul, Patricia 231-234
Pauley, Bernadette 224-226
Paulin, Scott 185-188
Paulsen, Pat 176-178
Payne, Bruce 216-220
Pearl, Mel 53-55
Pecic, Bogdan 124-126, 146-149
Pedone, Mario 12
Pelshaw, Mary Beth 78-81
Perez, Jack 159-161
Perkins, Millie 218
Perlmutter, David 279-281
Peters, Noel 156-158
Petersen, Curtis 209-211
Petry, Cherie 169-170
Peyton, Chuck 107-110
Pfeiffer, Michelle 188
Pfeiffer, Scott 202-204
Phantasm (1979) 97
Phantasm II (1988) 97-99
Phillips, Samantha 97-99
Piccirilli, Tom 224-226
Pike, David 78-81
Pike, Vanessa 258-261
Piper, "Rowdy" Roddy 72-74, 202, 212-215, 254-257, 265-267
Pirana, P. Floyd 82
Pit and the Pendulum, The (1991) 40, 182
Plan 9 From Outer Space (1959) 49, 51
Planet of the Apes franchise 12, 37, 73, 282
Pleasence, Donald 15-18, 28
Plummer, Scott P. 169-170
Plutonium Baby (1987) 78-81
Poli, Maurice 66-68
Pollard, Michael J. 193-197
Porter Rockwell: A Biography (book) 223
Porter Rockwell Chronicles, The (book) 223
Postlethwaite, Pete 197
Potter, Terry 60-61
Pouget, Eli 241-243

Powers, Tim 135
Pray for Death (1985) 38-39
Predator (1987) 187
Presley, Elvis 288
Prime Target (1991) 115
Princess Bride, The (1987) 186
Pritzker, Gigi 279-281
Proteus (1995) 200
Prototype X29A (1992) 189-192
Psycho (1960) 140, 170
Psycho Weene (2006) 115
Pumpkinhead (1988) 100-103
Pyun, Albert 22-24, 37, 185-188
Quadros, Stephen 177
Quarry, Robert 141, 236
Queen, Ron 75-77
Quezada, Robert A. 97-99
Quick and the Dead, The (1995) 248
Quigley, Linnea 104-106, 146-149
Radar Men From the Moon (1952) 202
Radell, Daniel 44-46
Radioactive Dreams (1984) 22-24
Ragsdale, Tex 121-123
Raiders of the Lost Ark (1981) 17, 32, 39, 126
Railsback, Steve 268-270
Raimi, Sam 124-126, 248
Rand, Craig 44-46
Rao, Krishna 262-264
Rao, Roman 262-264
"Rats in the Walls, The" (short story) 217
Rausch, Kasey 206
Ray, Fred Olen 140, 235-237, 250-252, 253, 290
Raybourne, Richard 265-267
Re-Animator (1985) 40, 182, 216
Rear Window (1954) 67
Rebeca, Maria 28-31
Red Elvises, The 288
Reder, Benjamin R. 268-270
Redneck Zombies (1987) 82-84, 85-87
Reeves, Keanu 275
Relentless 4 (1994) 256
Remsen, Bert 141, 142
Ren & Stimpy Show, The (TV) 60
Rennard, Deborah 44-46

Resort to Kill (see *Immortal Combat*)
Restivo, Joe 268-270
Restivo, Steve 268-270
Return of the Jedi, The (1983) 9
Return of the Living Dead franchise 82
Return of the Living Dead Part 3 (see *Zombie 4: After Death*)
Return to Frogtown (1993) 202-204
Revenge (1986) 82
Revenge of the Ninja (1983) 64
Revenge of the Sun Demon (see *What's Up, Hideous Sun Demon?*)
Reyes, Pia 177
Rhys-Davies, John 285
Rice, Anne 169
Richardson, Jay 271
Riffel, James (see Mason, Lowell)
Rifkin, Adam 156-158
Ridenour, Raymond 134
Ripper, The (1986) 50-52, 82
Ritter, Tim 231-234
Road Warrior, The (1981) 32, 67, 183, 190
Roadblock (1951) 274
Robertson, Joseph F. 176-178
Robocop 3 (1993) 49
Robot Holocaust (1986) 55
Robot Jox (1990) 182
Robot Ninja (1990) 146-149, 150-151
Rockhold, Brad 276-278
Rockwell, Orrin Porter 221-223
Rockwell: A Legend of the Wild West (1994) 221-223
Rockwell: A Novel 223
Romancing the Stone (1984) 32, 35, 236
Romano, Rino 281
Romero, George A. 85, 124, 174
Rose, Kristine Anne 176-178
Rose, Jamie 111-114
Rosenblatt, Michael 19-21
Rosenthal, Helen 79
Rosenthal, Stuart 25-27
Rosskowick, Patrick 133-135
Ross, Kimberly 100-103
Ross, Robert R., Jr. 156-158
Rossner, Danny 265-267, 284-287
Rosten, Peter 247-249

Roth, Andrea 262-264
Roth, Phillip 189-192
Rourke, Mickey 274
Rowlands, Joanna 227-230
Rubinek, Saul 279-281
Runyon, Jennifer 198-201
Russell, Karen 104-106
Ruud, Michael 221-223
Ryan, Terry 182-184
Sademura, Takehito 152-155
Sagarino, Frank 153
Sahara, Kenji 162
Santiago, Cirio H. 32-37
Santini, Bucky 83
Sarkissian, Arthur M. 111-114
Sarlui-Tucker, Helen 91-93
Sasaki, Katsuhiko 163
Satsuma, Kenpachiro 162-168
Savage, John 279-281
Savini, Tom 50-52, 88
Sbarge, Raphael 198-201
Scandiuzzi, Gian-Carlo 189-192
Scandiuzzi, Sebastian 189-192
Scarface (1983) 149
Schauffler, Florence 101
Scheik, Sandra 19-21
Schofield, Annabel 152-155
Schorer, Clifford J. 78-81
Schreier, Tom 50-52
Schroetter, Walter 44-46
Schwarzenegger, Arnold 62, 179, 211
Sci-Fighters (1996) 256, **265-267**
Scott, Betty S. 69-71
Scott, George 82-84
Scott, Jill 69-71
Scrimm, Angus 97-99, 143-145
Sea of Love (1989) 274
Seagal, Steven 179
Searchers of the Voodoo Mountain (see *Warriors of the Apocalypse*)
Segan, Lloyd 262-264
Serafian, Richard C. 152-155
Sergei, Ivan 247-249
Severed Ties (1992) 145
Sevi, Mark 254-257, 265-267
Sha, Sunil R. 38-39
Sharian, John 241-243
Shark Attack 2 (2002) 15
Shark Attack 3 (2003) 15
Sharp, Ian 193-197
Shatner, William 282-283
Shaw, George Bernard 175

Shaw, Scott 204
Sheehan, Ciaran 80
Sheets, Chad 53
Sheets, Todd 205-208
Shendal, Margaret 53-55
Shepard, Hilary 24
Shinas, Sofia 279-281
Shor, Dan 155
Shostak, Murray 265-267, 284-287
Shostrom, Mark 55
Shriner, Kin 235-237
Siegel, Michael 91-93
Silence of the Lambs, The (1991) 258
Silent Hill (2006) 217
Silke, James R. 62-65
Simon, Adam 198-201
Sinelkinoff, Michael 284-287
Singer, Linda 204
Singer, Marc 235-237, 268-270, 271-273
Singhe, Sanjeey 258-261
Singin' in the Rain (1952) 76
Six-String Samurai (1998) 276, **288-289**
Skaggs, Jimmie F. 155
Skinned Alive (1989) 149
Skyscraper (1996) 254
Slate, Jeremy 129-132
Sloane, Rick 104-106
Small Soldiers (1998) 158
Smellman, Fester 82-84
Smith, Anna Nicole 254
Smith, Craig 60-61
Smith, Joseph 221
Smith, Kurtwood 182-184
Smith, William 72-74
Smithee, Alan 152-155
Snyder, Maria 111-114
Snyder, Suzanne 91-93
Soble, Ron 270
Soisson, Joel 53-55
Solar Crisis (1990) 152-155
Solomon, Alan N. 121-123
Somtow, S.P. (see Sucharitkul, Somtow)
Sorority Babes in the Slimeball Bowl-O-Rama (1988) 146
Soylent Green (1973) 145, 283
Space: 1999 (TV) 123
Speed Racer (TV) 283
Spellos, Peter 237, 275
Spiegel, Scott 124
Spielberg, Steven 198-201
Spirtas, Kevin 88-90

Split Second **(1992) 193-197**
Spring, Helena 258-261
St-Pierre, Leopold 284-287
Stait, Brent 249
Stakeout (1987) 274
Stallone, Sylvester 66, 179
Stambler, Deborah Sharon 244-246
Star Hunter (1995) 237
Star Slammer (1986) 238
Star Trek (The Original Series) 209, 269
Star Trek: Enterprise (TV) 49
Star Trek: The Motion Picture (1979) 16, 164, 282
Star Trek 6 (1991) 195
Star Wars (1977) 9, 16
Stargate SG-1 (TV) 153
Stefani, Michael 40-43
Stein, Gerald 176-178
Stephan, Tom 169-170
Stephens, Brynne 135
Stevens, Andrew 235-237, 238, 250-252, 253, 271-273
Stevens, Brinke 237, 239
Stevens, Stella 250-239
Steward, Stephen 105
Stewart, Catherine Mary 19-21
Stiglitz, Hugo 28-31
Stockwell, John 22-22
Stoff, Erwin 179-181
Stone, Dee Wallace 250-252, 253
Stone, Gus 12
Storm, T.J. 244-246
Strain, Julie 271-273, 274
Street Corner Justice **(1996) 268-270**
Stroud, Don 203
Stryker, Jeff (see Peyton, Chuck)
Suarez, Bobby 56-59
Sucharitkul, Somtow 133-135
Sullivan, Susan Jennifer 88-90
Sullivan, Tim 133-135
Supernaturals, The **(1986) 53-55**
Survivor (TV) 160
Svatek, Peter 265-267
Swalve, Darwyn 115-120
Swanson, Brenda 189-192
Swanson, Jandi 103
Swanson, Rochelle 235-237
Sword and the Sorcerer, The (1982) 22, 185
Sybil War (comic) 147
SyFy Channel 264

TJ Hooker (TV) 283
Tales From the Crypt (TV) 49
Tamblyn, Russ 238, 250-252
Tanaka, Tomoyuki 162-168
TARDIS, The 263
Taylor, Wally 47-49
Teasedale, Boo 83
Teenage Mutant Ninja Turtles (comic) 147
Tempe Entertainment 147
Temple, George 189-192
Terminal Rush **(1995) 254-257**
Terminator, The (1984) 32, 41, 211, 245
Terminator 2: Judgment Day (1991) 283
Terminator 3: Rise of the Machines (2003) 145
Terminator: Salvation (2009) 145
Texas Chainsaw Massacre, The (1974) 84, 258
Texas Chainsaw Massacre 2, The (1986) 145
Texas Nailgun Massacre (see *Nail Gun Massacre*)
That '70s Show (TV) 183
They Live (1987) 72, 202
Thomas, Craig 90
Thomerson, Tim 40-43
Thompson, Brian 68
Thompson, Gary Scott 193-197
Thompson, J.L. 32-37
Thompson, John 62-65
Thornton, Billy Bob 112
Thorsen, Sven-Ole 209-211
Three Stooges, The 85
Tigar, Kenneth 99
Toad Warrior (1996) 204
Todd, Michael 146-149
Todd, Tony 179-181
Tombs of the Blind Dead (1972) 283
Tomiyama, Shogo 162-168
Tossberg, Robert 189-192
Tower, Wade 50-52
Towers, Harry Alan 258-261
Towles, Tom 182
Town That Dreaded Sundown, The (1977) 76
Toxic Avenger franchise 82, 86, 111
Toyohara, Kosuke 162-168
Trancers **(1985) 40-43**
Trancers sequels 42
Treacherous (1993) 274

Treasure Island (novel) 285
Troma 82, 86, 93, 111
Trotter, Charles L. 69-71
Tsuchiya, Yoshio 163
Tweed, Shannon 271-273
Twisted Justice (1990) 115
Tyler, Dan 79
Ueda, Koichi 162
Ukmar, Frank 12
Unforgiven (1992) 248
USA Up All Night (TV) 106
V: The Final Battle (1984) 20
Van Atta, Don 38-39
Van Damme, Jean-Claude 274
Van Dyke, Phillip 251
Van Pernis, Mona 50-52
Van Valkenburgh, Deborah 283
Vance, James 25-27
Vanni, Massimo 107-110
Velasco, Usi 28-31
Vengable, David 182-184
Vengeance: The Demon (see *Pumpkinhead*)
Ventura, Jesse 209-211
Verhoeven, Paul 157
Verkaik, Petra 177
Verkaik, Tim 136-139
Vernon, John 91-93
Verrell, Cec 72-74
Vest, Sonny 44-46
Vice Academy **(1988) 104-106**
Vickers, Yvette 141
Victim of Desire **(1996) 271-273**, 274-275
Victor, James 249
Village People, The 56
Viviani, Joe 78-81
Von Franckenstein, Slement 158
Walsh, Christopher 12
Walsh, Matthew Jason 169-170, 171
Walters, Melora 159-161
Ward, Burt 146-149
Ward, Dave 248
Warner, David 216-220
Warren, Bill 135
Warren, Brian 254-257
Warrior of the Lost World **(1983) 15-18**, 66
Warriors of the Apocalypse **(1986) 56-59**
Wayne, John 185, 247
Wayne, Keith 173-175
Webb, Wendy 133-135
Webster, Christopher 143-145

Weekend at Bernie's (1989) 19
Weigel, Rafer 282-283
Weigel, Teri 177
Wein, Len 135
Weinman, Richard C. 100-103
Welback, Peter (see Towers, Harry Alan)
Wells, Vernon 183
West Wing, The (TV) 153
What's Up, Hideous Sun Demon? (1983) 173
What's Up, Tiger Lily? (1966) 173
"Whisperer in Darkness, The" (short story) 219
Whitlow, Jill 47-49
Whitman, Stuart 115-120
Who's the Boss? (TV) 73
Will & Grace (TV) 282
Willets, Kathy 231-234
Williams, Freeman 69-71
Williams, Johnny 271-273
Williams, Mollena 159-161
Williams, Nat 12
Williams, Paul 153
Williamson, Fred 15-18, 66-68
Willis, Bruce 179, 256
Wilsey, Shannon 156-158
Wilson, Chuck 162-168
Wilson, Don 107-110
Wilson, Don "The Dragon" 107, 254-257
Wilson, Stuart 262-264
Winston, Stan 100-103
Winters, Marc 115-120
Wiseman, Michael 264
Wisniewski, Andreas 242
Wizard Video 55
Wolfman, Martin J. 83
Wonder Woman (TV) 283
Woon 212
Woronov, Mary 19-21
Worth, David 15-18
Worth, Nicholas 74
Wu, William 135
Wynhoff, Mick 159-161
Wynkoop, Joel D. 231-234
Wynorski, Jim 271-273
Yamanouchi, Al 11-14
York, Tanya 202-204
Young, Brigham 221
Young, Burt 179-181
Young Frankenstein (1974) 153
Yuen, Russell 285
Yuzna, Brian 216-220
Z'Dar, Robert 202-204
Zombie 2 (1979) 107
Zombie 3 (1988) 107
Zombie 4: After Death (1988) 107-110
Zombie Bloodbath (1993) 205-208
Zombie Cop (1991) 146, 171
Zombie Flesh Eaters 3 (see *Zombie 4: After Death*)
Zombie Rampage (1992) 206
Zombieland (2009) 277
Zombies of the Stratosphere (1952) 203
Zoofeet 82-84

www.ingramcontent.com/pod-product-compliance
Lightning Source LLC
Chambersburg PA
CBHW061152010526
44118CB00027B/2950